Jazz Radio America

MUSIC IN AMERICAN LIFE

The Music in American Life series documents and celebrates the dynamic and multifaceted relationship between music and American culture. From its first publication in 1972 through its half-century mark and beyond, the series has embraced a wide variety of methodologies, from biography and memoir to history and musical analysis, and spans the full range of musical forms, from classical through all types of vernacular music. The series showcases the wealth of musical practice and expression that characterizes American music, as well as the rich diversity of its stylistic, regional, racial, ethnic, and gendered contexts. Characterized by a firm grounding in material culture, whether archival or ethnographic, and by work that honors the musical activities of ordinary people and their communities, Music in American Life continually redefines and expands the very definition of what constitutes music in American culture, whose voices are heard, and how music and musical practices are understood and valued.

For a list of books in the series, please see our website at www.press.uillinois.edu.

Jazz Radio America

AARON J. JOHNSON

UNIVERSITY OF ILLINOIS PRESS
Urbana, Chicago, and Springfield

© 2024 by the Board of Trustees
of the University of Illinois
All rights reserved
1 2 3 4 5 C P 5 4 3 2 1
♾ This book is printed on acid-free paper.

Publication of this book was supported in part by a grant
from the Judith McCulloh Endowment for American Music
and the AMS 75 PAYS Fund of the American Musicological
Society, supported in part by the National Endowment for
the Humanities and the Andrew W. Mellon Foundation.

Cataloging data available from the Library of Congress
LCCN 2024026872
ISBN 978-0-252-04622-3 (cloth : alk.)
ISBN 978-0-252-08830-8 (paper : alk.)
ISBN 978-0-252-04749-7 (ebook)

*With loving memories of Yewande Kelley-Johnson
and of putting the radio under my pillow at bedtime.*

> You might keep us off the radio,
> but you can't keep us out of the air.
>
> —Rashaan Roland Kirk

Contents

Preface ix

Acknowledgments xiii

Introduction 1

PART I. JAZZ ON COMMERCIAL RADIO

1 Jazz Here and Jazz There: Jazz Rides the Omnibus 35

2 Independent Contractors: Jazz Shows Outside the Format 71

3 Jazz Around the Clock: Jazz as a Radio Format 108

PART II. JAZZ ON NONCOMMERCIAL RADIO

4 Paradise Found, Paradise Lost: The Rise and Fall of Jazz on Noncommercial Radio 137

5 Don't Get Too Far Out: Programming Jazz on Noncommercial Radio 170

6 Jazz Is for Everybody: Missions, Precursors, Models, and Ownership 193

Postscript: Jazz Radio Present and Future 235

Appendix A: Notable Jazz Disc Jockeys   249

Appendix B: Jazz Radio Stations circa 2020   253

Notes   257

Bibliography   285

Index   295

Preface

It has been said that the difficulty in writing about music is that it is ineffable, but of course people write about it anyway. Writing about radio is difficult not only because it is a widely practiced simultaneous and dispersed activity, not only because of the vast amount of material we would wish to study, but also because the central object, the broadcasts themselves, are evanescent. What a research tool we would have if, like the opening of the 1997 film *Contact*, we could travel out into space to catch up with radio waves from decades past.

Before the technology existed to preserve musical performances—among the first being the piano rolls that allow today's listeners not to hear Scott Joplin and Maurice Ravel but allow their physical gestures to be preserved and applied to modern instruments—music was not only ineffable but also fleeting, and we had only earwitness accounts of how things actually sounded. Fortunately, for nearly all of radio broadcast history, means of recording it have been available. Unfortunately, only the tiniest fraction of broadcasts has been preserved. Why? Expense: Until very recently, recording audio to keep has had a non-trivial cost. Storage: Again, until recently, recording media were bulky and fragile enough to require significant dry, temperature-controlled, and sheltered space—witness the disastrous 2008 Universal Studios fire that destroyed countless master recordings of blues, jazz, pop, and classical music. Disinterest: Even a daytime-only radio station will produce almost five thousand hours of programming yearly, and most of that from records. Yawn.

So there is one great hurdle to radio research: a lack of archival records that extends, by the way, to business records and operating logs, which stations, to avoid liability, often deliberately destroy as soon as is legally permissible. In the case of a generalized study such as this one on jazz radio in the United States, the problems multiply: There are so many stations in so many markets and so many have changed hands so many times. And the most difficult thing of all is that the most important participant, the audience, is the most difficult to research, especially in a historical study.

Let me, then, talk about what this book is not. It is not a thorough and comprehensive catalog of all the important jazz broadcasters in the history of the medium, nor a compendium of jazz radio's top hit records. It is not a close examination of any pivotal broadcasts. It is not a biography of Felix Grant, Herb Wong, Rhonda Hamilton, Ray Scott, Harrison Ridley, Helen Borgers, Dick Buckley, Chuck Niles, Willard Jenkins, China Valles, Willis Conover, Yvonne Daniels, Jae Sinnett, Del Shields, or Bob Parlocha. As far as I am concerned, each of these figures deserves a chapter in a comprehensive book on jazz DJs.

Instead, *Jazz Radio America* is about major trends. It so happens that radio is an industry small enough and imitative enough that innovations and successful practices quickly reverberate from one end of the country to the other and back. This book is concerned with the exercise and application of power—by which I mean, first of all, the power to own and operate a radio station, the power to shape programming, make programming decisions, and otherwise determine the content of radio broadcasts—in the jazz radio world, where, at a minimum, the recording, live music, and music services sectors have forged working relationships with first the commercial and later the noncommercial radio industries. In order to study the use of power it is necessary to identify power and those who wield it. One must also locate those who do not have power, at least in the conventional sense, and those objects on which power operates.

In the jazz radio world, one could argue that the wielded powers are financial, political, and cultural and that the first disproportionately affects the others. The cultural theorist Stuart Hall observed that race was the modality of class/race is ever-present in affairs of jazz radio, with African Americans consistently underrepresented as decision makers, as they have always been underrepresented on the business side of jazz. Radio is a mass medium, and the masses—the listeners—also hold a great though typically a diffuse and unfocused power. From time to time, the masses demand justice and respect; on occasion they win. but usually the powers yield as little as necessary to maintain control. Radio also has a history of determined, inspired, inventive, and audacious individuals who have managed to flip radio convention on its head. I have tried to pay particular attention to these struggles, triumphs, and failures in *Jazz Radio America*.

One note on method: I have used a lot of news sources to recover discourses shrouded in the fog of history, including trade papers and magazines about radio, records, and the entertainment business. I have tried to be cautious and skeptical about their original purposes and intent. Trade papers are vital research assets but must be eyed with suspicion because they are as often a tool of promotion or manipulation as they are a source of information. They can be wildly optimistic. For example, a May 12, 1980, *Washington Post* story whose sources were mainly industry press releases celebrated the imminent arrival of electric vehicles in time to deliver drivers from the energy crisis. (That very summer an OPEC initiative limited gasoline supplies, and consumers had to face "odd-even" rationing at stations.) The article, "Electric Cars Humming Along: Battery Cars Speed Up as Gasoline Alternative," declared that "a rapid series of technological breakthroughs in battery design have made it possible to mass-produce electric cars and vans by 1985, according to industry officials." As it happened, the less-than-successful General Motors EV 1 debuted in 1996, followed by the celebrated hybrid Toyota Prius in 1997, the plug-in hybrid Chevy Volt in 2010, and finally the Tesla Model S in 2012. With trade papers the lesson is, as Public Enemy said, "Don't believe the hype."

It is also true that jazz radio was being broadcast all across the United States, with additional programming coming from Canadian radio stations whose broadcast signals failed to respect political boundaries. Readers will not fail to notice that *Jazz Radio America* lacks comprehensive coverage of all stations and markets that were part of jazz radio. Such a study would be wonderful but difficult to compile in the absence of extensive radio archives. Readers will note that communities with African American newspapers—Chicago, Baltimore, New York, Pittsburgh, and Los Angeles—are better represented in this volume. As always, researchers revel in rich archival collections such as the Smithsonian Museum of American History's trove on the black appeal station WANN in Annapolis, Maryland. Although I tried not to miss any all-jazz stations, please forgive me for not including your local jazz DJ and his wonderful overnight or weekend jazz show on that stuffy old station your dad used to listen to.

I come to jazz and radio as a practitioner of both. I am an African American jazz musician and composer who plays trombone, bass trombone, tuba, conch shells, and bass clarinet, a professional musician since at least 1980. My radio days are long behind me. As a high schooler, I was a technician and board operator at WGTS-FM, Takoma Park, Maryland, a station owned by a Seventh Day Adventist university just outside the border of my hometown, Washington, DC. In college I was a DJ, assistant general manager, and for a time, chief operator (I had a second-class radiotelephone license from the FCC) of WRCT-FM, a college radio station owned and operated by the Carnegie Mellon Student Government Corporation. I also had one exciting summer as a summer intern in the engineering department of the CBS television network in New York.

With electrical engineering degrees from Carnegie Mellon and Georgia Tech, I spent about twenty-five years mostly in the telecommunications industry working on optical fiber technology, optical fiber networks, access networks, and digital television. Not only did writing about jazz and radio thus seem to be a natural blend of my interests, but both fields are tremendously rewarding ones in which to study the application of race, power, and privilege, as well as opportunities for innovation and change. Also, both jazz and radio studies profit from detailed studies of the borders of accepted and conventional practices. Sadly, jazz and radio are struggling to hold onto their places of cultural prestige and influence. On a positive note, both are still beloved by many, many fans, practitioners, and listeners.

I hope that despite the limitations discussed above you will find *Jazz Radio America* informative and entertaining.

Acknowledgments

As the author of *Jazz Radio America*, I take full responsibility for misstatements, leaky arguments, and assertations about radio that are just wrong. But the process of constructing this study involved the cooperation and assistance of a great number of archivists, librarians, collectors, historians, radio practitioners and radio lovers, and I wish to thank them all, those I name and those I have forgotten to name.

First, let me recognize the three broadcast entities that gave me my start in the 1970s. WGTS-FM is now a highly rated Christian Contemporary station run by a non-profit corporation, but in 1975 it was a small, sleepy, NPR-affiliated radio station that I stumbled into on the campus of (then named) Columbia Union College in Takoma Park, MD, while looking for a brass ensemble concert. On that particular night, it was the retired dentist Walter Dorn ("Musical Memories") who welcomed me and made me an informal station intern. I am forever indebted to the kind folks at the station that took in this DC city kid and trained him to be a radio operator.

Armed with radio experience, I immediately sought out the student-run station WRCT-FM (88.3) when I matriculated at Carnegie Mellon University. During my tenure, I was a jazz DJ, the station's chief operator (as I held an FCC second class radiotelephone license), and assistant General Manager. I got a glimpse of big-time broadcasting during the summer of 1978 as a summer intern in the CBS television network's engineering department. Although my engineering career went in other directions, a piece of my heart has always belonged to radio, and writing this book has allowed me to come full circle.

Several archives have been crucial to this project, and I wish to thank them and their helpful archivists. Let me thank Laura Schnitker at the Broadcasting Archives at the University of Maryland; Judith Korey and the staff at the Felix E. Grant Jazz Archives at the University of the District of Columbia;

Brenda Nelson-Strauss and William Vanden Dries at the Archives of African American Music and Culture at Indiana University and the wonderful series *Black Radio: Telling it Like it Was* and its rich body of interviews conducted by Sonja Williams and series director Jacquie Gales-Webb; Kay Peterson at the Smithsonian Institution American History Archives; all the folks, including Dan Morgenstern, Vince Pelote, and Elizabeth Surles at the Institute of Jazz Studies at Rutgers University–Newark; Kathy Kienholz at the Carnegie Museum of Art in Pittsburgh; Ricky Riccardi at the Louis Armstrong House Museum; and all the helpful folk in the Performing Arts Division at the Library of Congress. Also, thanks to the libraries and librarians where vast chunks of text were typed: many thanks to Nick Patterson, Eli Lara, and Elizabeth Davis at the Columbia University Music and Arts Library; and Leighan Cazier and Barry Devlin at the Millburn Free Public Library and all the various other public libraries I holed up in in New Jersey, Washington, DC, New York, and Pittsburgh.

The research for *Jazz Radio America* was greatly aided by free and partly free radio web resources. The website WorldRadioHistory.com was most critical to the project. It was created by David E. F. Gleason, recipient of the 2023 Library of American Broadcasting Foundation Excellence in Broadcast Preservation Award. WorldRadioHistory.com has over nine million scanned and searchable(!) pages of important radio related trade publications, books, and magazines dating back to the 1920s and music trade publications back to the 1890s. Astonishingly, WorldRadioHistory.com is completely free to use, as is the Airhead Radio Survey Archive, which, to date, has almost 175,000 music surveys from almost more than 4,500 radio stations. These radio surveys, which were never created using reliable analytic methods, nonetheless provide insight into past radio programming where researchers can only wish there existed airchecks or detailed program logs. Theodoric Young's Radio-Locator.com is a useful database that merges FCC license and technical data with useful station streaming and website links.

There are so many individuals to thank, such as the anonymous contributors who submit and update the radio station histories on Wikipedia that provide leads to be checked and investigated using other sources. Thanks to the many blogs and web pages devoted to the radio histories of specific markets and to folks like Ron Rodrigues, Lauren Virshup, and Yulun Wang who let me peek at confidential data for sanity checks. Thanks to Ed Trefzger's JazzWeek and all the devoted jazz programmers that attend his annual JazzWeek Summit in San Jose. Thanks as well to the unique resource, GuideStar.com, invaluable in studying nonprofit radio stations owners.

I have been fortunate to have local access to Pittsburgh's Chuck Leavens and Scott Hanley, who lost the Battle of WDUQ but are now the proud principals at WZUM, the station that brought jazz back to town. I am grateful for conversations with several veteran jazz DJs, beginning with the Washington, DC, institution Rusty Hassan, Mark Ruffin, Evelyn Hawkins, Sharif Abdus-Salaam, Frank Greenlee, and Maxx Myrick. No matter who I talked to, all roads led to the late Dick LaPalm, who joyously shared his thoughts and insights on decades of jazz radio from the point of view of a record promoter.

If anything really got *Jazz Radio America* going, it was being named a 2019–20 fellow at Harvard University's Hutchins Center for African and African American Research under the welcoming gaze of Henry Louis Gates and his team.

I wish to express deep gratitude to the anonymous peer reviewers who made insightful and solid suggestions on how to improve the project and the book.

I am grateful for the backing of all my faculty colleagues at the University of Pittsburgh and would like to especially thank the late, great Geri Allen for her full faith and support in me as a contributor to jazz and jazz history. Thanks to Daphne Carr for helping me keep my head on straight. And I don't think anyone had more faith that this project and author had promise than Laurie Matheson, who more than once pulled me off the bench and back into the game.

Most of all, thanks for all the dedicated people who keep jazz radio alive.

Introduction

Meanwhile, at WBGO . . .

On the same day as the 2020 Iowa Caucuses and just a few weeks ahead of the impending COVID-19 pandemic, the board of directors of Newark Public Radio, license holders of WBGO-FM, held a public meeting at the New Jersey Historical Society, next door to the station's studios. The room was packed to overflowing, and the meeting was intense. Just a few days earlier the station's CEO had resigned under fire after an outside review supported accusations of perceived racial bias and a lack of effective internal reporting mechanisms. To weather the crisis, Bob Ottenhoff, WBGO's CEO from its 1978 founding, was called upon to bring peace and unity to the station and its community of listeners, paid staff, and volunteers. Ottenhoff promised to restore the station to harmony with "a simple but powerful concept: building a community of people that love jazz."[1] After an hour-long routine business session, the mostly white and male trustees listened to questions and comments from the mostly black attendees, who included current and former volunteer and employee staffers, community members, and musicians.

WBGO is considered by many to be the leading jazz radio station in the United States and, being the only full-time jazz station serving the world's largest community of jazz musicians, it can also claim to being the most important. In some respects, the crisis just described is merely a matter of management issues, common to many nonprofits. It does, however, touch on issues specific to radio, to public radio, and to jazz.

Many in attendance that night felt that the station's Newark roots had been sacrificed to its New York audience and its global fundraising aspirations. Many thought that the station was no longer engaged in Newark, the community that hosted it and to which it is licensed. There was more than an undercurrent of feeling that the increasingly professional operation had valued fundraising and audience research more than its original mission as a community-based jazz station. Several spoke up to bemoan its programming practices: the regimented on-air presentation of jazz on WBGO including the lack of staff autonomy, the practice of not reading musician credits on the air (and thus not celebrating the side musicians), the restriction to records from the music director–approved library, the use of programming clocks—schemes that structure each hour of airtime—to format the musical selections, and the absence of music from outside the station's sonic "wheelhouse" of hi-fi postwar swinging mainstream jazz.

A great deal of the strife in the WBGO meeting was related to unexpressed yet active tension over what jazz *is* and what jazz *means* as well as the meaning and purpose of public radio. An overly simplistic yet enduring binary has jazz representing a multiracial democratic ideal of egalitarian and meritocratic participation on one pole and a black music of protest, alienation, and critique of modernism (American modernism in particular) on the other. Jazz is a complicated social and cultural object with repudiations, critiques, affirmations, and embraces of American modernism all present in its practices. Even working with the simple binary, it is easy to understand the largely black and poor Newark community's fears. In a city that has fallen from its position as one of America's most prosperous and important manufacturing centers to that of a struggling city with high unemployment and troubled public schools, at odds with its own suburbanite-dominated state government and shivering in the long shadow of New York City, the fear that one of its prime cultural jewels, WBGO, is more concerned with its listening and fundraising numbers in cosmopolitan New York and among its worldwide audience of internet streamers is consistent with Newark's ongoing trauma.

To be sure, the professionalization of the top staff brought conflict between the increasingly white and peripatetic managers of WBGO and the community-based nonmanagerial staff. But as the meeting continued, issues of ownership—of WBGO and of jazz itself—begin to be openly aired. These issues underlay many disputes.

The question of who owns jazz is in some respects a ridiculous one, but in matters of cultural politics, cultural capital is a valuable asset. In an American culture that uniquely values property rights—to the extent that the ownership of people was written into its constitution—African American ownership of and authority concerning jazz have been challenged from the outset, right down to what we call the music. Not only did whites make the first jazz record, but even the music's name, highly contested by black musicians for more than one hundred years, was imposed from without. The power to name, to say what something is, or what it isn't, has been understood to be the original grant to humankind:

> And out of the ground the LORD God formed every beast of the field, and every fowl of the air; and brought them unto Adam to see what he would call them: and whatsoever Adam called every living creature, that was the name thereof.[2]

Rather than a trivial power, the power to name something is a fundamental and essential power of ownership. Over the years, radio has played an outsized role in maintaining the shifting, porous wall around the public conception of jazz, at times inclusive, lately rather exclusive.

Why Won't They Play My Record?

The question at the origin of this project a decade ago was simple to state but complicated to answer. "Why does some jazz music get played on the radio and why does some not get played?" This question, of course, begat others. "Why is jazz only heard on noncommercial and satellite radio today?" "With the amazing range of performed jazz styles, why does only a narrow subset of that range of receive consistent airplay?" And "Is that even true?" In order to resolve these questions, it is necessary to avoid writing a history comprised of anecdotes or a history of famous radio personalities and jazz musicians. Radio, like jazz, is a complex social structure that is constructed as much by its material conditions, technology, enterprises, social relationships, racial policies, industry practices, and politics as anything else. Radio, jazz, music lovers, innovators, the live music industry, the record industry, Congress, labor unions, and listeners all combined to create jazz radio as we have heard it.

Jazz Radio America is a study of the current media environment for jazz music and a history of jazz radio since the decline of network radio beginning shortly after World War II. The book has two overlapping parts. Part I is a history and analysis of jazz on commercial radio from roughly 1948 to 1980. It was around 1948 that the television networks began offering full evening schedules. And in 1948 a critically important radio programming innovation occurred: WDIA become the first station to offer a full programming schedule aimed at African American listeners. In marking the slow demise of commercial jazz radio, 1980 is as good a date as any; it was when New York's all-jazz WRVR-FM switched to country music.

Although the origin of today's noncommercial radio dates back far earlier than the 1945 FCC ruling that set aside twenty FM channels for educational use, Part II is concerned mainly with noncommercial jazz radio's mid-1980s peak and the decline to its current endangered status. Initially jazz enjoyed a warm welcome across noncommercial radio, but as the survival stakes have risen for the public radio sector, jazz has declined there as news, talk, and information programming has prospered. While jazz has fared better on community and college radio, it also faces serious challenges there.

Not quite simultaneously but in a broadly overlapping manner, jazz could be heard in any of four ways on U.S. radio for about two or three decades beginning in the 1950s:

1. Radio stations with omnibus or variety programming were disappearing, but middle-of-the-road AM stations (a reaction to youth-oriented Top 40) still played a little jazz, best found in regularly scheduled slots such as weekday evenings or weekends. Crossover jazz vocals like Frank Sinatra's or Nat Cole's and the occasional jazz instrumental hit record, for example, Toots Thielemans's "Bluesette," Henry Mancini's "The Pink Panther" (sax solo by Plas Johnson), or Kenny Ball's 1961 Dixieland hit "Midnight in Moscow" could, however, fit the inoffensive pop music format.[3] (Oh, how we cherished Bobby Bryant's cornet solo on Cole's "L-O-V-E.") This was also true of black radio, although these stations' jazz containment slots might at first have been more prominent mid-day, overnight, or weekend morning shows, and in addition to the vocals by such singers as Nancy Wilson, Dinah Washington, Etta James, Ray Charles, or Gil Scott-Heron, the crossover instrumental hits would be funkier tunes like Cannonball Adderley's "Mercy, Mercy, Mercy," Lee Morgan's "The Sidewinder," Quincy Jones' reworking of Benny Golson's "Killer Joe," or Herbie Hancock's "Chameleon."[4]

2. During this period, experimentation with radio formats flourished, and fortunate jazz listeners may have had one of the few dozen all-jazz commercial radio stations come to (and usually shortly thereafter, depart from) their market. There were both AM and FM all-jazz stations, the latter having additional appeal to hi-fi aficionados but limited audience potential until FM radios came into greater consumer use in the 1970s. Chapter 3 traces the all-jazz lives of about two dozen radio stations. The first half-dozen took up the format before 1959 and at the end of 1980 only about the same number were still operating.

3. Other products of that experimentation were the free-form, underground, and progressive formats, exciting and adventurous concepts in radio programming that could be found on both commercial and noncommercial FM radio in the late 1960s and early 1970s. Consistent with the growing anti-war and anti-establishment zeitgeist (Do Your Thing!), free-form radio gave DJ-programmers almost unlimited license to mix music styles from moment to moment, and jazz itself, resistant to commercialism, imbued with improvisational energy and spirit, and directly influential to an entire family of popular music styles, was often found here. Lacking prohibitions against long music tracks or extended solos, these loose formats emphasized music on albums rather than the record industry's heavily promoted singles.

4. Finally, some the educational radio stations set aside at FM's birth became havens for jazz music because of the allure of and interest in hi-fi that appealed to jazz fans, because jazz was popular with college radio programmers, because of jazz's rising cultural cachet and acceptance in academic environments, and because of ideological compatibility between jazz and many educational broadcasters. The collapse of commercial jazz radio would feed directly into noncommercial jazz radio's expansion.

Whereas the first mode limped along for decades (and is still available in a few places), the second and third modes, with rare exceptions, gave way completely by the mid-1970s. A confluence of technology and marketing made the commercial FM radio spectrum far too valuable in management's view for free-form or jazz programming. (Easy listening and classical continued to be profitable niche formats for selling advertising: Easy listening was ideal for reaching a subset of older listeners, and the perceived sophistication of the classical music audience was often enough to support at least one station in a moderately large market through the sponsorships of products and services "of distinction.")

With the progressive radio format, which grew out of free-form and underground radio, the music industry began to emphasize the LP (higher price, higher profit) for pop and rock sales at about the same time the consumer electronics sector realized there were more than just jazz, classical, and Broadway fans out there to sell hi-fi components to. Finally, FM radios became widely available in automobiles. Very rapidly, broadcasters that owned AM-FM combinations switched their emphasis to FM. (It took twenty years, but in the end, change was rapid.) Jazz's endangered status on commercial radio made an even stronger case for its preservation on noncommercial radio, and by the mid-1970s jazz was second only to (highbrow) classical music on those stations. It was the fourth mode that survived and grew until a reversal, which began as a trickle in the 1980s, led to an outright stampede away from jazz and music in general in the 1990s.

Jazz and noncommercial radio are partners in a curious dance of intersecting interests. The current world of noncommercial jazz radio manages to bridge a major institutional divide: the mission-centered world of noncommercial radio interacts with the market-oriented and profit-centered music industry and vice versa. In this clash of cultural, educational, and financial institutions within an artistically focused corner of larger and prosperous culture industries, all sides depend on one another. Together they have negotiated a common set of practices for jazz radio concerning the boundaries of musical content, recording studio and production norms, hosting styles, track lengths, and the distribution of music, liner notes, and liner art to programmers. Broadcasters depend on the industry to provide music programming (records), promote and nurture new talent, reframe and feature established artists, and define musical trends. And increasingly, today's musicians are functioning within jazz radio without corporate support and investing their own labor and money in order to participate.

Radio's jazz programmers supplement their meager pay by earning prestige and influence in the field they love. More than is the case with most other music genres, (older) jazz fans still listen to radio, and radio programmers have great power in determining the music aired. These days, jazz radio programmers are flooded with releases from established major labels and independent labels with rosters of jazz artists and with CDs, EPs, and digital download releases produced by the artists themselves. In the past the record industry whittled the material by legions of aspiring musicians down to a few hundred releases per year, with the breakout of only a handful of new artists. Today's jazz programmers are faced with evaluating twenty to forty label and DIY releases per week.[5] From among these, programmers have to choose which few new releases to feature in their limited airtime allotments alongside the established, sometimes classic, jazz tracks already in the permanent library. In this respect jazz radio is different from most commercial formats, which do not mix new and old music. Despite the rise of social media, blogging, and playlists as new music showcases, jazz radio's programmers, still positioned between the music makers and the radio audience, are now collectively the most influential gatekeepers in the jazz world.[6]

Jazz programmers and DJs choose artists and records subject to station library and format restrictions and, when allowed, according to taste (not all DJs can choose, as this may be the purview of the program or music director, especially on jazz-formatted stations). Gatekeepers employed by organizations in the culture industry—label managers or A&R (artist and repertoire) representatives and venue bookers—or nonprofit agencies—programmers, music directors, festival directors, and curators—discover, sponsor, and bring cultural objects to public attention. In potentially linking artists to audience, gatekeeping decisions in these organizations "can block or facilitate communication" within a complex network of organizations that both facilitate and regulate the innovation process.[7] The role and power of cultural gatekeepers in relation to fine and popular arts hints at the complex interweaving of profit-driven and mission-driven organizations and the ability of unpaid entities to thwart or propel aspiring artists, but it is worth considering that, given the organizational and managerial range of noncommercial radio as well as the increasing presence of internet-based listening options, gatekeepers cannot be narrowly defined or described.

Musicians look to jazz radio for help in creating visibility and maintaining a reputation with the jazz public, though they too now have new media alternatives to replace or supplement radio. Musicians' own initiative and "hustle" can place them in spots where their work is known to audiences in key cities, jazz journalists, club owners and festival bookers, and jazz radio programmers. Hustling artists may reach out personally to these figures or they may hire publicists, some of whom specialize in record promotion, radio distribution, news coverage, or all of the above. There is no set formula for using social media to get the word out about the music, performances, and recordings, but blogs, streaming, and special fan access opportunities work especially well for artists who already have a following that they wish to retain, nurture, and augment. (A prominent example is Emmett Cohen's *Live from Emmett's Place,* a professional-looking streaming series that has netted Cohen close to 175,000 YouTube subscribers.)[8] Also, by making live or recorded live content available to fans, artists can avoid drastically modifying their music just to please radio programmers.

Jazz Radio America argues that, historically, the range of jazz styles that make it past the combined gatekeepers to radio is limited, despite the wide variety of music makers either seeking harbor under or being unable to escape the label "jazz." The latter has especially been the case for generations of African American experimentalists for whom race has been a barrier to acceptance as concert hall composers. It is true as ever today, but those limitations are not uniform across all types of noncommercial radio, so it is vitally important to understand the range of noncommercial radio operations and their relation to jazz, which is the primary topic of Chapters 5 and 6.

Histories of radio often focus on programming, technology, finance, and regulatory policy. Cultural studies scholars have brought issues of gender, class, urban-rural interests, and with great difficulty and ingenuity, the agency of the radio audience into radio studies.[9] Ethnicity has probably been more often a topic of radio studies than has race, especially with regard to foreign-language broadcasting. Practically the only areas of radio studies to pay attention to race have been those that have been more concerned with the music-industrial complex than with radio. There are, however, two indispensable studies of race in radio: Barbara Savage's *Broadcasting Freedom* (1999), a study of serious programming aimed at African American listeners during World War II, and the late William Barlow's *Voice Over* (1999), the first overall history of U. S. black radio. Since then, Brian Ward's *Radio and the Struggle for Civil Rights in the South* (2004) addressed the open and covert coordination between black southern radio, usually white-owned and-managed, and the civil rights movement. Perhaps the most in-depth look at a single chapter in black radio history is Louis Cantor's *Wheelin' on Beale* (1992), which takes a book-length picture of the nation's first full-time station to appeal to blacks, Memphis's WDIA. Ryan Ellett's reference work *Encyclopedia of Black Radio in the United States* (2012) is also an essential resource.[10]

Race plays a part in both the commercial and noncommercial eras of jazz radio and is a factor in regulatory policy, ownership, employment and management, programming, and listenership. During broadcast radio's first half century, the absence of black elected officials resulted in impotence in regulatory matters for African Americans. For example, the primary regulatory authority for radio, with final approval of all licensing matters, is the Federal Communications Commission, established by the Communications Act of 1934.[11] Its five commissioners are appointed by the president and confirmed by the Senate to serve overlapping five-year terms. Until the 1972 appointment of former NAACP president Benjamin Hooks by Richard Nixon, only two women and no persons of color had ever served as an FCC commissioner. During that interval, exactly one African American had been elected to the Senate.[12] Clearly, African Americans were almost completely voiceless in federal policy matters concerning radio, including the value of diversity in ownership, racially offensive programming, the absence of programming serving black audiences, the limited employment of black talent on radio and behind the scenes, and decisions about who received radio broadcast licenses.

By the time the networks were forming in the late 1920s, radio was an important and growing business sector. As in other industries, de facto segregation practices affected radio, despite its occasional employment of black musical and comedy talent. More often the jazz heard on the air was played by whites rather than blacks, with the exceptions of Earl Hines, Duke Ellington, Cab Calloway, and Count Basie as frequently aired black bandleaders. A true indicator of their perilous status was the complete absence of sponsored broadcasts featuring black musicians.[13] Swing music, dominant on network radio in the 1930s, often used the envelope of African American jazz—jazz instrumentation, jazz arranging styles—but with limited emphasis on improvisation and often having a focus on novelty features. As a result, to undiscriminating ears Guy Lombardo and Erskine Hawkins were equally essential swing bands.[14]

Things began to change with bebop in the 1940s as among fans and DJs jazz started to develop a separate though sometimes fuzzy identity distinct from popular music. Radio stations, black and white, began to offer programs appealing directly to jazz fans. On shows not specifically featuring jazz, however, jazz vocals and catchy jazz instrumentals could still chart and be heard along with popular records. Gradually, white and black radio grew to favor different types of jazz crossovers. Black radio's rhythm and blues playlists would feature releases by artists such as Louis Jordan, Lionel Hampton, Lucky Millinder, and Ruth Brown that were performed by jazz musicians, had the familiar instrumentation of jazz combos or big bands, and consistently challenged the boundaries of jazz. This was temporary. As the 1950s wore on, the Top 40, Middle of the Road (MOR), good music/easy listening, and R&B formats had hardened against incursions by the rare crossover jazz hit such as "Madison Time" by Ray Bryant (which reached 30 on the Billboard Top

100). Otherwise, jazz records were to be heard only on jazz programs or jazz segments, although jazz, the formal language of a generation of commercial arrangers and musicians, was still frequently used in jingles, themes, commercials, and station identifications.

Jazz and Ideology Play out on Radio

As a matter of history, jazz and radio, icons of twentieth-century modernity, have been deeply engaged with one another. Jazz, however one defines its boundaries and essential elements, is the influential African American musical genre that emerged from a confluence of cultural streams in the century's first years. The music's concurrency with the United States' transition from agrarian-rural to industrial-urban to information age–suburban, from isolationist nation to global superpower, from Black Codes and Jim Crow through the Great Migration to the civil rights movement and the age of Obama allow it to be viewed from any number of ideological perspectives and to deliver a wide range of aspirational payloads, in addition to, of course, being appreciated for its inherent musical qualities. The same musical object, say, Louis Armstrong's recording of Fats Waller and Andy Razaf's "(What Did I Do to Be So) Black and Blue," could be appreciated for its earnest and innovative improvisational explorations, for its value as protest, for its subtextual claims for equality, for its humanitarian appeal for societal inclusion ("I'm white, inside . . ."), or for its blending of musical genres (blues, jazz, and Tin Pan Alley) into something uniquely "American." Jazz can simultaneously serve as American's model artistic contribution to the world, as black classical music, as evidence of the acceptance of black culture in America, as the soundtrack of rebellion and resistance to the marginalization of African Americans, and as an early warning system for sustainability and justice. These simultaneous constructions of meaning and significance in cultural, social, and political discourses allow jazz and related music forms to illuminate undercurrents of race, class, gender, and power that operate within radio and within society.

The question of how ideology and music interact, central to this examination of jazz radio, appears in each chapter. The network era that leads into Chapter 1 was a time when radio was rivaled only by newspapers and movies for mass media power. In those years, when socialism and fascism were vital and potent threats to American capitalism, federal policy favored broadcasters' using radio for profitable entertainment rather than social messaging, making it difficult for labor unions and reform organizations to obtain licenses. Hiding out as non-ideological natural law, market capitalism enjoyed a great and unseen victory consistent with Terry Eagleton's "vanishing mediator." Such victors enjoy power in its most essential and effective form, a power that is "not something confined to armies and parliaments: it is, rather, a pervasive, intangible network of force which weaves itself into our slightest gestures and most intimate utterances."[15] Employing the grandest rhetorical weapon, market ideology declared itself "normal" and "natural" and marked its rivals as ideologues and extremists.

In Part II it is proposed that in noncommercial radio, ideology is an important driver of programming philosophies. Even as these stations face increasing budgetary pressures, their mission, almost always stated in writing, is in competition with the listenership and membership goals thought to be needed for survival. Aesthetics competes with popularity mediated through ideology, such that a station's programming choices walk a line between simply surviving, serving the mission, attracting new listeners, and retaining contributing members.

Three interrelated questions of ideology seem important here. The first is how ideologies regarding radio enable or block jazz's access to the air. These ideologies address the market allocation of broadcast resources and opportunity, race, and the value of culture. The second is how station ideology situates the jazz that is played. The third, a major subject of Chapter 5, concerns the progressive and conservative nature of jazz production and performance, the music's own ideological potential.

Many ideological positions have formed with respect to jazz since its inception. These include positions regarding modernism (jazz's arrival coincides roughly with the modernist-primitivist push and pull exemplified by the arrival of cubism and the tumultuous premieres of Schoenberg and Stravinsky) and post-modernism, presaged by such figures as Thelonious Monk, Charles Mingus, Ornette Coleman, and Sun Ra.[16] However, jazz's dominant ideological metaphors are those of African American resistance to oppression and racism versus a stubbornly inclusive Americanism, together forming what Ingrid Monson calls a "familiar standoff between blackness and colorblindness."[17] Yet in the early days of jazz on radio, the music's very blackness was the attraction, if diluted by interpretation by white performers using templates familiar from minstrelsy and vaudeville. The ideology that jazz was American music developed gradually, displacing a narrative of racial essentialism and exceptionalism, paced by black social progress, embraced by blacks' desires for integration and widespread participation by whites in jazz, through cold war projections of American harmony instead of apartheid.

The American argument for meritocracy had and has many proponents. Its mythologizing allows a wide range of political stances to gather under its tent and feel invested in the music. Actor and director Clint Eastwood, long noted as both a jazz fan and a political conservative, considers jazz a uniquely American creation, "something that could only come out of such a diverse country as America," and [black] jazz players as "pioneers of integration," judged on talent and "ability in an era when people were judging people by a lot of other things."[18] Although Eastwood told this story in 2011, this kind of writing dates at least to the cold war, when the growing appreciation of jazz as highbrow art coincided with the geopolitical need to counter the negative global image of American racial segregation. John Szwed observed that "in America, critical writing on jazz (whether pro or con) began by recognizing that this music was born under the sign of race, and assumed its role to be oppositional, turning national values on their head. Only recently have some authors reevaluated jazz and found it reflecting core American values even in its subversion and opposition."[19] It is useful to note that the great majority of these critical writers were from outside the black jazz community; otherwise, they might have noted much sooner the wide potential of jazz to challenge America's segregated status quo, demanding inclusion and respect on their own terms.

Once planted so deeply in ideological furrows, and finding institutional cover as America's classical music, America's unique contribution to the arts, this notion of jazz as "reflecting core American values" has barely faded, though the flip side, "subversion and opposition," was just as readily on display. The United States' cold war opponent, the Union of Soviet Socialist Republics, certainly capitalized on this image of jazz. The Soviets "viewed jazz as the music of the class struggle—through jazz, subjugated black lower classes struggled for self-expression and autonomy from capitalist oppressors."[20] For the Soviets, jazz was indeed thoroughly American, since music expressing the "struggle for self-expression and autonomy" was obviously unneeded in the workers' paradise.

It may not be totally coincidental that the cold war significantly overlapped with the evolution and rapid growth of public radio from the almost dormant educational broadcasting sector. An ideological conflict in almost every sense, the cold war stimulated investment in education, particularly in science and technology, but the battlegrounds extended to matters as far afield as sports and culture. These educational institutions and their allies eventually come to dominate public radio; at this critical moment, jazz entered the mix as an intellectual, not merely hot, music. "It became a unique and enigmatic instrument of ideological and intellectual warfare," Lisa Davenport observed in *Jazz Diplomacy*, and in promoting the expressive voice of America's subaltern, came to symbolize the superior cultural inclusion of American democracy."[21]

One more complication in the 1950s picture, one that would endure for another two decades and eventually lead to smooth jazz (itself yet another complication), was the turn to soul jazz. With an embrace of musical elements from the black church and a renewal of its vows with the blues, black jazz musicians of the 1950s extended the black reclamation process that began with bebop. Pioneered by figures such as Horace Silver and perfected commercially by players like Ramsey Lewis, Cannonball Adderley, Groove Holmes, and

Bobby Timmons, soul jazz, sometimes conflated with hard bop, incorporated musical elements and gestures from black sanctified music. It was the cultural blackness of these elements that set white critics' hair on fire. If authenticity in jazz was so overtly connected to the black experience, what of jazz musicians and critics who lacked that experience?

In 1961 the historian Lerone Bennett Jr. wrote about soul jazz as blues fixative to a general but predominantly African American readership in the pages of *Ebony*:

> Outraged by the growth of classical-oriented jazz and inspired by the success of artists like Mahalia Jackson and Ray Charles, the young New York musicians began in the late Fifties to reassess the Negro folk idiom—the cries, chants, shouts, work songs and pulsating rhythmic vitality of gospel singers and shouting choirs. Then, in one of the most astounding about-faces in jazz history, the fundamentalists (most of them are conservatory-trained liberals) abandoned Bartok, Schönberg and "all that jazz" and immersed themselves in the music of Thomas A. Dorsey, Roberta Martin, and Howlin' Wolf. Jazz, which had been rolling merrily along on a fugue kick, turned from the academy and faced the store front church.
>
> The soul-sayers, in contrast to the rather anemic West Coast school, stressed a hard-swinging, gospel-flavored blues feeling and emphasized—some critics say flaunted—their spiritual ties to the cottonfield–collard greens tradition. In the beginning the qualities deemed soulful (earthiness, emotional and spiritual vigor) were canonized under the general term—funky.[22]

Bennett's recap of a decade's worth of developments in jazz is reductive, but it points to still-living controversies among jazz historians concerning the intentions of these black creative musicians. Did hard bop and soul jazz intentionally answer cool (West Coast) jazz and Third Stream music? Bennett's mention of the leaders of the Second Viennese school was surely claiming a total rejection of classical modernism to an extent with which black bebop musicians would not concur. And Bennett's consistent smirking at black "conservatory-trained" musicians needing to get back to their roots smacked of an embrace of primitivism.

Was this music designed to exclude whites? A decade of hurtful "Crow Jim" debates would follow. Bennett holds up as Exhibit A the critic John Tynan—infamous for later labeling the music of John Coltrane and Eric Dolphy "anti-jazz"—who claimed that the motivation of the black musicians was extramusical and political: "The motivation, in my opinion, can be traced more to racialistic feeling as Negroes than to further development of jazz as art." Tynan continued, "It is as if they hurl the challenge at their white colleagues: 'Copy this, if you can.'"[23] Tynan's use of "racialistic" was explosive; it was a soft term for *racist*. He implicitly endorsed an ideology of "art for art's sake" at the exact time the ideals of the black arts movement were shaping up, as well as a growing and vitally important black pride movement. Was Tynan aware that many of his favorite black jazz musicians were still "conking" their hair?

One point to consider in the controversy about soul jazz is its direct link to contemporaneous developments in black popular music, that is, soul music. I am unaware of Ray Charles, Sam Cooke, Booker T & the MGs, or Carla Thomas's ever being accused of using elements of black church music to keep whites out of R&B. Without question, at least to me, soul jazz celebrated the black experience in America and formed an important precursor to the "black is beautiful" movement, which also reflected the importance of the black church in the growing civil rights movement.

To the extent that it still could feature long playing times and extended instrumental solos, soul jazz was unlikely to be readily incorporated into soul radio stations' normal rotations, but edited to radio-friendly singles, soul jazz was surprisingly successful and sometimes enjoyed crossover success. On the backs of Hammond organs, shuffle beats, and modified gospel harmony, soul jazz, in partnership with black AM radio, helped form the basis of a modest 1960s jazz industry revival that has been mostly neglected by jazz historians. Respected or not, soul jazz was among the most successful jazz styles both in record sales and in radio airplay, and it has won the long-term battle for the hearts and minds of jazz listeners.

It should come as little surprise that jazz—the music, its recordings, forms, history, players, and practices—could simultaneously embody contradictory ideological meanings, given that the music emerged from the post-Reconstruction America of Du Bois's double consciousness; that the music might be received differently by the communities who nurtured it than by the communities it entertained, even where these communities overlapped. Under the extreme segregation of the era, black America's cultural utterances could only be expressed openly if they had a patina acceptable to white America. Beyond the specific paradigm of U.S. racial dialectics, Pierre Bourdieu demonstrated that even an object as simple as rice could have a wide range of social uses, concealed by the "apparent constancy of the product."[24] The ethnomusicologist Travis Jackson, noting the range of relationships that "performers and other participants in musical events" maintain with the music, also recognizes that "the meanings of jazz are not simply *in* the music; rather, they are constructed from the ongoing, dynamic relationship between what one encounters in musical events, the dispositions one brings to those events, and the relationships between the two."[25] Meaning in music, and perhaps especially radio-delivered music, is intricately tied to the way the music is used by all parties—programmers, listeners, musicians, and the music industry—and how they view one another.

This dipole of "musical embodiment of American values" and "resistance to hegemonic oppression" has dominated jazz discourse for quite some time. The cultural critic Albert Murray is often cited as resisting the resistance. Murray shared the view of Ralph Ellison, his close associate, that the burdens of black arts movement sociology, as exemplified by the writings of Amiri Baraka, were enough to "give the blues the blues."[26] Murray's project of locating the black experience at the very heart of the American experience saw jazz as key in this regard. Baraka and Murray were perhaps not so far apart; where Murray saw black music already nestled at the core of American culture, Baraka saw an American culture that refused to acknowledge it. Both lamented a bourgeois black establishment in denial about the music's power of protest and change. Murray wrote of Ellington as

> the quintessential American composer because it is his body of work more than any other that adds up to the most specific, comprehensive, universally appealing musical complement to what Constance Rourke, author of *American Humor: A Study of the National Character,* had in mind when she referred to "emblems for a pioneer people who require resilience as a prime trait." Nor can it be said too often that at its best an Ellington performance sounds as if it knows the truth about all the other music in the world and is looking for something better. Not even the Constitution represents a more intrinsically American statement and achievement than that.[27]

Jazz is a performed demonstration, Murray says, of American values and ideals. John A. Kouwenhoven is even more specific, citing jazz as the art form first and best representing the Emersonian ideal of "union which is perfect only 'when all the uniters are isolated,'" as jazz musicians are with their respective tasks during performance. Kouwenhoven, who also likens jazz's collective individuality to the New York skyline, extends the analogy between jazz and American democracy further:

> One need only remember that the Constitution itself, by providing for a federation of separate units, became the infinitely extendible framework for the process of reconciling liberty and unity over vast areas and conflicting interests. Its seven brief articles, providing for checks and balances between interests, classes, and branches of the government, establish, in effect, the underlying beat which gives momentum and direction to a political process Richard Hofstadter has called "a harmonious system of mutual frustration"— a description that fits a jazz performance as well as it fits our politics.[28]

At the dipole's other end are notions of the music's inherent resistance to the status quo. If the avant-garde music known as bebop propelled jazz from mere entertainment into high art, Eric Lott notes that this musical movement breathed the same vapors as the events around it. "Brilliantly outside," Lott writes, "bebop was intimately if indirectly related to the militancy of its moment. Militancy and music were undergirded by the same social facts; the music attempted to resolve at the level of style what the militancy combated in the streets. If bebop did not offer a call to arms, as one writer has said in another context, it at least acknowledged that the call had been made."[29] Going further, Lott maintains that "These elements originally made up what Amiri Baraka called the 'willfully harsh, anti-assimilationist sound of bebop,' which at once reclaimed jazz from its brief cooptation by white 'swing' bandleaders like the aptly named Paul Whiteman and made any future dilution that much harder."[30]

When jazz landed on noncommercial radio in the 1970s both of these ideologies explained its presence. The music of resistance was a welcome constituent on community, free-form, and alternative radio—each offering its own critique of commercial radio and mass culture—and the art music representing the best of America was a featured component of a public radio network controlled largely by universities and cultural institutions and funded in part by taxpayers.

Within the totality of noncommercial jazz radio, stations' programming of music appears to conform to either a conservative or a progressive philosophy, because within jazz, certain styles enjoy stronger sales and more reliable audience appeal than do others. For this study, I consider the most conservative programming position to be one that only includes mainstream styles, namely, cool, hard bop, post-bop, Latin jazz, and big band swing styles. Such music would typically feature acoustic instruments, steady tempos, swinging rhythmic playing styles, and functional or modal harmony. A progressive programming style would include free, experimental, or "outside" jazz as well as music considered too commercial by many jazz adherents, such as R&B crossover, smooth jazz, soul jazz, jazz fusion, jazz funk, acid jazz, and early jazz.

What is deemed conservative or progressive may be a somewhat arbitrary decision; it certainly has little to do with interpreting the music as inclusively American or resistively alienated, because almost any jazz performance can be read as either. Jazz can play a role in the politics of jazz radio. Political content can be topical and, as times change, its political content, often subject to dispute, can fade or flare. It seems impossible to ever separate "Strange Fruit" or "Fables of Faubus" from their political meanings, but perhaps a bit more knowledge of jazz history is needed to recognize the implication of Coltrane's "Alabama," the black nationalist meaning of "A Night in Tunisia," or the cultural politics of Don Pullen's "Big Alice." Progressive programming can include jazz that is overtly political, but so can conservative programming.

For the broadcast industry, resuming the development of television after World War II required massive investments of capital and steep increases in production expenses that, coupled with the nation's rapidly growing enthusiasm for the new medium, signaled a swift decline for network radio. The end of the war provided a clear and easy division of eras for the radio historian. In their standard one-volume history of U.S. broadcasting, Christopher Sterling and John Kittross call the start of the postwar period, 1945–1952, the "era of great change," followed by "the age of television."[31] Eric Rothenbuhler and Tom McCourt, noting the trebling of radio stations, the impact of transistor radios, and the migration of prime time variety, comedy, and drama programs to television, aptly titled an article about this period "Radio Redefines Itself, 1947–1962."[32]

Neither jazz nor radio has been a static, well-defined entity over the timeframe of this history, thus complicating the initial question of what did and didn't get played. Radio's redefining did not stop in 1962. Radio formats were spawned in dazzling numbers, as many, Phil Eberly observed, as "cereal brands on the grocery shelf."[33] For approximately thirty years jazz feinted, jabbed, and kept on its toes before effectively being knocked out in terms of commercial radio. In fact, knocked clear out of the ring, jazz was fortunate to make a soft landing in the newly energized and rapidly growing noncommercial radio sector. There, for ten to fifteen years, jazz enjoyed a remarkable broadcast revival until noncommercial radio began to resemble its for-profit kin. While slow to catch on with the public, FM broadcasting ultimately was a vehicle for the total overhaul of radio including the rebirth and exponential growth of public radio.

One assertion of this study is that the engagement of jazz with commercial radio helped lead to greater fluidity in its styles. This is sure to be a controversial view, so a bit more elaboration may (or may not) help. At any given time, musicians are creating music that some will call jazz and others will not. This discourse is participated in by those interested in jazz, some who are rewarded monetarily and others who are compensated by building reputations that increase their standing in the jazz or music community. Some are fans who vote with their bodies and wallets. My argument is that, especially through the relatively unusual adoption of the genre-based format of all-jazz radio, commercial radio conditionally welcomed certain boundary-stretching musics—bossa nova, jazz-rock fusion, world jazz, funk, and early smooth jazz come to mind—that shared attributes with more popular music genres.

Book-length publications about jazz radio as an institution are lacking. As one might expect, the topic has been grazed both by writers in music and by writers in media studies. The latter have long acknowledged the importance of jazz in early radio, but as jazz's popularity has waned, so has its role in media studies. Still, recent works about commercial and noncommercial broadcasting have been concerned with the ideological contest over the control of and access to radio, and with the agency of the radio audience, both centrally important to this work. Within music, though works regarding popular music and mass culture, notably rock and pop, have provided wonderful models, the specific issues and controversies pertaining to black music and specifically jazz music can be quite different.

Jazz historians (myself included) have directed some energy toward the early days of jazz radio, including the emergence of Duke Ellington, and wonderful work has been done in cataloging and collecting appearances by Ellington, Waller, Basie, and others in the form of reference books about network and local radio, though without much analysis.[34] In my own research I have profited from the work of writers concerned with the intersection of jazz and politics, and I have reinvested this work in considering jazz's access to the airwaves and its presence in the missions of prestigious cultural institutions.[35]

Writers in media studies have often considered the importance of the role of jazz at different points in radio history, though they seldom focus on the marriage of media and jazz specifically.[36] Yet these very meaningful and important studies rarely investigate the fluctuating meaning of the term *jazz* and, perhaps more important, fail to consider the specific discourses concerning race that accompany jazz. However, media studies writers have provided some very useful models for understanding the philosophies and practices of programmers, and I have again reinvested those models in understanding the uneasy alliance between the jazz sector of the music industry and commercial and noncommercial broadcast management.

Perhaps because of the visibility of its politics or because of the appropriation of public funds, and because NPR, PRX, and others have been wildly successful in engaging affluent and educated listeners, public radio has been the topic of several thorough studies. All of them mention jazz—it would be hard not to, given its signature presence on public radio stations, especially in the late 1970s—but the focus has largely been on the struggles over funding, audience appeal, the diversity of audiences and programming, and the future of public radio.

This topic, jazz and radio, is largely overlooked because it falls between music and media studies. With only a few exceptions, jazz studies, while moving quite effectively past history, biography, and style and into studies of cultural politics and social justice, has largely overlooked examining institutions that are important to jazz. And certainly, studies of institutions have seldom placed much importance on the impact that jazz has had on them.

Although the turn from mass culture to popular culture studies reflects a new respect for the agency of the audience, musicologists have only recently and reluctantly taken up the challenge of the mass media. According to Marcello Sorce Keller, "Probably the number-one reason why musicology is little inclined to deal with mass-media is that doing so would be tantamount [to] facing primarily the question of 'music listening,' *tout court*," which clearly challenges us to develop a different set of tools.[37] Fortunately, the interdisciplinary field of sound studies, which includes some participation by a new generation of musicologists, is beginning to pay significant attention to radio and related sound technologies. Important texts by Mark Katz, Jonathan Sterne, Timothy Dean Taylor, Tony Gradeja, Alexander G. Weheliye, Paul D. Greene and Thomas Porcello, and others have begun to admirably fill the gap.[38]

Jazz, Radio, and Records

It is doubtful that jazz would have had such a dramatic impact on music and American culture had it not been coupled to the technological capabilities of the newly developed mass media. One reason jazz was able to project American vitality around the world between the world wars was the availability of jazz records. The genre itself had been fashioned from a mix of cultural ingredients, many of them arriving from around the circum-Caribbean. Sailors and merchant seamen carried jazz records to ports around the world. The heavy hand of the United States in the Western hemisphere spread jazz through military installations, diplomatic functions, and the social activities of U.S. multinational corporations and their employees. Further, record companies on both sides of the Atlantic had distribution arrangements with each other. Radio waves did not respect borders, and jazz was spread abroad by both U.S. and international broadcasters. The mass media—let's not leave out motion pictures—functioned, as Warren R. Pickney called it, as the "cultural invader" that came into its own at precisely the right time for jazz.[39]

It was mass media, extending globally and benefiting from the newly emerging concept of international cooperation on compatible technical standards, that helped enable the rapid, cosmopolitan development of the music. Jazz was a major part of the mix of "software" that enabled the technological possibilities of radio and records to be realized as mature and profitable mass culture industries as broadcasting stations and networks and as record companies, each with other affiliated business enterprises. In short, jazz was one, but certainly not the only one, of the "killer apps" that lifted radio and records from fascinating and promising niche technologies to dominant social institutions, radio all the more so owing to its ability to function as life's daily audio wallpaper.

Jazz and the syncopated music styles associated with it dominated the schedules of early radio, especially in metropolitan areas. As early as 1928 stations large and small were devoting little more than a quarter of their music time to "serious and part-way serious" music and allotting up to three-quarters of their time to "syncopation." Charles Merz of the *New York Times* wrote, "At all the larger stations the usual procedure is to get the serious part of the program done with fairly early in the day, so as to have the evening free for sheer enjoyment. . . . The saxophones begin at seven."[40] Music of all kinds, but jazz in particular, was a key element in the financial profitability of early radio, even in the heyday of radio drama and comedy programs, which of course used music liberally in their productions; moreover, music was a cheaper but popular alternative to these costlier scripted programs. In that regard, live music programs enjoyed cost savings akin to today's reality television.

In the 1950s, when television decimated the mass audience of network radio, local radio found a new, highly successful business model built on the already evolving use of records rather than scripted programs and live music performances. Sadly for jazz, its moment as popular music had peaked. Although jazz was no longer the main interest of youth in general, it still had appeal to its existing fans and some new fans as well. A sonic culture emerged in the 1950s and 1960s that combined record collecting (already a hobby for pre-war jazz fans) and high-fidelity audio equipment that would grow to include FM stereo broadcasting. This culture, described so well in Tim Anderson's *Making Easy Listening*, was far bigger than jazz, but jazz, and music made by studio jazz musicians and arrangers, could be found at its center. It was a culture gendered male: record collections that strived for possessive completeness and music equipment that reflected a fascination with electronics stemming from their G.I. experience. Although I remember when seemingly every middle-class household had an electric organ, it was the family's hi-fi system, including the radio receiver—if Dad let the kids use it—that became the "dominant space for music audition."[41]

As for the record industry itself, the 1930s saw the depressed sales of classical, opera, show music, and race records eclipsed by the jazz subgenre called swing. Like a multi-stage rocket, swing powered the first "big business" stage of the record industry, from which successive stages—R&B, rock and roll, soul, rock, disco, pop, and rap—each propelled the industry higher until the onset of its long-term slump in the late 1990s.

The secret of the mass media was "mass"; economies of scale permitted content to be distributed (and sold) at costs that were astonishingly small considering the numbers. A record that sold tens or hundreds of thousands of copies cost only a few hundred dollars to record and manufacture, plus promotional costs contingent on success, yet could be sold at profit margins sufficient to cover the losses of all the less successful records. As jazz fans, we appreciate this legacy; big-selling popular records supported a large number of records that are considered jazz classics today, just as the strong sales of jazz and popular music supported the expenses associated with classical music recordings that had great prestige but small sales volumes. Radio became a singularly important means of promoting records; by similar economies of scale, a radio station serving a major metropolitan area could easily reach a potential audience of more than million a people. A radio network could multiply that by a factor of ten.[42]

For a variety of reasons however, the process of getting music from the performer to the audience cannot be looked on as organic, automatic, or transparent. For one thing, the demands of the media have always left an imprint on the music as obvious as the length limits of 78 rpm records. The orchestration of early recordings reflected the recording process's limitations, such as when Zutty Singleton used hand-held percussion in lieu of drums on Armstrong's 1928 "West End Blues." The earliest examples of the crooning style of singing, predating its development as a strategy for use with the amplification of public address systems, were associated with the limited dynamic range of early radio equipment.[43] Once the style was in place, crooners could hold their own with much louder blues shouters, operatic and Broadway singers, and vaudevillians; the potentiometer (the volume knob on the control board), Wald suggests, "leveled the playing surface" between loud and soft.[44] Finally, there is considerable uncertainty about the origins of the three-minute length of early recordings, but there can be no doubt that this limitation shaped several generations of recorded popular music.

Gatekeeping is another shaping process. One of the salient features of "old media" such as radio and television is the fierce competition for access to production and distribution resources. Record companies have to be selective about the products they release. Despite the relatively low cost of record production with respect to potential sales revenue, those costs, plus much higher distribution costs, require a significant amount of financing. The most significant expense in selling physical recordings (LPs, CDs, and so on) is distribution, which places the product on shelves in individual stores.[45] This distribution cost has been the primary expense (and hence a barrier to competition) for independent record labels. For major and independent record labels, the cost structure ultimately plays a large role in shaping their roster of artists.

Ostensibly independent decisions can result in business success all around, as radio broadcasts from the Cotton Club helped establish Duke Ellington. Early on it was recognized that radio was good for business at live venues and that being heard on the radio was beneficial to musicians' careers, despite the music business's concerns about "free" music compromising live attendance and record sales. Although many wish to be featured on radio, one of broadcasting's core functions is programming, which involves the selection, and rejection, of material for use on the air. Radio began as a scarce resource, with a relatively small number of radio licenses available. This scarcity had a technological basis—avoiding interference between stations—but anticompetitive desires drove policies that ensured that scarcity. As a result, radio gatekeeping, which extended to radio station ownership, involves the interaction of artist popularity, social and political ideologies, economic pressures, and the individual preferences of programmers.

In old media, gatekeeping thrived at every opportunity for choice, from decisions about what artists to record and which recordings to sprinkle with promotional resources to which tracks and artists to play on the radio. Though a significant barrier to aspiring artists, gatekeeping has economic value to the audience, as "people want information checked, evaluated, and edited for them by professionals," so long as they trust those processes.[46] Sifting through the avalanche of content available on the internet is a big job, and media companies recognize these gatekeeping locations as a valuable spot to wield influence and control commerce.

Any such gatekeeping opportunity has potential for generating revenue, extracting concessions, or exercising power. Song pluggers showered cash and favors on popular bandleaders in exchange for performing songs from their catalogs. Bandleaders had already figured out this game. For on-air performances, many bandleaders favored songs for which they owned a cut of the publishing, so-called self-payola. They could obtain that share by any of a number of routes.[47] Later, record promoters did the same with DJs and station managers. Other opportunities arise. For example, after the inclusion on its web-based rundowns of artist information concerning musical bumpers used on *All Things Considered* initially saved NPR's staff time spent answering email inquiries, a revenue source was created by adding "buy" links to partner music retailers. In a *New York Times* op-ed, Nancy Sinatra complained about gatekeeping profiteering by Clear Channel (now iHeartRadio) in demanding $24,000 per song for "backselling" announcements—merely mentioning the name and performer of the song that was just played.[48] Announcing the selections played since the last announcement, often in reverse order, is a common practice on noncommercial radio that informs the listeners as to what they have been hearing. The type of thinking that recognizes it as "backselling" and sees an opportunity for revenue is all too familiar; some airlines charge a fee for assigning a seat.

Finally, performers are aware of their limited access to these media and of the tastes of influential gatekeepers. They consider such access crucial, or at least helpful, to their careers. Not only do gatekeepers influence the success of individual artists, but they also participate in genre-defining discourse, as the programmers of 1970s all-jazz radio did. Fabian Holt described how gatekeepers' ideologies come into play in Chicago, the home of the Association for the Advancement of Creative Musicians and a hotbed of experimental music. Despite a tradition of "politically engaged" jazz that includes Ed Wilkerson's jazz opera about Harold Washington (Chicago's first African

American mayor) and Ernest Dawkins's large-scale work about the Chicago 7, the influential home-market voices of *DownBeat* and Chicago Public Radio rarely acknowledge the home-grown talent.[49] The mainstream jazz favored by the establishment voices of its most august and leading magazine and a major public broadcasting nonprofit avoids the direct political engagement of the city's own jazz experimentalists. This does not negate the political meanings of mainstream jazz; it merely restricts them. One of the enjoyable complications of writing about black music is the multiple and simultaneous meanings that it can carry. For many, the straightforward demand to be recognized as a human being is still a radical political statement inherent in black music. For others, mainstream jazz is full of subversive messages specifically aimed at the status quo of racial and economic injustice. And for yet others, jazz carries as a message that affirms a universal joy in living.

Though there are exceptions, few jazz musicians are aligned with conservative politics. Yet the mapping of musicians, programmers, and presenting institutions into conservative and progressive camps (more on this in Chapter 5) can have more to do with music than with politics of the electoral kind. In part the ambiguity is born of mixed feelings within the jazz-making community about commercially popular and experimental music. Charles Mingus and Miles Davis made some of the most overtly political music of the mid-twentieth century and both were extremely critical of free jazz though both were really important figures in free jazz themselves. Their critiques had to do more with what they considered the unearned success of some free jazz figures (and one cannot rule out envy) than with the style's musical principles. Similarly, jazz musicians who place a high value on technical mastery are sometimes dumbfounded by the commercial success of "lesser talents" playing "simple" music marketed to the public as jazz. Their critiques are often meant to return our gaze once again to the gatekeepers, and Davis and Mingus were not alone in questioning the gatekeepers' motives and qualifications.

The Jazz DJ

For many years, jazz listening was inextricably bound up with radio. During the age of network radio, 1927–1946, swing music performed live in-studio or, more often, carried as remote broadcasts from nightclubs, ballrooms, or theaters was a programming fixture hosted by announcers. After the war, remotes continued, often hosted by the DJs who continued the program by spinning the latest jazz platters into the night after the performance ended. Increasingly, though, the broadcast involved just a DJ, perhaps a technician, and a stack of jazz records, and the DJ became the constant companion of the jazz listener. Like other radio personalities, they were the human focal point of the show and sometimes the face of the station at public jazz events. But in addition, jazz DJs as programmers have typically had a curatorial role. These gatekeeping DJs served as guides who steered listeners through the maze of constantly reconstituting performer combinations, translated and explained musical lingo, decoded lively and sometimes naughty musician nicknames and slang tune titles, and made listeners feel less confused about jazz in general. There have always been exceptions to the curated presentation of jazz, and some early hosts presented jazz as they would any other music. "Symphony" Sid Torin, a famed early supporter of bebop, or modern jazz, saw radio as entertainment distinct from the lecture hall and believed his fans were "more interested in music than talk."[50] On his noon-hour jazz program on WANN (Annapolis, Maryland) as late as 1983, "Hoppy" Adams might announce simply, "That was Miles Davis and the group," sometimes without even giving the song title. Similarly, Hal Jackson's holdover "Sunday [Morning] Classics" on WBLS-FM, which ran until 2012, included some jazz records amid co-host chatter, public service announcements, and live commercial reads but few record details, with all of the dialog over an uncredited sonic bed of Miles Davis's "Someday My Prince Will Come."

Presentation style is a balancing act. Some DJs will tell long stories and anecdotes, contributing to the legend and folklore about famous musicians, while others cultivate a hosting style with a minimum of talk, only announcing the last song and the next song. As one consultant report states, "Mainstream jazz listeners pay attention to the recordings played and the information given by announcers because they want to continue learning about the music. The station turns them on to artists they might hear in person or recordings they might purchase." Further, "Mainstream jazz listeners value authoritative air personalities. They look up to jocks that know the music and can explain the significance of each recording. But too much talk—any talking beyond a tidbit of musical information—can cause a tune out."[51] Gary Walker, music director at WBGO, decries the holier-than-thou DJ who engages in "top-to-bottom speak where they say things like, 'of course that was Roy Haynes on the drums.' They just made us all sound really fucking stupid, and that's ridiculous."[52]

Increasingly however, this attitude has become the exception. Buying into a widely shared but unproven belief that education will make jazz more popular, DJs have often served as information sources. In his gentle style, Washington, DC's longtime evening jazz host Felix Grant gave fans the latest news about the artists he featured. At the other extreme, the durable Columbia University radio host and 2021 National Endowment for the Arts Jazz Master Phil Schaap was (in)famous for his rambling and detailed contextualizing, sometimes complementing a master take with each of the available alternate and aborted takes, and his own lengthy commentary. Most longtime jazz DJs have forged relationships as trusted teachers, promoters, and explainers of jazz for their followers.

The jazz specialist DJ began to emerge with bebop and usually occupied a regular corner of the lineup on stations that had yet to develop strong formats. Indeed, "position wanted" classified ads for these specialists started to appear in broadcasting trade magazines in the 1950s.[53] Via these DJs, jazz was available for at least some hours each week on perhaps a hundred commercial radio stations until well into the 1970s. Unlike their colleagues, who were subject to management directives and increasingly rigid format requirements, off-format jazz specialists typically had nearly complete freedom in terms of programming music, so long as the ads were sold and the audience wasn't too small.

Jazz DJs served important functions within the jazz world that served to cement their relationships with listeners. Until the rise of social media, jazz radio had become practically the only regular source of jazz coverage. In the 1930s jazz was considered an important enough phenomenon (requiring cultural exegesis!) to merit regular coverage and columns in big-city daily newspapers and the black press but also in columns, reviews, and articles in *Harpers*, the *New Republic*, *Town and Country*, *Esquire*, *Mademoiselle*, *New Masses*, The *Daily Worker*, and of course in the widely read show-business oriented magazines, *Variety*, *Billboard*, *DownBeat*, and *Metronome*.[54] Today, in the United States, *JazzTimes* and the venerable *DownBeat* are in print, and the website allaboutjazz.com and a number of blogs are available, but as the general-interest press lost interest in jazz, the jazz DJ stepped in to help spread jazz news.

Postwar radio emphasized the local, and much jazz news was local. It took a much more determined effort than it does today for musicians to produce and release their own recordings, but local musicians did record, as well as perform gigs at clubs, bars, and concerts, and they appreciated it when DJs announced those events. National and international jazz artists toured as they do today, but there were far more performance venues at the time. Sometimes the DJ was the emcee or the event's promoter. The DJ let listeners know who was coming to town and announced the band's personnel changes since its last visit, where it was appearing, and when it was there last.

Promoters working for record companies and performers would make their clients available to jazz DJs according to the performer's available time, the need to promote new product or ticket sales, their perception of the DJs' influence, and the artist's own relationship with the DJ for live in-studio or in-advance telephone interviews. Notables would record station identification spots—"Hi! This is Duke Ellington. Whenever I'm in Washington I listen to Felix Grant on WMAL Radio 63"—both to encourage smooth relations with the DJ and to be heard regularly on the station. Making talent available for interviews was part of the bartered exchange of favors and courtesies that characterized the interactions between DJs and programmers, artists, their management, and record companies in the wider music industry. As would happen later with rock and roll, musicians named tunes for important and influential DJs both to honor them and to curry favor with them.[55]

In particular, the black DJ had an outsized influence on African American consumption of jazz. Disc jockeys were among the few blacks with an authorial public voice, and apart from the black press mass media advertising ignored black buyers. In the 1940s and 1950s African American elected officials were rare and confined to the largest northern cities, but in the cities with large black populations, North and South, black DJs could speak, however cautiously, to the entire community.[56] The bulk of this power may have been used to sell soap, beer, groceries, and furniture, but through hidden transcripts black folks found out about breakthroughs, setbacks, and community news.[57] It should be recognized, too, that the entertainment the DJs provided delivered large audiences to early black radio newscasters who gave straight reports of interest to the black listeners.

Brian Ward described the DJs of the civil rights era as "local idols" and "charismatic authorities on all manner of important social and cultural" matters. Especially influential with young fans, the DJs created solidarity all while weaving "coded messages" into their sonic mix of DJ patter and hit records.[58] In the early days of black radio, the DJs played a role similar to that of today's social media influencers, whose impact is attributable to their established credibility, their reach, and their perceived authenticity.[59] By speaking listeners' language and personalizing the advertising copy in the course of "live reads"—when the DJ goes directly to or from the entertainment content of the show with no break—the host's jiving and rhyming creates an authentic persona that can be trusted to give good information. Using hip street language, rhymes, and southern or "up-south" accents and referencing rituals and practices from "back home" to connect with recent migrants from southern states, the black DJ traded on this relationship for commerce and was a "major agent of socialization for the newly urbanized blacks. He told them what to buy, and stores at which to buy them."[60]

This included jazz records. Jazz radio and its DJs have been counted on to introduce new releases by established artists and to provide a showcase for new artists as part of larger promotional campaigns. The close relationships between the suppliers of records and the broadcasters who depend on them, especially on commercial radio, create an environment where preferred or prioritized records can be "pushed" to DJs, though perhaps not as forcefully as in genres in which Billboard Top 100 results are expected.

Influential jazz DJs were considered important to record sales. The legendary record promoter Dick LaPalm reported that black radio was the key to jazz sales for his principal client, Nat "King" Cole.[61] The jazz record producer and eventual label owner Creed Taylor also understood the power of black radio in the late 1950s when he was a producer for ABC-Paramount, noting,

> Jazz still sold primarily through radio shows, particularly black radio, which reached an influential record-buying audience and started what we now call

"word of mouth." As a producer, I had to know the disc jockeys and the names of the record buyers. In some cases, they were one [and] the same. For example, the buyer for New York's Korvette's department store had his own radio show. So I got to know the people who worked for him and arranged a lot of in-store displays for my jazz albums.[62]

Taylor's report that a major chain store's jazz record buyer was also a jazz DJ reinforces the notion that jazz knowledge was specialized and complicated and that DJs could play important roles in the industry. And note that, for the sake of business, Taylor had to personally know the DJs.

Finally, although generally low-key in their on-air personas and matching the jazz trope of being cool, today's jazz DJs tend to be holdovers from a more personality-dominated era of radio broadcasting. Music DJs on AM radio were expected to have outsized personalities with loud voices and attention-getting patter. They were at least as important to the station's ratings, sales, and identity as the endlessly repetitive music mix that could be heard on similar stations. The jazz DJs of the commercial era were more in keeping with those times, more likely to "rap" over a tune's introduction (or any other spot for that matter), less likely to tell long stories about the music, unlikely to read a full credit list of the tracks' performers, but able to create a music flow, segue in and out of recorded commercials, and weave live reads into the program flow. In an era when hip-talking DJs were fluent in jive, jazz DJs needed to be just as hip but cooler. As jazz faded from commercial radio, most of the surviving jazz DJs of the period 1950–1980 moved on to other things, but a few transitioned to noncommercial jazz broadcasting, and a few are still on the air today.

What Is This Thing Called Jazz?

Defining jazz has been a troublesome endeavor for as long as there has been jazz, and in reality, a task worth avoiding. But it is useful to have some understanding about what kind of music was being played as jazz on the air at different times, under different circumstances, and under sometimes fluctuating marketing names. Some of the music featured on the airwaves in the 1930s would be called jazz today but at the time might have been called swing, dance, or hot music. Much of the music performed by bandleaders such as the King of Jazz, Paul Whiteman (1890–1967), and Raymond Scott (1908–1994) would not be considered jazz by most jazz scholars today. The conflicts about what is and isn't jazz in the music marketed as jazz have been enduring and often divide music aficionados, casual fans, writers, and music promoters.[63]

The history of musicians, particularly African American musicians, and their acceptance or rejection of the jazz label is far too complex to do justice to here. Some musicians embrace it fully and proudly, while others, equally proud of the musical tradition and heritage, have issues with the term's etymology, its connotations, and its power to constrain their participation in the music business. A few examples outline the issues. Nina Simone, whose training and ambitions as a concert pianist were steered by stark racial and economic realities into a career as a jazz singer-pianist, deeply resented the term. "To most white people, jazz means black and jazz means dirt, and that's not what I play. I play black classical music. That's why I don't like the term 'jazz,' and Duke Ellington didn't either. It's a term simply used to identify black people."[64] Simone invokes "black classical music" to demand respect for her art on par with that accorded to Western classical music.

Others would say that *jazz* has been used to contain black musical creativity and generally restrict black musicians' opportunities to participate in music commerce. Earl Klugh (b. 1953), whose technique on the guitar and the construction of his recordings show the clear influence of jazz, is an example of a top musician wary of the genre's constricted economic space. Early on, as a teen prodigy, Klugh recognized the career limitations of being called a jazz musician. Asked if he considered himself one, Klugh's response alluded to the power struggle over jazz's boundaries. Klugh is careful to avoid disrespecting jazz but determined to avoid its limits:

> No, not in the traditional sense.... There's been so much, especially through the '80s and the '90s, so many people who want to claim that I'm a jazz player, or that this is jazz music and this isn't. I don't have time for all that. I like it all. I enjoy it all. I incorporate as much as I can from all the different idioms, from classical to blues to jazz. I'm a fan of all of it. I don't want to lay claim; I enjoy and love it all.[65]

The term *jazz*, in addition to restricting individual careers, was a discursive battle point among critics and commercial interests. The early structured, polyphonic, and often collectively improvised music most associated with New Orleans was called jazz very early on, and marketers tried to get the public excited about a new jazz music which they branded "swing." Bernard Gendron observes that as a brand name, swing was whatever its proponents said it was, noting the power of brand names to elude definition because their meanings are "determined less by the class of objects they refer to, than by the necessarily hazy, unarticulated, and frequently revised imagery with which they are irretrievably associated in advertisements and promotions," in other words, how they are marketed.[66]

Beyond the matter of who is and who is not a jazz musician, it is important to have some grasp on the many jazz styles that could be heard or not heard on radio. Much as hip-hop has exceeded its genre and finds its stylistic elements embedded all over the popular music spectrum, jazz elements could be found in a great many genres of popular and concert music. The styles of ragtime and early jazz, called New Orleans jazz by some and in its revival called Dixieland, emphasizing syncopation, variation of melody, ragging of thematic material, collective improvisation, and so-called Latin rhythms, greatly influenced commercial music. The same was true later in the twentieth century as swing, bebop, and post-bebop styles influenced music as diverse as Broadway show music, klezmer, country and western, western swing, ska, reggae, salsa, mambo, merengue, and the emerging styles of rhythm and blues, rock and roll, popular music of the 1950s and 1960s, and film and television scores. Evidence of the ubiquity of jazz elements in popular music is the question asked on first meeting, often at the musicians' union, between instrumentalists: "Do you play jazz or 'legit'?" meaning, do you play commercial music, with all its stylistic conventions from jazz, or classical?[67]

Perhaps a more useful distinction between styles during the network radio era was that between "sweet" and "hot." Sweet music was not simply ballads or music using strings, though it often did; it was popular music without or with a minimum of jazz elements. Indeed, sweet music styles pre-dated jazz, and it was the existence and popularity of music deemed "hot" that created the opposition "sweet."[68] The musicologist Christopher Wilkinson described sweet bands as having similar instrumentation to hot ones but playing fully arranged music with little or no improvisation, with little or no swing or unexpected rhythms, and "straight" tones.[69] Confusingly, *sweet* and *hot* could be used in the opposite manner, as well: Hot music was usually (but not always) up-tempo music and *sweet* could be applied to swinging performances such as Duke Ellington's "Mood Indigo."

Hot was used to suggest the qualities of rhythmic drive, excitement, passion, and intensity, and was the music the jazz connoisseurs desired, promoted, and collected.[70] Hot music was connected to the black vernacular styles of early jazz and ragtime and could be performed by musicians regardless of race. In general, collectors were less interested in the slick commercial swing music that came to dominate the airwaves in the 1930s and 1940s and more interested in the "primitive" elements of the earlier music that, in their view, provided its authenticity. One aspect of the gap between the connoisseur and the general music fan was the support of the former for the Dixieland revival of the early jazz style, which came even at the expense of support for the new and powerfully swinging Kansas City style associated with Count Basie.[71]

Both *swing* and *big band*, words with other more or less specific yet elusive meanings, came to be marketing terms for musical performances that were not always considered jazz by the most demanding critics. They were also commercial terms that could create space between the African American origins of jazz and the many white practitioners in the field. One example of the erasure of black musicians from this category was a big band retrospective series broadcast to apparent listener delight over Philadelphia's KYW during 1954. The series was inspired by the release of a Glenn Miller memorial album by RCA, and the list of bands given one-per-night, four-hour tributes is enlightening; featured were "Miller, Benny Goodman, Jimmy Dorsey, Tommy Dorsey, Glen Gray, Woody Herman, Jan Savitt, Larry Clinton, Duke Ellington, and others," with Ellington the only black bandleader.[72]

On the eve of World War II, jazz on the radio meant at least four things: small-group swing music, sometimes with vocals (Benny Goodman, Nat Cole, Errol Garner, Billie Holiday, Ella Fitzgerald), big band swing music, often with featured vocalists (Count Basie, Benny Goodman), Dixieland revival music (Lu Watters, Eddie Condon), and jazz-influenced popular vocal music (Peggy Lee, Frank Sinatra). Jazz as a category was still under construction. Jazz advocate and critic Leonard Feather wrote to and spoke for the jazz fans who could tell the difference between "real" swing bands that, for the sake of business, "made minor concessions to popular tastes" and organizations that looked like swing bands but who "devote[d] seventy-five per cent or ninety per cent of their time to straight melody, conventional crooning, vocal groups, comedy routines, and novelty numbers."[73] In the immediate postwar years, such conflation was a mechanism allowing many jazz musicians to enjoy airplay as popular music moved away from jazz.

Bebop seemed all the more mysterious to casual listeners because of a lack of recordings attributed to the prolonged music industry dispute that resulted in the American Federation of Musician's recording ban of 1942–1944. Jazz fans observed yet another community fracture between the "moldy figs" who supported the older, more dance-oriented styles and the "modernists" who supported bebop. While expressing deep respect for their older swing colleagues, the black musicians who created bop generally distanced themselves from early jazz and its supporters. That music had been created under deep and severe racially restrictive conditions, and its apparent primitivism was compatible with the kind of America in which a black person knew better than to look too intelligent before hostile whites. By contrast, bebop musicians performed with a serious and dignified demeanor befitting the attitudes of African Americans on the cusp of initiating the civil rights movement. This put them at odds with the body of jazz enthusiast critics who complained that the professional values and aesthetics of modernist jazz players had lost the joyful and primitive "real" feeling of early jazz.

Despite these disputes among hardliners, all of these styles of jazz and nearly jazz (for example, Louis Prima and Keely Smith or Jonah Jones) coexisted in this period. Paul Lopes has called this period the "New Jazz Age," a final period of robust economic vitality for both live performance and recording activity in jazz, and also a turning point in the music's cultural standing.[74] The arrival of bebop roughly coincided with the beginning of the end of the network era in radio. Bop was enthusiastically supported by jazz-loving DJs and perhaps not so well loved by general radio audiences. The establishment of bebop, its supporters in the jazz press, and its players' demands for respect as artists helped solidify jazz into a category of its own, rather than just a part of the popular music industry. In his insightful volume *Rise of a Jazz Art World* Lopes identifies sometimes contradictory impulses that helped jazz begin to take on an identity distinct from popular music. In the 1940s the modernist professionalism and commercial orientation of swing musicians and the outsider attitude of bebop players collided with the "connoisseurship of jazz enthusiasts" and the progressive politics of the American left. Lopes observes, "While earlier professional musicians struggled with the commercial market to mediate between the cultivated and the vernacular, the new generation of professional 'jazz' musician rejected the role of mediator, moving into a new trajectory as an American music."[75]

The production of easy listening, the successor of the sweet music of the 1920s, further illustrated how popular music could be distinct from jazz. The Canadian bandleader Percy Faith (1980–1976) was one of the pioneering popularizers of easy listening. In parsing a review that found Faith's arrangements "spine tingling" but not losing sight of the basic melodies such that his musical ideas would "run away" from the original work, Keir Keightley also rather neatly describes the growing divide between jazz and jazz-like popular music:

> Unlike jazz improvisations (whose radical alterations of melody privilege the soloist's right to self-expression and may thereby exclude some listeners), easy listening privileges the audience and its desire for familiarity ("easy recognition"). Thus, Faith is positioned as middle of the road: he remains faithful to the art music tradition of respecting the composer's intentions, yet still writes "spine tingling arrangements" (arrangements that nonetheless resist the excesses of jazz, where the composition is rendered subservient to the musician's improvisatory individualism).[76]

This was really what distinguished bebop from popular music in a way swing had not, for even as it featured powerful and sometimes virtuosic improvisation, in a swing performance each musician played with a deep and unified commitment to the groove. Less noticeable than the music's frantic tempos and angular rhythms was the bebop musicians' adherence to a polyphonic improvisatory philosophy in which the rhythm section players were in a constant dialog with the soloist and each other rather than singularly focused on supporting the soloist and the groove. Adding to that the proliferation of longer solos that jazz musicians demanded beginning with bebop, it is easy to see how jazz and pop music could manage to intersect yet remain at arms' length from one another. Jazz musicians, especially vocalists, could emphasize the melody strongly, employ short and melodic solo improvisations, and emphasize the groove and create music that strongly resembled early rhythm and blues, early rock and roll, or pop music that utilized similar instrumentation.

During the remainder of the 1950s, four more significant stylistic developments took place in jazz. Actually, cool jazz dates to the 1949 singles released on the 1957 Miles Davis LP *Birth of the Cool*, the first important collaboration between Davis and the Canadian arranger Gil Evans. Cool, as it was called, was an arranger-focused music that countered bebop's fiery tempos, unison lines, and rhythmic complexity with an emphasis on softer instrumental textures, dense harmonies, and the foregrounding of composed ensemble material both as interludes and in support of the soloist.

Just as cool jazz is often positioned as a white response to bebop, hard bop is perhaps just as often positioned as a black response to cool jazz. Hard bop and the closely related style soul jazz both have strong bebop elements but are also infused with gestures from blues, rhythm and blues, and the black church. A strong case can be made that hard bop and soul jazz represented the reincorporation of black popular music styles into jazz. For example, in rhythm and blues of the 1940s and 1950s the same jazz instrumentation is often used, with an emphasis on a strong driving beat and less complicated harmony than that found in bebop. Meanwhile, if the origin of soul music was the common-law marriage of rhythm and blues and gospel—Ray Charles is said to have sung "Oh baby!" instead of "Oh Lord!"—then hard bop and soul jazz are really tied to the emergence of soul music. Importantly for jazz radio, cool jazz along with hard bop and soul jazz would be important styles that could find some space on commercial radio, often along those racial lines.

Free jazz (or the New Thing) would emerge at decade's end. Whereas bebop is the basis of the post-bop family of styles that underlies most jazz activity today, free jazz has had limited acceptance with jazz audiences, even though many free jazz principles have become standard.[77] Two more significant styles would be added over the next decades: jazz fusion—a combination of jazz with funk or rock elements including non-acoustic instruments—and smooth jazz, a style using instrumental and vocal R&B with acoustic and electric instruments associated with jazz and jazz fusion but emphasizing melody and groove and de-emphasizing improvisation.

Perhaps no debate about what should be included under the jazz umbrella was more vigorously contested than the one regarding smooth jazz. As with every other style, definitions are elusive, and perhaps a better substitute is to name some artists generally considered to work within the smooth jazz style. Among the earliest was the saxophonist Grover Washington Jr (1948–1999), who came to prominence on records produced by Creed Taylor. Other early smooth jazz stars include John Klemmer, Chuck Mangione, the group Spyro

Gyra, and perhaps the person most closely associated with the style, saxophonist Kenny G. Indeed, the name *smooth jazz* is as arbitrary as the name *jazz* itself; the name appears to have been coined by a listener in an industry focus group.[78] The musicologist Charles Carson identifies smooth jazz as follows:

> Generally speaking, smooth jazz blends jazz instrumentation, pop production techniques, and an R&B aesthetic into a style that foregrounds the instrumental soloist similar to the manner in which the vocalist is featured in popular music. In fact, the repertoire for the style consists not of jazz works, but also includes covers of popular contemporary R&B songs.[79]

Smooth jazz does include vocalists as well, but the notion that smooth jazz equals instrumental R&B is a sound one. Smooth jazz was a pretty successful commercial radio format that peaked in the 1990s, though it may be in terminal decline.[80] Despite the crossover activity of jazz musicians in smooth jazz, it will receive little consideration in these pages, primarily because of the decline of the radio format. It is, however, worth noting that one of the few places where jazz and smooth jazz mix is on black college radio, where it is not uncommon to hear jazz, R&B, hip hop, and smooth jazz mixed with other black styles.

From the beginning, each new style or proposed style of jazz has faced opposition from its opponents and generated support from its proponents. Both groups, regardless of era, have typically comprised musicians, critics, fans, and music businesspeople. Critics, fans, and critical fans, the so-called jazz police, have often been the among the most energetic opponents, while musicians and music businesspeople have often had the largest stake in advocating for new styles. Radio programmers and DJs can operate anywhere on this spectrum, of course, according to their tastes, but also with respect to how they relate to the music—as fans, as critical fans, as musicians or friends of musicians, or as part of the music business. Disc jockeys and radio stations will have to take a position on the new music at each juncture, be it big band swing, swing combos and vocals, sweet and symphonic jazz, bebop, cool, hard bop, soul jazz, free jazz, jazz fusion, smooth jazz, and beyond.

Over the course of the seventy years covered in *Jazz Radio America* nothing has been static, not jazz, nor radio, nor America. If there has been one constant, it may be that radio, like all of us, has always struggled to capture the full measure of jazz.

PART I

Jazz on Commercial Radio

In the three chapters of this part, postwar commercial jazz radio will be examined. The timelines of all three chapters, by necessity, overlap. Chapter 1 is concerned with the development of the practices of radio stations with regard to jazz records during a transitional period of omnibus or variety programming that had its origins in network radio and was still the model of radio programming for several years after World War II. The history of jazz on commercial radio as organized into and dominated by radio formats such as Top 40, MOR, and Black Appeal is the subject of Chapter 2. Chapter 3 recounts the history of the all-jazz commercial radio format. There was a period in the late 1950s when jazz could be found on all three kinds of stations: omnibus, formatted as something other than jazz, and formatted as jazz.

1

Jazz Here and Jazz There

Jazz Rides the Omnibus

> Jumpin' with my boy, Sid, in the City
> Mr. President of the DJ committee
> We're gonna be up all night gettin' with it
> We want you to spin the sounds by the witty
> —King Pleasure and Lester Young

World War II provided American radio with great opportunities to distinguish itself. News reporting from the European and Pacific theaters demonstrated that network radio had the ability to bring complex breaking events into U.S. homes. Wartime coverage established models for broadcast journalism that lasted until the birth of cable news channels and shrinking network television viewership. Franklin D. Roosevelt used network radio to build national support for total wartime mobilization. Radio's entertainers, actors, and musicians sold war bonds, promoted blood drives, and encouraged listeners to collect and donate materials that could be used for military purposes. Network radio was so important for morale, information, and propaganda that it was largely spared the kind of sacrifices other industries endured in terms of material and labor.

But with the war's end radio's days, in its network form, were numbered, and the way most people heard music over the air began to change. The FCC was poised to license thousands more stations and to create the new FM and television services. Recorded music was rapidly displacing live music, comedy, and drama as the major source of radio programming. In reality, the use of records as programming was a pre-war development that had started on small and independent stations and was growing, in part, because so many hours of radio broadcasting were taking place on newly licensed independent and local stations rather than network-affiliated radio stations, and in part because those expensive radio programs were moving to television. As network radio's primetime audience left it for television, bringing the national advertisers along with them, the medium stayed alive by Darwinian adaptation—it sought local advertising and sought listeners in places where TV couldn't compete: in automobiles, in workplaces, and in the private spaces of teenagers.[1] But programs constructed from stacks of records were hardly new and had been airing for some time.

Record Playing Discouraged, but Not Forbidden

Network radio dominated broadcasting from 1927 to 1946, and live music was one of its predominant features. Although totaling only third of the nation's stations, the networks and their affiliates had accounted for almost 90 percent of the kilowatt power allocated for U.S. standard (or AM) broadcasting.[2] The very largest independent radio stations emulated the practice of live programming as well. Not only was live music used on music programs, but radio orchestras provided program themes, interludes, underscores for radio dramas, filler music if programs ran short, and music for commercial jingles.[3] Even on radio programs recorded on special discs for later broadcast, so-called transcription programs, the music was typically provided by live musicians in the transcription recording studios rather than by commercially released records. Radio musicians were usually represented by the American Federation of Musicians (AFM) through an individual local. Although the AFM had black members, either in segregated locals or, less commonly, integrated locals such as New York's Local 802, radio orchestras were plum jobs seldom held by black musicians. Black bands were not infrequently heard on radio as guest attractions or via remote broadcasts; Duke Ellington, Fats Waller, Earl Hines, Ethel Waters, and Cab Calloway were big name examples. The music of African Americans was heard on network radio, but the nation's practice of segregation significantly limited their opportunities.

There were technical, competitive, and political reasons why live music dominated early radio. Many engineers thought live music, captured by microphones, sounded better than records played over the air. But as quality audio amplifiers were developed to amplify the weak signals from record pickups, that rationale faded. Rather, favoring live programming had a strategic business advantage. Requiring it created an effective barrier to entry for the many smaller firms and private individuals who wanted to get into (or remain in) radio. Programming live entertainment required studio facilities and a stable of radio-compatible performers at the ready. And in particular, live radio networking—and nationwide networking was the business model on which radio corporations such as AT&T and RCA began to converge—required expensive and advanced technological facilities that further discouraged undercapitalized competitors. To simultaneously cover all of the largest radio markets effectively required either the use of super-high-powered radio stations, the relay of radio programming to local stations by shortwave radio, or the relay to local stations by expensive, conditioned long-distance phone lines, and it was the last that won out. Comparing the expense on a cost-per-listener basis of a radio program with high production values airing on a network to one airing on a single station, it is easy to see that the corporations effectively discouraged direct local competition.

Along with the scarcity of radio spectrum, these entry barriers were effective in limiting early network radio to only a few players—NBC, which owned the national Red Network (former AT&T stations) and Blue Network (RCA's stations) and eventually the smaller Orange/Gold (West Coast) Network, CBS, and the cooperatively owned Mutual Broadcasting System (MBS)—and they perpetuated the notion that live programming was a superior listening experience. Collectively they defined "radio in general and quality radio specifically as live, networked, and national."[4]

Of course, these corporations did not present themselves as opposed to competition. Rather, they promoted the aesthetic of liveness as the superior mode of listening while lobbying for rules and regulations that inhibited competition. Publicly, NBC boasted that even when imperfect, live broadcasting had advantages over recorded programs.

> But one of the most appealing things about the radio program is its spontaneity, the feeling that one is listening to living voices; top music just as it is being played by the artist himself. There is nothing of the set precision of a phonograph record in the radio program picked up at a studio microphone and broadcast directly. The little hesitancies of a speaker, the very realities of human imperfection, even among the finest instrumentalists, all tend to make the program, instantaneously broadcast, fascinating and intriguing. These are advantages hardly possessed by phonograph records.[5]

Always attuned to business interests, the third Secretary of Commerce, Herbert Hoover, backed this corporate play. As early as 1922 the requirements for the new Class B "superior" entertainment wavelength at four hundred meters[6] established by the Department of Commerce's Federal Radio Commission (FRC) to ease spectrum congestion favored live programming by imposing technical standards that allowed these new stations to transmit at up to one thousand watts but prohibited "mechanically reproduced" programs.[7] This set the regulatory tone of disfavoring licensees that proposed to use recorded music for programming. The FRC went further. Its Special Order 16, issued on August 9, 1927, equated failing to disclose mechanical broadcasting of music with fraud and implicitly normalized live music performed before microphones by requiring that "all broadcasts of music performed through the agency of mechanical reproductions shall be clearly announced as such with the announcement of each and every number thus broadcast," subject to a $500 fine for each offense.[8]

It was probably the clever evasion of such announcements that resulted in Special Order 49 (October 26, 1928), which mandated specific wording for records and piano rolls. Each such program item required a preceding announcement that the following was, for example, a "phonograph record."[9] But the reality of the wide use of transcription programs led to amending that language. A month later, Special Order 52 was issued, which allowed less direct language to be used when the recording in question was not intended for sale to consumers.[10] Again, the emphasis was on the notion that the public would be deceived into thinking that recorded performers were live in the studio or at the point of network origination. But Special Order 52 reflected the reality that a great number of smaller stations, many located in smaller markets, needed to broadcast recorded material in order to survive.

The networks, in particular market-leading NBC, continually defended liveness as a desirable aesthetic for quality radio, at least until they began to make limited exceptions for themselves starting in 1934. The National Broadcasting Company was caught in a corporate conflict, not only regarding its own opportunities to profit from the sale of transcriptions and transcription services and to save money by reusing programs via transcriptions—the idea of reruns as we know them on television today had not yet been formulated—but also because its owner, RCA, had business prospects both in manufacturing and selling sound equipment used in recording studios and in the growing business of selling records directly to the public through the RCA Victor Record Company

Digging through the NBC archives, the historian Alexander Russo found that a significant cause of the network's revised policy regarding recorded programming was the drive to use and produce radio programs on transcription discs. Transcriptions, sixteen-inch platters that played for fifteen minutes per side at 33–1/3 rpm, were a practical and useful method of distributing radio programs to stations. The discs could be delivered by rail or air or simply mailed in advance to distant cities around the globe, at a cost of only a fraction of the expensive AT&T Long Lines used by the networks to connect affiliates. These were not new—before NBC picked up *Amos 'n' Andy* from its Chicago originating station WMAQ, its creators, Freeman Gosden and Charles Correll, distributed the show to more than thirty stations via transcription disc—but the business of producing and supplying programs was destined to grow as the number of stations grew. As with many policies, competing opportunities created tensions. For NBC, the "networks' commitment to liveness protected their market position, but it also curtailed their ability to evaluate and respond to new methods of programming production and distribution" and thus hurt their bottom line.[11]

Transcriptions, and the business of making and distributing them, were a direct threat to the networks and the way they did business. Not only could transcriptions deliver competitive network-quality programming produced by other organizations, they also represented a threat to the networks themselves. For one thing, transcribed radio programs came complete with presold national advertising and thus competed with the networks in making the advertising sales. Competitors such as the World Broadcasting System succeeded in selling their transcriptions to stations, including those in small markets skipped over by the networks. There were many such undervalued markets in the South, where, despite large total populations, black consumers were not considered real customers by white ad buyers. The national networks were frustrated by ad buyers happy to pay low prices rather than network rates in order to get on transcription recordings.[12] The WBS was successful enough to get NBC's attention. It had sold transcription playback equipment to more than 150 stations, including network affiliates, and *Variety* estimated that 75 percent of radio stations used some transcriptions by 1930.[13]

The "Make Believe Ballroom" and the First DJ

Radio historians have long sought to name the first radio DJ, with most of the debate centering around the two men most closely associated with programs called *The Make-Believe Ballroom*: the West Coast's Al Jarvis at KFWB (Los Angeles) and the East Coast's Martin Block at WNEW (New York).[14] Both programs sought to play down their reliance on phonograph records, typically evading the FCC regulations requiring an announcement before each recorded tune was played, and invited their audiences to suspend their disbelief and participate in a radio imaginary: a faux concert with big-name stars. Despite the titular confession, Jarvis's *Make-Believe Ballroom* pretended to have a rotation of bands on stage. Jarvis created the fiction that a top-name band was performing an actual set by surrounding the records with announcements such those as a host would make at a live remote.[15]

Jarvis chose to interpret the FCC regulations as only requiring periodic announcements that he would be playing recorded music. "To everyone's amazement we discovered that it was unnecessary to say 'this is a phonograph record' before and after each time you played one," he noted. "That all the Federal Communications Commission required was the identification of the program as being recorded, on the average of once each quarter [hour].[16] Jarvis recalled that he came up with this idea in March 1932 on Los Angeles station KFWB and that his friend Martin Block carried the idea east to New York at WNEW.

Both Block and Jarvis may have been preceded in the disc jockey format by black radio pioneer Jack Cooper in 1931. Cooper had already written and performed comedy skits on WCAP (Washington, DC) in 1925 and produced and hosted the first weekly show featuring African Americans on radio, *The All-Negro Hour*, on WSBC (Chicago) in 1929.[17] That station, which carried ethnic programming, shared its frequency assignment with two other local stations. While general interest programming predominated on radio, stations such as WSBC chopped the broadcast day up to reach different ethnic audiences, in their case Polish, Jewish, or Swedish immigrant listeners. Such operations did not require owners like WSBC's Joseph Silverstein to understand these communities; rather, blocks of airtime would be sold to entrepreneurs from one of those communities, who would in turn sell advertisements on programs created for those listeners.

Apocryphally, Cooper's inauguration of the DJ format was an accident. When a gospel pianist walked seeking for more money, Cooper is said to have improvised with a record player and a microphone. His innovation was helped along by the ready availability of race records of gospel music. Here he caught a break. Because of the high rates that ASCAP charged radio stations for performances, live or recorded, of songs in their catalogs, broadcasters used non-ASCAP material when they could—a practice that culminated in the creation of Broadcast Music, Inc. by the broadcast industry in 1939 to create more favorable rates for using songs. The Jim Crow practices at ASCAP—Ellington was one of the exceptions—largely excluded the songs on race records and give Cooper the opportunity to play recorded non-ASCAP black music for free on his *All-Negro Hour*.[18]

Cooper expanded on the brokered time model and came to have a team of announcers working for him. By the 1940s he had more than forty hours of weekly Chicago airtime on WSBC, WHFC, WAAF, and WBEE and employed or trained broadcasters Oliver Edwards, Eddie Plique, Manny Mauldin, William Kinnison, and his third wife, Trudy Cooper.[19] Cooper was an ambitious and race-conscious businessman who saw in radio a means to build his own media empire but also to achieve black advancement. He was marked by his initial experiences at Washington's WCAP, where the only roles for blacks were in buffoonish comedy.[20] Described by Bill Barlow as "the voice of the urban black bourgeoisie and a symbol of racial uplift," Cooper insisted on maintaining his personal dignity; he spoke proper English in direct contrast to the stereotypical dialect of the blackface hit *Amos 'n' Andy* and in contrast to many of the Black Appeal DJs that would achieve fame with "Up-South" audiences after him.[21] Cooper's Sunday lineup included religious material—gospel DJ shows, *Know Your Bible*, and broadcasts of live church services—and sports-oriented programming, but the heart of his weekday show was jazz programming that showcased well-established black and white swing bands and vocalists, "scrupulously avoiding the more pedestrian and often risqué vaudeville and urban blues recordings."[22]

The economic case for recorded music and record playing never completely disappeared from the American airwaves. Indeed, stations in rural areas and smaller urban operations always used music from records, and they were a dependable source of fill-in programming on stations of any size. The programming schedule for a typical Monday for Cincinnati's WSAI in 1931 included *Records* eight times between 8 a.m. and the 11 p.m. sign-off. These segments fit in between named programs and ran from fifteen to forty-five minutes in length.[23] Even with the use of records, WSAI listed live local and network music programs including a 10:30 p.m. show featuring a local orchestra.

The practices of the smaller stations are underrepresented in broadcasting history at the expense of network radio stations. In neglecting their histories, the highbrow/lowbrow distinction in network programming, with jazz often considered as the kind of lowbrow programming that independent stations forced the networks to match, is not properly contextualized. There was a correlation between income and education with station listenership. Listeners at lower educational and income levels were more likely to listen to smaller unaffiliated stations that favored lowbrow programming (country or fiddle music, for example), and those stations were not shy about accepting "low class" advertising.[24]

The combined forces of network practices, opposition from the musicians' union, and federal regulatory policy was effective in keeping recorded music in check on network stations and at the largest competing non-network stations, but playing records always made sense for smaller and rural stations. The case for records was obvious, and over time even the networks' owned-and-operated stations began the practice for certain time slots.[25]

Early television star Arthur Godfrey began as a morning DJ on the CBS network–owned WJSV[26] (now WTOP) in Washington, DC, from 1934 to 1945, and another CBS-owned station, WBBM (Chicago), had *The Musical Clock*, a highly formatted record-based morning show. As early as the summer of 1942 the NBC Blue network offered *Say It with Music*, a 1 a.m. to 7 a.m. record show originating from its New York City flagship, WJZ, and heard over forty-four stations.[27] Placed among a general programming lineup of news, variety shows, lectures, church services, women's shows, sports roundups, and classical music shows, these DJ shows could be as short as fifteen minutes and as long as two or three hours. Instead of promoting the DJs by name, these shows tended to have titles such as *Breakfast Club, Anything Goes, Milkman's Matinee*, or *Tune Inn*, the last hosted by Willis Conover at the Washington, DC, station WWDC before he garnered worldwide fame presenting jazz on the U.S. government's Voice of America shortwave broadcasts.[28] With time, more and more local programming was DJ-hosted, with the DJs becoming the stars.

By 1949 there were about 2,000 DJs on about 2,000 AM and 750 FM stations.[29] That works out to about one per AM station on average, supporting the notion that a great deal of radio programming did not consist of DJs spinning records. Many of the newer stations served listening audiences largely neglected by the networks and their large independent competitors. In the largest urban centers, many stations catered to non-English-speaking recent European immigrants and African American audiences, usually via block time arrangements. In rural areas, they played music that the networks ignored: religious music and what came to be known as hillbilly (later country and western) music. While the big money was thought to be gained by programming to a large share of the broadest audience—seen as a white, mythically American audience—there was plenty of business to be had servicing the underserved. Black radio pioneer Jack Cooper's four-station brokered-time empire in Chicago was grossing him perhaps $2 million a year, and the following observation in a 1945 issue of *Billboard* made a case for the coming rise of disk jockey programming replacing the old network model.[30]

> An exec of a large agency drags out the dossier on a large Southern city in which the sole competition for a 50,000-watt NBC outlet is a 250-watt indie station that uses nothing but disks all the livelong day. The one lung outlet beats the pants off the webber [network affiliate] most of the day and in the lushest evening hours, too. Performance of this little station is, of course, a rare exception, but it dramatizes something not at all rare. It is, in fact, the rule from one end of the country to the other that stations which use no live music are doing very well, thank you. Translation: Stations which use records are doing very well indeed. Translation: Records make radio.[31]

Records were making radio, and records were displacing songs as the key musical commodity.

Hit Records Rather Than Hit Songs

When bands performed songs live on network radio they produced immediate royalty income and promoted sheet music sales for the songwriters and publisher, regardless of which band performed it.[32] Figure 1 gives an example—an advertisement, perhaps from 1929, for Triangle Music Publishers with forty-five performers, including Paul Whiteman, Rudy Vallee, Guy Lombardo, Vincent Lopez, Red Nichols, and Louis Armstrong associated with "After You've Gone." The switch from live orchestras to records on radio, coupled with the vibrant and still important jukebox industry, created a change in emphasis in the music industry from songs to records, and shifted the location of a crucial gatekeeping function. Sheet music sales still mattered, though less and less, and record sales had always mattered, but the best place to influence commerce changed from bandleaders choosing songs to spotlight on network broadcasts to DJs choosing which sides to spin on the air. Consistent with this switch was the debut in 1955 of the *Billboard* Hot 100 record chart (called the Top 100 until 1958). The exact method and weighting of the criteria used in the Hot 100 are a trade secret that has changed over time (in recent years it has needed to account for streaming and digital downloads, for example) but from the outset it emphasized some combination of record sales, jukebox plays, and radio airplay. It supplanted the 1945–55 Honor Roll of Hits, which included sheet music sales in its computation and competed with the lists at *Cash Box*, a trade magazine for all kinds of coin-operated diversions including jukeboxes. It was in this era that the record replaced sheet music as the "dominant material of unit of exchange and musical distribution."[33]

FIG. 1. Triangle Music ad with images of performers of "After You've Gone." (Courtesy of the Louis Armstrong Museum.)

Prior to the Honor Roll of Hits, *Billboard* tracked music in a list titled Songs with Most Radio Plugs, a title reflecting the effort of publishing house "song pluggers" to place songs in the repertoire of leading bands, especially those making regular network radio appearances, because it was the bandleaders who had the most say about repertoire.[34] With the emphasis on live music, a radio listener might have heard several artists perform the same hit song on a given day.[35] And contrary to the practices of today, a steady listener then might only hear a specific popular version of a hit song only once every day or two.

It could be argued that the music industry's fealty to songwriters and publishers during the network era obscured the audience's preferences for specific performers. For example, three different recordings of "Don't Fence Me In," along with competing versions of "I Dream of You" and "There Goes That Song Again," collectively occupy seven spots on the *Billboard* Top Record Sales list of January 20, 1945 (see table 1). Jazz record buyers did not operate in this mode; fans drawn to the store to buy Coleman Hawkins's version of

TABLE 1. Harlem Hit Parade and *Billboard* top record sales for January 20, 1945, compared.

Harlem Hit Parade			Best-Selling Retail Records	
Song	Artist		Song	Artist
Into Each Life Some Rain Must Fall	Ink Spots and Ella Fitzgerald	1	Don't Fence Me In	Bing Crosby/ Andrews Sisters
Somebody's Gotta Go	Cootie Williams	2	Ac-cent-tchu-ate the Positive	Johnny Mercer
I Wonder	Pvt. Cecil Gant	3	I'm Making Believe*	The Ink Spots and Ella Fitzgerald
I'm Lost	King Cole Trio	4	Don't Fence Me In	Sammy Kaye
I'm Beginning to See the Light	Duke Ellington	5	Rum and Coca-Cola	Andrews Sisters
Gee, Baby, Ain't I Good to You?	King Cole Trio	6	I Dream of You	Tommy Dorsey
Rum and Coca-Cola	Andrews Sisters	7	There Goes That Song Again	Kay Kyser
Cherry Red Blues	Cootie Williams	8	Don't Fence Me In	Kate Smith
Don't Fence Me In	Bing Crosby/ Andrews Sisters	9	I Dream of You	Andy Russell
You Always Hurt the One You Love	Mills Brothers	9	The Trolley Song	Vaughn Monroe
Hamp's Boogie-Woogie	Lionel Hampton	10	There Goes That Song Again	Russ Morgan

Source: *Billboard*, January 20, 1945, 18–19.

44   JAZZ ON COMMERCIAL RADIO

"Body and Soul" would tend not to leave with a version by Django Reinhardt or the one by Chu Berry and Roy Eldridge; they were more likely to buy the artist's performance rather than the song.[36] Of course, multiple versions of songs continue to exist to this day—the practice saw a particularly egregious pinnacle in the early years of rock and roll with softened white covers sidelining "offensive" black hits—but with the focused and coordinated promotion applied to records rather than on behalf of songs, today's record charts are no longer littered with simultaneous competing versions of a single song.

It was foreseeable that the power of DJs to "break" hits (create a buzz or demand for a new release) and otherwise give exposure to records resulted in payola, inducing DJs to play records for cash and other considerations. However, DJ reports also played a role in record charts. There were several kinds: trade magazine charts of spins, sales, and requests, but also radio station charts listing hits. Most of these charts had mysterious methods of construction and unclear ranking criteria. Yet participation in these DJ reports gave the DJs visibility and respect in the record industry.

Radio and Records Form a Partnership

The lingering death of the networks after World War II changed more than radio; it drove the radio and record industries into each other's loving arms. In order to stay alive, radio became focused on the local. But local radio did not benefit from the economies of scale that would allow it to present live music or scripted programs on a regular basis. Scaling up was the very principle that had driven the formation of the radio networks in the 1920s, but now that television owned the hearts, minds, and investment capital of network executives (as well as of advertisers, shareholders, and viewers), music, and specifically records, exploded into importance at radio stations big and small.

Radio, music publishers, the recording industry, and the concert, theater, and nightclub sector had completed three uneasy decades of suspicion-filled mutual existence and occasional but amateurish cross-promotion, but by the 1950s, just as the federal courts and U.S. Justice Department were breaking up the vertically organized film studio monopolies, which ran from film production to ownership of movie theater chains, the entertainment industry was reorganizing into cross-media conglomerates.

Before the formation of the conglomerates, record companies and radio networks gazed at each other and saw competitors even as musicians, who tended to pocket more money from touring than from recording, always saw a promotional ally in radio. Bandleaders such as Ellington and Goodman and their management noticed increased booking fees after a period of network radio broadcasts. Likewise, these artists drew larger crowds and appeared in larger venues on the tails of radio exposure. But the record industry was not as certain of the benefits of free airplay. While a live radio performance of "Mood Indigo" might get some fans to run to the record shop, the recording industry suspected that many more were content to wait until the next time it aired. Furthermore, whereas the Great Depression barely slowed radio, it all but crippled the record industry, which saw 1927 sales of $104 million plummet to $4 million by 1932.[37]

Today, radio stations are given free promotional copies of records. It may come as a surprise that this practice only began in the 1950s, when record labels began to court influential DJs. Before that stations that wanted to play new hit records had to buy them. The provision of recorded music in the form of transcription libraries for radio stations was a viable business for music transcription companies provided that the discs already included ASCAP licensing in the subscription price, but this was an arrangement that could hardly keep up with the hits.

Milt Gabler, uncle of comedian-actor Billy Crystal, was a longtime industry stalwart who owned the Commodore Music Shop in New York and later the Commodore music label. His record store claimed New York's widest range of records. Potential record buyers who asked radio stations where they could find particular numbers were sent to Gabler's shop. Soon Gabler recognized a business opportunity, especially with the large number of record plants operating in metropolitan New York. He recalled:

> In fact, in those days, when disc jockeys started on small stations, I used to sell one each of every release to every radio station in N.Y. I used to have a route and I would pick the records up so that they would have them even before the dealers. Early on Thursday morning I would take my car and pick up the records from the various manufacturers and make up the bundles, like a newspaper route, and take them to Martin Block and everybody else, and send them a bill at the end of the month and the station would pay it. They appreciated the service.[38]

Not only was the relationship between record companies and radio in flux, but specifically the relationship between the companies and individual DJs was evolving as well. Gabler's service attempted to get releases before they hit stores, but the ability of DJs to "break" records was not yet recognized. In the early growth period of DJ-based shows, high on their lists of demands, expressed through the nascent DJ associations, was better service from record companies in terms of timely and broad access to the new releases and accompanying biographical and publicity materials. To this day, jazz DJs, especially at small college and community stations, have issues and concerns with record service; a major concern for jazz programmers today is the avalanche of independent and self-published releases to be evaluated each month.

Black and general record sales as a 1945 snapshot in time are compared in table 1, where several things are worthy of note. Although both lists have artists associated with jazz, the selections on the Best Selling list tend to be in the swing era style with vocals, a style that, over time, was becoming the dominant pop music vocal style until well into the 1960s: a singer backed by a swinging, if commercial, orchestra with big-band instrumentation at its core, perhaps with strings, the kind of vocals that would move on to adult MOR radio. The Harlem Hit Parade list, on the other hand, is already showing a tendency to embrace the urban electrified blues with the kind of hard-driving swing that will become rhythm and blues. (Pvt. Cecil Grant's "I Wonder" is a beautiful and melancholy blues number with only Grant on vocals and piano!)[39]

Early in this postwar period the now-iconic jazz figures that appear in table 1, Duke Ellington, Count Basie, Lionel Hampton, Nat Cole, Ella Fitzgerald, and Cootie Williams, could be played on the radio alongside Bing Crosby, the Andrews Sisters, Vaughn Monroe, and Kate Smith. On the other hand, the music of Dizzy Gillespie, Thelonious Monk, Charlie Parker, Bud Powell, Lester Young, and Coleman Hawkins was more likely to be heard on a "jazz" radio show.[40] Toward the mid-to-late 1950s, this separation was even more complete. Jazz instrumentation and arranging styles were still used to support pop vocalists. Strongly melodic and show-business-oriented jazz entertainers like Louis Prima and Jonah Jones and R&B and soul crossover artists such as Ray Charles, Louis Jordan, Dinah Washington, and Lionel Hampton, and marketing exceptions like Dave Brubeck and Stan Getz could still get airplay outside jazz programs. But the rise of rock and roll and the arrival of radio music formats as station-wide programming philosophies largely pushed jazz artists into specific shows designed to reach jazz fans.

Remotes and Transcription Programs

Live remotes were a staple of jazz radio in the network era and continued on a diminished basis as postwar radio programming. Remote broadcasts exploit radio's intrinsic abilities to capture and transmit the moment, to paint pictures in the mind's eye, and to create a simultaneously shared experience. Late-night jazz sets broadcast from big-city nightclubs met listeners' expectations about the sophistication and coolness of urban nightlife. And via remotes, a New York, Chicago, or Los Angeles radio station could originate a network program that earned it fees in an arrangement that benefited both the performance venue and the network.

Since the 1920s, New York stations such as WHN had established dedicated "wires"—specially engineered phone lines that established permanent, high-quality audio connections between the remote location and the studio—to cabarets, clubs, and theaters such as the Kentucky Club, whence the

Ellington-led band was heard in 1926, before its more famous Cotton Club residency. In an early business model, WHN charged a cabaret $50 to allow its talent to be featured on WHN twice per week.[41] These permanent wires gave WHN and other stations multiple live programming options. Permanent lines to clubs and other sites of recurring remote broadcasts were a standard feature of the network era, and originating stations continued the practice after World War II. The cost of installing a wire was enough that any chance of needing it again justified simply leaving it in place. Figure 2 is taken from a WNEW engineer's 1934 notebook of that station's installed audio wires.

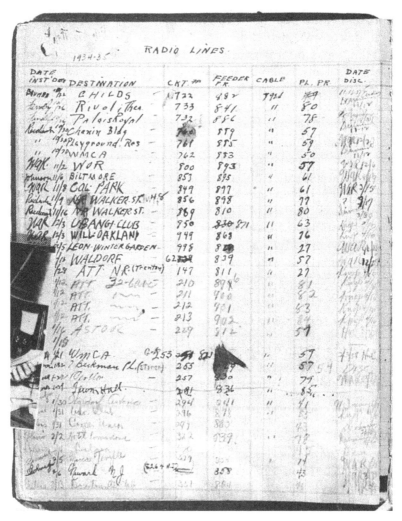

FIG. 2. WNEW engineer's notebook of remote lines. (Nightingale Gordon, WNEW: Where the Melody Lingers On [New York: Nightingale Gordon, 1984].)

(Note the reciprocal wires to stations WMCA and WOR and multiple links to an AT&T office.)[42]

Live music remotes gradually faded as regular programming but can still be heard on occasion.[43] This author, though born in 1958, has several personal experiences with live remotes that demonstrate their enduring appeal. While working in the studio of WGTS-FM (Takoma Park, MD) he made a recording of a live performance by Gil Scott-Heron with Brian Jackson and the Midnight Band c. 1977 originating from Howard University's Cramton Auditorium and carried over WHUR-FM. Thirty years later, the author played tuba in the fiftieth-anniversary re-creation of the Thelonious Monk at Town Hall concert of 1959 broadcast live over WNYC-FM. One of the longest-running jazz remote series is NPR's *Toast of the Nation*, which began as a *Jazz Alive* special broadcast in 1977.[44] Now produced by WBGO-FM (Newark) and Jazz at Lincoln Center, *Toast of the Nation* rings in the New Year in each of the four time zones of the contiguous forty-eight United States. The author also had the privilege of playing trombone and conch shells with Steve Turre and Sanctified Shells, along with Pharoah Sanders, for the Pacific time zone countdown from Yoshi's in Oakland, California, on New Year's Eve 1999 and New Year's Day 2000.

As an alternative to live remotes, recorded live performances were offered to radio stations as transcriptions. One example is shown in figure 3, a transcription offering from RCA, parent company of NBC, featuring broadcast-quality performances and interviews culled from record producer and concert promoter Norman Granz's *Jazz at the Philharmonic* series. Live remotes, recordings of live concerts, and live albums appeal to the audience's sense of looking in on the action. The musicologist Scott DeVeaux identified the tendency of serious jazz fans of the 1930s and 1940s to consider the after-hours jam session as the "real thing," as jazz in its most authentic and least commercial embodiment.[45]

Hardcore jazz enthusiasts read of after-hours jam sessions that took place in small and mostly inaccessible Harlem clubs and imagined performances that went beyond the three-minute limitations of 78 rpm records, performances they believed to be wilder and purer than what was being filtered by the studio recording process. The fans' highly romanticized view of the jam session

Jazz at the Philharmonic A Special bonus package of 100 classics by the greatest men of jazz, including Count Basie, Gene Krupa, Teddy Wilson, Oscar Peterson . . . Plus 100 voice-track interviews with Norman Granz for your DJs.	**RECORDED PROGRAM SERVICES** 155 East 24th Street, New York 10, N. Y., MUrray Hill 9-7200 445 N. Lake Shore Drive, Chicago, Ill., WHitehall 4-3530 522 Forsyth Building, Atlanta 3, Ga., Jackson 4-7703 1907 McKinney Avenue, Dallas 1, Texas, RIverside 1371 1016 N. Sycamore Avenue, Hollywood 38, Calif., OLdfield 4-1668

FIG. 3. Trade paper ad for Jazz at the Philharmonic. (Source: *Broadcasting*, n.d.)

reflected a simplistic but durable tension between the commercial success of swing and the perceived authenticity of hot jazz. Late-night sets broadcast as remotes inherited the aura of pure jazz jam sessions as home listeners peeked into the faraway clubs.[46]

Granz's Jazz at the Philharmonic concerts were structured to create a jam session feeling in a concert setting, with different collections of stars rotating onstage during the concert. Although the club remotes usually featured working bands, the late hour helped deliver that after-hours feeling to homebound, shift-working, or cab-driving fans. But with inexpensive disc-based jazz programs on the increase, the number and regularity of remotes declined as DJ shows increased.

Local, But Still Omnibus: Jazz Before the Format Boom

Entering the 1950s, radio, for the most part, was still an omnibus affair, with different kinds of shows airing at different hours of the day. The largest and most popular general-interest stations retained this programming strategy until well into the 1960s. The variety programming approach was consistent with that of other big-time show business genres. It was only over the course of a decade starting in the late 1950s that movie exhibitors eliminated cartoons, newsreels, short features, and the double feature. The notion of something for everyone could still be found at the circus, in live theater and cabaret revues, and, not surprisingly, on television. It was true for black show business, too. At the Apollo in New York, the Howard in Washington, DC, the Lincoln in Los Angeles, or the Royal in Baltimore, black audiences in the 1950s would get cartoons, a tap dancer, chorus dances, a comedian, and various other acts before the headliner came on, the same as at the big white theaters. Broadcast television would replicate this omnibus strategy at both the macro and the micro level; its programming schedules contained all those elements plus news and public affairs, as did its variety shows—the long-running *Ed Sullivan Show* for example—sans the cartoons, news, and public affairs. It is no wonder, then, that radio would continue in this way until it was unable to compete with new business models such as Top 40.

At the end of World War II, jazz was deeply intertwined with pop music. The big band instrumentation and swing musical styles and gestures are widely found, though sometimes scaled down and slicked up, in both pop music and the black urban style becoming known as rhythm and blues.[47] Yet a distinct (if not quite distinguishable) jazz identity was being formed and supported by fans, critics, and advocates who insisted that jazz was a different thing. Conversely, some fans of show tunes and vocals that relied on the swing aesthetic were just as eager to reject jazz for its bohemian reputation. It is not surprising, then, that with jazz still relatively popular, the omnibus lineups would include shows appealing to jazz fans.

One such program aired in Chicago; Dave Garroway, the future original host of television's longest-running franchise, the *Today* program, was an important jazz presenter on WMAQ, a powerful clear channel station owned by NBC and an important station on its Red Network since 1931.[48] Besides serving as one of the first television hosts with *Garroway at Large* (1949–1951) and *Today* (1952–1961), he had hosted a late-night jazz program on WMAQ, "The 1160 Club," its title being a clever play on its start time and a slick reference to "11:60 PM," a 1945 recording by the Harry James Orchestra (vocal by Kitty Kallen).[49] Garroway, a rare broadcasting talent on a par with Arthur Godfrey and Steve Allen, helped carve out postwar DJ space for jazz in Chicago. He consistently presented jazz on his other programs such as the *Dave Garroway Show*, promoted jazz concerts, and was an outspoken champion of the young singer Sarah Vaughan.[50] Garroway not only dubbed her "The Divine One," he once took to the stage microphone to defend her when bigoted fans tossed tomatoes at her at a concert where he was the emcee.[51] One of Garroway's enduring contributions to jazz radio was his influence on the styles of Daddy-O Daylie and Sid McCoy, both DJs who would be among the leading black jazz voices, along with Yvonne Daniels, on Chicago radio.

Pre-Format Jazz DJs: Symphony Sid, Fred Robbins, Hal Jackson, Joe Adams

From the beginning, the voices heard on radio were those of the stars. Actors, comedians, singers, bandleaders, and even the mellifluous voices of the program announcers were attractions. As radio began to use records as programming, the importance of air personalities continued but entered into a period of long, slow decline while the specific music content steadily ascended in importance. Over the course of a few decades in the postwar era, radio went from hot DJs to announcerless music. Some of this was deliberate. One of the most important innovations in broadcasting was the introduction of the first practical automated programming systems, called simply "automation" in the trade, in 1966. It was particularly well suited to the easy listening format, so that by 1969 the two thousand automated stations were able to cut payroll costs. By the late 1960s, on certain radio stations, most notably Easy Listening and Good Music (and especially on the not-yet-profitable FM radio stations), automation had replaced or downplayed the DJ altogether. The impact of air personalities on the sonic identity of automated stations was minimized, as was DJs' leverage in salary negotiations.[52] But at the start of the wave of DJ programming, the radio industry was not quite sure of the balance between celebrities and music.

In the late 1940s, celebrity DJs Paul Whiteman, Duke Ellington, Kate Smith, and Tommy Dorsey were among those hired to present records on the assumption that listeners would tune in more for the stars than for the

FIG. 4. Duke Ellington, the disc jockey. (Getty Images.)

music (figure 4). The celebrity record spinners, hosting a fifteen-, thirty-, or sixty-minute program live or via transcription, soon gave way to local DJs with longer air shifts. Given the economies of networking, the local DJs may or may not have been cheaper—not being famous at the start, they probably were—but they and their colleagues could host enough hours per week to create an identifiable persona for the station. Most AM radio stations, especially those using Top 40, soul, MOR, and country and western formats, relied on strong DJ personalities to differentiate themselves in the market. Such stations expected star DJs to produce star ratings and to drive sales.

In New York . . .

Music programming presided over by the DJ proved a versatile arrangement. In 1949 the trade weekly *Sponsor* (1946–1964) explained the growing practice to its readership of radio and television advertising buyers:

> Perhaps the greatest single reason for the success of the disk-jockey format, aside from the personality of the platter spinners, lies in its flexibility. Programs may run from 15 minutes to two or three hours; not a few past and present shows have been and are midnight-to-dawn sessions. The type of recordings played may range from pop songs to the classics. From hillbilly

music to bee-bop. From Crosby to spiritual singers. The chatter accompanying the disks can be straight, comedy, serious, explanatory, or a combination of all four. Records can be grouped—the top dozen tunes of the week or the month or the year; musical-comedy songs of previous years; outstanding platters made by the late Glenn Miller or Tommy Dorsey or Dinah Shore—or they can be totally unrelated. Program selections may be carefully thought out by the disk jockey himself, or they may be arrived at via the requests-from-listeners route. The elasticity and latitude in programming a disk-jockey show are limited only by the normal consideration of good taste and the imagination of those handling the program.[53]

These observations from 1949 are for the most part true of music programming today, but they describe DJs' activities at general-interest stations particularly well. Casey Kasem succeeded with the "count down the hits" format for more than thirty years, and shows in which the records share a theme or concept are still commonplace as weekly offerings. "By request" shows have diminished in proportion to increasing corporate control over content, but before the advent of sophisticated radio ratings services they were considered an important source of audience data. Today's DJs often have overnight programs, but hosted fifteen- or thirty-minute record programs wedged in between news or sports wrap-ups are no longer found. And more prophetically, some of the presentation styles present in 1949 (ways "records can be grouped") have become not only the basis for radio formats themselves such as Oldies, Soft Rock, and Sinatra and Friends but also the concept underlying algorithmic playlists in today's streaming services.

One such grouping of records was the jazz DJ show. Whatever jazz meant, as the war ended it still had fans, and new releases, especially on the new LP format, were prevalent. Bebop was the new style, promoted by independent record labels such as Blue Note, Savoy, and Dial, run by equally enthusiastic owners Alfred Lion, Herman Lubinsky, and Ross Russell, respectively, and by DJs excited and entranced by the new music. One of those so captivated by bebop would become one its most famous radio voices, "Symphony" Sid Torin (figure 5). The cartoonist Bill Griffith devoted a *Zippy the Pinhead* cartoon to telling the story of Symphony Sid, including a URL that directs readers to King Pleasure's "Jumping with Symphony Sid."

Identifying himself on his overnight show with the phrase "This is your all-night, all-frantic one," Symphony Sid (Sidney Tarnopol, 1909–1984) was an icon of bebop and beat culture. Sal Paradise, the narrator in Jack Kerouac's 1957 novel *On the Road*, describes the last leg of hitching a ride to New York in 1949 thus: "The man got tired near Pennsylvania and Dean took the wheel and drove clear the rest of the way to New York, and we began to hear the Symphony Sid show on the radio with all the latest bop, and now we were entering the great and final city of America."[54]

FIG. 5. Symphony Sid depicted in a cartoon. (Bill Griffith, King Syndicate.)

This was an experience shared by Dan Morgenstern, an NEA Jazz Master (2007) and eight-time Grammy winner (all for album notes), then newly arrived from war-torn Europe. "My first night in New York I listened to the radio and I had this mistaken impression that I would find a lot of jazz on the radio. This, of course, was in the days when it was AM only, in 1947. And I finally found something at the tail end of the dial, and that was Symphony Sid."[55] An expatriate lover of modern jazz, Morgenstern, who knew the difference between jazz and pop music with jazz overtones, was disappointed in the radio offerings in New York, finding only Ted Husing (the man who connected Duke Ellington and the Cotton Club to CBS radio in 1927) hosting "Ted Husing's Bandstand" swing program on WHN at 10 a.m., Dr. Jazz with traditional jazz on WMGM, and Rudi Blesh, whose New Orleans revival *This Is Jazz* broadcasts on WOR were heard nationally. Modern jazz, bebop, was hard to find on the air at that time.

Morgenstern was grateful to find Symphony Sid, who by this time didn't play anything old. Enjoying a questionable reputation as the first to play bop on the radio, Torin's thirty-minute *After School Swing Session* ran for more than three years on the Bronx's WBNX. In 1940 he moved to WHOM (Elizabeth, New Jersey), where, in addition to his Wednesday and Saturday *Brother Sid* gospel shows, Torin settled into a long run with his overnight jazz show, *After Hours Swing Session*. WBNX and WHOM were among the first New York–area stations to offer programing that appealed to African Americans.

Symphony Sid later worked at the large New York independent station WMCA. There he straddled the programming divide, mixing live-music remotes from bebop strongholds like the Royal Roost, the Three Deuces, and Birdland with the latest bebop records between and after sets. (Long-playing records were issued of 1948 and 1949 airchecks of Torin hosting Count Basie, Charlie Parker, and Dizzy Gillespie.)

Because Torin worked in New York and was closely and personally associated with major bebop players, many aspects of his career and of his relationships have been written about. Torin only played modern jazz; he wouldn't play Louis Armstrong, for example.[56] Since he was the major figure exclusively promoting bebop on the New York airwaves, jazz labels, including Capitol Records, made regular payments to Torin.[57] His influence is also reflected in the number of songs mentioning him by name or reference (see table 2).

TABLE 2. Jazz disc jockey tributes.

Year	Artist/Composer	DJ Honored	Composition
1940	Louis Jordan	"Symphony" Sid Torin	After School Swing Session
1946	Lester Young/ King Pleasure		Jumpin' with Symphony Sid
1947	Illinois Jacquet		Symphony in Sid
1947	Arnett Cobb		Walkin' with Sid
1947	Erskine Hawkins		After Hours (Torin used this as a theme song)
1947	Sir Charles Thompson/ Illinois Jaquet	Fred Robbins	Robbins' Nest
1956	Billy Strayhorn		Snibor
1950	Charlie Parker/ Dizzy Gillespie	Oscar Treadwell	An Oscar for Treadwell
1958	Red Garland	Mort Fega	Mort's Report
1959	Quincy Jones	Daddy-O Daylie	Daylie Double
1957	Clark Terry		Blues for Daddy-O's Jazz Patio Blues*
1958	Cannonball Adderley/ Nat Adderley		One for Daddy-O
1953	J. J. Johnson (The Emminent J J Johnson)		Daylie Double
1996	Horace Silver	Chuck Niles	Hippest Cat in Hollywood
1980	Louis Belson		Niles Blues
1979, 1998	Bob Florence		Bebop Charlie, Nilestones
2016	George Cables	Monifa Brown	The Mystery of Monifa Brown
1995	André Previn	Evelyn Hawkins	Dr. DJ
1981	Tal Farlow	Art Vincent	Blue Art, Too
1949	Lionel Hampton	Al Benson	Benson's Boogie
1950	Max Miller Quartet		Jump for Al Benson Lumbar Ganglion Jump
1948	Paul Williams and his Sextette		Bouncin' with Benson
1956	Gerry Mulligan	Jimmy Lyons	Lines for Lyons
1997	Gerald Wilson		Lyon's Roar (from Theme for Monterey)

Source: Compiled by the author from various archival sources.

* This should not be confused with the "Daddy-Oh on the Patio" show on WAAA in Winston-Salem, North Carolina, in the 1950s with Oscar Daddy-Oh Alexander.

But Torin was not without critics, and not just for how often, in Morgenstern's words, he "mangled" the English language in attempts to be hip. His use of "jive" and hip lingo could be seen as an affinity for black culture or as a mocking appropriation. In this matter, Sid wasn't the only one talking jive. In an interview, Pittsburgh's Bettelou Purvis described her approach to her radio program, saying, "I'm strictly a jazz fiend, and really wig myself on these sessions."[58] In contrast, the earliest black radio announcers, who pre-dated the explosion of Negro Appeal radio, had consciously chosen to speak proper English for the express purpose of countering racist stereotypes and presenting black voices with dignity. Later, many successful black DJs chose to use slang and hip lingo to create bonds within the black community. These DJs spoke a common dialect with common folks, and black DJs both borrowed from the language of the street and contributed to it.[59]

Despite or because of his embrace of the veneer of black culture, Torin was hailed by some as the "accepted white voice of the New York Negro."[60] He proudly claimed to be in tune with black jazz fans. For example, Torin knew that Stan Kenton's recordings were unexpectedly popular with his young black listeners even as they were criticized by musicians and critics.[61] Further, as a public figure associated with jazz, Torin had many opportunities to promote concerts and participate in the management of such ventures, though apparently not to the satisfaction of all the musicians he employed. In his autobiography Miles Davis expressed little affection for Torin, who organized a 1952 tour that resulted in a lot of friction about billing and about the disparities in pay between emcee and promoter Torin and the musicians.[62]

Torin obtained a prominent spot on the ABC flagship station WJZ with nightly live remotes from Birdland that could be heard nationally. In 1952 Torin was fired in New York. He moved to Boston for a few years, only to return in 1958 with a typically grueling schedule—a weekday 4 to 5 p.m. show and his midnight to 3 a.m. daily program, both replacing classical music shows on WEVD.[63] In Fairfield, Connecticut, high school jazz fan Rusty Hassan, who would go on to a long and venerated career as a jazz DJ in Washington, DC, listened to Torin in the early 1960s, as well as to competitors Mort Fega, Ed Beach, and Billy Taylor. Hassan recalled hearing Maynard Ferguson ("Olé," *Maynard '61*), Oscar Brown Jr. ("Dat Dere," *Sin & Soul*), and Stan Getz ("I'm Late, I'm Late," *Focus*) on Torin's programs.[64]

During his time at WJZ Torin faced competition from Fega (1921–2005), whose WEVD overnight show (11:30 p.m. to 3:45 a.m.) ran from 1959 to 1966. WEVD was an ethnic AM/FM simulcaster owned by *The Forward*, the socialist-leaning Yiddish-language newspaper founded in New York in 1897. He quipped that "they program Yiddish, Greek, and Mort Fega."[65] Fega played plenty of bebop but also included a wider range of music on his show. In addition to Miles and Monk, Fega drew from his own record collection to play big bands, singers, and even stand-up comedy, reflecting the range of performers in New York clubs.[66]

Fega was clearly a favorite with *Metronome*'s New York–based editorial staff, as they did at least three profiles of him between 1957 and 1961, including one by Morgenstern himself.[67] Fega's approach was distinct from that of his chief competitor, Torin:

> Mort is one of those blessed jazz jockeys who talks little and plays much. That doesn't mean that he leaves the listener hanging for information. On the contrary, he's a firm believer in giving all pertinent information: "I sure get unhappy when I hear a record and the jockey hasn't told me who all the sidemen are." But it does mean that the unnecessary chatter is seldom there and the music is given the star billing.[68]

On his arrival in New York, Morgenstern may have also missed Fred Robbins (Fred Rubin, 1919–1992), a DJ that *New York Times* music critic Carter Harmon cited as a major supporter of bebop.[69] Robbins, another DJ immortalized in song (see table 2), would go on to more general success on radio and later television, but in 1942, after a start in radio in his hometown of Baltimore, he became a jazz-playing DJ at WHN in New York. Like Torin and unlike Fega, Robbins laid on the heavy jive. "He would begin by intoning such slangy verbal riffs as: 'Hiya cat, wipe your feet on the mat. Let's slap on the fat and dish out some scat.'"[70] By 1948 he was hosting the *1280 Club* on WOV, a New Rochelle station that had studios in Harlem and decent coverage throughout New York, before stints at WABC, WNEW, and WINS with his *Robbins' Nest* jazz program. Typical of stations with "Negro" programming, WOV faced all kinds of market encumbrances. Radio blogger Jose Fritz describes its labyrinthian licensing complications:

> WOV ditched a cumbersome three-way time share [of its frequency assignment] in 1940 to become the powerhouse it is today. Greater New York Broadcasting Corporation bought 1130 WPG and absorbed it into WOV. Then asked the FCC to delete the WOV license and shut down WOV and WPG for interfering with 1100 WBIL then deftly they moved WBIL to 1130, changing its calls to WOV. That all happened in 1940. The next year they swapped call letters[,] moving WOV to 1280 and WNEW to 1130. Without that complicated series of changes, they couldn't have maintained the listenership to become what they did. More complicated is that 1280 still was a share time with WHBI. That was not resolved until March of 1962, when WHBI was sold to Greater New York Broadcasting for $635,000. WHBI was bumped off shortly thereafter. . . . But that happens long after our tale. . . . So in the 1940s WOV is running ethnic Italian programming in the mornings. In the evenings they were running what we now call Rhythm

and Blues marketed at African Americans. (The ethnic Italian programming continued until 1962 under the WADO calls.)[71]

As we have seen, it was not atypical for stations with low power and license issues to turn to ethnic and Black Appeal programming to salvage their situation.

"Robbins' Nest" ran six nights per week from 6:30 to 9:00 p.m., and one hour was extracted and made available to other stations by transcription each night. A trade advertisement for the transcription program (figure 6) emphasizes that Robbins's "jive" is authentic and up to date, claims that his show on underpowered WOV draws an oversized listening audience, and stresses his "integrity" in choosing records according to his own taste. Such claims about large and loyal jazz listening audiences would become routine as radio stations would continue to struggle selling mainstream advertisers on the value of black audiences. And a full decade before the Congress would investigate payola, the trade magazines such as *Sponsor* featured a number of articles reflecting concerns about music selection in the emerging DJ show trend.

Despite Harmon's praise of Robbins as a great advocate of bop and the advertising copy's claims of a certain diplomatic stature within the jazz community, Robin D. G. Kelley offers a tale of a not-so-patient Fred Robbins in his groundbreaking biography of Thelonious Monk:

> Lorraine Lion was Blue Note's marketing department. On the night of January 12, she, Alfred [Lion], and Frank [Francis Wolff] took Thelonious to three different radio stations to promote the record. Although Monk wasn't always the best interviewee, he took the job seriously. He went in a dark suit and tie, with his classic gold-rimmed glasses, but no beret. Accompanying Wolff and the Lions that night was artist, critic, and amateur musician Paul Bacon, an old friend of Lorraine's from the Newark Hot Club. Just out of the service, he had begun working for Blue Note designing album covers. What Bacon thought would be a pretty routine evening turned out to be an unforgettable experience, from the moment he got in the car. "I got to ride in the back seat and Monk captivated me in thirty seconds." He found Monk's performance on Fred Robbins' radio show that night particularly amusing. Robbins, host of the 1280 Club Show on station WOV, was perhaps the most prominent radio personality in support of the new music. (Sir Charles Thompson had written "Robbins' Nest" for Fred.) "Robbins wasn't too deep," recalled Bacon, "and was expecting a light interview with some young musician who was hot to get his records played and make it. But Monk was incurably honest and simply couldn't engage in superficialities even if he wanted to. By the end of the show, Fred took Lorraine aside and told her in harsh terms never to bring this so-and-so up to his studio again. It was a funny scene."[72]

FIG. 6. Advertisement for the "Robbins' Nest" transcription program. (*Broadcasting and Telecasting*, August 30, 1948, 40.)

Torin, Fega, and Robbins were just a few of the jazz DJs promoting modern jazz in the immediate postwar period, but like the overwhelming majority of DJs in the country, they were white men, regardless of whether they were on stations programming to black audiences. Black DJs were still scarce, and female DJs and announcers were even rarer.

Women Spin Jazz: Mary Dee and Bettelou Purvis in Pittsburgh

Mary Dee Dudley (Mary Elizabeth Goode, 1912–1964), from Homestead, Pennsylvania, and a Howard University graduate, was a pioneering black woman DJ. The sister of early African American radio and television news reporter Mal Goode, Dee had a significant career in radio, first in Pittsburgh and later in Baltimore and Philadelphia, though it was cut short by her early death in 1964. In general, the few women who were on air tended to be restricted to women's shows. On black radio, black women were also found hosting gospel music programs, and later in her career Dee did exactly that, six days a week at WHAT in Philadelphia. But at the start of her career in 1948, she was one of the first general-duty black woman DJs in the industry at WHOD in Pittsburgh (figures 7 and 8). As was typical of the earliest black radio hosts, she got the job on the condition that she first sell the time for her show. She did so, selling time to a florist, her brother James's real estate business, and her father's twenty-four-hour pharmacy, located in Pittsburgh's Hill District.[73] Her "Movin' Around" show, perhaps the first entertainment show hosted by an African American woman, eventually expanded from fifteen minutes to two hours. By the time she left for Baltimore in 1956, Dee was on four hours a day, at times broadcasting from WAMO's Hill District storefront studios (figure 9; WAMO was formerly WHOD). Mary Dee was not known as a jazz DJ, but given her start in 1948, she would have certainly

FIG. 7. Mary Dee at WHOD in Pittsburgh. Lang-Worth Transcription Service discs are visible behind her. (Teenie Harris photo courtesy of the Carnegie Museum.)

FIG. 8. Mary Dee in the control booth (note the upcoming Dizzy Gillespie appearance, April 18, 1952). (Teenie Harris photo courtesy of the Carnegie Museum.)

FIG. 9. The WHOD studio at Herron and Centre Avenue in Pittsburgh's Hill District on August 1, 1951. (Photo by Charles "Teenie" Harris.)

played her share and reportedly played "the latest records by African American artists, introduced local talent, and interviewed national celebrities like Sarah Vaughan, Cab Calloway, and Jackie Robinson."[74]

Also in Pittsburgh, not as well known today as Mary Dee, was Betty Lou Purvis (Marks) (1927–1976), a self-described "music bug" who leveraged her position as a music librarian and continuity director at daytime-only WPGH (1947–1954) into several on-air positions and the role of music director.[75] It is clear from her *Metronome* profile that she had performed many roles at WPGH before hosting *For Women Only* and her initial jazz program, the 4 p.m. daily *Jazz You Like It*.[76]

> The show is three years old, its sponsors "are the kind of people who cater to my audience . . . clubs, music shops and wine companies," and she is proud of the fact that she features "ONLY BOP!" Perhaps Bettelou is stretching a point when she says she plays only bop, as her list of typical artists includes Miles Davis, Kenton, Sonny Stitt, Wardell Gray, Benny Green and Stan Getz, but the program definitely caters to the modernists. "When I obtained my show," she explains, "I wanted to make it a show for musicians only. From talking with local boys who played I learned that there was no outlet for the type of music they wanted to hear, and that's why, even though there are arguments against bop, I keep my format the same. I plug local groups and interview young musicians whom I hear and like. It's really a musicians' exchange."[77]

Purvis's profile seemed determined to link her bona fides as a jazz expert to her well-known trumpeter father, and that relationship could have played a role in her approach to the Pittsburgh jazz community. But Purvis was just as much of a hustler as any of the early figures who wanted "in" regarding radio and music. An article in the record collectors' magazine *Playback* from 1949 announced that she had bought inventory from a failing record company and was releasing it on her own label.[78] From 1947 to 1949 Purvis was a frequent contributor to *DownBeat*, supplying news items about Pittsburgh jazz and keeping the activities of the city's artists in the most important national jazz periodical. At this time, *DownBeat* was a bi-weekly and contained detailed coverage about engagements, band personnel changes, and box office reports and served as much as a trade magazine as one oriented toward fans. Purvis's reports reveal a thorough familiarity with the working musicians, black and white, in the then-vibrant Pittsburgh jazz scene.

It is fortunate that two Top 10 lists compiled by Music Director Purvis from October 1948 survive (table 3).[79] One list is a jazz Top 10; the second is labeled "Top 40," but because that term was not used in 1948, it may have been added by the collector. It does give some idea of the growing divide between jazz and pop.

TABLE 3. WPGH October 1948 Jazz and Pop Top-10 lists.

WPGH Jazz Top 10, October 16, 1948			WPGH Pop Top 10, October 1, 1948	
Artist	Song		Artist	Song
Billy Eckstine	Sophisticated Lady	1	Billy Eckstine	Solitude
Charlie Ventura	East of Suez	2	Bill Farrell	You've Changed
Tadd Dameron	The Tadd Walk	3	Bill Darnell	So Much
Dizzy Gillespie	Manteca	4	Helen Forrest	Just Got to Have Him Around
Sarah Vaughan	I Get a Kick Out of You	5	Derry Falligane	Deep as the River
Buddy Johnson	Li'l Dog	6	The Ravens	Someday
Stan Kenton	Bongo Riff	7	Fran Warren	Envy
La Vere's Chicago Loopers	Subdivided in F	8	Kate Smith	Over the Hillside
Erroll Garner	Pastel	9	Perry Como	I Wish I Had a Record
Arnett Cobb	Cobb's Boogie	10	Buddy Johnson	Lovely in Her Evening Gown

Sources: Both surveys come from a large collection on the Airheads Radio Survey Archive, http://www.las-solanas.com/arsa/. The lists were compiled by Bettelou Purvis.

(Woodrow Wilson) Buddy Johnson, whose music straddled the blues, R&B, and jazz borders, appears on both charts. "Li'l Dog" is a backbeat-heavy blues instrumental, whereas "Lovely in Her Evening Gown" is a melodramatic vocal ballad. At first glance "Subdivided in F" by La Vere's Chicago Loopers seems just a catchy novelty number, but on closer examination it has the hard-swinging Joe Venuti on violin and Pittsburgh's own Billy May on trumpet, and the placing of this record on her list may also be evidence of her commitment to support the local musicians. (May would go on to be one of the music industry's most sought-after arrangers.) The placement of Tadd Dameron at number 3 verifies that this list is oriented toward jazz fans. Dameron was a musician of considerable note, better known as composer and arranger than as a pianist, and always better appreciated by players than by fans.[80]

As for Billy Eckstine, who tops the lists, both tracks are ballads with a jazz orchestra accompanying his deep baritone voice. Neither recording, by the way, reflects the spirit of Eckstine's legendary 1944–1947 big band, an incubator for young bebop talent that included Dizzy Gillespie, Charlie Parker, Dexter Gordon, Art Blakey, Fats Navarro, Miles Davis, and Sarah Vaughan, with arrangements by Gil Fuller and Dameron. But it may be that Purvis placed the deservedly popular Eckstine at the top lists because he was from Pittsburgh.

Purvis moved to New York in 1949, and while working in a music publicity office, had a show on WLIB from 8:45 to 9:15 on Saturday and Sunday nights called *Spinner Sanctum*, featuring jazz and interviews with jazz musicians.[81] There is not much of trace of Bettelou Purvis after the move to New York.[82]

African American DJs with Jazz in the Mix

As an African American, Hal Jackson (1915–2012) had a tougher time getting started in radio than did Torin or Purvis. Like Jack Cooper, Jackson was rebuffed by Washington, DC, radio stations and like Cooper, Jackson used a friendly intermediary to gain surreptitious access to the air. Earlier he had approached the manager of WINX, owned by the *Washington Post* at the time, proposing to broadcast Negro League baseball games from Griffith Stadium. Told flatly that "no nigger will ever go on this radio station," Jackson concocted a plan.[83] Working with a cooperative white advertising man, he bought fifteen minutes of Monday through Friday airtime on WINX at 11 p.m. for $35 per night.[84] Because he showed up only a few minutes before airtime, the absent station manager was unavailable to block him, and Jackson went on the air. One reason for Jackson's end-run success was the ignorance of whites about black activities. Before airtime, Jackson had made feverish efforts to promote the show in the black press. Even as he bought the airtime, white management could not decode his message of appeal to the black audience. In proposing *The Bronze Review*, featuring music, interviews, and news, the station managers were unaware that *bronze*, like *sepia*, was a way of signifying *black*. The show was a hit with black Washington and featured guests such as First Lady Eleanor Roosevelt, entertainer Lena Horne, and Representative Adam Clayton Powell Jr. In the end, money talked; "I knew the station was getting flak for letting me on, but they liked that money they were making."[85]

Reflecting the low wages paid to black DJs, Jackson eventually was working simultaneously at WINX and WOOK in Washington and at WANN (Annapolis) and WSID (Baltimore), playing race records and doing sports reports at different times of the day at each of them. By 1954 Jackson was in New York and working at WMCA, where his *All-American Revue* had wide appeal playing Duke Ellington, Frank Sinatra, Sarah Vaughn, and Xavier Cugat from 8 to 10 p.m.[86] A couple of months later Jackson added a 4 to 6 p.m. show six days a week on Newark's WNJR, which Rollins Broadcasting was converting into a Black Appeal station. One month after starting at WNJR, Jackson began hosting live remotes from Birdland as Symphony Sid had done before him over network flagship WABC (previously WJZ).[87]

In his autobiography, Jackson provided details about how the nightly broadcasts and his taxing career were structured:

> The show over WABC was six hours, midnight to 6 AM, which meant that I would have very little time for sleep. But I couldn't leave Al Lamphian

[WNJR] and I couldn't leave WMCA. So I decided to work all three shows. And so it was that I became the first New York radio personality to have daily shows on three separate stations. Only the first hour of the show was broadcast live from Birdland. At 1 AM, we went over to the studio, which held about 300 people, and from there we would record a music-and-interview show. The audience would drift in and out all night, and so would the big-name celebrities who happened to be in town. Between the broadcast from Birdland and the broadcast from the ABC studios, I got to work with many of the big artists of the day—Stan Kenton, Charlie Parker, Nat Cole, Billy Eckstine, Sarah Vaughan, Dizzy Gillespie, Billie Holiday . . . In the Studio show, we talked about a variety of music and artists, then I'd play the records. It was basically a hosting job. Morris Levy handled the other matters, such as selling time and booking acts. But there was still a lot to do, what with interviews, record announcements, and commercials.[88]

As with Torin, the live remote portion was carried by the ABC network—fifty-four stations, according to Jackson. Some stations carried the studio show as well. Because he worked overnight, Jackson believed that many executives and listeners at ABC were unaware that he was black and only became aware once the transition to his hosting was already successful.

Like Martin Block with his *Make Believe Ballroom*, Jackson used a framing imaginary to introduce artists. Using the premise of "the House that Jack Built" to present records, he had artists performing in fictional rooms:

I chose all the records myself, although [WOOK owner] Richard Eaton made it clear that I was to stick to those by Black artists—"race music," as it was called then. I played Nat Cole and Dinah Washington and the Ink Spots because they were great artists, and once in a while I would slip in a record by Peggy Lee or some other White performers whose work I liked. To me, it was the quality of the music, not the color of the performer, that mattered.[89]

Jackson was one of the black DJs who spoke in a low-key manner and avoided the hyperbolic jive that would later become commonplace among white and black DJs:

"How are you?" he would begin. "This is Hal Jackson, the host that loves you the most, welcoming you to 'The House That Jack Built.' We're rolling out the musical carpet, and we'll be spinning a few just for you. So come on in, sit back, relax and enjoy your favorite recording stars from here to Mars."[90]

Reading this quotation, one might question Jackson's jive avoidance, but reciting it a various speeds and with a range of inflections can provide some insights into how different DJs might have sounded.

Hal Jackson was a jazz fan and played jazz records at times but did not sacrifice his career for jazz. He played the popular artists and records of the day throughout his extraordinarily long career. Like Chicago's Al Benson, who once dropped leaflets of the United States Constitution from an airplane over segregated Mississippi, Jackson was politically active. Early in his career he used his influence to help desegregate stores, performance venues, amusement parks, swimming pools, and other public spaces and to organize radio employees seeking higher wages. His influence, pioneer reputation, and history of activism led to his ownership stake and management position with the Inner City Broadcasting Corporation, which would become the first large black-owned broadcasting company beginning with the acquisition of WLIB in 1972 and WLIB-FM in 1974. These stations became influential trendsetters in black radio broadcasting. WLIB-FM (later changed to WBLS-FM) had had a jazz format under previous owners. For a brief period after its acquisition, jazz was at least part of the programming mix at WBLS and other stations emulating its style, in contrast to most commercial radio at the time, on which it was almost always heard on jazz specialty shows. (See Chapter 3.)

On the West coast, Joe Adams (1922–2018) also managed to get on the radio. The 1949 *Sponsor* magazine annual special issue on the Negro radio market noted, "Joe Adams on KOWL in Santa Monica, California is typical of the 100-odd Negro disk jockeys [recall that there were more than 2000 DJs by 1947] who have sprung up around the country in the past year or so."[91] Adams had a remarkably diverse career; a Tuskegee Airman who convinced Al Jarvis (*Make Believe Ballroom*) to take him on as an assistant, Adams was also a ruggedly handsome bandleader who became best known for his acting roles as a psychiatrist in John Frankenheimer's *Manchurian Candidate* (1962), his Golden Globe–winning role as boxing champ Husky Miller in Otto Preminger's all-black production *Carmen Jones* (1954), and his real-life role as Ray Charles's manager and corporation head. Adams owed much of that show business success to his early breakthrough on radio.

Adams also represents the danger of assuming that African American radio DJs at that time were playing a great deal of jazz on their programs. Adams claimed to have only "played the best music. T-Bone Walker followed by Duke Ellington, Tommy Dorsey if it's a good song, Wynonie Harris followed by AquaViva something pretty like 'That's All' (easy listening)."[92] Adams claimed that because of his music choices and his smooth vocal delivery, he had a wide crossover audience and that his film career came from his show being piped into movie studio sets between setups. A white Los Angeles DJ, Hunter Hancock, corroborated that account, noting, "Joe Adams did have a show that started a couple of months before mine, he was playing sort of pop music. He was a black announcer playing white music."[93]

Hancock (1916– or 1914–2004) was another fabled early DJ presenting black music on the radio in southern California and a good example of the tough times jazz was already having with younger radio audiences in the late 1940s. As with many figures, Hancock's youth, perseverance, and enthusiasm for radio got him in the door. He waited at KFVD for the program director to arrive and talked his way onto the air as a weekend DJ. A critical factor was the addition of an apparel sponsor that wanted to reach black Los Angeles shoppers with a one-hour Sunday show in 1943. Despite little knowledge of black music outside of jazz, Hancock hosted "Harlem Holiday," using Chick Webb's similarly titled "Holiday in Harlem" as a theme. ("Harlem" indicated "pertaining to Negroes," as, for example, the Chicago-based Harlem Globetrotters basketball team.) In 1947 Hancock had a daily half-hour show, "Harlemtime," on which he initially played jazz until a race record promoter persuaded him to play music from his catalog of black southern hits. Soon Hancock was being supplied by all the race record firms for his now three-and-a-half-hour show, which was becoming a pioneering rhythm and blues program. Hancock still had his Sunday jazz show, but it was clear that R&B drew larger audiences than did jazz.[94] As was typical of the time, Hancock's career was affected by the primacy of Top 40 and by the increasing practice of managerial control over the playlist. Yet he continued to be associated with jazz in Los Angeles through the 1950s at least, because of his Sunday jazz program and as the master of ceremonies for the Cavalcade of Jazz. The Cavalcade (1945–1958) was the first large outdoor jazz entertainment event of its kind, produced by an African American, Leon Hefflin, Sr., and was a prominent event in the life of the Central Avenue music scene.[95]

No Jazz, Please

Jazz wasn't loved by all, and it was downright unwelcome on some radio stations. Over the history of radio, promotional claims regarding music excluded from programming have recurred, and they have repeatedly involved music associated with African Americans. From the language used by these stations it can be inferred that race played a significant part in these policies. "No rock and roll" policies at MOR stations did not totally exclude black music—Nat Cole, Johnny Mathis, and later, some Motown acts were all right—but the raucous beat and screaming vocals of Little Richard, James Brown, and Ike Turner were not. The late 1970s "disco sucks" bias on the part of fans and stations had as much to do with its being black party music and its currency in queer culture as it did with irritation with its repetitive nature and production excesses. In the 1980s, criticized for rejecting black artists, MTV lamely responded with a "we're a rock station" defense. (It took the Michael Jackson phenomenon to break MTV's informal black music ban.) Today, the distinction between the Urban Contemporary (which includes hip hop) and the Urban Adult Contemporary (which excludes hip hop) formats, descendants of the soul or R&B formats, reflects a generational divide over hip hop that echoes the 1940s black middle-class discomfort with jazz in that it includes internalized negativity about hip hop artists and culture.

From the beginning, jazz faced resistance across races. Some whites feared and despised the growing influence of black culture on their young people, while some blacks harbored complex and interwoven embarrassments and resentments about jazz and the enthusiasm it aroused in white fans. For many white fans, jazz expressed the organic primitivism which they enviously thought blacks effortlessly retained during modern times, and many African American intellectuals feared that such beliefs were obstacles to racial progress. It was jazz's raw and energetic qualities that offended some, while its direct appeal to bodily pleasure caused concern in others. Further, jazz was associated with places of social pleasure and drinking at a time when American moral tensions were reflected in Prohibition. These sinful associations led to further reservations among those in the striving black middle class concerned with their image in the eyes of white America. Music educators decried its appeal to impressionable young music students and feared the music's power to distract students in their studies and to disrupt their career paths. By the 1940s jazz had another image problem: its reputation as a community tainted by the use of narcotics and as a music led by drug addicts.[96] Major jazz figures including Louis Armstrong, Billie Holiday, Lester Young, Anita O'Day, Gerry Mulligan, Chet Baker, and Jimmy Heath were all targets of aggressive drug prosecutions.

This subcultural view of jazz and jazz fans also extended to black slang (sometimes called "jive") that was picked up by whites intrigued or infatuated with black culture.[97] Norman Mailer's 1957 essay "The White Negro" expressed this attraction of male white youth culture to the alienation and perceived sexual and social freedom of African Americans in rejection of the staid status quo, although many black writers found the essay, and the concept, hollow. Ralph Ellison, for example, called Mailer's essay "the same old primitivism crap in a new package."[98] With this notion that jazz was part of a subculture subverting American values, it should come as no surprise that there were radio stations that proudly announced no-jazz or no-jive policies.

One "no jazz" station, ironically, was New York's WLIB, which would become one of the most prominent Black Appeal stations in 1949, feature Bettelou Purvis's jazz programs, and become a leading jazz station in the 1960s; it was one of the first of a new wave of black-owned radio properties after its 1972 purchase by Inner City Broadcasting. Originally a "good music" station, playing classical music and popular standards in direct competition with WQXR (long owned by the *New York Times*), WLIB made its "no jazz" policy an attribute of its appeal. In 1944 ads, WLIB, "The Voice of Liberty," claimed to attract the listener "who likes *a variety of good music* just for the endless pleasure it gives" (emphasis original). Its mix of "familiar music and famous artists" plus news was claimed to be "distinctly different from the daytime soap-operas, women's programs, 'jazz, jive and swing,' sports results, talks, and the deep-serious music heard on contemporary stations."[99] WLIB's list of included music and the critique of network staples such as soap operas and women's programs points away from omnibus programming and toward a future format that would come to be known as easy listening. But also, "jazz, jive and swing" are called out as disturbing and jarring. This was made explicit in an ad for Fort Worth station WBAP's weekday afternoon "good music" haven. A close look at the copy shows that WBAP was linking its "no jazz, no jive, no hillbilly" policy to good citizenship and its programming earning the unsolicited endorsement of church-goers, educators, and civic-minded community groups.[100]

"Good" or inoffensive music became a central concept to the Easy Listening and Good Music formats that emerged late in the following decade. Yet the programming at stations like WLIB and WBAP in the 1940s was distinct from that of stations employing those later formats. They still tended toward omnibus programming, only theirs was an inclusivity that did not extend to black people or rural Americans—no Negroes, no white trash. Also, the style of jazz DJ-ing established by Torin and early Black Appeal DJs as, in fact, black, was itself offensive to white radio stations that attempted to erect barriers between what they believed was degenerate Negro culture and respectable culture. This, of course, was much of the basis for the opposition to rock and roll and a motivation for the era's payola investigations: the conviction that "crude crap" like rock and roll and rhythm and blues could not possibly be that popular with young white kids without a conspiracy between record companies and DJs, aided by substantial payments, to foist this music on white America.

Black music could be used as a boogieman summoned whenever needed to support a position, for example, a claim that rock and roll had insidious effects. When FM service was established, AM station owners were quick to grab FM licenses for future prospects and to keep them from competing broadcasters. Although there were immediate calls for nonduplicating programming, station owners and managers lobbied to resist the additional expense that, in reality, would not likely produce any more real revenue at the time. James L. Howe, president and general manager of Chanticleer Broadcasting in New Brunswick, New Jersey, invoked the specter of black music in his defense of simulcasting when he asked rhetorically, "What shall we do to give different and more exclusive service on FM—change our broadcast time, write different news, use new announcers, or what?" Continuing in this vein, he threatened to unleash jazz on the community should he be forced to offer separate programming:

> Our station policy at present is not to use boogie-woogie or jazz on the air. Will we be providing an additional worthwhile service if we program

boogie-woogie and jazz on FM? Will the added fidelity of 15,000 cycles add to the pleasure of Benny Goodman's clarinet?[101]

Capitulating to the limited yet energetic demand for jazz, some stations sought to contain it to hours when fewer ears might be offended. Baltimore station WITH, for instance, was promoted in a trade magazine feature that purported to explain its success at surviving against television. It stated that extreme music was avoided, "symphonies got the cold shoulder," and "hot jazz was permitted only in the 10 pm to 1 am period," when WITH "programs for the 300,000 Negro population in the coverage area and from 1:30 to 2:30 am when a special jazz classics show" was aired.[102]

WITH may have been the first Baltimore station to devote some airtime to black audiences. In 1951 WITH brought "Hot Rod" Hulbert from Memphis, where he had been on staff at WDIA. Hulbert would have a legendary career in broadcasting, later serving as program director of each of Baltimore's fulltime Black Appeal stations, WWIN and WEBB. In 1963 Hulbert held down shifts in Baltimore (WITH), Philadelphia (WHAT), and New York (WDES) at the same time.[103]

These policies had long-term implications. Jazz programs as late-night offerings continue to this day, especially on noncommercial radio. Perhaps it is thought to belong there, with jazz representing nightlife in some folks' minds, but also those hours are safely distant from the ratings-crucial morning and evening rush hours.

Radio stations portrayed themselves as playing "no jazz, no jive," and so did individual radio personalities. In 1956 a DJ named Frank Ford hyperbolically promoted himself as "the world's only living disc jockey who doesn't play jazz, barrelhouse, or rock 'n' roll,"[104] while a help wanted advertisement for a group of stations in Alaska, with harsh wording attempting to sift out nonserious responses, warned:

> Four hours board and air work. All shows are heavy commercial. Unless you are willing to work the above hours and can sell hard commercial copy and lots of it, do not apply. If you expect to play rhythm and blues, Rock and Roll of all varieties, progressive jazz, or "cool" music, please do not waste your time and ours. Strictly enforced music policy of the stations prohibit all of the above. Pay good but hours permanent, music policy strict. No humorist or character expected or desired. If you feel that you do a good country and western show say so but not necessary to get the position.[105]

North to Alaska indeed!

2

Independent Contractors

Jazz Shows Outside the Format

> I'm Doctor Hep Cat, on the scene,
> with a stack of shellac in my record machine.
> I'm hip to the tip, and bop to the top.
> I'm long time coming and I just won't stop.
> —Doctor Hep Cat (Lavada Durst)

With the end of the war the FCC approved a flood of new radio licenses. At the time of the attack on Pearl Harbor, about 900 radio stations had been licensed for regular operation, and this number remained stable for the war's duration. However, by the end of 1946, more than 1,500 stations were on the air, with almost 500 more under authorized construction permits. By the middle of 1955 radio's gross income was divvied up by 2,748 AM and 538 FM radio stations.[1] It is not surprising that almost none of these new licenses went to African American entrepreneurs. The first five black-owned stations were WERD in Atlanta (1948), KPRS in Kansas City (1950), WCHB in Detroit (1956), WEUP in Huntsville, Alabama (1958), and WVOE in Chadbourn, North Carolina (1962).

The explosion of radio licenses after World War II left many station owners with a marginal business in an oversaturated market. The postwar radio economy caused some broadcasters to seek out untapped markets. One strategy for an unsuccessful station remained unchanged from early radio: avoid head-to-head competition with the most well-entrenched and successful stations and instead target the underserved with programming aimed at ethnic communities. The turn to African American listeners became known as Black Appeal or Negro Appeal radio. Few stations would openly acknowledge the black community in the twenties and thirties, but there were stations that sold wholesale blocks of time to foreign-language ethnic groups and, only reluctantly, to black entrepreneurs. By the forties, in each market with a significant black presence at least one station kept afloat by devoting some hours to those listeners.

In Memphis, WDIA's white owners went further and made theirs the nation's first full-time Negro Appeal station. It launched in June 1947, becoming the sixth station in the Memphis market. Making no headway as a country and western station nor later as a classical music station, owners John Pepper and Bert Ferguson imagined there was potential business in appealing to the area's large black population and in directly selling ad time to both white and black businesses desiring to reach black listeners. Rather than openly orienting their station towards blacks, Pepper and Ferguson avoided criticism from local segregationists by doing it in stages. By the time they were fully committed to black audiences, they expected to be so successful as to be impervious to criticism. Wisely, they tapped local Booker T. Washington High School educator Nat D. Williams (1907–1983) to gradually steer them to a full schedule of black programming. By the spring of 1949, WDIA went from last to second in its market and on to place first, now one of eight stations, with 28 percent of all listeners in the Memphis market by the end of the year.

With each group having differing goals, a synergetic relationship developed between the white owners and black staff at WDIA, and the station became a pioneering social experiment that benefited all. The color line was ever present at WDIA, with white employees receiving higher pay than the black staff, but the station was nonetheless a vehicle for local black empowerment. The indignity of the unfair wage scale was at least partly offset by what was created for the black community—in the words of pioneering DJ Martha Jean the Queen, a platform "to serve, to sell, to inform, to entertain, and to educate our community."[2] The owners and management saw the enterprise as a sound investment, and the staff considered it an opportunity to create change for the better in the black community.

WDIA's programming became the template for early Black Appeal radio across the nation; blues, gospel, rhythm and blues or black-oriented rock and roll, homemaker shows, call-in shows for relationship advice, and some jazz highlighted the still omnibus offerings. At stations like WDIA jazz artists began to slip out of the playlists in favor of rhythm and blues, but jazz survived for a time either as the focus of a specific show or because the DJ would set aside a half-hour or so for jazz records on a regular basis. At WDIA, it was Nat D. Williams himself who preferred to play Ellington, Basie, Fats Waller, Jimmy Lunceford, and Ella Fitzgerald on his program, but much more airtime went to Ruth Brown, Laverne Baker, the Clovers, and the Drifters.[3]

The station's success was noticed. In cities north and south with substantial African American populations, programming to the black community became a viable if not prestigious path to success in the flooded broadcasting industry. Stations with disadvantageous frequency assignments above 1100 kHz, often limited to 250 W (not kW) or less and to sunrise-to-sundown operating hours, were most likely to try Black Appeal. With limited coverage and possibly with an inferior-sounding airchain, these stations had a difficult time competing with the full-power (as much as 50 kW) and full-time stations for advertising and listenership.[4] To be clear, black radio stations were not found on the right end of the radio dial because of any kind of direct radio redlining, but because these less valuable broadcast properties had operating constraints that limited their business potential with general audiences.

Despite the black staffers' subversive use of these stations to help the community, one imagines that most Black Appeal broadcasters were not at all interested in the social or political aspects but were focused intently on the bottom line. Black Appeal programming was no civic service, though the owners often took that pose; it was strictly a profitable business strategy with lower entry costs than more desirable radio properties. Former KDKO (Denver) owner David Segal crudely recalled his motivations: "Going black was the two dirtiest words in the business. Radio is a fucking money machine. I wasn't in it to win black friends. Our rates were a lot lower than on the white stations, but we made money. Enough so I'm sitting on my ass in Rancho Mirage."[5] Industry observers noted WDIA's success, and the model spread to every part of the country with African American populations, as William Barlow notes, often without desegregation of their staffs and with mixed results.[6]

With one of the nation's largest black populations, Chicago became a center for Black Appeal radio. Indeed, from the pioneer broadcasts of Jack Cooper to the production of "Destination Freedom" to the afternoon show of "Fly Jock" Tom Joyner, Chicago holds an important place in the history of black radio.[7]

Al Benson, Daddy-O Daylie, Sid McCoy, and Yvonne Daniels

The Old Swingmaster

After radio pioneer Jack Cooper established a black presence on Chicago radio with his purchased time arrangements, the next three decades of developments encapsulated commercial jazz radio there. It really got going with a preacher named Al Benson, who took to the air with religious programming and soon found a career playing blues and R&B to the African American audience in Chicago. Benson's success opened the doors for others to enter city's jazz radio history.

Chicago has been a fruitful source for illustrating the market forces impinging on jazz radio. Owing to the city's industrial might, its due-north location relative to the masses of blacks suffering under Jim Crow, and the advocacy of Robert Sengstacke Abbott's *Chicago Defender*, the Great Migration pushed the postwar African American population in Chicago to almost half a million by 1950 and to more than one million by 1970. This moment spawned a rich history of black entrepreneurial activity. Besides the hair care and cosmetics company Johnson Products (makers of Afro Sheen and Ultra Sheen), Chicago was home to the Johnson Publishing Company (1942–2019), once black America's largest, publishers of *Ebony*, *Jet*, *Black World* (1961–1970), and *Negro Digest* (1942–1951), as well as Vee-Jay records, founded by Vivian Carter and James Bracken in 1953 (but now owned by the Concord Music Group). Chicago's black broadcasting tradition can be traced back to the ambitious Jack Cooper.

Cooper's *All-Negro Hour*, which premiered in 1929, led to an empire of brokered-time black broadcasts on four Chicago stations, WSBC, WHFC, WAAF, and WBEE, several of which would play important roles in the city's jazz radio history. Al Benson (born Arthur Bernard Leaner in Jackson, Mississippi, in 1908 and died in 1978) was a graduate of Jackson State College who moved to Chicago and founded a storefront church in the 1930s. Supporting himself at various times as a Pennsylvania Railroad cook, a probation officer, and a Works Progress Administration interviewer, Leaner had made contacts with African American Congressman William Dawson's political machine and served as a precinct captain.[8] His radio career began on WGES in 1945. As Reverend Al Leaner, he ran a Sunday evening religious program that did okay but didn't allow him to sell advertising. As Al Benson, "The Old Swingmaster," he was a runaway business success, augmenting his meager DJ's salary with commissions on the ads he sold on WGES and later (and simultaneously) on WJJD, appearing on air as much as twenty hours per week playing what nobody up to that time was playing in Chicago, the blues.

William Barlow explained his success thus:

> Benson's phenomenal appeal on the airwaves undoubtedly stemmed from his black-identified style. He was the first radio announcer in the Chicago market to speak with a black Southern accent and use black street slang on the air, and he was the first local disc jockey to feature the popular—and previously taboo—urban blues hits of the era on his shows. He also proved to be the consummate radio pitchman. Prior to his career in broadcasting, Benson had worked closely with migrant and working-class African Americans in Chicago, in both a religious and a social service capacity. He was well aware of their daily lives, as well as their dreams and aspirations. Equally important, he spoke to them in their own vernacular—"native talk," as he called it.[9]

Equally adept at selling advertising and playing the pitchman on the air, thus showing his mastery of the business side of radio, Benson had a great understanding of his audience and what they liked in terms of programming as well. He initially played a fair amount of jazz, which he personally liked—his theme song was Duke Ellington's version of "Dear Old Southland"—but, according to his junior colleague Sid McCoy, jazz was weeded out in favor of blues and R&B.[10] Another leading DJ who developed under Benson, Herb "The Cool Gent" Kent, recollected that their predecessor Cooper had regularly played such music as "Creole Love Call" (Duke Ellington), Louis Armstrong, and even ragtime, setting the tone for the station.[11] Barlow credits Benson with "almost single-handedly" pioneering the transition to rhythm and blues in Chicago.[12]

> In Chicago, Jack Cooper's big band jazz format continued to dominate the "black appeal" programming on the air. Moreover, he and his protégés refused to play R&B releases on the air because of their "suggestive" lyrics and "lowlife" cultural connotations. Al Benson changed this situation dramatically. In consultation with two of his nephews who operated a Southside record store, he learned not only that R&B discs were selling better than their jazz counterparts, but also which new releases were in the greatest demand locally. These were the records he would feature on his shows.[13]

Disc jockeys such as Benson, attuned to the rising popularity of R&B, played a major role in the decline of jazz on the radio, or at least its exile to the sanctuary of jazz shows. Another Benson protégé, Lucky Cordell, saw it as a market-driven affair:

> What happened, Al Benson saw a need, an opening, and filled it. There was no one at the time playing blues on radio. There was only one other deejay in Chicago and that was Jack L. Cooper. He played jazz and/or ballads; Ella Fitzgerald, Dinah Washington, acts like that. He would not play what he considered "gut bucket blues."[14]

It is fascinating to see how jazz played a role in the social politics of aspiration and respectability of black America; this pattern would repeat with soul, funk, disco, and hip hop. However, there were DJs in Chicago who wanted to play jazz and did play jazz on the radio to the extent that they could and remain popular with their audiences. Several of the DJs had lengthy programs that allowed them to emphasize different music styles, especially when the time was sold to different types of businesses. One of Benson's main rivals, Sam Evans, had a 10 p.m. to midnight show on WGES in 1955 that switched gears at 11 p.m. According to Robert Pruter,

> [The] *Jam with Sam* show was greasing the airwave[s] with recordings by the Flamingos, Ravens, Danderliers, and all the great groups of the time, who were waxing solid jumps and smooth ballads. After he had played vocal group recordings from 10 to 11 PM, he stopped smoothly and mellowly

oiling the megacycles with pastels for Gold Medal flour and velvet intonations of "I love you madly." Then, through the speaker came the first haunting bars of Little Walter's great chromatic Hohner wailing "Blue Light" as the theme for the next hour of music.[15]

This description reflects several facts about black radio. First, it was a sparse resource that had to serve a black audience that spanned several generations and included recent southern transplants as well as native northerners by playing doo-wop, R&B, jazz, and blues. Second, advertisers were beginning to see the value of selling to the black audience. And third, the programmers—in this era, the DJs themselves—had wide discretion to play music they liked, but they could not totally ignore what was popular with their audience. In this regard the DJ's path to success was similar to that of many musicians. One could imagine Benson telling the same story as saxophonist David "Fathead" Newman, who came to fame with Ray Charles.

> "I was brought up a bebop musician, but it wasn't so acceptable, especially in Dallas," Mr. Newman told the Dallas Morning News some years ago. "You couldn't make a living doing that, so I had to play rhythm and blues. I adapted to it easily being from an area where blues was prevalent."[16]

Norm Spaulding, an eyewitness to this era as a DJ on Chicago stations for many years, took a free-market view of jazz and labeled the jazz DJs "elitists" who saw themselves as "uplifters of the community's taste and guardians of an art form." Spaulding noted that the more popular Chicago blues DJs out-earned their jazz counterparts, but he also sensed a lack of reciprocity or perhaps respect: "While a blues disc jockey often played a jazz selection, the jazz jockey seldom played a rhythm-and-blues record."[17]

By taking phoned-in requests, consulting with trusted contacts at record stores, befriending the artists, and maintaining contacts with the record companies, DJs blended information streams. As the historian Elena Razlogova writes, "Disc jockey culture mediated between the scientific and informal aspects of the music business," where the scientific was formal research and hard sales data and the informal was requests, word of mouth, and gut feelings about hit potential.[18]

In this era almost all DJs had control of their playlists, but black DJs would maintain this control well into the 1970s, primarily because white station owners and managers had little feel for black music. Without reliable research materials such as the record reports and tout sheets that guided them in choosing pop music, they relied on the expertise of their underpaid black DJs but rarely thought to hire African Americans for management positions. Top DJs like Benson enjoyed close relationships with companies that made black records and were frequently credited with "breaking" hits—being the

DJ responsible for making a new release popular, a reputation which could bring a DJ considerable financial benefits and a power that would only increase with the size of the record industry in the 1960s and 1970s.

A discussion of jazz on Black Appeal radio in Al Benson's Chicago is not complete without the stories of Sid McCoy, Yvonne Daniels, and Daddy-O Daylie, each of them direct beneficiaries of Cooper's and Benson's success in opening Chicago radio for African Americans.

Daddy-O, Sid, and Yvonne

Holmes Bailey (1920–2003) had been an outstanding high school basketball player who spent some time as a professional with the Harlem Globetrotters. He applied his showmanship and slick ball-handling skills to bartending at an upscale drinking establishment. Tossing glasses, ice cubes, and ingredients all while rhyming, he caught the attention of enough people in radio that "Daddy-O Daylie" soon had a nightly show playing his favorite music, jazz and bebop, on "Jazz from Dad's Pad" on WAIT in 1948. More significant, Daylie would have overnight shows through the 1950s on WGN, owned at the time by the *Chicago Tribune*, and NBC-owned WMAQ, where Dave Garroway once held court. Both stations were radio powerhouses.

Whereas Jack Cooper purposefully avoided any hint of a stereotypical black dialect and Al Benson had embraced sounding "country," Daddy-O Daylie's radio patter resonated with the hip slang associated with bebop musicians and told the black audience that one of their own was at the microphone. Disc jockeys like "Symphony" Sid Torin, and later white R&B DJs such as George "Porky" Chedwick (Pittsburgh), William "Hoss" Allen (Nashville) and the famous "Wolfman" Jack (Robert Smith), used black slang to manufacture racial authenticity with their listeners, often successfully, just one aspect of a practice Barlow called, after historian Mel Watkins, "racial ventriloquy."[19] Daylie not only used slang, but like many other early black DJs, used rhyme to establish his persona. Sid McCoy described his act:

> Daddy-O's whole thing was rhyme. He was the precursor of today's rappers because back when he did his radio show—he did it in rhyme. And he developed that thing as a bartender. People would come from miles around to be at his bar—all the celebrities liked to hang out with Daddy-O. He would get up there with a glass and pour that drink and he'd be rhyming all the time that he was making it. He would wrap the glass in a napkin, and at the end of a couplet he would set the glass down.[20]

Daylie and his black rhyming contemporaries connect to the black oral tradition of signifying that extends to the earnest "raps" of soul artists such as Isaac Hayes ("By the Time I Get to Phoenix"), political artists such as the

Last Poets and Gil Scott-Heron and Brian Jackson, to hip hop rappers and even to the current uses of social media by African American influencers. In "The Black Disc Jockey as Cultural Hero" Gilbert Williams assesses the cultural work of the "rapping" DJ beyond mere ear-catching entertainment, noting that "the black disc jockeys' ability to 'rap' and speak eloquently made them instant heroes in the community where such language skills are highly valued."[21] Daylie was a fervent supporter of bebop on the radio and connected several up-and-coming artists with record labels. Connected and durable, Daylie continued on radio in Chicago until the 1970s.

After starting as a Benson associate and having a radio gig in Denver (WNER), Sid McCoy (1922–2009) returned to Chicago and Benson at WGES with a thirty-minute religious program that lasted three years and ultimately was distributed to sixty cities. The program, sponsored by Pet Milk, illustrated what was required of Benson's team: They were assigned a block of time for which it was their responsibility to sell ads and share the revenue with Benson.

McCoy was impressed with Dave Garroway's relaxed conversational style, and it was an influence on his own style, featuring his smooth baritone voice. One reason McCoy may have been able to concentrate on jazz as a DJ was his multiple roles; he was an A&R person at VeeJay and Chess, he produced recording sessions with Wayne Shorter and Ramsey Lewis, and he promoted jazz concerts. Before he was a DJ, McCoy was an announcer and actor on a couple of episodes of "Destination Freedom," the groundbreaking black radio history-drama program produced at Chicago's WMAQ.[22]

For the better part of a decade McCoy was a leading overnight voice of jazz in Chicago, spending seven years beginning in the late 1950s at WCFL. When WCFL converted completely to Top 40 in 1963, his time there was running out. McCoy left Chicago for Los Angeles, where he did some radio work at KGIL but mainly participated in the television and film industry. His previous experience as a voice-over actor opened some doors and his contacts in the jazz industry opened others. McCoy first played the school principal on jazz lover Bill Cosby's first sitcom, *The Bill Cosby Show* (1969–1971), and later directed two episodes. He directed many episodes of *Soul Train* with his former DJ colleague Don Cornelius. (It was McCoy's voice you would hear introducing each episode's lineup. Not the one howling "The Sooooouuuuuul Train"—that was the voice of WVON DJ Joe Cobb!)

Like many jazz DJs, McCoy operated around the fringes of the core business at WGES, WCFL, and KGIL.[23] Keeping their accounts sold and maintaining their audience probably shielded many in his field from scrutiny by management. McCoy may have spoken for many jazz DJs when he told an interviewer, "I was really very fortunate when the rock and roll and format radio—by and large format radio whether rock and roll or rhythm and blues—it was something I didn't have to put up with and never had to contend with. It was always my thing to do with as I wanted to[,] the thing I did at night."[24]

Sid McCoy had an interesting, at times competitive and at times collegial, relationship with DJ Yvonne Daniels. McCoy told radio historian Sonja Williams that "she was one of the best radio talents I have ever heard." He continued, "Her musical knowledge was way beyond her years. Her father was Billy Daniels the singer."[25] Daniels (1937–1991) was born in Jacksonville, Florida, and began her radio career there at WOBS. After stints in East Saint Louis and back home in Jacksonville, she moved to Chicago and radio station WYNR. The former WGES of Al Benson fame, WYNR changed from a brokered-time station to full-time Black Appeal on its purchase by Gordon McClendon, known in the industry as one of the innovators who, along with Todd Storz, created Top 40 in the 1950s. Yvonne was brought to WYNR specifically to compete with McCoy at WCFL, and the two developed a friendly rivalry, often phoning each other during shows.[26] With its owner dissatisfied with its performance in this format, WYNR became one of the first all-news stations (WNUS) in 1964. McCoy brought Daniels on board, making the overnight jazz program a team show at WCFL, where "their lively repartee and staged 'feuds' over the 50,000 watt station caught the attention of listeners all over the country."[27] After their show ended, she spent nine years as the evening jazz host at WSDM, a Chicago FM station that boasted an all-female air staff. A measure of the esteem in which Daniels was held was that at WSDM she was the only DJ who programmed her own show.

Black Appeal stations popped up in large metropolises such as Chicago, Los Angeles, Washington, DC, and New York, but also in smaller cities such as Annapolis, Maryland, Richmond, Virginia, and in Pittsburgh, where at WHOD, Mary Dee became, according to some, the first African American female DJ in the country. After Dee's time, the jazz duties at WHOD and later, when the station became WAMO, were handled by local bandleader Walt Harper (figure 10).

In Washington, DC, Al Jefferson (1919–2014) worked at WOOK from 1955 to 1963. That station was owned by Richard Eaton's Black Appeal radio group, United Broadcasting. When he arrived at WOOK, the late-night jazz duties were handled by Tex Gathings, whom the more versatile Jefferson described as somewhat of a snob who "wouldn't think about playing B.B. King, blues, and all that kind of thing. He played jazz."[28] Recognizing the declining mass appeal of jazz, Jefferson attributed his success to his ear, his ability to pick hits, and his versatility. Describing his time at WOOK, he recalled,

> Luckily for me, anywhere you put me I could make it go because I was pretty well-rounded music-wise. At one time on this station I did not only the current popular things, but also gospel and jazz. I was doing a jazz show and called it "Jazz after Midnight." It was one of the most popular shows in Washington. I used to have cab drivers and the all-night people and the post office people and everybody tuned it. The cab drivers would come by

FIG. 10. Front row, left to right: Art Blakey, Walt Harper, and Horace Silver; back row, left to right: Jon Morris, Skeets Talbot, Early Mays, and Hank Mobley, July 1955 at WHOD. (Teenie Harris photo courtesy of the Carnegie Museum.)

[8th and I Sts., NW] and bring donuts and coffee and stuff like that. It was one of the best shows that ever originated out of that station, but you know in young radio at that time all black guys had problems with making money. We just didn't make any money. I think I was making about $70 a week and putting in all that time.[29]

Not far away, and almost equidistant to Washington and Baltimore, was the nation's third capital, Annapolis, Maryland, the location of WANN. The progressive Jewish businessman Morris Blum obtained one of the many licenses issued right after World War II. His initial freewheeling "Bach to Bebop" format struggled, and in 1951 he turned to gospel programming and focused on serving the black community. The station's marketing material (figure 11) claimed to give advertisers access to a coverage area with more African Americans (600,000 spending $250 million annually) than any other station outside New York. More than most, Blum's station became quite involved with the community. "My dad put public service ahead of profits," his son Larry Blum explained. "That was part of the mystique of WANN. It was a

FIG. 11. WANN ad sales flyer. (Smithsonian National Museum of American History.)

place where people could express themselves freely. Remember, Annapolis, at that time, had perforated borders. People lived a public life, but lived another when they were among themselves, before the racial lines became somewhat blurred when the Civil Rights movement ended Jim Crow by the mid-'60s."[30]

A prominent part of WANN's success was its connection to summer concerts at Carr's Beach. Charles "Hoppy" Adams (1926–2005) became a WANN DJ in 1951 and hosted Sunday afternoon remotes from that spot. Carr's and Sparrow's beaches were Chesapeake Bay properties owned by two African American sisters, Elizabeth and Sparrow Carr. The beaches they provided were among the few in the region that catered to blacks between the 1930s and the 1960s. After the death of Elizabeth Carr, the properties came under the control of William L. "Little Willie" Adams in 1948. Adams was a "West Baltimore businessman, real estate tycoon, venture capitalist, and political heavyweight" with an underworld past—he gave testimony before Congress that admitted to his activities in the numbers racket, telling investigators, "I used the illegal lottery to get into legitimate business."[31] Adams made Carr's Beach into a prominent stop for top performers on the "Chitlin' Circuit" because it was proximate to Washington, DC, Baltimore, and Philadelphia.

Hoppy Adams was the principal emcee at Carr's Beach, and his remotes were carried on WANN. Among the acts that appeared there in the 1950s were jazz notables such as Billie Holiday, Count Basie, Dinah Washington, and Lionel Hampton.[32] Figures 12–15 bear witness that jazz figures Bill Doggett, Sarah Vaughan, Dizzy Gillespie, and Ella Fitzgerald also appeared at Carr's Beach in the 1950s and provides evidence that there was demand in the 1950s for jazz on black radio, even as R&B was the main attraction. Hoppy Adams and Morris Blum had a thirty-year collaboration; eventually Adams would become station manager.[33] As late as 1984, Hoppy Adams still hosted a noon-hour weekday jazz program on WANN.[34]

FIG. 12. Carr's Beach, the Hoppy Adams Show, Sunday, July 15, 1956. (Smithsonian National Museum of American History.)

FIG. 13. Sarah Vaughan singing at Carr's Beach in August 1956. (Photo by Thomas Baden, from the WANN collection at the Smithsonian National Museum of American History.)

FIG. 14. Dizzy Gillespie at Carr's Beach. (WANN collection at the Smithsonian National Museum of American History.)

FIG. 15. Ella Fitzgerald at Carr's Beach. (WANN collection at the Smithsonian National Museum of American History.)

AM Rules: The 1960s

Today, there are literally dozens of radio formats.[35] As the 1960s opened, a few basic formats dominated music-based radio broadcasting. Top 40 had evolved from a simple, short playlist of the most popular records into a youth-oriented format featuring a mix of rock and roll and pop, while MOR was its adult-oriented counterpart with a greater emphasis on pop music. Easy Listening, featuring soothing and jolt-free music, was successful on early FM but also was the format of some AM stations. Having a classical music format was prestigious but limited to advertisers that wanted to reach listeners with elite tastes. In general, a market could only accommodate one classical station, and a competing Easy Listening/Good Music station could nibble away at the classical audience with light classical offerings. The Country and Western (later simply Country) format would grow to become a huge success in the following decade.

With these formats aimed at the general public, specialty formats—Negro Appeal, Religious, Gospel, and Ethnic—targeted what were considered niche audiences. Because the ethnic stations were all that African American, Greek, Serbian, or Polish listeners had, they tended to operate somewhat as the old omnibus model had, either with programs of general interest or a slate of specific offerings for homemakers, the elderly, patriots, and businesspeople.

By the 1960s jazz was seen as distinctly different from pop music. Even within rhythm and blues it was now less common to have songs based on blues progressions, and the sound of the electric bass and electric guitars, not to mention slick studio production elements, moved black music further away from jazz practices. Jazz sounds were still ubiquitous in the broadcasting soundscape, however. Starting in the 1950s, as film scores moved steadily away from Romantic-era symphonic music, they began to incorporate atonality, popular songs, and country and western but also jazz, especially in the film noir, detective, and spy genres and in diegetic or source music in contemporary scenes. In television, almost all nightlife scenes were underscored with jazz. Even the cartoon music of the 1960s moved away from Carl Stallings's amazing orchestral scores for Warner Brothers and toward the overtly jazz-oriented underscores that Hoyt Curtin and others composed for Hanna-Barbera.[36]

For U.S. listeners, jazz was an active, if subliminal, component of AM radio for many years. Indeed, production of radio and television themes and jingles was firmly in the hands of arrangers, musicians, and producers schooled in jazz. Speaking of the 1960s, pianist and educator Billy Taylor commented that he "rarely heard a radio or TV commercial or studio band that was not primarily jazz-based."[37] Vocalists, especially those still singing from the American Songbook, would be accompanied by jazz-styled combos and big bands. Prominent examples include albums by Frank Sinatra backed by the Count Basie band and by Nat King Cole with an orchestra conducted by Billy May; in fact, the prominent credits given to the bandleaders and arrangers is a testament to the connection of this style to its jazz aesthetics.[38] Soul vocalists often fronted bands with the same instrumentation as jazz ensembles, but with rhythm sections playing grooves associated with soul and, increasingly, funk. A few highly successful R&B or soul artists such as Lloyd Price, James Brown, and Ray Charles performed and toured with big bands staffed by jazz musicians, while other artists saved money by touring with their rhythm sections and hiring local musicians, again usually jazz musicians, to play their arrangements.[39]

An unintended consequence of the segregation of the nation's radio airwaves was the comparative confluence of styles on Black Appeal radio, which led to a remarkably unified music listening culture that spanned classes and generations among black Americans. Because station ownership by black was scarce, the underserved black community had to make do with white-owned stations in each market that only reluctantly programmed for African American audiences. Black Appeal radio in the 1960s and 1970s played music meant for mature adults (for example, Brook Benton, Billy Paul, and Nancy Wilson), young women and men (Millie Jackson, Al Green, Isaac Hayes, and the O'Jays) and teens and preteens (the Jackson 5, Stacy Lattisaw, and the Brighter Side of Darkness ["Love Jones"]). It wasn't until the appearance of rap in the late 1970s—strongly resisted by establishment white and black programmers at first—that black radio experienced a true "generation gap" similar to the way white radio split into youth (Top 40) and adult (MOR) formats.

Despite the diminishing position of jazz on radio relative to R&B, pop, and rock and roll (just beginning to be called rock), airplay was still important to jazz commerce, however airplay could be obtained. In 1967, when Chicago's WCFL canceled Sid McCoy and Yvonne Daniels's overnight jazz show and all-jazz WAAF was expected to change format shortly after a change of ownership (it did) the record industry voiced despair. "This means a blow to the exposure of good jazz musicians," said one record executive. Dick LaPalm, a veteran record promoter known for working with Nat Cole and Chess Records, complained "This deprives AM radio listeners of the third largest jazz market in the country."[40] It is worth noting that, although jazz was still available on FM radio in Chicago in 1965, only a small portion of the listening public, certainly less than 15 percent, owned FM receivers (see table 7).

Even so, radio still mattered to jazz in the 1960s. Jazz on LPs was a significant business sector throughout the 1960s, with soul jazz an especially reliable seller. Tables 4a and 4b show the *Billboard* R&B LP chart for November 19, 1966, and the corresponding *Billboard* R&B Singles chart. In this accounting *R&B* meant sales and airplay via the usual channels through which black music was sold; the term doesn't distinguish between musical styles. Jazz giants Sonny Rollins, Nina Simone, and Wes Montgomery lead a cadre of nine jazz artists (or artists closely associated with jazz) taking eleven of the twenty-five spots on the LP chart. Many jazz fans would consider Ray Charles's *Ray's Moods* only a borderline jazz record, but Charles had already produced and performed on the jazz classic *Fathead: Ray Charles Presents David 'Fathead' Newman*, recorded in 1958 but not released by Atlantic Records until 1960. They might have similar feelings about Lou Rawl's *Soulin'* but would have had warmer feelings for his breakthrough *Live!* LP. In fact, *Soulin'* represented a change in direction for Rawls; up to that point his recordings had been considered jazz.

Nancy Wilson was a versatile vocalist and actress who, like Sarah Vaughan and Dinah Washington before her, was difficult to categorize. Wilson made frequent appearances on the record charts between 1961 and 1997, placing 9

TABLE 4A. *Billboard* top-selling R&B LPs, November 19, 1966.

This Week	Last Week	Title, Artist, Label, & No.	Weeks on Chart	This Week	Last Week	Title, Artist, Label, & No.	Weeks on Chart
1	2	LOU RAWLS SOULIN' Capitol T 2506 (M); ST 2566 (S)	12	14	13	HOLD ON! I'M COMIN' Sam & Dave, Stax 708 (M); SD 708 (S)	17
2	1	SUPREMES A' GO-GO Motown MLP 649 (M); SLP 649 (S)	9	15	15	SOUL BROTHER #1 James Brown & His Famous Flames, King 985 (M); S 985 (S)	11
3	5	THE EXCITING WILSON PICKETT Atlantic 8129 (M); SD 8129 (S)	13	16	16	TENDER LOVING CARE Nancy Wilson, Capitol T 2555 (M); ST 2555 (S)	13
4	4	WADE IN THE WATER Ramsey Lewis, Cadet LP 774 (M); LPS 774 (S)	12	17	20	ALFIE Sonny Rollins, Impulse A 9111 (M); AS 9111 (S)	4
5	3	ON TOP Four Tops, Motown MLP 647 (M); SLP 647 (S)	13	18	18	THE NEW LEE DORSEY Amy 8011 (M); 8011 (S)	4
6	6	GETTIN' READY Temptations, Gordy GLP 918 (M); SLP 918 (S)	20	19	19	A CHANGE IS GONNA COME Brother Jack McDuff, Atlantic 1463 (M); SD 1463 (S)	14
7	7	RAY'S MOODS Ray Charles, His Ork & Chorus, ABC ABC 550 (M); ABCS 550 (S)	8	20	22	SOUL MESSAGE Richard (Groove) Holmes, Prestige PR 7435 (M); PRS 7435 (S)	2
8	9	TEQUILA Wes Montgomery, Verve V 8653 (M); VC-8653 (S)	13	21	17	SOUL OF THE MAN Bobby Bland, Duke DLP 79 (M); SLP 79 (S)	6
9	10	LIVING SOUL Richard (Groove) Holmes, Prestige PR 7468 (M); PRS 7468 (S)	7	22	—	WARM AND TENDER SOUL Percy Sledge, Atlantic 8132 (M); SD 8132 (S)	1
10	8	LOU RAWLS LIVE! Capitol T 2459 (M); ST 2459 (S)	30	23	—	HE'LL BE BACK Players, Minit LP 40006 (M); LP 24006 (S)	1
11	11	CARLA Carla Thomas, Stax 709 (M); SD 709 (S)	5	24	—	A COLLECTION OF 16 BIG HITS, VOL 5 Various Artists, Motown M 651 (M); S 651 (S)	1
12	14	WILD IS THE WIND Nina Simone, Phillips PHM 200-207 (M); PHS 600-207 (S)	12	25	—	THE OTIS REDDING DICTIONARY OF SOUL Volt 415 (M); S 415 (S)	1
13	12	ROAD RUNNER Jr. Walker & the All Stars, Soul SLP 703 (M); S 703 (S)	12				

Source: *Billboard* Special Survey for the week ending November 19, 1966, Billboard, November 19, 1966, 44.

TABLE 4B. *Billboard* top-selling R&B singles, November 19, 1966.

This Week	Last Week	Title, Artist, Label, & No.	Weeks on Chart	This Week	Last Week	Title, Artist, Label, & No.	Weeks on Chart
1	3	KNOCK ON WOOD Eddie Floyd, Stax 194 (East, BMI)	13	14	7	BEAUTY IS ONLY SKIN DEEP Temptations, Gordy 7055 (Jobete, BMI)	13
2	2	REACH OUT, I'LL BE THERE Four Tops, Motown 1098 (Jobete, BMI)	11	15	14	FA-FA-FA-FA-FA Otis Redding, Volt 138 (East-Redwal, BMI)	7
3	1	LOVE IS A HURTIN' THING Lou Rawls, Capitol 5709 (Rawlou, BMI)	12	16	18	SECRET LOVE Billy Stewart, Chess 1978 (Remick, ASCAP)	5
4	4	BUT IT'S ALRIGHT J. J. Jackson, Calla 119 (Tamelrosa, BMI)	8	17	17	WHAT BECOMES OF THE BROKEN-HEARTED Jimmy Ruffin, Soul 35022 (Jobete, BMI)	16
5	5	WHISPERS Jackie Wilson, Brunswick 55300 (Jalynne-BRC, BMI)	7	18	19	SHAKE YOUR TAMBOURINE Bobby Marchan, Cameo 429 (Tree, BMI)	7
6	8	DON'T ANSWER THE DOOR B. B. King, ABC 10856 (Mercedes, BMI)	6	19	25	IT TEARS ME UP Percy Sledge, Atlantic 2358 (Fame, BMI)	9
7	9	DON'T BE A DROP OUT James Brown & His Famous Flames, King 6056 (Dynatone, BMI)	6	20	23	I JUST DON'T KNOW WHAT TO DO Dionne Warwick, Scepter 12167 (U.S. Songs, ASCAP)	6
8	44	YOU KEEP ME HANGIN' ON Supremes, Motown 1101 (Jobete, BMI)	2	21	22	BANG! BANG! Joe Cuba Sextet, Tico 475 (Cordon, BMI)	6
9	45	I'M READY FOR LOVE Martha & the Vandellas, Gordy 7056 (Jobete, BMI)	2	22	20	I'VE GOT TO DO A LITTLE BIT BETTER Joe Tex, Dial 4045 (Tree, BMI)	6
10	10	I'M YOUR PUPPET James & Bobby Purify, Bell 649 (Fame, BMI)	9	23	24	SAID I WASN'T GONNA TELL NOBODY Sam & Dave, Stax 198 (East-Pronto, BMI)	9
11	11	STAY WITH ME Loraine Ellison, Warner Bros. 5850 (Ragmar-Crenshaw, BMI)	6	24	12	STAND IN FOR LOVE O'Jays, Imperial 66197 (Metric-Barnew, BMI)	9
12	13	HEAVEN MUST HAVE SENT YOU Elgins, V.I.P. 25037 (Jobete, BMI)	9	25	26	NEVER LET ME GO Van Dykes, Mala 539 (Cha-Stew, BMI)	5
13	6	B-A-B-Y Carla Thomas, Stax 195 (East, BMI)	12	26	15	DAY TRIPPER Vontastics, St. Lawerence 1014 (Maclen, BMI)	12

This Week	Last Week	Title, Artist, Label, & No.	Weeks on Chart	This Week	Last Week	Title, Artist, Label, & No.	Weeks on Chart
27	16	I WANT TO BE WITH YOU Dee Dee Warwick, Mercury 72584 (Morley, ASCAP)	13	39	40	I'LL MAKE IT EASY (If You'll Come on Home) Incredibles, Audio Arts 60.001 (Madelon, BMI)	4
28	27	BABY, DO THE PHILLY DOG Olympics, Mirwood 5523 (Keymen-Mirwood, BMI)	7	40	35	CAN YOU BLAME ME Jimmy Norman, Samar 116 (StaBox Art, BMI)	5
29	32	STANDING ON GUARD Falcons, Big Wheel 1967 (Maples & Big Wheel, BMI)	5	41	—	BOOKER-LOO Booker T & the MG's, Stax 196 (East-Bell, BMI)	1
30	36	POURING WATER ON A DROWNING MAN James Carr, Goldwax 311 (Pronto-Quinvy, BMI)	16	42	30	UP TIGHT Ramsey Lewis, Cadet 5547 (Jobete, BMI)	5
31	47	DON'T PASS ME BY Big Maybelle, Ro Jac 14969 (Streetcar, BMI)	7	43	43	FUNCTION AT THE JUNCTION Shorty Long, Soul 35021 (Jobete, BMI)	8
32	48	HYMN #5 Mighty Hannibal, Shurfine 021 (Bold lad, BMI)	9	44	—	A PLACE IN THE SUN Stevie Wonder, Tamla 54139 (Stein-Vanstock, ASCAP)	1
33	46	PEAK OF LOVE Bobby McClure, Checker 1156 (Chevis, BMI)	6	45	—	DEVIL WITH AN ANGEL'S SMILE Intruders, Gamble 203 (Razorsharpe, BMI)	1
34	31	HE'LL BE BACK Players, Minit 32001 (Stanc, BMI)	6	46	—	HOLY COW Lee Dorsey, Amy 905 (Marsaint, BMI)	1
35	34	POVERTY Bobby Bland, Duke 408 (Don, BMI)	6	47	—	A CORNER IN THE SUN Walter Jackson, Okeh 7260 (Blackwood-Blue Chip, BMI)	1
36	41	I BET'CHA (COULDN'T LOVE ME) Manhattans, Carnival 522 (Sanavan, BMI)	9	48	—	AND I LOVE HER Vibrations, Okeh 7257 (Maclen, ASCAP)	1
37	42	COME BACK 5 Stair-Steps, Windy C 603 (Camad, BMI)	9	49	50	I FOOLED YOU THIS TIME Gene Chandler, Checker 1155 (Cachand-Jalynne, BMI)	2
38	49	AM I A LOSER Eddie Holman, Parkway 106 (Harthon/Cameo, Parkway, BMI)	5	50	—	CRY LIKE A BABY Aretha Franklin, Columbia 43827 (Blackwood, BMI)	1

Source: *Billboard* Special Survey for the week ending November 19, 1966, *Billboard*, November 19, 1966, 44.

songs on *Billboard*'s Hot 100 and 22 songs and 1 Top 10 hit, "You're as Right as Rain," on the R&B Hot 100. Nina Simone also had established herself, against her wishes, as a jazz singer and pianist, but around 1963 had begun to raise her profile in the black community with her artistic leadership in the civil rights movement. This LP, *Wild Is the Wind*, not only included a stunning performance of "Black Is the Color of My True Love's Hair" but perhaps more significant, the controversial "Four Women," which had been banned by many record stations. Simone had two Top 10 R&B hits, "I Loves You, Porgy" in 1959 and "To Be Young, Gifted and Black" in 1970.

Sonny Rollins and the Impulse jazz label received a real boost from the 1966 LP *Alfie* and its tie-in to the 1966 film of the same name. Rollins was on the original soundtrack, and his "Alfie's Theme" is distinct from the Bert Bacharach–Hal David title song "Alfie." What Rollins's album does have in common with those of guitarist Wes Montgomery, pianist Ramsey Lewis, and organists Richard "Groove" Holmes and Brother Jack McDuff are the principles of soul jazz: strong melodies and funky grooves. Indeed, the stage nicknames "Groove" and "Brother" allude to their rhythmic drive and soulful playing, and Lewis's massive hit "Wade in the Water" was driving, grooving take on the spiritual of the same name. Here it is showing strong album sales two months after its peak at #3 on the R&B singles chart.

While making no claims about the consistency of the appearances of jazz in the charts used as examples in table 4, they help demonstrate the possibilities that still existed for jazz artists' sales in the 1960s. Only the dedicated jazz programs played mainstream jazz, so opportunities for airplay were best for jazz records that meshed well with the leading formats: vocalists that fit with Pop or R&B playlists, or instrumentals—soul jazz compatible with black radio or melodious tunes compatible with Pop or MOR. For example, Hugh Masekela's soul jazz hit "Grazing in the Grass" was a number one *Billboard* Hot 100 hit in 1968l. The jazz music most likely to get airplay was by artists who would produce reliable crossover product such as Ramsey Lewis, who had seventeen Hot 100 songs and a number five hit with "The 'In' Crowd" in 1965.

The jazz record companies saw what succeeded and tried to replicate those hits. A mid-1960s program director told *Billboard* that several record companies

> noticed the popular appeal of certain types of jazz and are now releasing jazz singles. This, and the fact that they are putting shorter cuts on LP's—cuts of about three or four minutes in length—certainly makes it easier for us to program new jazz releases. We don't play anything longer than four minutes and it used to be that we had to edit the records ourselves in order to be able to use them on our program.[41]

As stations adhered ever more rigorously to their core format, jazz was more likely to be sidelined by placement late at night or on weekends. Even overnight jazz shows became vulnerable to station managers' concerns; where radios were tuned overnight might affect the morning drivetime ratings. The jazz programs that held on did so because advertisers bought time in order to reach jazz listeners. As long as the jazz programs were successful at selling time, program directors and general managers initially had little reason to tamper with jazz shows. Whereas a decade earlier most stations had had a variety format, it became increasingly rare in the 1960s for top stations to have many weekday hours airing content outside the established format. This crowded other subjects—local sports roundups, gardening shows, cooking shows, programs featuring barbershop quartets, jazz hours, and public affairs programs—into weekend hours.[42]

A comparison between 1957 and 1969 data volunteered by DJs reveals significant trends affecting jazz on radio. These data, summarized in table 5, are subject to several important caveats. They may sometimes represent wishful thinking. A DJ who liked jazz may have overrepresented the jazz content of their program. Similarly, it would be hard to account for missing information. The data from *DownBeat* magazine almost certainly underreports jazz programming because it was based on DJ-dependent correspondence rather than a methodical census.

Also, the presentation of these data has introduced limitations. In order to display the data compactly, four daypart bins, day, evening, overnight, and weekend, are generously applied and undoubtedly mix dissimilar shows. (For example, three-hour morning drive shows are included in "Day," as are fifteen-minute programs that are really segments featuring only three or four quick jazz numbers.) In this analysis, "Day" includes morning drive, noon hour, and afternoon shows, and "Evening" includes evening drive and programming up until about 11 p.m. "Overnight" includes shown running from midnight to 5 a.m. shows as well as from 11 p.m. 1 a.m. programs. And the "Over Weekend" combined bin has any programming appearing at any time on Saturday or Sunday. Finally, what DJs list as a jazz radio show may have only a jazz feature spot (for example, a rush-hour wind-down from 6:00 to 6:30 pm. or a segment of a longer show like "Turnpike Jazz," which aired during Sir Johnny O's five-hour overnight on WWIN (Baltimore).[43]

The station listings arranged by format in *Broadcasting Yearbook*, which only began to be compiled in 1975, also present issues. Stations can be listed in multiple formats because any report of twenty hours or more per week qualifies the listing. Thus, a single overnight DJ show could result in a station's being listed as a jazz station. Harry Abraham's twenty-five weekly overnight hours at WHAM in the 1970s could have earned a jazz listing but did not. A significant amount of jazz could also have been aired on stations listed as

TABLE 5. Jazz shows and stations with jazz shows, 1957–1985.

Jazz Shows	AM	Day	Evening	Over	Weekend	FM	Day	Evening	Over	Weekend
1957	139	45	38	9	47	25	3	12	2	8
1969	78	17	19	9	33	86	23	28	4	31

Jazz Shows	AM and FM Simulcast Shows	Day	Evening	Over	Weekend
1957	165	48	50	11	55
1969	168	40	47	13	64

Stations with Jazz Shows	Commercial AM	Noncommercial AM	Commercial FM	Noncommercial FM	Simulcasting	Noncommercial Simulcasting
1957	102	—	9	—	8	—
1969	38	—	63	3	17	2
1977	19	3	28	97	—	—
1985	17	4	39	211	—	—

Sources: 1957 data taken from "On the Dial," *DownBeat*, October, 3, 1957, 68; 1969 data taken from "On the Dial," *DownBeat*, May 1, 1969, 44; 1977 data taken from "Programming on Radio Station in the United States," *Broadcasting Yearbook 1978*, D70–96; 1985 data taken from "Programming on Radio Stations in the United States," *Broadcasting Yearbook 1986*, F62–108.

"progressive," which also combined "free form" and "underground." Similarly, stations may have listed "black" as their format, though some jazz was played during the week.

Even with these cautions, table 5 holds some surprises. The number of jazz programs in 1957 and 1969 are roughly equal rather than showing the expected decline (though there could be fewer total hours of jazz). The probable reason: There was no abatement of the astonishing growth in the number of licensed stations from 3,640 (3,113 AM, 527 FM) in 1957 to 6,658 (4,255 AM, 2,025 FM, 378 educational FM) in 1969.[44] It is clear, however, that jazz was becoming more marginal in broadcasting. As shown in table 6, in 1957, 3 percent of all radio stations had jazz shows; by 1969, 3.1 percent of all FM stations had jazz shows, but in a much larger field of AM stations, just under 1 percent had them. The eventual move to noncommercial radio was evident in the 1977 data—10.9 percent of educational FM stations had jazz shows.

Throughout the decade there was a significant move out of daytime and evening and into the weekends and overnight slots for jazz. Moreover, the shift to FM stations reflects at least two trends. The first was increasing format-rigidity in the AM radio business, where Top 40, MOR, Soul, Country and Western, and Easy Listening were growing in market share and less core time could be devoted to other programming that deviated from the core business. The second factor was the impact of the FCC rulemaking relating to simulcasting. A rule that went into effect in 1965, with certain exceptions, limited to 50 percent the amount of duplication of programming between FM and AM in stations in larger markets. Owners of AM/FM combinations were forced to find new FM programming. These simulcasting rules disrupted the sleepy FM business and eventually upended the AM business.

The explosion of noncommercial jazz stations during the 1970s and 1980s is not so surprising considering the overall growth of noncommercial FM broadcasting. In 1970 there were about 2,597 FM stations, which included

TABLE 6. Percentage of radio stations with jazz shows, 1957, 1969, 1977, and 1985.

Year	All stations	AM stations	Commercial FM stations	Noncommercial FM stations
1957	3.0	3.3	1.7	—
1969	1.6	0.9	3.1	0.8
1977	1.7	0.4	1.0	10.9
1985	2.7	0.4	1.0	17.4

Sources: 1957 data taken from "On the Dial," *DownBeat*, October, 3, 1957, 68; 1969 data taken from "On the Dial," *DownBeat*, May 1, 1969, 44; 1977 data taken from "Programming on Radio Station in the United States," *Broadcasting Yearbook* 1978, D70-96; 1985 data taken from "Programming on Radio Stations in the United States," *Broadcasting Yearbook* 1986, F62-108. Percentages were computed according to FCC yearly station data.

413 noncommercial stations. By 1985 there were 4,888 FM stations and 1,172 noncommercial stations of all types, or 24 percent of all FMs.[45]

Fundamental changes begun in the 1950s drove society and radio in the 1960s. Widespread home ownership became a goal of national policy and a principal, if unevenly distributed, benefit of the group of postwar compensations that became known as the G.I. Bill. The growth in home ownership that took place on the edges of the large metropolitan areas began to overrun the close-in suburban communities and would lead to the sprawl of the outer suburbs. Highway building and car ownership grew apace with the housing boom. Radio listeners and music consumers simultaneously had more commuting time in their automobiles and space in their larger homes for radios, phonographs, and televisions, though television continued to be the dominant mass medium around which all other media—newspapers, movies, radio, and records—had to compete.

One more important development in the 1960s was the transistor radio. First commercially available in 1954 and much improved in reliability and function over the next several years, transistor radios could fit in a pocket or handbag and could run for hours on standard batteries, making radio listening possible and popular in places it had never been in before, such as beaches, parks, and playgrounds. Broadcasts using AM had a narrow audio bandwidth to begin with. In order to fit into a 20 kHz channel its audio content cannot exceed 10 kHz and, as a practical matter, its frequency response begins to roll off rapidly after 7.5 kHz. For different reasons, the low-frequency signals below 20 Hz are filtered out as well. The filters used in radio transmitters are of high quality, but very often this is not the case in the filters used in inexpensive radio receivers. There were two modes of listening to transistor radios. One could listen through the built-in speaker. On larger units, speakers five inches in diameter or greater could provide decent bass response, but transistor pocket radios with speakers as small as 2.5 inches were also in circulation. Alternatively, a listener could use an earplug—a monaural precursor to the hi-fi earbuds of today—but the output power for a transistor radio typically could not drive high-quality headphones.

With 1960s radio dominated by formats that ranged from the broad, Top 100–based crossover of MOR to the always relaxing elevator music of Easy Listening, to the regimented, rigid, heavy rotation of Top 40, jazz DJs functioned almost as independent contractors who were free to program their shows as they saw fit. (By comparison to what was to soon follow, even this era's mainstream "personality" DJs enjoyed considerable freedom.) Looked at another way, the independent contractor jazz DJ operated largely outside the direct supervision of station management, the program and music directors who were charged with establishing the station's identity. As radio stations that had jazz increasingly left it in the hands of these specialists, their independent contractor status became significant, because it implies that the DJs' relationships with the music industry were subject to less management intervention than others on the same station. For example, since a station was unlikely to have a jazz library, the DJ would use their own collection on the air. Jazz record labels knew these DJs and their musical tastes and worked to get their product, sometimes at or beyond the margins of those tastes, aired by these deejays, who had an immediate and direct relationship with their listeners.

A good example was the career of Felix Grant in Washington, DC (figure 16). Grant had a show on middle-of-the-road WMAL, a pioneering AM radio station with a long affiliation with ABC and its predecessor, the NBC Blue network. In 1993 Grant told the *Washington Post* that when he started (on Washington station WWDC) in 1954, "jazz was as popular on college campuses as rock and rap are today."[46] Despite perennial struggles with management—"for most of his career, Grant was battling station managers suspicious of both his music and his popular appeal"—he lasted on commercial WMAL until 1984. As Grant recalled:

> "I had played as much jazz as possible at WWDC—I just loved the inventiveness of it—but WMAL was a good bit different," he remembers. His

FIG. 16. Felix Grant and Cab Calloway (Courtesy Felix E. Grant Jazz Archives, University of the District of Columbia.)

new employer carried the Metropolitan Opera and some other fairly highbrow programs such as "Town Meeting of the Air," but the station managers were leery of jazz, thinking it either too cerebral or too ethnic for the broad audiences they were trying to attract. Grant realized, however, that most managers knew almost nothing about music. "I dealt with them in the beginning by never using the word "jazz." . . . They sold a lot of spots and the station was happy."[47]

Grant's remarks touch on one of the major fault lines of jazz reception in this era: its split perception as either too cerebral or too primitive, either too artistic in ambition, or, if just swinging good fun, too black. In addition, he notes the ironic lack of musical expertise by the management of an enterprise quite dependent on music for its success, which illustrates the degree to which the jazz radio enterprise (or that of any music) constructs practices between participants with diverse skills and seeking divergent goals and rewards.

In Washington, Grant maintained a large and loyal following that perplexed station executives for years. When he was finally forced out by having his relationship with his audience repeatedly disrupted by frequent preemptions for sports broadcasts, Grant followed a path parallel to that of jazz itself; he went to noncommercial WDCU-FM, operated in the community-radio model by the University of the District of Columbia.

FM: From '60s Sleepy to '70s Domination

It took almost three decades for FM to fully bloom. The relocation and long-term launch of the FM broadcast service (U.S. FM used 42–50 MHz until the 1945 move to 88–108 MHz) was one of the FCC's first orders of postwar business. Soon after came the beginning of the hi-fi industry. The new formats of FM radio, reel-to-reel audio tape, and microgroove records (leading to the long-playing record, or LP), combined with a fascination with electronics nurtured by military veterans who had learned electronics in the service. They were willing and able to build from kits and parts audio systems that outperformed the console radios and record players sold in department stores. Keir Keightley suggests that the hi-fi culture was part of a masculine reclaiming of domestic space from their wives in white middle-class postwar suburbia, regarding which one should note that African American men were hardly immune to the kinds of marketing campaigns that encouraged smoking pipes, driving wood-paneled station wagons, and wearing jackets with patches on the elbows.[48] These early adopters, mostly men, would form the core of a hi-fi and record-collecting culture that would be the basis of a rapidly growing home audio industry in the 1960s and 1970s.

The 1970s would bring a dramatic rise in FM radio's market power. Spurred on by the FCC's nonduplication rules, the take-off of FM automobile radios, and the ear-catching programming innovations on FM that had roots in the 1960s, FM began attracting more of the younger listeners, and its revenues began to overtake AM's; suddenly, an FM air slot had a much larger value. The progressive format, with its emphasis on music and comedy beyond pop and Top 40, and with its high degree of DJ independence, would soon be housetrained by the industry and form the basis of the AOR, or album-oriented rock, format.

Jazz, classical, and easy listening formed a trio of music genres that, each for their own reason, held particular appeal for the early audiophile listeners to FM. Classical music demanded the widest dynamic range from audio equipment; a symphony orchestra or opera recording could go from pianissimo to fortissimo and back in just a few beats but also over a wide frequency range. The best jazz records also covered a wide frequency range, with high energy in the upper frequencies from the drummer's cymbals, the low frequencies of the bass and the bass drum, and the challenge of capturing the percussive crispness of the piano. Easy listening had some similarity with classical in terms of frequency range but often had exaggerated stereo separation and ambitious and innovative uses of studio processing such as compression and reverb that challenged the most elaborate home audio systems.

An unsigned feature on the future of hi-fi appeared in the jazz-oriented magazine *Metronome* in 1954. Ignoring black jazz artists but enraptured with the new technology, it asked,

> How, of all people, can a jazz fan help being deeply impressed by the Hi-Fi achievement? Jazz is a music of nuances, of tints and shades, of violent eruptions, yes, but also nowadays of the tenderest understatement, too. To capture everything from a Stan Kenton blast to a Gerry Mulligan murmur, that is the aim and accomplishment of Hi-Fi in America's own music. What is more, if you have topnotch equipment, even the old records take on new life, for all that is in them now can be fully heard.[49]

The article that followed gave advice for listening to jazz on a hi-fi. Both the article and the prelude quoted above make clear the connection between the cultures of jazz listening, record collecting, and amassing hi-fi equipment. Recording engineers, previously totally anonymous culture workers, would begin to earn fans of their own. Promoted and given a high profile by Blue Note principal Alfred Lion, Rudy Van Gelder and his Hackensack and Englewood Cliffs studios would become icons among jazz and hi-fi enthusiasts who would develop similar reverence for engineers like Tom Dowd at Atlantic Records and Al Schmitt at various labels in Los Angeles.

TABLE 7. FM receiver sales and market share, 1960–1980.

	1960	1965	1970	1975	1980
FM sets sold (x1,000)	1,994	6,337	21,332	22,420	39,822
FM as a percentage of all radios sold	8%	15%	48%	65%	78%
FM car radios sold (x1,000)	<75	636	1,427	3,482	8,892
FM car radios as a percentage of all car radios sold	<1%	6%	14%	38%	78%

Source: Christopher H. Sterling and Michael C. Keith, "Sounds of Change: A History of FM Broadcasting in America," *Journal of Popular Music Studies* 21, no. 3 (2009): 238.

This mating of jazz fandom and hi-fi audio culture in the 1950s developed slowly, perhaps owing to the costs and technical skills needed to fully engage audiophilia at the outset. The 1960s, however, saw a rapid expansion of FM radio (table 7). The coupling of stereo records and stereo FM broadcasting (introduced in 1961) helped home hi-fi electronics take off. Data from the Electronics Industry of America data show the remarkable growth in the number of FM radios in homes and cars in this period.[50] It is not clear whether innovative programming led to the purchase of more FM receivers or if the uptick in FM receiver sales led to better programming. What is clear is that FM broadcasting was largely underutilized through much of the 1960s but was primed for prominence in the 1970s.

The number of stations continued to grow, increasing from almost 700 commercial FM stations on the air in 1960 to more than 1,250 by 1965.[51] Broadcasting was a good business that was expected to continue to grow, but for the most part, in the 1960s the FM band was an undiscovered country. As a consequence, it was a playground for radio innovation. "FM stereo was commercial radio's laboratory," writes radio historian Michael Keith. He continues:

> It was where experimentation was allowed, because there was so little to lose. Until the mid-1960s, FM moved along in low gear. A nearly negligible listenership provided it with little status and currency among the general public and industry. It was perceived as the province of eggheads and the terminally unhip—the place to tune for Stravinsky and fine arts programming.[52]

In some way or other, radio listeners were discovering two things about FM: (1) the sound quality, as its inventor Edwin Armstrong promised, was better because FM was static-free, delivered a greater audio bandwidth, and could deliver music in stereo, and (2) exciting and interesting things were happening on these neglected stations.

Within the nearly fallow band lay opportunity. These stations were not so profitable as to preclude experimentation. A group of radio innovators and malcontents rebelled against the hegemony of Top 40 and the blandness of MOR. On what became underground or progressive commercial (and noncommercial) radio, jazz could sometimes be heard! It is thought that KMPX, for instance, a leading underground commercial FM station, played a blend of about "60 percent rock and roll, 20 percent blues and R&B, and 20 percent jazz, electronic music, and poetry."[53] The underground radio of the 1960s led first to progressive radio and eventually to the AOR format. By the mid-1970s, FM was the place to be, and it was AM that was beginning a tumble that only bottomed out with its later rebirth as talk radio.

Specifically, underground or progressive radio, quietly attracting listeners during the late 60s, was becoming commercialized as the AOR format and challenging Top 40. The initial growth of FM radio listenership was largely a matter of the generation gap. "FM," according to the media journalist Marc Fisher, "sounded like a different plane of consciousness. The clarity of FM's signal, the freshness of stereo sound, and the smooth calm of the new deejay's patter combined to attract the people President Richard Nixon derided: 'They call themselves flower children,' he said in 1968. 'I call them spoiled rotten.'"[54] In addition to its inherent technical qualities, programming was developing on the FM band that excited and attracted a new audience of music fans.

An important factor in FM's rise was that FM receivers were finally reaching a high level of consumer market penetration. In 1970 only 14 percent of car radios could receive FM. By 1980, keeping in mind that automobiles are durable goods that people drive for years, 78 percent could, and there were more than three thousand commercial FM stations to listen to. Although Senate Bill S.585 (1974), which required all but the cheapest radios to be able to receive FM as well as AM, failed in the House, it put pressure on auto manufacturers to make AM/FM radios standard equipment.[55] This wasn't good news for commercial jazz radio. Its initial gains on commercial FM turned out to be short-lived, and its historic migration to noncommercial FM would begin in the 1970s.

Jazz and Progressive Radio

The underground or progressive radio movement of the late 1960s established free-form radio as an alternative anti-format to slicked-up, predictable commercial radio.[56] In the 1960s the revenue was still all in AM radio, and the commercial portion of the FM band was home primarily to three types of broadcasters, with the first by far the largest: those unimaginatively simulcasting their AM programming to a small FM audience, those broadcasting music that inherently would benefit from the greater FM fidelity (easy listening, classical, and jazz for hi-fi enthusiasts), and those looking to get on the air with unconventional ideas about broadcasting. Free-form programming in its purest form meant that any type of music could follow any other—for example, James Brown, J. S. Bach, Gullah field recordings, Cream, Robert Johnson, Lenny Bruce, John Coltrane, the Kingston Trio, Monteverdi, Odetta, Led Zeppelin—but as a matter of practice the programming followed the range of interests of the programmers or hosts, subject to any restrictions imposed by management. For example, at underground pioneer KMPX, Tom Donahue essentially banned Motown records as just "too slick and commercial."[57]

In many ways, the progressive format was ideal for jazz. Progressive DJs looked beyond the singles that the record companies promoted and would often select other tracks from albums. Jazz fans were already album-oriented because few jazz records were released as singles. Since the 1950s the leading jazz labels had been releasing albums that featured extended instrumental solos and contained as few as two or three tracks on a twenty-two-minute LP side. Since they were on stations with less sold commercial time than on AM, FM progressive DJs could and would play longer tracks.

By no means did jazz dominate the progressive stations' playlist, but jazz selections could be heard in its eclectic mixes. Progressive radio began to attract Top 40's restless listeners, and the former's initial DJ practitioners migrated to new opportunities on other commercial FM stations. With the format now formalized as Album-Oriented Rock (AOR), its managers installed some of the same programming controls and research tools used in Top 40. According to Kim Simpson, competing Top 40 management never really took progressive radio seriously, perceiving its followers as "wild-eyed hippies, the progressive drug and sex crowd right out of *Easy Rider*."[58] Instead, the radio insiders carved out the features that were attracting the desired demographics and tightened their playlists, leading to AOR. The eclecticism and racial diversity of progressive radio gave way to mostly white rock, to the detriment of jazz and, many would say, to the detriment of the pop music to follow.[59]

Surveys from four commercial progressive radio stations are presented in table 8. All four surveys are from a six-week period in early 1972. As expected, rock, soul, funk, and folk are well represented, but so are jazz artists Tom Scott, Les McCann, Idris Muhammad, Charles Mingus, and Charles Lloyd.

For comparison, surveys from all-jazz commercial KBCA, Los Angeles (1970), and from mostly classical noncommercial WBJC, Baltimore (1973), which programmed about twenty hours of jazz per week, are provided in table 9 and table 10.

The diversity of styles on these two playlists is, to modern eyes and ears, astonishing, and the possible reasons for such diversity are discussed next Chapter 3.

TABLE 8. A sample of progressive FM stations' music surveys, circa March 1972.

	KOL 94.1FM Seattle March 18, 1972	KMET 94.7 FM Los Angeles March 18, 1972	WMMR 93.3 FM Philadelphia March 25, 1972	KSAN 94.9 FM San Francisco March 4, 1972
1	Tom Scott, Great Scott	Stevie Wonder, Music of My Mind	Jesse Ed Davis, Ululu	Neil Young, Harvest
2	Steve Miller Band, Recall the Beginning	Edgar Winter's White Trash, Roadwork	Charles Mingus, Let My Children Hear Music	Alex Taylor, Dinnertime
3	Colin Blunstone, One Year	Joe Tex, From the Roots Came the Rapper	Rory Gallagher, Deuce	Les McCann, Invitation to Openness
4	John Roman Jackson, John Roman Jackson	Charles Mingus, Let My Children Hear Music	Bobby Whitlock, Bobby Whitlock	Jimi Hendrix, In the West
5	Edgar Winter's White Trash, Roadwork	Nick Drake, Pink Moon	Edgar Winter's White Trash, Roadwork	Little Feat, Sailin' Shoes
6	Idris Muhammad, Peace & Rhythm	Brinsley Schwartz, Silver Pistol	Steve Miller Band, Recall the Beginning	Jackie Lomax, Three
7	James Gang, Straight Shooter	Eddy Senay, Hot Thang	60,000,000 Buffalo, Nevada Jukebox	—
8	Doc Watson, Elementary Doc Watson	Steve Miller Band, Recall the Beginning	Wild Turkey, Battle Hymn	—
9	Bernard Purdie, Shaft	Cream, Live, Volume II	Lee Michaels, Space and First Takes	—
10	—	Rufus Thomas, Did You Heard Me?	Tim Rose, Tim Rose	—

Note: For comparison, here is a top ten from KOL AM 1300 for January 22, 1972: 1. Don McLean, "American Pie"; 2. Nilsson, "Without You"; 3. Jonathan Edwards, "Sunshine"; 4. Al Green, "Let's Stay Together"; 5. Dennis Coffey, "Scorpio"; 6. Climax, "Precious and Few"; 7. Badfinger, "Day After Day"; 8. The Chi-Lites, "Have You Seen Her"; 9. Melanie, "Brand New Key"; 10. Apollo 100, "Joy." This also illustrates Top 40 KOL-AM's focus on hit singles as opposed to KOL-FM's progressive radio's album orientation.

Source: Airheads Radio Survey Archive, http://www.las-solanas.com/arsa/index.php.

Jazz After Hours

A fitting way to conclude this chapter is to return to DJs operating outside their station's format. Like Felix Grant, discussed above, was Daddy-O Daylie. Table 11 presents a rare aircheck, a document that indexes the content of a sample of a radio show, in this case Daylie's show from Sunday, June 25, 1972.[60] By then, Daylie was one of the few links to the WGRT's previous identity as all-jazz WAAF. He was now, like many other surviving jazz DJs, playing jazz

TABLE 9. KBCA survey, September 7, 1970.

	Album	Artist	Label
1	Chapter 2	Roberta Flack	Atlantic
2	Black Talk	Charles Erland	Prestige
3	Gula-Matari	Quincy Jones	A&M
4	First Take	Roberta Flack	Atlantic
5	Right On Brother	Boogaloo Joe Jones	Prestige
6	Fat Albert Rotunda	Herbie Hancock	Warner Bros.
7	Isaac Hayes Movement	Issac Hayes	Enterprise
8	Lena & Gabor	Lena Horne & Gabor Szabo	Skye
9	Ebony Woman	Billy Paul	Neptune
10	Everything I Play Is Funky	Lou Donaldson	Blue Note
11	Green Is Beautiful	Grant Green	Blue Note
12	That's the Way It Is	Milt Jackson	Impulse
13	Bitches Brew	Miles Davis	Columbia
14	Happy & In Love	Gloria Lynn	Canyon
15	My Kind of Jazz	Ray Charles	ABC
16	Just a Little Lovin'	Carmen McRae	Atlantic
17	Transitions	John Coltrane	Impulse
18	Old Socks, New Shoes	The Jazz Crusaders	Chisa
19	Swiss Movement	Les McCann & Eddie Harris	Atlantic
20	Soul Symphony	The Three Sounds	Blue Note
21	Give Peace a Chance	The Jazz Crusaders	Liberty
22	Red Clay	Freddie Hubbard	CTI
23	Move Your Hand	Lonnie Smith	Blue Note
24	The Boss Is Back	Gene Ammons	Prestige
25	Love Country Style	Ray Charles	ABC

KBCA Jazz Artist of the Week . . . Gary [sic] Mulligan

The Dee Jays of Radio KBCA!

Jim Herrin			Jim Gosa
Rick Holmes	Chuck Niles	Stu Cronan	Gary Bell
Richard Leos	Bob Summers	Jai Rich	Dennis Smith
Kogi Sayama	Tollie Strode	Calvin Jackson	Johnnie Swift

Source: Flyer produced by KBCA-FM, September 1970.

Note: The survey is based on requests received at KBCA and on actual sales at leading retail stores in southern California.

TABLE 10. Survey, "WBJC's Favorite Jazz Things," December 26, 1973.

	Artist	Album
1	Billy Cobham	Spectrum
2	Stanley Turrentine	Don't Mess With Mr. T
3	Deodato	Deodato 2
4	Weather Report	Sweetnighter
5	Herbie Mann	Turtle Bay
6	Brian Auger	Closer to It
7	George Benson	Body Talk
8	Chick Corea	Light as a Feather
9	Funk Inc.	Superfunk
10	Gato Barbieri	Chapter One
11	Ahmad Jamal	'73
12	John Coltrane	Concert in Japan
13	Lou Donaldson	Sassy Soul Street
14	Chick Corea	Hymn of the Seventh
15	Gene Ammons	Big Bad Jug
16	Maynard Ferguson	M. F. Horn III
17	Chuck Mangione	Land of Make Believe
18	Ramsey Lewis	Golden Hits
19	Miles Davis	Basic Miles
20	Milt Jackson	Sun Flower
21	Various Artists	The Saxophone
22	Doug Carn	Spirit
23	Sonny Rollins	Horn Culture
24	Black Heat	Black Heat
25	Gato Barbieri	The Legend of Gato Barbieri
26	Dave Brubeck	Two Generations
27	Sam Rivers	Streams
28	Herbie Hancock	Succotash
29	Mal Waldron	On Steinway
30	Catalyst	Perception

Source: Flyer produced by WJBC-FM for distribution to the public, 1973.

records on an otherwise-formatted radio station. In his case, the station had gone soul. Unlike most, though, Daylie had also retained a prominent mid-morning spot in the lineup rather than an out-of-the-way late-night show. This made Daylie, and his jazz programming, subject to intense management scrutiny concerning his ratings and sales performance.

The Daddy-O Daylie tape is a valuable sample of his Sunday show, which ran an hour or so before sundown and sign-off on WGRT. Daylie's playlist would not sound out of place for today's jazz radio listeners. Its featured music was bebop and later genres, despite Daylie's known love of Billie Holiday. It had no free jazz, but it did include some relatively new straight-ahead releases: Grady Tate's "Lost in the Stars" is from 1969 and Esther Phillips's "Cry Me

TABLE 11. Rundown of a surviving aircheck of Daddy-O Daylie from June 25, 1972.

Start: Kenny Clarke, "Hear Me Talkin' to Ya" (Daylie named all the players)
1:00: Public service announcement
1:45: Grant Green, "I Didn't Know What Time It Was," swinging guitar
2:45: Live ad, Competition Motors
4:00: Louis Smith, "Stardust"
5:15: News
5:37: Isaac Hayes concert commercial
6:13: "SMTWTFSS Blues," Sahib Shihab (Daylie named all the players)
7:11: Ad for George Benson's *White Rabbit* with live read tag
8:12: Hank Mobley sextet, "Easy to Love" (Daylie named all the players)
9:50: Live ad for Bachelor Quarters menswear
10:40: Immediately into PSA for youth program Brainard Little League
12:40: Esther Phillips, "Cry Me a River"
13:45: Live read, furniture store ad
15:10: Count Basie, "Backwater Blues" with Irene Reid
15:50: PSA
16:25: Cándido Camero, "Indian Summer"
17:24: News, then into PSA for Brainard L.L.
18:19: Back to news
18:50: Bill Harris, "Perdido," likes the acoustic!!
19:40: Competition Motors live read, "treat you twice as nice as a mother's advice"

21:08: Same as 7:11
22:09: Station ID, then Gene Ammons, "Brother Jug's Sermon"
23:00: Commercial
23:16: Live ad for jazz records at Ralphs's ($2.88 for any Daddy-o specials at Ralphs)
24:48: Grady Tate, "Lost in the Stars," Jimmy Smith, "Grab and Hold"
25:37: Ray Charles, "Feel So Bad"
25:55: Teddy Charles, "When Your Lover Has Gone"
26:43: Weather
27:08: Same as 7:11, then
27:10: Esther Phillips concert ad live read
27:30: Daylie announces he will "change the mood and play some things for lovers"; Phineas Newborn, "Moonlight in Vermont"
28:15: PSA with Jerome Richardson in background, "Way In Blues"
29:42: Live read for Competition Motors
31:22: Announces his end of show, Kenny Burrell, "Yes Baby, Yes"
32:01: "Gotta wrap it up . . ."; promo for other DJs at WGRT; "Be gentle to yourselves, don't borrow from sorrow"
32:25: "Peace is what this whole world needs"
33:07: Station sign-off at dusk

Note: This is a typical radio hobbyist aircheck in that the focus is on the announcer rather than the music. This thirty-minute clip has most of the music removed. https://soundcloud.com/gbarman/wgrt-daddy-o-daylie-jazz-padio.

a River" is from 1972. Daylie played Jerome Richardson's "Way in Blues" from his 1959 LP *Midnight Oil* as background to a public service announcement. Although Richardson was top side musician with a long and versatile recording résumé, he was little known as a bandleader, and Daylie's selection of Richardson's music is evidence of his deep knowledge of jazz. There is also a live read by Daylie promoting an upcoming Esther Phillips engagement in Chicago; it would not be uncommon for a DJ to play the music of artists who were soon to make a local appearance, and it would not be uncommon for clubs or promoters to buy ads, provide complimentary tickets, or otherwise curry favor with the host of an influential show prior to an appearance.

That Daylie was still on the air in 1972 was the result of negotiation and outside pressure.[61] The station had a soul music format.[62] Daylie fought off an attempt in 1971 to reduce his weekday jazz programming and his public service program "Rap Session" to thirty minutes each starting with jazz at 11 a.m. rather than starting at 10 a.m.[63] The changes were not at all unusual in the broadcast industry, but Daylie's longevity at this station was. Its call sign had only recently been changed from WAAF to WGRT. Before the sale to Ralph Atlas and change to WGRT and soul, WAAF had employed an all-jazz format since 1956. In the near future, WGRT would be bought by Johnson Publishing, publishers of *Ebony* and *Jet* magazines, operate under the call sign WJPC, and become Chicago's first black-owned radio station.

The acquisition of WGRT by Johnson Publications is not unrelated to the battle over ownership and content. One prominent voice of support for Daylie's full ninety-minute jazz show was Reverend Jesse Jackson. He sent Atlas a wire that, when read closely, was quite threatening. It began,

> WGRT's changing schedule that effectively removes Daddy-O Daylie from significant broadcasting is a deep blow to the black community and to Chicago audiences seeking appreciation of jazz as a major black art.... We cannot idly stand by to allow the federal communications facility WGRT to destroy Daddy-O's role as a major communication to and for black people. Our fight to see that Daddy-O has decent air time for jazz and rap on issues will increase throughout the community that listens to WGRT. Black men as air personalities and as listeners will no longer be disrespected by radio facilities under review of the FCC. We will take our struggle wherever is necessary to see that Daddy-O Daylie is neither limited nor degraded in his broadcast time at decent hours on WRGT. —Rev. Jesse L. Jackson, National Director, SCLC Operation Breadbasket.[64]

Jackson twice implies and finally names the FCC, an invocation that implies that unhappy opponents would use the community service requirements of the renewal process to threaten Atlas's license. It is probably no coincidence that the station would soon be under African American ownership.

Another example of the jazz deejay on an otherwise non-jazz station was Harry Abraham, heard all over the eastern United States from 1969 to 1978 on clear channel WHAM (1180 kHz) in Rochester, New York.[65] AM stations assigned to clear channels were allowed to broadcast at night with maximum power, typically 50,000 watts, on a frequency that they either did not have to share or they shared with lower-powered stations that were obliged to "protect" (not interfere with) the dominant station. Abraham's "The Best of All Possible Worlds" ran six nights per week, midnight to five a.m., on a station otherwise programmed as MOR. Abraham outlined his programming philosophy in a letter responding to an out-of-state fan who was a college radio station jazz DJ. Abraham identified his consideration of audience, artists, his own tastes, and first and foremost, his non-jazz fans:

> Forget, for the moment, all the people who are jazz buffs, for they will listen as long as you don't offend them. Who else might be listening? What can you play to keep them tuned, get them back next time, and recommend you to their friends? . . . WHAM is commercial radio and even though I'm outside of the norm of their broadcasting, I wouldn't be here if I offended their regular listeners. Without playing commercial music, I manage to garner 50 percent shares with 6 to 8 stations in the market on all night.[66]

Abraham's letter dates from the mid-1970s, a time when jazz was becoming a programming staple on noncommercial radio. It is revealing of this trend that Abraham was already equating jazz with noncommercial or describing jazz with crossover appeal as "commercial," echoing a durable commercial-versus-artistic tension among jazz advocates. The degree to which he was thinking strategically, worried about keeping his inherited non-jazz-fan audience, even growing it proportionally while maintaining his core one, is also revealing. Abraham claimed to draw half of the overnight listeners in an eight-station market, which certainly flew in the face of perceptions of the unpopularity of jazz.

Abraham was open about his commitment to featuring the current work of artists. He felt that one of the "burdens" of being a jazz broadcaster was providing exposure to "the cats that need it most." He was aware that he was part of an art world, perhaps more sensitive to the needs of the artists than to those of the industry but clearly desiring to avoid a purely curatorial approach to programming. He felt the need to play music that represented the current work of the musicians—that is, if he liked their music. Abraham counseled aspiring broadcasters to trust their own taste and remain open to the music:

> Play something you dislike intensely and you'll lose your entire audience. If they don't believe that you like it, they can't justify listening to it, either. So it's up to you to broaden your tastes as widely as possible. There is no

artist whose records I've received that haven't had some exposure on my program. But some artists require a lot more digging to come up with something decent. And sometimes, quite unexpectedly, you find your own tastes turning around.[67]

During the period when this correspondence took place, "jazz" DJs like Abraham were being asked to play funk and instrumental soul tracks such as Pleasure, Grover Washington Jr., Dexter Wansel, and the Blackbyrds, free jazz by artists and groups such as Air, Anthony Braxton, Leroy Jenkins, and Archie Shepp, and the jazz-rock fusion of Return to Forever, Weather Report, Jean-Luc Ponty, and Billy Cobham. All of these artists had their music marketed as jazz, and undoubtedly some of the soul-searching that Abraham was describing concerns his handling of these kinds of records. He struck a blow against a research-driven programming model or one driven by industry record-plugging. His approach was to trust his own tastes in music but also to be cognizant of audience tastes, which since he was an overnight deejay, could vary by the hour.

While the DJs of Top 40, R&B, and country and western—that's what they called it back then—were larger than life, high-decibel personalities, and classical music announcers (hardly DJs, they) were dignified identifiers of composers, conductors, and Köchel numbers, the jazz DJ was a personal guide and interpreter for the jazz listener.

The jazz DJ was a specialist, but like the jazz musicians they paralleled, they often wore many hats. Although most working jazz musicians preferred to play jazz at all times, they performed in whatever styles provided a living, or close to it. Similarly, many of the best-loved jazz DJs would also work as Top 40, MOR, or Soul DJs, newscasters, sports show hosts, or whatever showbiz capacity would pay their bills. When the opportunity came to do a weekly or daily jazz show, they were most pleased.

Format radio had begun the process of narrowcasting, and though jazzy music could fit those formats, jazz rarely could. Progressive radio temporarily reversed the format trend and, at least until the era of digital downloads and streaming, permanently ended the reign of the single while opening up albums as the focus of music retailing and listening.

3

Jazz Around the Clock

Jazz as a Radio Format

> There were times during the '60s when jazz had . . . well, how can I put this? . . . an elitist appeal. Now, it is becoming a popular music again and we like to feel that KBCA played some part in keeping it going . . . the artists have broadened their appeal. Sure, they're accused of compromising, but this isn't a compromise. The jazz artist recognizes that his music can now influence a greater number of people.
> —Saul Levine, founder of KBCA radio

Across the United States, from New York's WLIB-FM to Philadelphia's WHAT-FM to Cincinnati's floating radio station WNOP, and to L.A.'s KNOB, there was a two-decade attempt to make commercial jazz radio work. Beginning in the 1950s a handful of commercial radio stations adopted all-jazz or mostly jazz formats, though today it is not always clear what range of music was included in their programming. By and large, these stations were located in the largest American radio markets—Los Angeles, Philadelphia, New York, San Francisco, Chicago, Detroit—but were also found in Minneapolis, Cincinnati, Pittsburgh, Richmond, and Miami. And for a time, they coexisted with early noncommercial jazz programming, which was likely to turn up in any market with educational or community based broadcasters. Eventually the commercial format disappeared, the last of them hanging on into the twenty-first century, not so much for lack of listeners, but almost certainly for a lack of advertisers.

All-Jazz Pioneers: KJAZ-FM, KNOB-FM, KBCA-FM, WAAF, WHAT-FM

It is far from clear as to which was the first radio station to program jazz full-time (or nearly full-time). The picture is further clouded by those claiming at various times to be the oldest all-jazz stations; as stations abandoned the format, the title of "oldest" could change hands. Nevertheless, the pioneers in this era began operation between 1955 and 1960, not surprisingly about the same time jazz became a genre distinct from popular music in the mind of the public.

Radio programming and innovation are highly imitative, and with the geographical limits that stations faced, ideas from one market could be implemented in others without direct competition. Whereas intra-market competition can lead to bitter rivalries between stations, inter-market competition is minimal (restricted, perhaps, to human resources) and the widespread adoption of a format has benefits for all, especially in creating a proven advertising market for it.[1]

The San Francisco Bay area's KJAZ-FM dates its all-jazz start to August 1, 1959.[2] It programmed jazz eighteen or more hours a day for thirty years until August 1994. From the outset it marketed its audience to advertisers as selective and desirable and clearly sought to have its sales pitch resonate with the jazz fan among the ad buyers as well, asserting that it listeners were "aware," or "in jazz parlance . . . hip."

Its sales brochure, "the KJAZ story," while touting the station as the place to be for jazz, illustrates the technologically determinist pattern of FM broadcasting before the maturity of the medium:

> There are over a dozen FM classical music stations in northern California that the FM listener can choose from. The big network stations provide excellent newscasts and commentary through their FM outlets, and there are about 20 FM stations offering popular and light classical music for "background" listening.
>
> But there is only one FM station programming jazz every hour of the broadcast day.
>
> When the FM listener wants to hear jazz, he must turn to KJAZ, northern California's first and only fulltime station.[3]

The brochure pretty well summed up the underutilized state of the early days of the FM radio band. Because of its superior hi-fi characteristics, the medium was thought suitable for classical, light classical, and so-called beautiful music, but the presence of a dozen classical and twenty Easy Listening stations was contrary to any reasonable market demand. Meanwhile, the unimaginative AM-FM duplication of network stations and other established broadcasters undervalued the business potential of FM. Finally, KJAZ was careful to restrict its claims to the northern California market, perhaps because a parallel initiative was already under way to the south.

Southern California's KNOB, "the jazz knob," began operation with a jazz format two years earlier, on August 25, 1957, in Long Beach, though the station only gradually increased its hours of operation to twenty-four as it increased power and moved from 97.9 to 103.1 MHz a year later.[4] A 1961 *Billboard* column *about* the use of LPs on radio provides a snapshot of KNOB's programming and lineup (table 12).

> Until KNOB-FM, Los Angeles, adopted an all-jazz format in August 1957, jazz LPs enjoyed only scant air play. Rarely does AM programming permit broadcast of complete tracks, due to pressure of commercials, and even non-specializing FM stations devote only brief time slots to jazz. Sleepy Stein [KNOB's owner and a former DJ] took the station (oldest FM outlet in Southern California [1947]) over in 1957, and since that date every note broadcast by KNOB has been jazz. Even sponsors, such as Buergermeister, wrote the commercials in the jazz idiom.[5]

The 1961 KNOB lineup (table 12) illustrates the variety approach taken in many all-jazz stations, with different styles featured at different times. (One can only imagine a world with competing all-jazz stations forced to find its niche by specializing in free jazz, swing, vocals, or piano music!) Note that the DJ lineup included Joe Adams, the early black DJ from the late 1940s noted in Chapter 1.

Stein had ambitions for a jazz radio network. The *Billboard* article mentions a potential new station in Detroit, operating as WIPE. Radio station WIPE never materialized, though Stein and a group that included Henry Mancini were granted a construction permit.[6] Another group bought the permit and brought WLIN-FM to the air in late 1962 as a general-interest station. It was unsuccessful in that form, and in 1963 finally adopted an all-jazz format that lasted perhaps a year. In 1964, WILN was bought by Hy Levinson, owner of "Good Music" WCAR (1130 AM) and renamed WCAR-FM. Though Detroit didn't quite work out, KNOB did enter into a programming agreement with WAZZ-FM, a short-lived all-jazz launch in Pittsburgh from 1961 to 1964 that ultimately became the longtime soul station WAMO-FM, in which KNOB agreed to send up to ten hours per day of programming, "patter plus music," less commercials, and sent a KNOB DJ, John Eastman, to get it started.[7] Sleepy Stein and KNOB anticipated the kind of jazz satellite programming service that would become a staple of public broadcasting (see Chapter 5).

In 1961, feeling pressure from, of all things, that overheated classical music market, KBCA changed formats to become an active jazz competitor of KNOB in Los Angeles, eventually outlasting it. Although KBCA won the jazz battle with KNOB, it was perhaps only in a Pyrrhic sense. KNOB dropped all-jazz in 1966 in favor of an "adult request" music format—clearly placing itself in opposition to Top 40—and reportedly experienced a 500 percent revenue gain.[8] Remarkably, KNOB's bright jazz future had been trumpeted just months earlier in a 1965 *Billboard* story that, while boasting of a 13 percent increase in ad revenue, also quoted the station president as who lamented that "many

TABLE 12. KNOB-FM lineup, spring 1961.

Time	DJ	Show Information
7 a.m.	Al Fox	Start the Day Swingin' (big bands, vocals)
9 a.m.	Al Rieman	Dixieland A.M.
10 a.m.	Ed Young	Jazz for Housewives ("sweet and pretty jazz . . . Red Garland, Erroll Garner, George Shearing, and Dave Brubeck")
Noon	Joe Adams	("leans to the blues . . . Ray Charles, Count Basie . . . Cannonball Adderley, Jimmy Smith)
3 p.m.	Ed Young	Young in the Afternoon ("in contradiction to the housewives show, this features more pure and modern jazz." Jazz Messengers, Benny Golson, Miles Davis)
5 p.m.	El Dormido	"Jazz con Savor Latino" (both Latin styled—Herbie Mann—and Latin jazz—Tito Puente)
6 p.m.	Jack Rockwell	Dinner Jazz (modern)
7 p.m.	Sleepy Stein	Sleepy's Hollow (A show directly sponsored by a group of record labels and airing remotely from Sam's Record Shop.) A different theme each night.
10 p.m.	Al Fox	The Fox's Den (modern jazz)
Not specified, but 30–60 minutes	Various	A live remote from one of the following: Bob Gafell (The Summit, Hollywood), Shelly Manne (Shelly's Manne Hole, Hollywood), or Howard Rumsey (The Lighthouse, Hermosa Beach)
Until 3 a.m.	Bob Cook	(record show from the Summit)
3 a.m.	Archi Stein	Steinways of Jazz (also from the Summit)
Sunday, 8 a.m.	Pat Collette	Jazz Goes to Church (gospel jazz, spirituals, Ray Charles, Les McCann)
Sundays, 7 p.m.	Howard Lucraft	Jazz International

Source: Lee Zhito, "LP Programming," *Billboard*, March 27, 1961, 8, 22.
Note: The labels sponsoring "Sleepy's Hollow" included Contemporary, World Pacific, Prestige, Riverside, Fantasy, Blue Note, Argo, Roulette, Impulse, Mercury, Atlantic, Veejay, Savoy, Epic, Capitol, and Columbia.

advertisers don't think jazz is dignified."[9] After dropping its all-jazz format, *Billboard* gave it to "the jazz KNOB," reporting that the station "slipped away to a fate midway between jazz and Nancy Sinatra singing 'These Boots Are Made for Walkin'."[10] Today there is an online webstream that plays jazz around the clock at www.jazzknob.com inspired by and in the spirit of KNOB.

KBCA is fondly remembered by listeners from that period. (The content of a 1970 KBCA-FM survey is reported in table 9 in Chapter 2.) "It's hard to believe that there was once a jazz station that would use John Coltrane's song 'Spiritual' as a morning drive-time theme, but it's true," wrote current KCRW-FM host Tom Schnabel, who recalled that he "installed a Delco FM receiver in his VW just to hear this station."[11] Schnabel, KCRW-FM's first music director and the author of *Rhythm Planet: The Great World Music Makers* (1980) and *Stolen Moments: Conversations with Contemporary Musicians* (1988), had warm recollections of the KBCA of his youth:

> The KBCA deejays were my and my friends' heroes: Tommy Bee in the afternoon, with "Miles Ahead" as his theme and fill music. There was Kogyo Sayama, who I recall had a hell of a time doing the voiceover ad for Mr. Jim's Barbeque: "You need no teeth to eat Mr. Jim's beef." Mr. Jim's was located at 102nd and Avalon in Compton, and though it's been closed for many years, there are still people who crave the BBQ sauce and the ribs there. There was Tolley Strode, who asked listeners to change lanes on the freeways when he segued cuts. Jai Rich, "Rosita's Little Boy Jay," the Jammin' Jay Rich, was the morning host from what he called "the lion's den." He used Oscar Brown's classic "Mr. Kicks" as his theme, and Coltrane's "Spiritual" as his fill music in between cuts. Finally, the late, great bandleader/educator Gerald Wilson had a noontime show called "Jazz Capsule." He always referred to musicians as "fine young men" regardless of their ages.[12]

The station would eventually change its call letters to KKGO, adopt a country music format in 1979, and swap jazz programming at the time to KKGO-AM, only to finally drop jazz on AM on September 14, 1990, also for lack of advertising revenue. The story of KBCA/KKGO/KKJZ-AM is an ironic one. The last of these switched to country in September 1990. According to a writer for the *Los Angeles Times*, "'We just didn't receive any support from either listeners or advertisers,' said [KBCA founder] Levine. 'Nine months had gone by [since KKJZ took over KKGO's jazz format], we hoped for some kind of audience, any kind of audience, even a .1 [Arbitron ratings] share, but it simply failed to materialize.'"[13] As it shut down, KKJZ literally passed the baton to noncommercial KLON. The KKJZ music library was given to the station, and its top veteran announcers, Chuck Niles and Sam Fields, were given shows at KLON that they continued for many years. The demise of KKJZ acted out in miniature the passing of jazz from commercial radio to noncommercial radio.

Chicago's WAAF was a daytime-only AM station at 950 kHz that had an all-jazz format in 1966. It has been claimed by several sources that WAAF had been using the all-jazz format since 1957, but a 1957 survey flyer from WAAF is strong evidence that rhythm and blues was featured at least as much as jazz in that year.[14] At any rate, its owners, Corn Belt Publishers, had featured pop music, news, and sports until 1956. Retaining some of their versatile announcers and adding Daddy-O Daylie and Jesse Owens, the winner of four gold medals at the 1936 Olympic Games, gave WAAF an integrated on-air staff, and the station sought to appeal to the upper-class Negro market but claimed to have an integrated audience.[15] The WAAF staff also included the venerable Dick Buckley, who had been playing jazz records over the air in Chicago since

1956 on WAAF, for another ten years at WAIT, and another twenty-one years at noncommercial WBEZ-FM until his retirement in 2008. Buckley's retirement was in part a result of the drastic reduction of jazz programming on WBEZ. Like several other all-jazz stations, WAAF would also play comedy recordings, perhaps simulating the typical nightclub mix of jazz and stand-up comedy. Table 13 contains the prime on-air voices at WAAF in 1966, its last full year of all-jazz operation and some idea of how the DJs differentiated their shows.[16]

In 1967 WAAF was sold to Ralph Atlas and was converted to a soul music format, eventually under the call sign WGRT. The new owners probably saw an opportunity because the city's almost one million African Americans were only being addressed by three stations: (1) WBEE, an underpowered Harvey, Illinois, station that could be heard on part of the South Side, (2) a newcomer, the recently licensed WMPP (Working More for People's Progress), another daytime-only station, owned by the black-owned Seaway Broadcasting, and (3) WVON (the Voice of the Negro), owned by Leonard and Phil Chess, owners of Chess Records. When the change was made Daddy-O was retained at first, but his hours were chipped away until his weekday show on WGRT was only thirty minutes in 1971.[17] In 1973 it became a black-owned station when Johnson Publishing purchased it in 1973 and renamed in WJPC.

In 1956 Philadelphia's WHAT-FM broadcast Sid Mark's overnight jazz program before resuming the AM-FM simulcast of rhythm and blues in the

TABLE 13. WAAF jazz host lineup, April 1966.

Time Slot	DJ	Typical Artists
6 a.m.	Marty Faye	Ramsey Lewis, Richard "Groove" Holmes, Jimmy Smith, Barbra Streisand, Nancy Wilson, Frank Sinatra
8 a.m.	Vince Garrity	(For a time hosted "Sounds of the City" with Studs Terkel)
9 a.m.	Daddy-O	See Chapter 2, table 8
12 noon	Jesse Owens	Art Tatum, Duke Ellington, Sarah Vaughan*
1:30 p.m.	Dick Buckley	Sonny Rollins, Wes Montgomery, Thelonious Monk, Duke Ellington
3 p.m.	Norm Spaulding	Jazz and commentary**
4:30 p.m.	Daddy-O Daylie	As above
Weekend	Dick Buckley	Jelly Roll Morton, Coleman Hawkins, Louis Armstrong, Jimmy Lunceford
Weekend	Lou House	Jazz Crusaders, Eddie Harris, Jimmy McGriff
Weekend	Mary Merridee	Count Basie, Lou Rawls, Quincy Jones

Source: Earl Paige, "WAAF: Stock in Yards & Jazz," *Billboard*, November 19, 1966, 36.

* This information comes from an internet mailing list conversation between two jazz radio heavyweights, Jae Sinnett of WRV-FM and the late Dick LaPalm, who is providing an answer about Jesse Owens as a DJ. http://archive.jazzweek.com/2008-May/026815.html.

** Norman W. Spaulding, "History of Black Oriented Radio in Chicago 1929–1963" (PhD diss., University of Illinois), 98.

TABLE 14. WHAT-FM weekday program schedule, 1966.

Host	Times	Format
George Lyle	6:00 a.m.	Light jazz
Stu Chase	9:00 a.m.	Piano sounds ("diapers, dishes, and Dave Brubeck")
Joel Dorn	12:00 p.m.	Modern sounds
Sid Mark	4 p.m.	Modern big bands, vocalists, trios
Joel Dorn	10 p.m.	"Hard-school of honkers and expressionists"
Vince Garrett	12 p.m.–6 a.m.	A bit of all

morning. The surprising popularity of Mark's show encouraged the station's owners, siblings Dolly and William Banks, to launch an all-jazz format on WHAT-FM on November 11, 1957.[18] The station limped into 1975, when as WWDB it became the nation's first FM talk radio station; Sid Mark remained a fixture with a weekend Frank Sinatra program. A 1966 *Billboard* story delineated the jazz station's offerings.[19] Its weekday lineup (table 14) appears to have provided its listeners with reliable separation of styles, though these descriptions are somewhat vague.

The station made claims about its audience demographics that track well with the claims of KJAZ. It maintained that more than 30 percent of its listeners had incomes between $8,000 and $12,000, with another 25 percent earning between $6,000 and $8,000, and that its largest listener segment, 34 percent, was in the twenty-one to twenty-eight age bracket. The WHAT-FM program director, Sid Mark, told *Billboard* that the station's success followed from good management practices and a strong relationship with the recording industry: "Each member of our staff programs his own show under supervision of management, all of the record companies have always given us excellent service and, in most instances, we have the pleasure of being the first to preview new record albums."[20] This close supervision by management differentiates the DJ on the all-jazz station from the DJs discussed in Chapter 2, whose programming was anomalous to the station's format. That WHAT-FM felt satisfied with the "service" it received from record companies is also in part a testament to management's efforts at building strong relationships with them; complaints about service are common among jazz programmers across the decades, and even today, service is critical issue.

WBEE: The Little Jazz Station That Could— Until It Couldn't

Black Appeal AM station WBEE, licensed to the city of Harvey, Illinois, in 1955 with the goal of reaching Chicago's black South Side, would eventually become a jazz station after many years with a soul format with some jazz programming here and there. It began as a 250W daytime-only operation broadcasting at 1570 kHz. Its first owner, O. Wayne Rollins, took advantage of the television-induced plunge in radio station prices to purchase inexpensive broadcast properties on which to advertise his brother John's automotive businesses. In 1964, Rollins bought the Orkin pest control company in what may have been the first leveraged buyout in the United States. In some markets Rollins aimed the stations at the African American audience,[21] including three other Black Appeal stations: WGEE (Indianapolis), WNJR (Newark, New Jersey), and WRAP (Norfolk, Virginia). Rollins Broadcasting, along with Sonderling, Rounsaville, Speidel, and United Broadcasting, would constitute the big five white-owned "soul radio" chains that led an industry of more than three hundred Black Appeal radio stations, of which only nine were black-owned by 1969. This format was strictly a profitable business strategy with lower entry costs than more desirable radio properties.

The black community saw white-owned Black Appeal radio as at best meeting a need and at worst as exploitative and parasitic. In the wake of the turbulent 1960s, the lack of black radio ownership became a public policy issue. In the wake of a decade of civil unrest, a study of black radio identified several deficiencies including the lack of nationwide black news services, a paucity of black executives, and an excess of radio programming "based almost entirely on 'Rhythm-n-Blues' or 'rock' music, with little or no emphasis on black performances in jazz, 'pop,' folk, or other music modes."[22] Charles Sherrell II had been one of the few black radio executives—he had already served thirteen years as WBEE's general manager and vice president—when he purchased it in the late 1980s. Sherrell retained the all-jazz format that WBEE adopted in about 1966, although WBEE would alter its lineup, for instance, announcing in 1990 the addition of more blues and African music, in search of greater listenership.[23]

Over the years Sherrell championed the "real" jazz played on his AM station as opposed to the smooth variety available elsewhere in the market. Sherrell provided the following description of WBEE for a website that was still available in 2011 though the station was sold in 2003.

WBEE Chicago CD1570AM, 24 hours of Real Jazz—"The New Blues Groove"

Real Jazz Music created by jazz masters: Duke Ellington, Louis Armstrong, Charlie Parker, Milt Jackson, Ella Fitzgerald, et al. Now recorded by Oscar Peterson, Clark Terry, Sonny Rollins, Wynton Marsalis, Mark Whitfield, Marcus Roberts, et al.

Jazz music exemplifies the basic tenet of American democracy: freedom amidst structure. Jazz music is serious music, it sounds good, feels good, and it means peace, joy, serenity, happiness, hope and good fortune.

> Real Jazz (as opposed to "smooth" jazz) is an art form, much like dance, theater, literary writing, oratory and painting. Listen to the masters, the beautiful music of the young stars, and the soulful singing of the new and talented vocalists.
>
> Deliver this music to the children; make them know about Milt Jackson (not just Michael Jackson), Dizzy Gillespie, Duke Ellington, Clifford Brown, Count Basie and so many other supremely gifted men and women who continue to create such marvelous music.
>
> Finally, buy at least one Real Jazz CD a month. See our Real Jazz Airplay list, or visit our websites to determine what to buy: www.cd1570.com, www.realjazzradio.com, and www.realjazzmusic.com[.]
>
> Remember: no music has given as much to American culture as jazz, and nothing sounds sweeter, richer, lovelier, or hipper than the music for all ages: jazz.[24]

However, throughout its existence, even with increased daytime power of 1 kW, WBEE's weak signal severely restricted its reach.

With only forty thousand to sixty thousand listeners, Sherrell lamented the circumstances leading to the sale.[25] "It's all but impossible to get dollars from advertising agencies if you don't have ratings," he told the *Sun-Times*. "The market is becoming more and more competitive to the point where if you don't have ratings, you can't even get local retailers [to advertise] anymore."[26] With ratings below the Arbitron threshold, WBEE had difficulty signing advertisers—Sherrell claimed $2 million in advertising revenues in 2001—even with pitches that emphasized jazz listeners' good taste and spending power.[27] Sherrell had also gone on record accusing mainstream Chicago cultural institutions of ignoring black audiences and black media. For example, he cited the exclusion of WBEE and WVON from receiving advertising from and promotional materials for of the Chicago Symphony Orchestra's annual jazz series despite his station's ability to reach jazz fans. Sherrell further claimed that the station was snubbed with regard to everyday promotion, "demonstrating a very subtle kind of racism. In some cases, when (WBEE staff) would call and ask for tickets, they would offer to sell them to us. That's an insult to a radio station like ours."[28]

He summed up his uphill battle thus: "If you're a small AM station like WBEE—with only 1,000 watts of power that can only be heard on the South Side of Chicago and in the south suburbs—and if you're programming an art form like jazz, which is only appreciated by a small percentage of the listening public, you cannot expect to get ratings. You're just not going to get the numbers."[29]

In 2003, after almost thirty years of offering various amounts of jazz programming augmented with brokered time sales to gospel and talk shows,

Sherrell announced the sale of WBEE for approximately $2 million to owners expected to establish a gospel station.

WSDM-FM: The Chicago Station with All Those Girls

"Smack dab in the middle with girls and all that jazz" was the slogan of 97.9 WSDM-FM Chicago, the FM partner of WVON. In 1965 WSDM-FM began an all-jazz format in direct competition with WAAF. It aspired to serve an audience that wanted the "latest and best in jazz and breezy night club style comedy interspersed with sultry feminine voices."[30] The tagline compressed the station's marketing portfolio neatly. Its position at 97.9 MHz put it in the actual center of the FM band, the station featured jazz, and, uniquely, had an all-female air staff anchored by the exceptionally talented Yvonne Daniels, freshly relieved of her "Sid and Yvonne" duties when WCFL changed formats.

The WSDM women, "a gaggle of girl deejays called 'Den Pals,'" spoke in soft and sultry voices and used pseudonyms: Fascination (Pam Eberhardt), Solid State, Maybe, Dawn, Peppermint Patty, Copper, Pennie Lane, and Petite (Yvonne Daniels).[31] The station's presentation evoked *Playboy*-era men with pipes, smoking jackets, and brandy snifters as listeners. Linda Ellerbee, later a journalist with NBC, came through WSDM as program director ("Hush Puppy" on the air) and recalled, "Looking back it was incredibly sexist, but at least they hired women."[32] In fact, the concept did provide on-air opportunities for women as DJs, announcers, newscasters, and copywriters.

Besides the formula of female voices and the appeal to the male gaze, WSDM looked to present music that might grow a large audience rather than a niche. For most of the broadcast day, playlists were under the control of program manager Bert Burdeen, but the veteran Daniels was given a free hand to program her own show. The station capitalized on a 1960s jazz marketing trend of jazz artists recording versions of pop songs: swinging and tuneful covers that ranged from Count Basie doing the Beatles (1966's *Basie's Beatle Bag* and 1969's *Basie on the Beatles*) to Wes Montgomery doing the Mamas and the Papas (1966's *California Dreaming*) to Miles Davis doing Disney (1961's *Someday My Prince Will Come*). WSDM wanted to "reach everyone too old for the Rolling Stones and too young for Lawrence Welk," and claimed, "our record programming formula is this: Pop-oriented jazz and jazz-oriented pop."[33] It was also an album-oriented station, the better to take advantage of its ability to broadcast in stereo. It is easy to imagine that a lot of WSDM's music would fit on easy listening and MOR stations as well. The formula was immediately successful, at least in the underutilized FM band. In 1966 WSDM was number two among Chicago FMs, behind the fine arts and classical music station WFMT, the venerable public radio station with commercial roots. More important, WSDM was outperforming AM WAAF, the established all-jazz station in the market, leading to WAAF's ultimate sale and format change.

Starting in 1968, WSDM started programming progressive rock on some of the weekend hours. A bit later, in 1971, it started to aggressively mix jazz and rock, reflecting the mainstreaming of the inroads made by underground and progressive stations.

> Music director Burt Burdeen said the combination of jazz and rock at WSDM-FM reflects what is happening in both the jazz and rock idioms and is still evolving. When he gets together the new system he's working on, the WSDM-FM mix will be nearly equally divided between jazz and rock. Thus, the six-year-old outlet's traditional slogan "smack dab in the middle" (meaning Chicago's FM dial) will put it squarely between two basic musical idioms that are in themselves coalescing.[34]

It is curious that WSDM was coming to progressive radio from jazz rather than from Top 40 or rock. As for the two idioms coalescing, given the mix of music on commercial jazz stations around this time, it is an interesting speculative exercise to think about the directions jazz would take if it were still dependent on commercial radio.

Burdeen struggled a bit with his jazz history but saw a blended future and the role WSDM (and stations like it) would play in bringing it into being. Defining the boundaries of jazz was as difficult for Burdeen as anyone else:

> Arnett Coleman [sic] once said he created "sheets of sound." I sometimes think of our sound as a "superhighway of sound." Actually, it's not easy to characterize our sound, you quickly get meaningless clichés like saying we're not MOR or we're not this or that. There are perimeters: the group War, without Eric Burden; Creedence Clearwater Revival but never Lynn Anderson, if you're talking about something in the country direction at all; Chicago and many of the rock groups, but never Grand Funk Railroad; many of the pop stars from B.J. Thomas to even a Julius LaRosa; but always that foundation rooted in jazz with now and then an oldie Glenn Miller to maybe show that that was part of the jazz tradition too.[35]

Representing the industry-friendly view that commercial radio offered, Burdeen rather defensively scolded the purists, those traditionally aligned with that durable connoisseurial voice that dominated jazz criticism, the jazz police:

> Switching from a pure jazz format was not a copout. I think the jazz buff is a rather selfish and stingy person. I mean, it's just not fair for a person not to listen to anything but jazz. Look at the survival list in jazz and you see that Ramsey Lewis, Herbie Mann, Cannonball Adderley and the others

have combined jazz and rock and have advanced because of it. But they have a foundation in jazz.[36]

The mix of jazz and rock lasted until the 1977 format change to AOR, which brought an end to WSDM as a jazz radio station, just a couple of years before the much-noted demise of New York's commercial jazz station WRVR in 1979.

Black Progressive Radio and Jazz

As we have seen, there was often a connection to black radio within the ranks of all-jazz radio stations. A few originated as jazz stations, but most had a prior format, and a subsequent format after giving up as jazz stations. In the case of jazz stations that were part of AM-FM joint license arrangements, it can be informative to look at the prior, current, and subsequent formats of the sibling station (see table 15). For Chicago's WAAF, for example, the prior format was MOR and the subsequent format was soul. For all-jazz WHAT-FM, sibling WHAT was a top-rated Philadelphia R&B or soul station. As with WWDB-FM, the station left jazz for FM talk radio. From the 1970s on, format "churn" became a common practice in the radio business, yet one cannot help but notice that stations usually turned to black programming out of distress. Indeed, the all-jazz format often depended on black listeners but in the mind of advertisers may have suffered from that same listenership. The managers of all-jazz stations constantly bemoaned the lack of interest on the part of advertisers who seemed nonplussed by the income and purchasing demographic claims made by the jazz stations.

The format was never adopted on a truly widespread basis. As new stations implemented jazz formats, others, disappointed with the resulting ratings and ad sales, abandoned it. For the most part, stations turned to jazz in varying degrees to counterprogram the dominant and youthful Top 40 variants or to go after MOR listeners.

During the 1960s, all-jazz commercial radio came to—and left—Bridgeport, Connecticut (WJZZ-FM), Cleveland (WCUY-FM), Boston (WUPY-FM), Pittsburgh (WAZZ-FM), Richmond (WRGM), Miami (WMBM, one of the Rounsaville Negro Appeal stations), and to Cincinnati via a durable station floating in the Ohio River (WNOP) off Florence, Kentucky. In 1967 all-jazz radio arrived in New York at WLIB-FM and competition in jazz radio came to Chicago (WSDM-FM). It is significant that full-time jazz programming was also adopted at several AM stations, though almost always on stations with service limitations similar to those described for WBEE—lower power, directional antenna patterns, and restricted hours—all to protect more dominant stations. Some of these stations described their format as "jazz" to trade publications and ad representatives, but to today's listeners the mix of

TABLE 15. Prominent all-jazz stations—years and format histories.

	Years as a jazz station	Previous format	Subsequent format	Sibling station format
KAZZ-FM (Austin)	1988	—	black/Top 40	—
KNOB-FM (S.F.)	1957–1966	MOR	all-request	—
WAAF (Chicago)	1958–1964	MOR	soul	—
WHAT-FM (Phila.)	1959–1975	soul	talk	soul
KBCA-FM (later AM) (L.A.)	1959–1990	—	classical	jazz transfer
KJAZ-FM (S.F.)	1959–1994	—	Spanish	—
KHIP-FM/KMPX-FM (S.F.)	1960–1964	—	free-form	—
WJZZ (CT)	1960–1964	—	classical	MOR
WUPY (Bos.)	1961–1963	—	off-air	—
WAZZ (Pgh.)	1961–1964	—	soul	soul
WNOP (Cinc.)	1962–2000	country	religious talk	—
KBVU (Bellevue, WA)	1964–1967	—	—	—
WBEE (Harvey, IL)	1966–2000	soul	gospel	—
WYDD (Pgh.)	1967–1976	—	UG AOR	—
WSDM-FM (Chi.)	1967–1977	brokered	AOR	soul
WCUY (Clev.)	1967–1974	—	oldies	soul
WLIB-FM (NY)	1965–1972	—	Urban Cont.	soul
WRGM (Rich.)	1971–1973	Top 40	Solid Gold	—
KADX-FM (Denver)	1973–1981	MOR	country	MOR/
WBUS-FM (Miami)	1974–1976	prog rock	soft AC	—
WRVR-FM (NY)	1974–1980	classical/edu.	country	—
WCHD/WCHB/WJZZ-FM (Det.)	1960–1996	—	Urban	soul
KTWN (Minn.)	1978–1983	—	AC/oldies	various
WBBY-FM	1978–1990	rock	revoked	—
KJZZ (Bellevue, WA)	1981–1984	AOR	AC	AC
KTCJ (Minn.)	1983–1997?	country	country	—
KRML (Carmel, CA)	1985–2012	MOR	free-form	—
KKUL	1986–1988	hot AC	news/business	—

Source: Compiled by the author.

AC: Adult Contemporary (an heir to Top 40); AOR: Album-Oriented Rock; Brokered: Stations sold blocks of time to outside programmers; UC: Urban Contemporary (an heir to Top 40); UG: Underground; Urban: black.

styles presented side by side on these stations would appear far afield of jazz. In this regard, these black-oriented AM stations were not so much adopting a jazz format as, for various reasons, emphasizing jazz to create an identity with listeners or advertisers, however successful. For example, in *Billboard's* largely mysterious "rapid response ratings" of January 23, 1965, for the St. Louis radio market, deejays from KATZ and KXLW dominated the jazz ranking.[37] While both stations had jazz shows, elsewhere in that issue KATZ is described as a R&B, religious, and jazz station and KXLW as R&B and gospel.

Except for a handful of black-owned radio stations, Black Appeal radio had long been dominated by the white-owned "soul" chains. Beginning in 1971, and lasting only a few years, an influential period of innovative programming took place at a few black-owned commercial radio stations including WBLS (New York) and WHUR (Washington, DC) that was to have long-term effects on black radio programming.

Coinciding with the format experimentation on FM was the first real wave of rising African American political power since Reconstruction. The Voting Rights Act of 1965 succeeded in increasing black voter registrations. The election of a number of black officials and the recognition of black voting power produced policymaking that led to greater participation in broadcasting at the management and ownership levels. New voices came to the microphone and to management as a set of physical, political, and cultural movements, the Great Migration, the civil rights movement, the black arts movement, and "black is beautiful" empowered unprecedented progress in broadcasting. In 1967 the Kerner Commission, convened after a summer of widespread urban unrest, recommended "increasing communication across racial lines to destroy stereotypes, to halt polarization, end distrust and hostility, and create common ground for efforts toward public order and social justice."[38] Along with calls for increased participation of black journalists, there were efforts to increase African American media ownership. Such remedies were desperately needed in radio, where only sixteen of forty-five hundred stations were owned by African Americans as the 1970s began.[39] Burgeoning black nationalism coupled black artistic and musical energy to increased social awareness in business and politics. Black radio ownership and management opportunities were on the rise, and with them, at least for a few years, a politically progressive black aesthetic was let loose to varying degrees on black radio.

In the forefront were two radio operations, each located in flagship communities for black America. In New York black media entrepreneurs, led by the politically connected Percy Sutton (former Manhattan borough president and the personal attorney of Malcolm X), purchased WLIB AM/FM from white owner Harry Novick, while Washington DC's Howard University received WTOP-FM as a charitable gift from the *Washington Post*.[40] Although these stations were in the vanguard of what Marc Fisher and others have called "Black Liberation Radio," other broadcasters, with access to college or community radio and occasionally black-owned commercial radio, enthusiastically participated as well, modeling their stations to varying degrees on these leaders.

WLIB (AM) had been featuring a mixed jazz and soul format since at least 1960. In the 1940s WLIB was a "good music" and "no jazz" station, but in 1949, under the new ownership of brothers Harry and Morris Novick, it would turn first to ethnic broadcasting, with only some of the programming aimed at the black audience. In the 1950s WLIB had a DJ named Phil Gordon, one of several DJs using the name "Dr. Jive." First appearing in 1959 as Dr. Jive's sub, and then his replacement, was Billy Taylor, the great jazz pianist who would go on to a remarkable career in jazz education and broadcasting. Taylor was a founder of Jazzmobile, which brought both concerts and musical training to New York's poorest neighborhoods as well as its parks, and spent much of his life devoted to the promotion of jazz through radio and television. As a broadcaster, Taylor had a long association with WLIB and WLIB-FM (where he served as program director for a time), worked for a time at AM powerhouse WNEW in New York, was the lead in a group that purchased WSOK in Augusta, Georgia, from Speidel Broadcasting (one of the major white-owned Black Appeal station group owners), and for many years was the jazz correspondent for CBS's *Sunday Morning*.[41]

In 1965 WLIB-FM began operation and, avoiding the AM-FM duplication restrictions, initiated a jazz format. In a hopeful 1966 article titled "Jazz Sales Spurting in New York—Thanks to Airplay by WLIB-FM," the station was lauded for its jazz programming, which featured generous helpings of such soul jazz stalwarts as Groove Holmes, Willis "Gator" Jackson, and "Brother" Jack McDuff. An approving record industry executive cooed, "Things we call jazz today that sell big are much more pop-oriented. Jazz has come back to the people. It's too early to judge what total effect the station will have on sales, but in my opinion the station is certainly helping."[42]

Although this article stressed the soul jazz formula, the tenures of Billy Taylor and later Del Shields as WLIB-FM program director is enough to confirm that a wide range of jazz styles, including less commercial forms, were present on WLIB playlists. Shields called his own show "The Total Black Experience in Sound." His program mix was militantly eclectic: new, trendsetting jazz from John Coltrane and Miles Davis, message soul from Curtis Mayfield and Nina Simone, poetry from Nikki Giovanni and the Last Poets, and speeches from Martin Luther King, Jr. and Malcolm X."[43]

With the station under new black ownership and now renamed WBLS, the ambitious program director Frankie Crocker soon reined in the Shields-era political activism and taste for the avant-garde but kept the slogan. Crocker let the music, with jazz in the mix, carry the political dialogue, albeit a more subdued one. As a fan and present-day blogger remembered,

> Frankie said that as WBLS Program Director it was his responsibility to bring to us the listener, "The Total Black Experience in Sound." That meant that we would hear:
> —Both Little Richard & Richard Pryor.
> —Both James Brown & James Baldwin.

—Both Jackie Wilson & Jackie Robinson.
—Both Miles Davis & Buddy Miles.
—Both John Lee Hooker and Dr. John "The Night Tripper."
—We would hear Dukes, & Counts, Kings (BB) and Queens (Aretha)
—We would hear Doo Wop & Funk & Rock & Blues & Soul & Jazz.[44]

As the '70s progressed, the ratings game and increased financial pressure began to homogenize the content. By mid-decade Crocker's playlists, according to Barlow, "featured the best-selling jazz artists of the day, such as Grover Washington, Jr., and Weather Report" along with "Aretha Franklin, Stevie Wonder, Marvin Gaye, and Isaac Hayes, and the latest disco tracks," a lineup that disappointed jazz fans at the time but would be retro-novel today.[45]

Crocker was, according to Nelson George, "a child of integration" who sought to attract a wider (that is, whiter) audience for WBLS by having more white artists in the WBLS mix.[46] These artists included Elton John, Bette Midler, the Bee Gees, and Hall and Oats. Crocker and his team of DJs were smooth but did not speak jive. For Crocker, the station needed to be something that black people could play on their jobs without embarrassment—no one "selling roaches [pesticides] and cheap wine and saying you didn't need any credit"—or "feeling ashamed of the kind of music they want."[47] Eventually WBLS's programming, with the inclusion of "white artists who ranked high on the pop charts and whose sound was compatible with the current black popular music," led directly to the durable urban contemporary format, a clever creation to attract white listeners while retaining black ones.[48]

Meanwhile, in Washington, DC, unprecedented directions in programming were taking place at WHUR-FM (the former WTOP-FM) beginning in August 1971.[49] The newly acquired station was originally conceived as being a part of a larger media training laboratory at Howard University with a high level of student participation. Instead, under the direction of Phil Watson, a veteran black media activist with experience at the Pacifica network, WHUR implemented "360 Degrees: The Black Experience in Sound." In musical terms, the "360 Degrees" concept was free-form and eclectic:

> Jazz, blues, R&B, gospel, soul, and reggae were all regularly featured—and often mixed together. The DJs, who initially controlled their own playlists, gravitated toward the new free-form style of programming popular in progressive FM circles. They combined the avant-garde jazz of John Coltrane and Sun Ra with the deep blues of Muddy Waters and Howling Wolf; the politically charged reggae of Bob Marley and Jimmy Cliff with the urban soul of Marvin Gaye and Curtis Mayfield, and the civil rights songs of the SNCC Freedom Singers and the Staple Singers with the militant street poetry of the Last Poets and Gil Scott-Heron.[50]

WHUR attempted something quite challenging, offering difficult jazz pieces, lectures, political speeches, readings of folk tales, and concerts of Delta blues shouters. Its programming was described as "a mélange of jazz, R&B, gospel, message music, black nationalism, and point-of-view public affairs programming . . . free-form, diamond-rough, and inventive."[51] Kojo Nnamdi, now a semi-retired senior figure on public radio giant WAMU but in 1971 a radio novice, was startled by the experiment at WHUR:

> "I'd never heard radio like this before—days-long discussions of the future of black people, hearings on government abuses, the entire score of *Ain't Supposed to Die a Natural Death*, the Broadway musical by Melvin Van Peebles," Nnamdi said, "and it affected me so much. The station had a strong black identity, and it developed such a loyalty. I just felt drawn to it."[52]

It comes as no real surprise that, though widely lauded, this progressive programming approach did not last. For one thing, the station ran afoul of political infighting; Howard president James Cheek was a moderate black Republican who desired closer ties with the Nixon administration, both personally and to protect the university's significant federal funding. For another, the station was costing the school a lot of money while not generating much by way of advertising revenues, even though it inherited a commercial frequency from the *Post*, at 96.3 MHz. Under constant top-down pressure to operate in a more businesslike manner, the station began to scale back the politically conscious programming. The "experimental stuff" was discouraged to make room for "the more melodic jazz" and a "more contemporary sound—Al Jarreau and Herbie Hancock, as well as some more popular hits—The O'Jays and that sort." Said music director Jesse Fax of these changes, "It didn't go over well with some of the staff, but I knew that FM would eventually use whatever music philosophies had worked on AM."[53] With these changes WHUR experienced dramatically higher ratings and "billed over $1 million in advertising for the first time in its history."[54] It eventually became a perennially top-rated station in the Washington, DC market.

As Fax had observed, the AM experience had shown that for making money, an eclectic music programming strategy could not match a more narrowly focused one that concentrated on building a loyal audience and claiming advertising revenues. Despite the political and cultural inclinations of the stations' owners and management, jazz was on the way out of the most progressive of black radio formats in Washington, DC, and New York, so what chance could it have at more mercantile operations? Although this period of highly idealized and ideological programming was brief, before yielding to bottom-line concerns, it reflected the aspirational positioning of black music, integrating jazz with other styles as it had seldom been before in commercial broadcasting.

Preceding the era of black liberation radio by a decade and establishing a clear model for it was the offshore broadcasting of Robert and Mabel Williams. The black nationalist Robert F. Williams (1925–1996), described by Malcolm X as "just a couple of years ahead of his time," was the militant branch president of the NAACP chapter in Monroe, North Carolina, where he confronted the Ku Klux Klan with armed self-defense including explosives and machine guns. As expected, his leadership drew the attention of law enforcement, and the FBI attempted to take him into custody. Soon after escaping to Cuba in 1963, the Williamses began a series of weekly broadcasts on Friday evenings called *Radio Free Dixie*, with "an hour of the latest jazz, soul, and rock and roll; news coverage of the black freedom movement; and Robert Williams's fiery invective against white supremacy."[55] Descriptions of the program bear a remarkable resemblance to the playlists of the black liberation radio period and of the politically active community radio stations in black communities ever since. Mixed in with Curtis Mayfield's "Keep on Pushin'," Nina Simone's "Mississippi Goddamn," and Sam Cooke's "A Change Is Gonna Come" would be Mabel Williams reading the poetry of Langston Hughes. Sometimes broadcasting with fifty thousand watts, *Radio Free Dixie* could at times be heard all over North America. A listener wrote that most stations "do not care or dare to broadcast the new music our musicians are really playing today and our people's hearts are beating to, because the new music is for freedom."[56] Listeners heard the blues of Leadbelly and Joe Turner, Abbey Lincoln and Max Roach's *Freedom Now Suite*, and the music of Ornette Coleman; friends of the Williamses such as Amiri Baraka and regular listeners kept them supplied with new music and news. In his book *Radio Free Dixie*, Timothy Tyson insightfully summarizes Williams's use of jazz.

> "Williams's innovative use of jazz was the show's musical cutting edge. "I did some experiments with some of Max Roach's stuff," he said, "and Ornette Coleman, he was producing this new type of way out jazz." Williams used the new jazz in an effort to create "a new psychological concept of propaganda" by combining "the type of music people could feel, that would motivate them."[57]

The Williamses' insistence on the centrality of jazz in the mix ran afoul of the Cuban Communists who, despite the strong relationship between jazz and Afro-Cuban music, took the standard Soviet position that jazz was degenerate music and a product of imperialism. Initially the Williamses' personal relationships with Fidel Castro and Che Guevara protected *Radio Free Dixie* from this dogmatic interference, but doctrinaire party operatives chipped away at both their output power and their time. Although the Williamses left Cuba for Beijing in 1965, their program had made an impact on U.S. broadcasters with black nationalist sensibilities, not only through direct listening but also via tapes of the program that circulated from person to person and were sometimes rebroadcast over Pacifica stations. For all its impact on black liberation radio and its successors, *Radio Free Dixie* was, ironically, suffocated by an ideological struggle over the meaning of jazz.

Perhaps the most visible and prominent exponents of black progressive radio, WLIB's and WHUR's influence was widespread as visitors to and expatriates of Chocolate City and the Big Apple implemented these concepts on college and community stations around the country. And I was one of them. In the best thieving radio tradition, my partner Michael Herron and I hosted *Sound, Color, and Movement*, the show's title stolen from a durable youth radio workshop on DC's WAMU. Each Sunday night on Carnegie Mellon's student-run WRCT we spun a playlist full of jazz fusion and jazz music with political or black nationalist leanings. Our program capped a day of black music at the station, but it was jazz that carried the overt and far too hip political content on our show. Our playlists were certain to include Gil Scott-Heron, Doug and Jean Carn, the Last Poets, and anything else that fit in with the spirit of our coming of age awareness of *The Autobiography of Malcom X*, *The Wretched of the Earth*, or *The Song of Solomon*.

Black progressive radio, or at least its descendants, had not yet finished impacting the boundaries of the jazz genre. One of the most successful subformats to emerge from Urban Contemporary was a programming concept begun on WHUR in 1977 called "The Quiet Storm." Named after a Smokey Robinson hit, this widely copied late-evening program, which featured low-key deejay announcements, romantic R&B ballads, and quiet grooving instrumentals, served as a precursor to the last commercial jazz format, smooth jazz. In spite of controversy as to whether it is really jazz at all, smooth jazz is the only jazz format regularly heard on commercial radio today and, ironically, it is connected to the black nationalist heritage of jazz. Although smooth jazz formats achieved something of a mixed-race audience that Quiet Storm formats did not, the number of stations using it peaked in the 1990s. Today, smooth jazz is no longer available over the air in several major cities, including New York.

WRVR and the Demise of Commercial Jazz Radio

The cause célèbre of American commercial jazz radio in the 1970s, seen as emblematic of the declining fortunes of jazz as a whole, was the slow-motion demise of WRVR-FM in New York. It began operation on New Year's Day 1961 as a noncommercial educational and cultural radio station. Because its owner, the Riverside Church—where Martin Luther King Jr. made his historic anti-Vietnam war speech on April 4, 1967, exactly one year before his assassination—was in possession of a frequency (106.7) that permitted commercial operation, there was tremendous temptation to sell because of the license's high market value.[58] In 1971 WRVR became a full-time commercial jazz station, programming about twenty-two hours of jazz each day. In 1974 WRVR was sold to Sonderling Broadcasting, one of the leading white-owned soul chains. Sonderling already owned New York's WWRL, an old-school, daytime-only AM Black Appeal station that lacked an FM station to counter the newly formed, black-owned Inner City Broadcasting's combination of WLIB-AM/FM. It is noteworthy that it was WLIB-FM (before being renamed WBLS-FM) that established extensive jazz commercial broadcasting in New York in the 1960s.

WRVR was not without critics of its jazz programming policies, and the sale to Sonderling only increased their number. Some found it erratic. Over its run as an all-jazz station, there would be less and less to please hardcore jazz fans. The shift to less acoustic jazz to more jazz fusion and early smooth jazz can be seen in the few surviving music surveys published by WRVR (see table 16).[59] These surveys are unfair representations of the on-air mix to some degree. My own memory is that there were plenty of older jazz classics (Dizzy Gillespie, John Coltrane, Miles Davis) on WRVR as well. These surveys are probably representative of the music in heavy rotation on the station.

Many jazz fans thought WRVR played too much pop music, while some industry professionals found the DJs too reverential about mainstream jazz. Charles Mitchell, himself a WRVR music director near the station's end wrote, "WRVR suffered from a surfeit of windy hipsters, not unlike those who plagued progressive rock radio with tedious anecdotes and minor trivia, not to mention drawn-out mentions of sidemen," the latter critique echoing "Symphony" Sid Torin's view (Chapter 1). "You got great music on WRVR, but you had to put up with a lot of dull guff to get it."[60]

Sonderling became involved in a drawn-out battle with community groups dedicated to preserving WRVR's jazz format. This campaign was richly steeped in the emerging discourse of jazz as "America's classical music." On several occasions, deals preserving the jazz format were announced, but they all fell apart when Sonderling's holdings were acquired by Viacom, which made an abrupt and unannounced change to country music. The end came on-air on September 8, 1980, at around 10 a.m., according to the recollections of several listeners, when Charles Mingus's "Good-bye Pork Pie Hat" was followed by Waylon Jennings's "Are You Ready for the Country."[61]

The Commercial Jazz Radio Partnership

Record company executives and jazz club owners, partners in jazz commerce, lamented the demise of WRVR. Where and how they would find comparable advertising opportunities and reach their customers without the station? The

TABLE 16. The shift in WRVR-FM's jazz programming, 1975–1979.

August 1, 1975
1. Liquid Love—Freddie Hubbard
   Esther Phillips w/Beck
   Expansions—Lonnie Liston Smith
2. The Chicago Theme—Hubert Laws
   Tale Spinnin'—Weather Report
3. Steppin' Into Tomorrow—Donald Byrd
   Renaissance—Ray Charles
4. Chocolate Chip—Isaac Hayes
   I Am Music—Carmen McCrae
   Mr. Magic—Grover Washington Jr.
   Come Get to This—Nancy Wilson
5. Phenix—Cannonball Adderley
   Beck—Joe Beck
   Universal Love—MFSB
   Silver 'N Brass—Horace Silver
6. A Tear to a Smile—Roy Ayers
   The Brecker Brothers
   Tell Me the Truth—Jon Hendrix
   Etta Jones '75—Etta Jones
   Who Is This Bitch, Anyway?—Marlena Shaw
7. Concierto—Jim Hall
   The Way We Were—Willis Jackson
   The Last Concert—Modern Jazz Quartet
   In The Pocket—Stanley Turrentine
8. I Need Some Money—Eddie Harris
   El Juicio—Keith Jarrett
   Sun Goddess—Ramsey Lewis
   Pressure Sensitive—Ronnie Laws
   The Boy's Doin' It—Hugh Masekela
   Native Dancer—Wayne Shorter

March 25, 1977
1. In Flight—George Benson
2. A Secret Place—Grover Washington
3. Main Squeeze—Chuck Mangione
4. My Spanish Heart—Chick Corea
5. Caliente—Gato Barbieri
6. Man with the Sad Face—Stanley Turrentine
7. Rising Sun—Ieruo Nakamura
8. Imaginary Voyage—Jean-Luc Ponty
9. Big City—Lenny White
10. School Days—Stanley Clarke
11. Unfinished Business—Blackbyrds
12. Renaissance—Lonnie Liston Smith
13. Nothing Will Be as It Was—Flora Purim
14. Sound of a Drum—Ralph McDonald
15. Body Language for Lovers—Bobbye Hall

May 12, 1978
1. Feels So Good—Chuck Mangione
2. Weekend In L.A.—George Benson
3. The Path—Ralph Macdonald
4. Casino—Al DeMeola
5. Modern Man—Stanley Clarke
6. Love Island—Deodato
7. Rainbow Seeker—Joe Sample
8. Say It with Silence—Hubert Laws
9. Live at the Bijou—Grover Washington Jr.
10. Magic in Your Eyes—Earl Klugh
11. Loveland—Lonnie Liston Smith
12. Hold On—Noel Pointer
13. Burchfield Nines—Michael Franks
14. The Mad Hatter—Chick Corea
15. Spyro Gyra—Spyro Gyra

January 13, 1979
1. Children of Sanchez—Chuck Mangione
2. Touchdown—Bob James
3. Pat Metheny Group—Pat Metheny Group
4. Reed Seed—Grover Washington Jr.
5. All Fly Home—Al Jarreau
6. Mr. Gone—Weather Report
7. Cosmic Messenger—Jean-Luc Ponty
8. Flame—Ronnie Laws
9. Secrets—Gil Scott-Heron & Brian Jackson
10. Tropico—Gato Barbieri
11. Friends—Chick Corea
12. My Song—Keith Jarrett
13. Images—The Crusaders
14. An Evening with Herbie Hancock & Chick Corea—Herbie Hancock & Chick Corea
15. Intimate Strangers—Tom Scott

Source: WRVR surveys at the ARSA (Airheads Radio Survey Archive), http://las-solanas.com/arsa/index.php.

Village Gate's venerable Art D'Lugoff told *Billboard*, "This is going to hurt. I don't know if we can keep booking jazz acts when we can't reach the public," while Vernon Slaughter of CBS Records complained, "We were one of the main advertisers on the station. We were set to run thirty-six spots for Ramsey Lewis.... We'll have to give more attention to print and urge other radio stations to play jazz." Joe Fields of Muse Records and Quincy McCoy of Fantasy/Prestige/Milestone/Stax predicted that future jazz releases would need to contain more crossover product to ensure airplay on non-jazz stations. Fields no doubt spoke for many when he added, "It's incredible to me that a city like New York, the center of jazz, cannot have a jazz station. It winds up that the big corporations beat us. Thank God for National Public Radio."[62]

Those engaged in jazz commerce could not have known how different their relationship with public and noncommercial jazz radio would be. Commercial jazz radio stations wanted commercial success; programming that brought both steady listeners and satisfied advertisers was preferable to programming that pleased a smaller number of jazz fans, critics, and musicians. Serving the world's largest jazz community, WRVR had pleased some while drawing frequent criticism of the music it called jazz.

The station had programmed some jazz from the very beginning, with Ed Beach's daily *Just Jazz* show as one of its fixtures. Over the years, with the change from noncommercial to commercial, listeners began to notice differences in what *jazz* meant on WRVR. While some jazz fans favored only acoustic mainstream jazz, the electrified jazz fusion of Spyro Gyra and the Mahavishnu Orchestra, and the mellow offerings of Earl Klugh and Hiroshima had fan bases that WRVR and other commercial jazz stations worked to attract that would be neglected on later noncommercial jazz radio. Blogger Will Layman, writing an appreciation of the diversity of jazz styles heard in the 1970s, recalled,

> Happily... I had WRVR to "hep" me to what was great from the past. But as the '70s progressed, RVR wanted to make money and played plenty of what it hoped was hipper, hookier jazz. Eventually, that would mean that they played the beginnings of "smooth jazz," but for a long time RVR's bread and butter was the down home soul jazz that thrived in the '60s and, yup, the '70s.[63]

On the site WRVRLives.org a fan commented, "The station moved from playing plenty of hard-hitting jazz, to losing its edge more and more as it approached its own death in late 1980." Another recalled, "The station provided you with new and old. You could here [*sic*] Duke and Louis on some shows, and Chick and Herbie on others. Jazz-rock fusion wouldn't have got the boost in 1970s without stations like WRVR."[64] Both of these comments, to varying degrees, reflect the greater battle over jazz authenticity and the rights to the jazz descriptor in the 1970s, as well as the role the all-jazz stations played in the contest. By proclaiming it had an all-jazz format, WRVR therefore asserted, by declaration, that whatever you heard on WRVR was jazz.

The commercial all-jazz format did bring a wide range of music into contact. On one of the few WRVR airchecks in circulation, the Ramsey Lewis–Earth, Wind, and Fire collaboration "Sun Goddess" was followed, after commercials, by Louis Armstrong. On another occasion a Patti Austin record led immediately into a commercial promoting an appearance by the adventurous Sam Rivers quartet, with Joe Daley, Barry Altschul, and Dave Holland, at the midtown club Storyville, a name evocative of traditional (Dixieland) jazz. But that contact was not always appreciated by jazz stalwarts.

The noted jazz critic Leonard Feather was a conniosseurial advocate for the jazz that agreed with his tastes. His 1975 article about the jazz crossover phenomenon attempts to take a largely neutral tone, recognizing the validity of soul, rock, and classical music as expressive forms while respecting the inclinations of *Billboard*'s largely non-jazz readership. Feather asks aloud how to categorize this crossover music and questions its entitlement to be described as jazz, even as radio stations such as WRVR explicitly did so in their crossover-rich jazz formats.[65] Throughout the article Feather uses the language of a rigid jazz purist. He approvingly describes the founders of Blue Note Records as "traditionalist-oriented purists" who created a label that produced hits organically. Alfred Lion and Francis Wolff's Blue Note was a place where "one artist after another, without any crossover motives and usually with no intention beyond that of expressing himself musically[,] came up with hit after hit." The label was "a classic case of artistic validity that was translated, over the years, into steady sales."[66] Herbie Hancock's pre-crossover music is lauded as "lyrical," "rhythmically subtle and harmonically oblique." Producer Creed Taylor, Feather explains, blended "legitimate, tasteful jazz" with elements from other styles without losing "much musical validity." Crossover jazz musicians armed with expertise in other styles were no longer restricted to "a pure, undiluted swinging form of jazz of the kind with which the word was once exclusively identified"—even though it is clear the word was seldom identified so clearly. Feather doubly invokes the notion of purity in this phrase, explicitly linking jazz first with purity, and second with the act of dilution by other music styles. More diplomatically, he defends the other boundary of jazz in describing ABC/Impulse's output as "avant garde and spiritually ethereal music, much of it composed and played by artists with a prior jazz reputation."[67] That is, the noisy output of these artists was at least grounded by earlier music of which Feather approved.

Gary Giddins, another noted jazz critic, wrote contemporaneously about the alliance of these commercially driven partners. "Radio and the recording industry are less concerned nowadays with jazz per se than with a momentarily lucrative trend," he warned. WRVR (and here WRVR is a stand-in for all the all-jazz commercial operations discussed in this chapter) was of the same mind as the record companies: Maybe this new thing will catch on, or if only Musician X would play more fan-friendly music we can sell more and get higher ratings. Noting the commitment to keeping WRVR playing jazz that Sonderling was forced into by all the public pressure, petitions, letter-writing, and threatened legal action, Giddins, although mistaking black soul radio for Top 40, pressed his case:

> By capitulating to top-40 jazz, WRVR simply became an outlet for the major record companies.... WRVR will play a jazz or quasi-jazz record if it is on Columbia or RCA, but not if it is on one of the many modernist independents, like India Navigation, or Sackville. To avoid internal friction, WRVR has replaced its authoritative jockeys (notably Ed Beach) with a staff of very cool snake-oil hustlers; in their hands, jazz, bereft of experimentation, innovation, and originality, becomes upper-middle-class party music. They will take a Bob James rehash over a Revolutionary Ensemble risk every time—which is one of the reasons the Ensemble has disbanded after six frustrating years.[68]

Giddins's observation about the preferential treatment, in terms of access to the air, given to the well-funded majors is insightful. In the 1970s the major record companies were engaged in an upward spiral of promotional spending on radio on behalf of pop music and rock, and the level of spending that would impress the commercial jazz radio world was paltry in the overall picture.[69] Further, there is an old distinction from deep in the heart of critical jazz discourse: the push and pull between the commerce, represented by the bottom-line-driven majors like Columbia and RCA, and devoted, music-loving discovery and authenticity, represented by the independents, which always seem to have actual music enthusiasts at the helm. The reference to upper-middle-class party music, though harsh, was just the demographic the stations sought.[70]

Giddins continued,

> Every few weeks WRVR sends me a playlist. Some of the albums are unrelated to jazz by any criteria, and all of them are on major labels. Jazz is desperate for a radio station—as an outlet for the best experimental *and* commercial music, for decent programming of the classics, and as a community bulletin board. WRVR demonstrates, if nothing else, how far underground the music continues to subsist.[71]

(Now is a good time to glance at the WRVR surveys from 1977 and 1979 [table 16].) Giddins went on to laud the jazz programming on WBAI (Pacifica's

New York Station) and WKCR (Columbia University) in a way that echoed the advertisers and promoters discussed above who, on losing WRVR, held out hope for noncommercial radio. But the record labels, advertisers, and promoters would never recover the kind of sales-oriented partnership that they had with all-jazz commercial radio. Needing only to find enough advertising to keep their shows solvent and largely exempt from managerial oversight, the independent contractor jazz DJs on commercial stations, who were more jazz fans than jazz retailers, would play the music they liked—acoustic mainstream jazz—and ignore the new releases they didn't.

Together with the record industry, radio in the 1960s and 1970s was broadening the public's understanding of jazz (that is, playing a role in genre definition) by welcoming this music under the jazz banner. Feather's writing can be seen as part of a discursive process of genre re-formation resisting that broadening. But this period would not last. As it became ever more commercially irrelevant and culturally prominent, jazz would disappear from commercial radio, as it did from WRVR.

The Move to Noncommercial Jazz Radio

The failure of the all-jazz commercial stations was just one more piece of evidence, along with declining record sales, that jazz was not commercially sustainable on a broad scale. In 1973, for the first time, the industry bible *Broadcasting and Cable Yearbook* began listing radio stations by format, but these lists were unreliable and perhaps more useful for examining large trends. The listings were refined with time. The initial list of thirty-six who reported their operations as jazz is misleading (WHAT-FM and KJAZ-FM are absent, though known to still be full-time jazz operations in 1972) and includes stations programming as little as two hours of jazz per week. By the following year's issue commercial and noncommercial stations were clearly distinguished, and by 1975 the publication had separate lists for the principal format and "special programming" presented fewer than twenty hours per week. Based on the data, the number of jazz stations seems to be increasing, but it must be noted that *Broadcasting and Cable*'s format lists are not unique, a station can be multiply listed (for example, WRVR-FM was listed under both the jazz and public affairs formats), and twenty hours per week can be achieved with just three hours per day of programming. Table 17, based solely on those listings, is therefore most useful in illustrating not the absolute number of stations programming jazz, but how noncommercial stations came to proportionately dominate jazz programming.[72]

National Public Radio, public radio stations, and noncommercial radio in general became the reasons why, in fact, the opposite of Fields and McCoy's hopeful predictions concerning jazz commerce came to pass. Rather than create more crossover content to compete on commercial radio, jazz and its supporters found a noncommercial sanctuary. The nearly exponential increase of noncommercial radio stations playing at least some jazz, many of them affiliated with institutions of higher education and other educational and cultural institutions, coincided with similar growth in jazz education in the applied side of music studies. With it came such institutionalizing gestures as the creation of the NEA Jazz Masters award (1982), the 1987 passage of H.R. 57 proclaiming jazz "a rare and valuable national American treasure to which we should devote our attention, support and resources to make certain it is preserved, understood and promulgated," and the founding of the Smithsonian Jazz Masterworks Orchestra (1990) and the Lincoln Center and Carnegie Hall bands (1996). In short, a confluence of movements, actions, and resources allowed jazz a refuge in an infrastructure far more isolated from market pressures than in times past. The result is a broadcast environment under the banner of "jazz" that supports art music—classically styled music and to a much lesser extent experimental music—but largely rejects styles with elements of contemporary popular music; that music must find a place in smooth jazz or dance music formats.

Finally, the 1970s pretty much marked the end stage for commercial jazz radio. There still were late-night, overnight, and weekend jazz shows, but increasingly these shows were either removed because they conflicted with the station's overall format or they were cancelled owing to other DJ-management issues and simply not replaced. Over the course of the decade scores of veteran jazz DJs, along with their listeners, transferred to new opportunities on noncommercial radio.

However, there were bright spots as individual jazz artists figured out how to get airplay, either in general rotation or on the jazz specialty shows. The soul jazz hits from the 1960s led not only to the early smooth jazz of Grover Washington Jr. but also the jazz-influenced music known as funk made by Sly and the Family Stone, Tower of Power, War, Mandrill, Earth, Wind, and Fire, Kool & the Gang, and Parliament-Funkadelic. It was also a time when, if temporarily, the black power movement took a measure of control over black radio and gave a privileged ideological position to jazz.

TABLE 17. The rise of noncommercial jazz radio stations.

Reporting Year	Commercial Jazz Stations	Noncommercial Jazz Stations
1974	15	18
1975	22	36
1978	40	73
1981	59	128

Source: *Broadcasting and Cable Yearbook* 1974, 1975, 1978, and 1981 (Washinton, DC: Broadcasting Publications).

Ironically, the only time jazz has been out of the hands of connoisseurs is when it has been popular enough to reach a mass audience and make mass money. The short-lived all-jazz commercial station era witnessed the completion of jazz's transition to highbrow music. In the mid-1950s, jazz still had enough market power for a few entrepreneurs to imagine that they could make a go of it on radio with only jazz. Yet they surely considered jazz to be much broader than the limited range of styles that dominate noncommercial radio jazz today. As it struggled to remain relevant, not only in a record-buying market with Motown and the Beatles but also in a radio industry rapidly slicing itself up into formats, jazz itself was simultaneously stretching out in multiple directions—adventurous free jazz, coalition-building jazz-rock fusion, funk and Afro-funk, and down-home soul jazz with a groove—and record company executives found kindred spirits at commercial radio stations who enthusiastically programmed these styles. At the end of the commercial era, the noncommercial sanctuary has largely been interested in jazz's classic repertoire and new music that reinforces rather than challenges those styles. Jazz was saved, but it seems something was lost.

PART II

Jazz on Noncommercial Radio

The following three chapters are concerned with noncommercial jazz radio. The blooming and evanescent decay of jazz on noncommercial radio is the subject of Chapter 4, which proposes that the tenuous status of jazz and music in general on noncommercial radio can be traced to a financial crisis at National Public Radio. Chapter 5 is concerned with the range of jazz programming in all sectors of noncommercial radio and the connections between the institutional values, ideologies, and philosophies that drive jazz programming. The chapter attempts to uncouple the conservative/progressive discourses regarding jazz music and jazz radio. Finally, the entire range of noncommercial jazz radio is examined in Chapter 6, including examples of public, community, college, and low-power jazz radio stations and their programming.

There are a number of fine books on the history of noncommercial broadcasting that describe in far greater detail the birth, growth, and flaws of the sector than space allows here, but a brief recap of how educational, community, and public radio were formed and what distinguishes them will be useful in understanding jazz on noncommercial radio.[1] An anti-corporate, public service model of radio broadcasting was first advocated in the 1920s. With few exceptions, this approach was all but crushed by the communications corporations' chokehold on policymaking, only to find new life on FM radio. Looking back on the FCC's reservation of a portion of the FM band for educational and noncommercial use in 1945, it is possible to see certain similarities with the 1967 legislation that enabled public radio. In both cases, advocates of "educational" radio benefited by the far greater attention given to television.

The early university-owned radio stations, the project of both communications (speech and rhetoric) and physics and electrical engineering departments, had a rough time from commercial industry in the 1920s and 1930s. Stations licensed to educational institutions faced constant attacks and procedural challenges to their licenses, and limitations on their power outputs and antenna radiation patterns limited their audiences and reach. However, with the broadcast industry's short- and long-range attention focused on the AM radio network and later the television network, advocates of educational broadcasting managed to get the lower 4 MHz, or twenty channels, set aside for noncommercial use in the 1945 relocation of the FM broadcast band.

The corpus of university or student-owned stations came to include FM stations that grew out of radio clubs and unlicensed AM carrier wave stations—distributed on campus via the electrical wiring in the buildings—that often indulged youthful, exploratory, and idealistic tastes in music, comedy, and drama. Public radio was another matter altogether, though these stations might be licensed to universities or other nonprofit institutions. Created by the largest of the educational broadcasters, and finally implemented by the organizational framework of the Corporation for Public Broadcasting, public radio evolved into a professional medium and drew talented and enthusiastic broadcasters, executives, writers, producers, journalists, hosts, and technicians that created NPR, its familiar programs, and its competing programming services.

Each of these sectors of noncommercial radio—public, college, and community—has a relationship with jazz radio, and for each, jazz has a range of meanings that contribute to its vitality and visibility on the medium. In the public radio sector, jazz is experiencing dramatic curtailment, if not extinction, as public radio stations look to establish a uniform programming identity across the broadcast day. Ripples from this shake-up are even reaching some community stations. Both jazz radio and jazz on radio are under threat.

4

Paradise Found, Paradise Lost
The Rise and Fall of Jazz on Noncommercial Radio

> Broadcasts of music, a public good of matchless nonfinancial value for human life, becomes a frill that can be traded away for news and information—another service that is also valuable but not interchangeable and that meets entirely different human needs.
> —David Duff

> Many stations could fulfill their mission without so much as a single person ever listening.
> —Tom Church

During the 1970s and well into the maturation of National Public Radio in the 1980s, classical music and jazz were critical components of noncommercial radio programming.[1] In the adolescence of the record industry in the 1950s, jazz and classical music were still important money makers. Considerable promotional resources were directed at those genres, and commercial radio continued to make some time for both. The major labels still enjoyed the prestige of their classical catalogs, and some of the younger executives supported jazz and folk music. But it was largely the independent labels that promoted the new developments in jazz, blues, rhythm and blues, and rock and roll. In particular it was pop singers, but also jazz, classical, Broadway show recordings, and folk music that accounted for the sales of the newly developed long-playing record, or LP (1948), which earned higher margins than did singles. Sales of 45 rpm singles (starting in 1949, when 78 rpm records were being phased out) continued the single-song-per-side tradition of music retailing that dated to Edison's wax cylinders.[2] Rock and roll was a catalyst for change, first developing a youthful and active market of singles purchasers and then transitioning them as older fans to buying LPs. By the 1970s, however, the now very large and very mature record industry was devoted mainly to selling rock and pop LPs and considered classical and jazz as legacy lines of business, still dependable and prestigious but small-time earners compared to pop, rock, and soul. Depending on your point of view, commercial radio either reflected this reordering or ushered it into existence.

By the 1970s these once-important music genres were being abandoned by commercial radio, and three sectors of noncommercial radio—public, community, and college—realized that programming them would be a real service to a significant radio audience, and service was paramount in mission-oriented community and public radio. There was a deliberate attempt in all corners of noncommercial radio to present alternatives to commercial radio programming. In this early period (1970s to mid-1980s), "Public radio was," according to public radio pioneer Jack W. Mitchell, "once the refuge of programming aimed at niches too small to interest commercial services . . . such as classical, opera, jazz, blues, folk, bluegrass, big band, or gospel."[3] Jazz has always had its fans and stalwarts. It made sense for noncommercial radio to grab jazz as it fell from commercial stations.

Jazz is heard overwhelmingly on noncommercial radio stations, yet it is hard to establish how many stations today play jazz. During a roundtable on the state of the field on NPR, Tom Thomas of the public radio research firm Station Research Group estimated that there were very few full-time jazz outlets in 2006. "Stations that really commit themselves to jazz programming—doing it day-in, day-out, across the week and throughout the year—actually are in pretty stable and, in fact, improving financial shape. But that's only about 20, 25 stations these days. It's not a huge number [out] of [the] public radio stations across the country," he noted.[4] Thomas clouded the issue a bit by including in his count only financially "stable" public radio stations, and his count neglected college, community, and low-power operations.

According to a 2012 Arbitron report on public radio listening, of a survey population of 1,235 noncommercial stations—note that the FCC had issued "educational" FM licenses to roughly 3,700 stations, but this figure includes religious broadcasters and a number of repeater stations that simulcast content—that fifty-eight, or 5 percent, were jazz-formatted, and another twenty-one were "News-Jazz," meaning 30 percent news and 30 percent daytime jazz programming.[5] This is in rough agreement with this author's findings (see appendix B) of sixty-three self-reported noncommercial radio stations, a total that includes community, low-power FM, and college radio stations.[6] More numbers? One industry insider who surveys jazz radio airplay tracks about seventy-five stations, while another count, provided by a record company executive involved in radio promotion, yielded eighty-nine (some, like KCRW, are definitely not considered jazz stations).

The 2010 *Broadcasting and Cable Yearbook* reported that of the 317 radio stations broadcasting a significant number of hours of jazz programming, 288 were noncommercial.[7] The 2010 yearbook also listed an additional 413 stations broadcasting fewer than twenty hours (and as little as a single hour) of jazz weekly. As impressive as these numbers are, they are already evidence of an erosion of jazz programming on U.S. airwaves. In 1986 there were 276 radio stations reporting a jazz format, 235 of them noncommercial, but there were also an additional 506 stations reporting twenty hours or less of jazz programming. More significant, over that period noncommercial radio was growing rapidly from fewer than 1,250 stations in 1986 to almost 3,300 stations by the end of 2010. Almost half of the stations surveyed in 1986 played some jazz; less than a quarter did so in 2010. Sadly, noncommercial jazz radio has been disappearing for more than thirty-five years.[8]

By the start of the new millennium, the movement to news, talk, and information was well under way in the industry, including those jazz-oriented stations. Stations that previously were likely to take an omnibus programming approach were, at minimum, programming news and talk in the periods of highest listening, morning drive and evening drive.

Noncommercial Radio's Jazz Audience

Noncommercial jazz radio has proved itself a valuable asset to the jazz community. Jazz radio serves jazz musicians, for whom the learning process never stops, and jazz fans, for whom there is always something new to hear and to learn. Both have internet-delivered alternatives, ironically including distant radio stations. Jazz radio has been a vital link between musicians and audiences. With the decline and demise of local print coverage of jazz, noncommercial jazz radio created the calendar feature. Heard on stations big (WBGO, WDCB) and small (WZUM), the jazz calendar would be unimaginable as a free service on a commercial station.

Both jazz and classical music have been proved to attract loyal audiences to noncommercial radio, and both formats can produce highly desirable audience demographics. An audience does not have to be large to be desirable, though of course an audience that is both would be best—television golf ratings are not particularly high, but the golf audience is thought to be disproportionately loaded with the kind of business decision makers that certain advertisers are keen to reach. Eric W. Rothenbuhler observes that in commercial radio, the goal is to maximize profit, not necessarily audience size, noting, "Maximum profits are not even tied to maximum audience size, but to maximum attractiveness of the ratings to those advertisers that do the most radio business."[9] Public radio audiences are notoriously affluent, and hence desirable. A 1998 report in *Broadcasting* cited the higher percentages of radio usage—that is, more hours per day spent listening—by affluent Americans than others, and correspondingly lower television viewing, perhaps the result of longer automobile commutes to more distant, wealthier suburban areas. As the report noted, "Radio formats that boast some of the highest concentrations of 'affluents' include the nearly extinct classical, all-news, all-sports, news-talk and smooth jazz." (It is likely that this report conflated jazz with smooth jazz.) As for all-news, all-sports, and news-talk, they each can be enjoyed by listeners who are trying to *not* hear music.[10]

A 2012 study found that for jazz-formatted public radio stations, 45 percent of listeners were college graduates, with another 32 percent having attended college, and that 34 percent of households had income in excess of $75,000, with another 18 percent in excess of $50,000. The jazz audience also demonstrates a significant gender gap, male and female listeners breaking down to 57.7 percent to 42.3 percent, respectively.[11]

The declining number of public radio stations airing jazz was by then a clear trend, with the growth of information and news programming coming at the expense of classical and jazz formats. In 1992, 83 percent of all public stations programmed jazz; that figure was predicted to be 77 percent over the course of the following three years.[12]

Worrisome to jazz and classical stations was the audience's median age. Approximately 50 percent of news and information station listeners were more than fifty-five years old, compared with 57 percent for jazz and 71 percent for classical.[13] The consequences of this aging demographic, and possible solutions, form a perennial discussion topic among jazz programmers. One paradoxical complication is that younger audiences, attracted by other formats, have not been found to contribute to public radio at the levels that older ones do, whether because of the greater income levels of older listeners, or because of a generational shift in attitudes about paying for music.[14] A consequence of these concerns about audience demographics has been a shift away from music programming on public radio and even at some community radio stations.

In 1995, 54 percent of the audience of stations qualified by the Corporation for Public Broadcasting as well as NPR affiliates was listening to public radio stations with a music formats; by 2005, this figure was only 39 percent. Noncommercial jazz and classical saw their audience share decline from 11 percent to 8 percent and from 31 percent to 21 percent respectively over the same time period.[15] National Public Radio's spending on cultural programming and news and information illustrates this trend. In 1977, NPR spent twice as much on news and information programming ($1.2 million) as it did on cultural programming ($671,000). But in less than twenty years, the gap had widened: $18.7 million compared to $7.3 million.[16] The year-to-year numbers (table 18) illustrate the rapid development of this spending differential.[17]

The startling thing about the 1988–1993 data is that while news spending increased every year, spending on cultural programming actually declined

Table 18. NPR spending for programming, 1988–1993 (in millions of dollars).

	1988	1989	1990	1991	1992	1993
News programs	$10.5	$12.5	$14.3	$16.1	$17.3	$18.7
Cultural programs	$8.5	$8.4	$9.2	$9.3	$5.7	$7.3

Source: After Tom McCourt, *Conflicting Communication Interests in America: The Case of National Public Radio* (London: Praeger, 1999).

over the period. (The narrowing of the gap in 1993 seems to have been a corrective.) Reports from 2017 show NPR spending $83.5 million on news and information programs, more than three times as much as the $25.6 million it spent on cultural programs.[18] The absolute difference is not in itself disturbing because original news coverage, as opposed to "talk," is expensive, and besides, shouldn't the local stations provide more of the locally based cultural programming?

Public radio has, however, become less local and less specific to its communities over the years. In 1981 the British journalist Simon Winchester studied U.S. public radio and noted that stations in both small and major markets were devoting 40 percent of their broadcast hours to NPR programming.[19] The amount of national programming from various sources is certain to be higher today. National Public Radio and its competitors have done a great job creating quality programming carried by member stations. At the same time, the individual stations purchasing those programs have felt the budgetary pressure associated with their costs, making less money available for their own production staffs and resulting in fewer locally produced programs. A few stations have succeeded in producing income-earning programs heard over other public and noncommercial radio stations.[20] In Washington, DC, WAMU produces several national programs, yet reflects the problem: In 2020, aside from three programs (*Hot Jazz Saturday Night*, *The Kojo Nnamdi Program*, and the old-time radio show *The Big Broadcast*), the station's entire schedule consisted of syndicated programs that could be heard without listening to WAMU.[21] Otherwise, from 1995 to 2005 the amount of local programming—including, of course, music programs such as local DJs playing jazz records and keeping the community informed about music happenings—decreased from 51 percent to 37 percent, and only 31 percent of all public radio consisted of locally produced music programs.[22] The case will be made that the influence of public radio consultants has been a catalyst for many of these changes.

The Glorious Peak

Since the broad reorganization of educational radio that began with the creation of the CPB in 1967 and NPR in 1970, jazz has been a staple of noncommercial radio, second only to classical. While some stations, notably community and college radio, had been playing jazz long before the CPB era, its adoption on noncommercial radio increased apace during the 1970s, coincident with the ouster of the music from commercial radio and the growing recognition of jazz as an art form by U.S. educational institutions. Jazz has remained a traditional noncommercial programming staple, but its place has grown increasingly insecure. The fortunes of jazz radio in Washington, DC, and Pittsburgh over the years illustrate the scope of this collapse and point to some of the underlying causes.

By the mid-1970s, free-form radio and the pluralist and anti-establishment principles that rode alongside led to an exciting but naïve period of broadcasting. Noncommercial broadcasters were often either subsidized by benefactors such as colleges and universities that paid the utility bills and provided physical space or they engaged in what would now be called DIY radio, operating on a shoestring, lurching from one crisis of shaky finances, balky equipment, or transient personnel to the next. Because these stations were in opposition to the commercial status quo and its formulaic repetition, they tended to emphasize inclusion and variety, often inscribing these principles in their bylaws and mission statements. True, they took several steps back from an authentic free-form approach, instead having program schedules that resembled a quilt. A typical broadcast day might have a blues show, a jazz show, an opera program, a discussion program, and a progressive rock show and end the day with reggae or more blues. And those shows could themselves wander a bit from their theme. It was a practice that allowed for jazz to be heard on a variety of broadcast outlets, sometimes by the same presenter. As will be discussed later, increasing professionalism and growing budget imperatives would result in major changes in noncommercial radio programming, especially in the public radio sector.

The Pittsburgh radio market illustrates well the shifting fortunes of jazz on commercial and noncommercial radio around the country. At the beginning of the 1970s, one- to four-hour jazz programs were still available on many commercial AM and FM stations in Pittsburgh. For example, Sterling Yates had two weekly programs with origins in the 1960s on clear channel AM powerhouse KDKA: Sunday morning 8 a.m. to noon playing "jazz, big band tunes, Broadway music, Steve and Edie, Sinatra and novelty songs," and Saturday night's *A Little Jazz*, which featured "hip progressive jazz introducing new releases every week."[23] Jazz could also be heard on black appeal radio: Bill Powell on Saturday mornings on WAMO (formerly WHOD) and DJs Tony Mowod and (Andrew) "Herschel" (Venezie) on WYDD-FM (figure 17), very briefly an all-jazz commercial station that morphed into a variety/underground/AOR format (see Chapter 3). To be sure, jazz programs were available on other commercial stations in various time slots, but increasingly, commercial broadcasters left the remaining vestiges of omnibus programming behind them and managed so as to fit more tightly their chosen formats.[24]

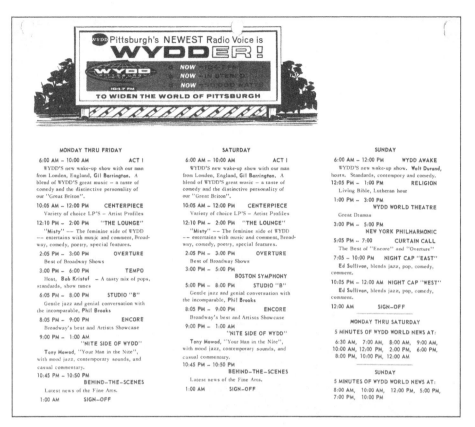

FIG. 17. An undated WYDD-FM Pittsburgh schedule. (Bob Kristoff collection, pbrtv.com, https://www.pbrtv.com/photo-gallery/bob-kristof-collection/.)

Although true free form programming was in decline, in the late 1970s omnibus programming was in full flower on noncommercial radio, and jazz could be heard in Pittsburgh, with regularity, on at least four stations: Duquesne University's mostly jazz WDUQ-FM, "Jazz Decades" on Pittsburgh Public Broadcasting's classical WQED-FM, jazz music at various points in the week on WYEP-FM (a free-form community radio station), and two or three jazz programs per week (including my own) on Carnegie Mellon University's mostly free-form WRCT-FM, licensed to the student body.[25]

What happened to the diverse presentation of jazz on Pittsburgh noncommercial radio? The coming turn in public radio to presenting consistent programming throughout the broadcast calendar would have a drastic effect on jazz radio in Pittsburgh and most other markets.

When the author returned to Pittsburgh in 2015 (after serving as one of those WRCT-FM jazz DJs in the late 1970s) jazz was regularly heard only on Sunday mornings from 6 a.m. to noon—Kevin Amos's twenty-year tenure on WRCT—and during the six-hour block on WESA-FM (formerly all-jazz WDUQ-FM) consisting of *Rhythm Sweet and Hot* and *Saturday Night Jazz* from 6 a.m. to midnight. There was no jazz during those mellow overnight hours; instead, WESA offered thirty-nine hours per week of BBC World Service.[26] And WQED-FM had tightened its classical schedule to the exclusion of popular NPR news programs such as *Morning Edition*, let alone jazz programming.[27] But it was the changes at WYEP and WDUQ that were most emblematic of the condition of jazz on public radio.

Aided by early adoption of the Triple A (Adult Album Alternative) format, WYEP grew from a humble community station known as "the granola station" or "the lesbian folk station" to a public radio powerhouse. Launched on April 30, 1974, WYEP was an all-volunteer station playing music, doing interviews with writers and artists, and making community announcements. As with most community broadcasters, its daunting mix of programming—"an Arabic Heritage Hour, an American Indian Hour, Irish music and jazz"—resulted in a small listening audience.[28] Under new and effective management and with its new Triple A format, WYEP prospered and by 2011 was in a position to purchase jazz station WDUQ when its owner Duquesne University, seeking an infusion of cash, put the station on the market. The result was the creation of a separate station dedicated to public radio news, talk, and information (NTI) programming, WESA-FM. After this change Pittsburgh's noncommercial stations had been neatly groomed; WQED was classical music, WYEP was Triple A, WESA was NTI, and WRCT remained a freeform-ish college station.

Over the same period of change, from the mid-1970s until about 2000, Washington, DC, underwent a process very similar to Pittsburgh's. Washington boasted jazz at various times on commercial WRC-AM (hosted by Paul Anthony—the voice of "You give us 22 minutes, we'll give you the world"), WLMD-AM, WMAL-AM, and WHUR-FM, and on noncommercial WETA-FM, WAMU-FM, WDCU-FM, and WPFW-FM in the 1970s. In 1977 the jazz boom was remarkable enough to draw the notice of *Washington Post* reporter Hollie West, who wrote:

> Saturday nights in Washington are fest time for people who listen to jazz on radio.
>
> Many people are torn about where to turn on the dial.
>
> What do you choose—Yale Lewis' comforting modern sounds on WETA-FM, Byron Morris' more contemporary offerings on WPFW-FM, or Russell Williams' avant-garde servings on WAMU-FM?
>
> And for the everyday jazz listener, there are healthy doses of jazz throughout the week. WGTB-FM, the Georgetown University station, has six different jazz shows. WAMU-FM, owned by American University, devotes

14-1/2 hours to jazz each week. Most of the jazz on WETA-FM comes in one chunk—the seven hours Lewis does on Saturday nights.

Leading the pack is WPFW, the newest radio station in town, which programs a healthy 104 hours of jazz a week.

Washington is in the midst of a resurgence of jazz on radio. It wasn't always this way. Five years ago, jazz on radio was confined to two local stations—WMAL and WHUR-FM. Since then, however, the latter, the Howard University station, has opted for more programming of the black disco sound.[29]

West's only mention of WMAL's nightly jazz host Felix Grant, the dean of Washington jazz DJs, was a comparison of style and content:

FM is much more experimental than the music on AM radio. Jazz purists, particularly the young, wouldn't pause to tune in Felix Grant, who might be playing Freddie Hubbard's disco records, when they can listen to an FM announcer playing a 45-minute clanging, dissonant solo by pianist Cecil Taylor or six different versions of "Star Dust" by various performers.[30]

West's critique of purists may have been a bit harsh, but it reflected a frustration common among jazz lovers. Grant had to work within the constraints of his MOR station, but he had nevertheless built a solid following among jazz fans. Also, Grant, who had a policy of featuring new releases and regularly interviewed internationally prominent musicians on his program, was considered a nationally important figure in the jazz industry.

Jazz radio in Washington, DC, peaked in the mid-1980s. "There's more now than there ever was," proclaimed Grant himself in 1986, when he was hosting a four-hour weekend show on AM station WWRC after the end of his thirty-year run weeknights on WMAL.[31] In addition to heavy jazz programming on WDCU and WPFW, there were weekly programs on WGMS (570 AM/103.5 FM), WAMU (88.5), WLTT (94.7), WDJY (100.3), and WETA (90.9).[32]

In 2024 only the Pacifica Foundation's WPFW (Jazz and Justice Radio) remains as a significant jazz voice in metro Washington, though it has been joined since 2016 by the low-power station WOWD. American University's WAMU, which featured weekend jazz and daily afternoon bluegrass during the 1970s and 1980s, has gone full time NTI. The nearly forty-year-old local program *Hot Jazz Saturday Night*, cancelled in 2018 but back on the air in 2021, is WAMU's only jazz program. The Washington Educational Telecommunications Association, owner of WETA-FM, has chosen to concentrate on classical music. Howard University (discussed in detail in Chapter 3) realized the earning possibilities of WHUR's location in the commercial portion of the FM band at 96.3 MHz and has become one of the nation's leading Urban

Contemporary stations. And WMAL's nightly *Album Sound* with Felix Grant ended with his departure first to WWRC and later to the now defunct WDCU in the early 1980s.

WDCU was a vital jazz radio resource in DC, and its loss is still felt by fans. It was owned by the University of the District of Columbia and featured a jazz, gospel, and community affairs lineup until its sale to National Cable Satellite Corporation on behalf of C-SPAN (the Cable Satellite Public Affairs Network) in 1997. In that year, facing a budget crisis, the District government sold the station for a one-time revenue bump of $13 million. The opportunity to own a radio station reaching listeners in the nation's capital reportedly drove the sale price to between five and ten times its perceived market value, though UDC had obtained the station from Georgetown University (then WGTB-FM) in 1980 for $1.[33] Ironically, whereas UDC had sold the station for fiscal relief, Georgetown had sold it after years of troublesome clashes between the students and its Jesuit administration over controversial program content, which often supported abortion and gay rights.[34]

Diminished Chords

It may very well be that the social conditions and aesthetic rationales that put jazz music on radio schedules in the 1980s and 1990s do not seem as compelling as they once were. That is, mission statements that prioritized the presentation of culturally valuable music to the public may have been amended since then. But listeners have not driven noncommercial radio to different music genres.[35] Rather, noncommercial radio, and in particular public radio, have turned away from music because news, talk, and information programming is thought to please more desirable listeners.

Beginning in the 1980s, diminished federal funding of public radio in real dollars, and the unease those reductions produced, resulted in stations' seeking stable, or better yet, growing audiences and alternative funding sources so as to continue operation. From the outset, the CPB gave local stations a strong push in this direction through the qualification standards it imposed on stations seeking federal funds for buying programs and improving facilities. The CPB choose to give financial support to a relatively small number of strong stations rather than sprinkling funds on stations throughout the sector.[36] Periodically, the CPB has ratcheted up the paid staffing and operating-hour requirements, and in 1996 it added audience standards to its qualification process. Stations had to meet either ratings standards or local fundraising targets to receive CPB funds. Those that did would be rated as CPB-eligible.[37]

Public radio stations with large budgets and those with in-market competition from other noncommercial broadcasters face acute pressure to achieve and maintain those audience numbers. Noncommercial radio has largely avoided offering fare that is available on commercial stations, but this doesn't mean that all noncommercial stations have been satisfied to merely offer alternative programming to small audiences. Conversely, student-run college stations, community stations with small budgets and large volunteer workforces, and stations whose mission is serving underserved communities seem somewhat more resistant, but not totally immune, to translating these budgetary pressures into programming decisions, and this seems to be due in part to these stations' avoiding CPB eligibility. Understanding the distinctions between different types of noncommercial radio stations, their missions, and their audiences is vital to understanding the nature of jazz radio programming today.

Most noncommercial stations are, to some degree, dependent on some combination of listener support and underwriting in order to meet their budgetary obligations and remain in operation. Exceptions include some college radio stations that are staffed by volunteers and receive space and utilities from the host institution, as well as certain religious broadcasters for whom dedication to the mission is not evaluated by audience size.

In any case, the sine qua non of noncommercial broadcasters is maintaining operations and fulfilling the mission of the station or the license-holding organization. Staying on the air is essential to fulfilling the mission. In contrast, the primary goal of the commercial broadcaster is producing operating profit and shareholder value. Naturally, there are exceptions—there have been commercial stations operated at a loss or near-loss by community service–oriented businesspersons or reflecting the political philosophy or values of an owner with a personal interest—but for the most part the content of commercial radio stations is secondary to the mission of earnings and profit, and this accounts for the frequent churn in their formats.

Radio formats are not only about audience size. In commercial radio, the value of the station's audience to advertisers, demonstrated by detailed demographics and other factors, is critically important. It can be the case that a much smaller but hard-to-reach audience of profligate spenders may produce more profit for a radio station than a larger audience that is perceived as parsimonious, impoverished, or undesirable.

Today, noncommercial stations, though in the game to fulfill their mission, are not immune to a similar calculus regarding audience. Public radio consultants, having applied scientific audience research to the noncommercial radio sector since the early 1980s, have used listener utility models to convince station boards and managers that public radio stations that offer more uniform programming attract listeners who tune in more hours per day and who are then more likely to support the station by subscribing. The change in strategy was a reassessment supported by fear, and it ran counter to the founding principles of public radio. National Public Radio founder Bill Siemering's 1970 mission statement declared that NPR "will not regard its audience as a 'market' . . . but as curious, complex individuals who are looking for some understanding, meaning, and joy," yet the adoption of market-based audience analysis strategies and principles has grown solid roots in public radio.[38]

This trend has had a decisively negative impact on jazz airplay since its 1980s peak because stations employing these programming strategies have accordingly abandoned variety programming for consistent programming, that is, instead of airing blocks of news, classical, bluegrass, and jazz, they turned the bulk of the lineup over to just one musical style or to news only. In small markets there may be no jazz on public radio as the station pursues a consistent classical or AAA format or the talk-intensive NTI. Even in markets with several noncommercial stations within range, where there were once several jazz programs, there may be none as one station moves to be the NTI station, another the AAA station, and yet another the classical-news station. In Boston, both leading public stations, WGBH and WBUR, are locked in combat as NTI stations.

By one measure, the share of public radio stations broadcasting a variety of music plummeted from 23 percent in 2004 to 3 percent in 2011.[39] Variety is out because public stations are looking for listeners who "don't touch that dial" during the programming day; fans of one musical style, say, jazz, are unlikely to stay to listen to alternative. By notions of listener utility, listeners who regularly tune in to a station but who do not stay with that station all day are less likely to become subscribers. By this reasoning, any consistent format is preferable to a mix, and those with higher subscription rates are even better.

Here the tradeoffs begin. Alternative and Triple A attract younger listeners, but they are less likely to become public radio station members. (This must only be getting worse as the notion of "buying" music fades from memory.) Classical and jazz listeners are loyal and subscribe, but the median age of this audience is of concern. The audience for the NTI format is similar in age but has a great advantage over the music formats; news programming has been the clear winner in attracting corporate underwriting. Public radio stations and their consultants have come to regard news and information programming as the best content for their goals of attracting loyal audiences that will yield the best subscription rates. In acknowledgment, and with a note of poorly edited self-congratulation, one consulting report notes: "As a result, public [sic] radio's service has shifted away from local production toward network production, away from music-based content toward news, information, and entertainment."[40]

Many listeners and critics find the trend away from local production quite disturbing and homogenizing. Sharing programs across markets exploits one of the natural economies of scale enabled by network broadcasting but conceivably reduces programming innovation. It is indeed ironic that now, when listening to virtually any radio station is possible via the internet, the number of local programs is much smaller than in the pre-internet era. (One need only look at the widespread availability of "1A," "Here and Now," and "On Point" across the country rather than local public affairs shows.)

There are examples all across the country, not only the markets detailed above. For example, the only music programs on early NPR station WBFO in Buffalo, New York, today are the Saturday and Sunday evening blues shows, and the closest thing to a local program is the nightly "Capital Pressroom," produced by New York Public Radio.[41] In 1978 WBFO had strong commitment to jazz, with seven hours of jazz daily (2 p.m. to 5 p.m. and 11 p.m. to 3 a.m.) and midnight-to-morning shows on the weekend.[42] All of those overnight hours are now filled with the ubiquitous *BBC NewsHour*. The result of the second trend, then, is that stations that formerly featured jazz programming have abandoned it altogether for news and information, or at least relegated music to less important times on the schedule.

The Turning Point: The 1983 Crisis

The 1983 financial crisis at NPR was the watershed moment for the change in the relationship between public radio and music. To be clear, there have been periodic budgetary crises over the life of public radio; for instance, NPR announced several rounds of job cuts in 2023, and cuts have spread to a number of public radio enterprises. Though boom-bust cycles now seem to be a fixture in public broadcasting, the 1983 crisis was its inconceivable first bust. Most of the changes precipitated by it were not immediately felt by listeners, but its trauma is engraved in the psyche of much of noncommercial radio.

It is perhaps emblematic that one of the immediate casualties of the $9 million budget deficit that exposed the crisis was *Jazz Alive*, a 1980 Peabody Award winner hosted by Billy Taylor that had presented live or recorded-live jazz concerts produced by NPR since 1977.[43] The 1983 crisis set in motion a reconsideration of how public radio was financed and programmed. And that reconsideration caused stations and institutions to find a new balance between ideals and survival.

If it is possible to identify a clear chain of events leading to the crisis, one could say it begins with the coalescence of the educational radio movement into public radio. Educators and educational institutions had advocated for a share of the radio spectrum since radio's beginning. Indeed, bringing education to the masses was one of radio's high-brow dreams. Educators, however, succeeded in getting a handful of AM stations in the early 1920s scramble for licenses, only to relinquish most of those licenses under pressure to commercial concerns by the mid-1930s.

When FM radio service as we know it—much delayed by World War II and the regulatory interference sponsored by the thriving yet wary radio industry—was finally launched in 1945, this time the educators managed to get 20 percent of the allocated spectrum, from 88 to 92 MHz, reserved for noncommercial use only (and, as always, noncommercial broadcasters could also operate in the nonreserved portion of the band or on AM if they could obtain a license). The powerful radio networks allowed FM to roll out in this way because they were focused on the next big thing, television. Despite there being almost three hundred stations in 1966, they were ineffectively organized as the National Association of Educational Broadcasters, and many were characterized by weak signals and irregular broadcast hours. Educational radio was largely unheard and ineffective, a "postwar renaissance in educational radio that was more apparent than real," and suffering from the public's disinterest in FM in general.[44]

Today's public radio may never have been organized if it were not for the capital needed to establish educational television in the 1960s. Efforts to identify both the needs and sources of funding to establish an effective educational television system involved the Ford Foundation and the Carnegie Corporation of New York and ultimately shaped legislation, the Public Broadcasting Act of 1967, that created the Corporation for Public Broadcasting.[45] The CPB was created to provide a buffer between the political process of appropriating funds for public broadcasting and its ultimate disbursement for programs, stations, and interconnection needs. During the process of creating public television, the comparatively modest needs of educational radio rode along almost as stowaways and managed somehow to get included in the Act.

The CPB distributes most of its allocation in the form of direct grants to television and radio stations, but it also provides programming grants (to stations, networks, and producers of programs) as well as systems support (for example, licenses and royalties). While doing so, the CPB spends an impressively low 5 percent of its budget on its own administrative costs, as mandated by law. For example, in FY 2010, 89 percent went to stations (about $210 million to television stations and about $61 million to radio stations).[46] The stations receiving the funds are those that are CPB-qualified or CPB-eligible. This concept, aimed at elevating and professionalizing public radio, was established early in the life of the CPB and was crucial to the growth of NPR and public radio. With fewer than 25 percent of educational stations CPB-qualified when NPR launched in 1971, the power, staffing, and budget requirements were designed to "encourage marginal stations to expand."[47]

For some stations the lure of funding was regarded as a hammer. Many small station managers bitterly opposed CPB qualification standards. As Ralph Engelman writes, "Robert C. Hinz, a member of CPB's Radio Advisory Council and the manager of an Oregon station, recalled 'fist pounding arguments' and bitterness because most educational stations would not qualify for federal funds and would have to change their operations and become answerable to a central authority to qualify for full participation in the public radio system."[48] Over time, CPB qualification standards have grown to require higher budgets, more staff, and most significant, audience rating thresholds.

In terms of fostering growth and stability, the CPB's strategy has been undeniably successful. National Public Radio celebrated fifty years of broadcasting in 2021. Its programs have become part of the fabric of U.S. cultural and political life even as it is troubled by diversity issues with regard to programming and listenership. Other consortiums of high-quality program providers have been spawned by the success of the CPB and NPR in creating a public radio sector.

Professionalism implied operational changes, however, and community stations saw those coming. Many declined to participate, valuing their independence and allegiance to their communities, but some could not resist the lure of funding. Indeed, growing professionalism and adoption of commercial radio principles have leaked out of the public radio sector into the community radio sector, although to a smaller degree. The growth and transformation of Pittsburgh's WYEP was an example.

Community stations that had scraped by without funding grants were answerable only to their mission and their oversight boards; CPB funding came with strings attached that affected programming. Critics such as Seattle-based journalist Jesse Walker—author of the position paper "With Friends Like These: Why Community Radio Does Not Need the Corporation for Public Broadcasting"—felt the pursuit of CPB funding distorted stations' goals:

> The CPB has fostered a new professional class within the community radio movement, a group that has accumulated power at volunteers' expense and promoted more streamlined, predictable programming. And while most community broadcasters continue to be grateful for any support their small stations can acquire, others are beginning to wonder if it is worth the price.[49]

With this as background, the crisis of 1983 was precipitated by the election of Ronald Reagan in 1980. Some conservatives consistently opposed public broadcasting, either claiming that it has a liberal bias in news and programming or objecting in principle to government involvement in media.[50] The Ninety-Seventh Congress had the first Republican majority in the Senate since 1955, and the GOP took aim at the CPB's budget. But wary of the funding threat from the very start of the Reagan administration, NPR's ambitious president, Frank Mankiewicz, an experienced Democratic Party operative who had served as press secretary for Robert Kennedy and George McGovern, was enthusiastically determined to grow the network with aggressive expansions in programming. Moreover, cognizant of the CPB's vulnerability to political swings, he was intent on developing funding sources outside the CPB to insulate NPR from those swings. In the fall of 1981 the charismatic Mankiewicz announced, "We're prepared to enter into almost any profession, except the oldest one.

... We intend to produce an entirely different source of revenue within the next five or six years."[51] The CPB budget process featured "forward funding," meaning that current appropriations went into effect in ensuing fiscal years, and with Republicans in power, Mankiewicz expected to receive 50 percent lower funding through the CPB by 1986.[52] The 1983 appropriation did fall from $172 million to $137 million, about 20 percent, giving credence to his dismal budget forecast. The budget hit was bad news at a bad time for NPR. As NPR pioneer Jack Mitchell explained, the ramifications for the network were more severe than for individual stations:

> The impact on public broadcasting as a whole was less serious than one might think. Federal support through CPB had never grown to the levels Lyndon Johnson and the Carnegie Commission envisioned. In 1982, CPB provided only about 20 percent of all the revenue for public radio and television. A 20 percent reduction in 20 percent of their budgets translated into a real cut for most public broadcasters of less than 4 percent of total revenue. Individual stations could cover the loss through increased revenues from nonfederal sources or reduced expenses, and all of the publicity over the Reagan "attack" on public broadcasting generated increased private donations to stations that in most cases more than made up for the federal cuts.
> Not so for National Public Radio. CPB had created National Public Radio and totally funded it. Having a single source of relatively assured funding helped give NPR the ability to create a distinctive program service over a period of a dozen years, in contrast to television[,] which faced constantly shifting fortunes. NPR's advantage turned into a significant disadvantage when its single source of funding was no longer assured. For NPR, a 20 percent cut in funding from CPB translated into a full 20 percent cut in its budget.[53]

Mankiewicz recognized the vulnerability caused by single-source funding and sought in advance to diversify NPR's revenues. What Mankiewicz and the NPR board approved was a plan to reduce dependence on CPB funds by aggressively seeking direct corporate underwriting of the network. Under his leadership, NPR hoped to develop "a new and invigorating underwriting campaign, sales of cassettes of NPR programs and other projects."[54] Mankiewicz also sought to develop profit-generating technological assets, notably by operating the network's own satellite system, whose excess capacity could be sold to other users. By comparison, NPR had paid $3.5 million for satellite service in 1981.[55]

The plan had merit. One can look at the value created today by public radio programming and see the revenue potential. A key factor was the focus on increased corporate underwriting. The rules concerning what was allowable in underwriting announcements have been gradually relaxed over the life of public radio to encourage this source of revenue.[56] Today, underwriting is the largest source of income for many public radio stations, and it is this dependence that has largely fueled its turn from music to news. While the Mankiewicz plan had merit on the revenue side, realizing those revenues, getting them flowing, called for spending, or investment, if you will, that threw the NPR budget entirely out of whack. A *Washington Post* interview explained:

> "Our fund-raising goals were . . . extremely ambitious, but at the time we were having active discussions with some major funders who could go a long way to making those goals realistic," said Tom Warnock, the second-in-command at NPR. But, those funders, he said in an interview, "dragged on, or helped out at a lower level." After that, NPR's financial difficulties "all sort of snowballed."
>
> Warnock said that, when contributions from private corporations and foundations lagged, he and Mankiewicz did not immediately turn their attention to vigorous cost-cutting because, "If you devote your time to cutting back and cutting staff, you can't devote your time to getting the increased revenue. It becomes a self-defeating spirit. . . . We were concerned with making the income projections come true instead of concentrating on cutting expenses."[57]

According to congressional testimony, when the 1983 fiscal year began in October 1982 NPR was spending at a $30 million annual rate while income was arriving at roughly a $20 million rate.[58] That spending included a 17 percent staff increase, employee raises, and startup spending on NPR Ventures, the subsidiary designed to ultimately reduce dependence on CPB funding.[59]

The crisis was resolved, but not without pain and changes. Eighty-four Washington-based staff members were fired, and NPR, seeking an advance on its future CPB disbursements, was instead permitted to borrow $7 million from the CPB to close its deficit. Within a week of the budget disclosures, on April 20, 1983, Frank Mankiewicz announced his impending departure.[60] National Public Radio would recover and eventually prosper, earning revenues from all sources of more than $220 million in 2015.[61] But the crisis damaged NPR's reputation and weakened the CPB's confidence in giving so much control over programming to one entity. After 1983, the CPB created the public radio program grant fund in order to bypass NPR's monopoly power with direct grants to the stations. Eligible stations would then purchase programs not only from NPR, but also from new players such as PRX (then known as American Public Radio and later as Public Radio International), dozens of other programming consortiums, and, as so many do in the overnight hours, the British Broadcasting Corporation. The new order drastically increased the importance of CPB eligibility because it shifted program funding to those stations in addition to money for station development. The era's political skirmishes drove home the importance of budgetary diversity, increasing nongovernmental revenue—subscriber memberships and corporate underwriting—for the future fiscal health of public radio stations.

Still, crisis-ridden NPR only cancelled two existing programs in 1983: *The Sunday Show* and *Jazz Alive*.[62]

Enter the Consultants

From the start there has been, within public radio, a constant tension between the maverick principles and ideals that found a degree of freedom in educational radio to fully utilize the power of radio and its creeping professionalism, the inclination to obey broadcasting norms as public radio stations often reflected the formality and hierarchical management style of the license-holding institutions. For noncommercial broadcasters, success was meeting the mission of "serving the public interest"—making good music available to listeners, giving arts and culture a chance to be heard, or giving underrepresented political voices access to the airwaves—and not in racking up big audience ratings or earned revenue (although enough money to stay on the air would be nice). Because stations desired to attain or maintain CPB-qualified status, they were increasingly willing to listen to public radio consultants, many funded by the CPB itself, who modified commercial radio management, programming, and audience measurement techniques and offered them as solutions to their problems. As early 1979 public radio general managers had begun hearing the format message: Public radio had to deliver its content in ways that followed the rules of radio.[63] The approaches these consultants urged have greatly affected the programs we hear.

During the self-proclaimed golden age of jazz radio just examined, many noncommercial programming schedules, including those at public and community radio stations, looked much like that of WVSP-FM (90.9), shown in figure 18. The station was founded by Valeria and Jim Lee in Warrenton, North Carolina, as a vehicle for "community development . . . [and] justice work." Operating from 1976 to 1986, WVSP, "Voices Serving the People," was an important achievement in African American community radio in the South (figure 19). Featuring jazz and blues, and producing progressive community affairs reporting, WVSP also gave local volunteers a chance to host their own programs and develop radio production skills. At the time, there was no other station like it in the region.[64]

The ideological and organizational differences between community and public radio stations are covered in some detail in Chapter 6, but the description above gives some insight into the vanishing similarities and growing divergence of the two sectors in the 1980s. At the time, stations in both sectors considered the presentation of jazz, classical, and other noncommercialized musics and quality news programming to be prime objectives. But WVSP,

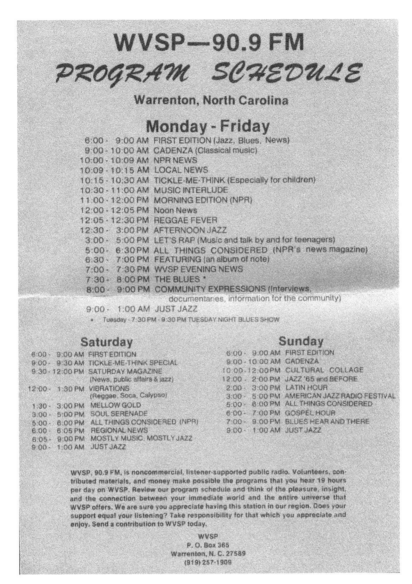

FIG. 18. A WVSP weekly schedule c. 1980.
(https://mediaandthemovement.unc.edu/2013/12/12/wvsp-90-9-fm/)

like most community stations, intended to give "any local volunteers willing to put in the requisite time and work the chance to host their own programs," whereas even at this stage public radio stations were employing (perhaps under-) paid staff and scheduling programs under the careful supervision of the general manager and program managers.[65]

A quick examination of the WVSP schedule given in figure 18 reveals that the station made few purchases of expensive outside programming. The lineup

FIG. 19. The WVSP-FM magazine and program guide. (https://mediaandthemovement.unc.edu/2013/12/12/wvsp-90-9-fm/)

does include NPR's flagship *All Things Considered* and most likely the station's newscasts, including those at 10 a.m. and noon, which were a combination of the NPR top-of-the-hour summaries and local content. The only other program that appears to be purchased is the late and lamented two-hour *American Jazz Radio Festival* produced by WBGO-FM (Newark, New Jersey) and distributed by NPR. There is also a nightly program called *Just Jazz* that, given its length, likely was locally produced. *First Edition*, a blend of music and news, looks particularly appealing.

These differences aside, the WVSP weekly schedule, though more black-oriented and militant than that of most public radio stations, was similar in structure to theirs at the time, with various types of programming sharing the broadcast day. The weekly programming schedule at WAMU during the summer of 1986 is reproduced in table 19.[66] For many years, WAMU had a strong commitment to bluegrass, airing it for *six hours* every weekday with six more weekend bluegrass hours. Even in 1986 the station had a strong weekday commitment to news, befitting a public radio station in the nation's

TABLE 19. WAMU Weekly Schedule, July–August 1986

	Monday–Friday	Saturday	Sunday
Midnight	**First Edition** news as early as you want it, from midnight to 6:00 a.m. with James White	**First Edition** news as early as you want it, from midnight to 7:00 a.m. with Aaron Hiter	(S) <u>Bluegrass Overnight</u> with hosts Bill Foster, Les McIntyre, and Carol Pittard
6:00 a.m.	**Morning Edition** four hours of news and features from 88.5 FM and National Public Radio	—	(S) <u>Gospeltime</u> with Walter Kennedy
7:00 a.m.		**Monitoradio** from the *Christian Science Monitor*	(S) <u>Stained Glass Bluegrass</u> with Red Shipley
8:00 a.m.		**Weekend Edition** "Sounds like Saturday" from NPR with Scott Simon	
9:00 a.m.			
10:00 a.m.	**The Diane Rehm Show** two hours of information, conversation, and call-in	(S) <u>Saturday Bluegrass</u> tradtional sounds with host Ray Davis	(S) <u>The Dick Spottswood Show</u> traditional music with country roots, the blues, and music of America's minorities
11:00 a.m.			
12:00 p.m.	(S) <u>Capital Bluegrass</u> an eclectic mix of traditional and current sounds, with host Lee Michael Demsey		
1:00 p.m.			
2:00 p.m.			(S) <u>Jazz Sunday</u> with Rusty Hassan
3:00 p.m.	(S) <u>Bluegrass Country</u> traditional and middle-of-the-road bluegrass with host Jerry Gray	(S) <u>The Jerry Gray Show</u> country music down through the years, songs of the Old West and a touch of western swing	
4:00 p.m.			
5:00 p.m.			
6:00 p.m.		**All Things Considered**	**All Things Considered**
6:30 p.m.	**All Things Considered** from National Public Radio	—	—
7:00 p.m.		**Hot Jazz Saturday Night** with Robert Bamberger, leading off with an hour of Duke Ellington music	**The Big Broadcast** vintage radio with host John Hickman
8:00 p.m.	**The Fred Fiske Show** three hours of guests and listener call-in		
9:00 p.m.			
10:00 p.m.			
11:00 p.m.	**As It Happens** Canadian news program	(S) <u>The Thistle and Shamrock</u> a program of Celtic folk music	(S) <u>Marian McPartland's Piano Jazz</u> featuring a special guest each week

(S) = Stereo programs; <u>underlined</u> = music programs.

capital, but somehow WAMU found room for thirty-one hours of music on its weekend schedule.

For comparison, recent weekly schedules for WETA (table 20) and WAMU (table 21) in Washington, DC, are shown. Other than the 7 p.m. broadcast of the audio portion of television's *PBS NewsHour* and NPR news headlines on the hour, the WETA schedule is 100 percent classical programming. (Remember Yale Lewis's seven-hour jazz block on Saturday nights in 1986?) The situation is mirrored over at WAMU, whose 2020 weekday schedule was 100 percent news and information programming; its daily program *1A* is offered to other news-and-talk-hungry stations around the country. Although music is sometimes the subject of *Fresh Air* or *Bullseye*, the schedule is all news,

Paradise Found, Paradise Lost   157

talk, and information. Fortunately for jazz listeners, the three-hour *Hot Jazz Saturday Night*, cancelled in 2018, was restored early in 2021.

The public noticed these changes. Writing in *Washingtonian* magazine, Drew Lindsay asked, "Has Success Spoiled NPR?"

> Over the years, as NPR grew in popularity, it came to dominate the public-radio airwaves and erase the homegrown, eclectic flavor of local stations. Hundreds of stations, like Washington's WAMU, ditched the locally produced shows that gave them their identities and hitched their fortunes to the NPR brand. Public radio—once a smorgasbord of music and cultural programs—today carries a steady stream of news and talk shows, most of them nationally produced.[67]

TABLE 20. WETA-FM weekly schedule, summer of 2018.

	Sunday	Monday	Tuesday	Wednesday	Thursday	Friday	Saturday
12:00 a.m.	Classical Music with Bill Bukowski	Classical Music with Bill Bukowski	Classical Music with Bill Bukowski	Classical Music with Bill Bukowski	Classical Music with Bill Bukowski	Classical Music with Bill Bukowski	Classical Music with Bill Bukowski
6:00 a.m.	Classical Music with James Jacobs	Classical Music with Linda Carducci	Classical Music with Linda Carducci	Classical Music with Linda Carducci	Classical Music with Linda Carducci	Classical Music with Linda Carducci	Classical Music with James Jacobs
10:00 a.m.	Classical Music with Trey Graham	Classical Music with Bill Bukowski	Classical Music with Bill Bukowski	Classical Music with Bill Bukowski	Classical Music with Bill Bukowski	Classical Music with Bill Bukowski	Classical Music with Trey Graham
12:00 a.m.							
1:00 p.m.							Classical WETA Opera House
3:00 p.m.		Classical Music with Nicole Lacroix	Classical Music with Nicole Lacroix	Classical Music with Nicole Lacroix	Classical Music with Nicole Lacroix	Classical Music with Nicole Lacroix	
4:30 p.m.							Classical Music with Trey Graham
6:00 p.m.		From the Top					Classical Music with Bill Bukowski
7:00 p.m.	Classical Music with Nicole Lacroix	PBS NewsHour	PBS NewsHour	PBS NewsHour	PBS NewsHour	PBS NewsHour	
8:00 p.m.		Classical Music with John Banther	Classical Music with James Jacobs	Classical Music with James Jacobs	Classical Music with James Jacobs	Classical Music with Trey Graham	
9:00 p.m.		Front Row Washington					
10:00 p.m.		Classical Music with John Banther					

Of the sixty-seven hours of music programming on WAMU in 1986, all but two hours were locally produced.

The replacement of variety, or "quilt," formats with homogenous formats is, from the point of view of music programming, the greatest change in public radio since its creation.

TABLE 21. WAMU-FM weekly schedule, February 2020.

	Monday	Tuesday	Wednesday	Thursday	Friday	Saturday	Sunday
Midnight	BBC World Service	BBC World Service					BBC World Service
12:30 a.m	With Good Reason						
1–5 a.m.	BBC World Service						
5:00 a.m.	Morning Edition					With Good Reason	The *New Yorker* Radio Hour
6:00 a.m.						Latino USA	Freakonomics Radio
7:00 a.m.						On the Media	On Being
8:00 a.m.						Weekend Edition Saturday	Weekend Edition Sunday
9:00 a.m.	BBC Newshour						
10:00 a.m.	1A						
11:00 a.m.						Wait, Wait . . . Don't Tell Me	
12:00 p.m.	The Kojo Nnamdi Show				The Politics Hour	Ask Me Another	TED Radio Hour
1:00 p.m.	Fresh Air					This American Life	Radiolab
2:00 p.m.	Here and Now					Snap Judgment	Hidden Brain
3:00 p.m.						The Moth Radio Hour	Reveal
3:30 p.m.	The Daily						
4:00 p.m.	All Things Considered					It's Been a Minute with Sam Sanders	Planet Money and How I Built This
5:00 p.m.						All Things Considered	
6:00 p.m.	Marketplace						
6:30 p.m.	All Things Considered						
7:00 p.m.						Special Program	The Big Broadcast
8:00 p.m.	The World					Live From Here with Chris Thile	
9:00 p.m.	PBS NewsHour						
10:00 p.m.	On Point				On Point	Live Wire	
11:00 p.m.	As It Happens					BBC World Service	Bullseye
				Schedule Change		Wa.m.U Productions	

Paradise Found, Paradise Lost   159

Why Jazz? Why Art Blakey?

In a 1988 CPB report, radio consultant and former NPR director of research David Giovannoni asked why there was so much music on public radio. "Is there any good reason why so many public radio stations devote so much of their airtime to classical music and jazz? And if there have been compelling reasons in the past, are they still valid?"[68] Giovannoni theorized, with some merit, that public radio's roots in educational institutions played a large role, because "classical and later jazz, are the only two kinds of music which have made it academically."[69] Giovannoni's clients were the public radio stations that mostly had roots in the educational radio movement, as reflected in the ownership and mission statements of these stations.

Because of the impact their recommendations have had on the mission (station programming), such consultants, who brought commercial broadcasting–styled audience research to public radio during the 1980s revenue crisis, remain controversial figures within public broadcasting and with public radio supporters and critics. For example, the awarding of the CPB's 1994 Edward R. Murrow Award for Service to Giovannoni and fellow consultant Tom Church prompted Pacifica Radio journalist and producer Larry Bensky to remark, "[N]ot since Henry Kissinger won the Nobel Peace Prize has there been a more inappropriate award."[70] We have already seen the effects of the professionalization of public radio on the quantity of music on the air. Giovannoni's not-quite-rhetorical question could be answered by the mission statements of public radio stations, but it was those compacts that he and his colleagues wished to sidestep.

In the opinion of many critics, this trend away from cultural programming and towards news, talk, and information is the result of following commercial radio research methodology too closely, with little or no adaptation to account for public radio's mission or the utility of its programming to the audience. It is not that public radio programming has grown indistinguishable from commercial programming; it has not. Rather, it is that the commercial radio tools used to improve public radio's bottom line—disciplined format rigidity and advanced audience metrics—have impacted programming in ways that directly affected the mission of public radio stations.

With regard to the latter point, the consultants have embraced, perhaps understandably, the simplest quantifiable measures of listener utility: average quarter hour (AQH) and daypart ratings.[71] Alabama Public Radio music director David Duff thinks these metrics forward a very limited concept of listener value:

> The love of music has waxed cold for many in public radio. The allure of younger audiences and greater revenue has seduced many of us to reduce or

eliminate music offerings in favor of news and talk programming. *Broadcasts of music, a public good of matchless nonfinancial value for human life, becomes a frill that can be traded away for news and information*—another service that is also valuable but not interchangeable and that meets entirely different human needs. The really important thing, apparently, is that we give our audiences lots of information. If we have time to spare for music, we'll throw a little on the air.[72]

Public radio stations truly are adapting commercial radio mindsets. Whereas accomplishing the mission was once primary, financial performance has an at least equal voice. In Boston, public radio giant WGBH decided to severely cut back on jazz and other music programming in order to better compete head-to-head with rival WBUR, already the news and information leader in that large, university-rich market. Longtime jazz writer and *Village Voice* columnist Nat Hentoff wrote about the Boston jazz community's reaction:

> Later, jazz musician and bandleader Ken Field observed: "I don't see the logic in having two NPR stations here in Boston both broadcasting primarily news and talk. There's an opportunity here for one of these stations—or another—to take on the arts and culture part and really focus on it . . . The community is not served by having two stations doing the exact same thing, leaving a huge gap when it comes to jazz music, which is, after all, a uniquely American art form."[73]

Actually, this is typical market behavior in commercial radio, and it is theorized by political economy. In commercial radio, if a station believes it will earn more revenue from a smaller piece of a more lucrative market segment than with a larger share of a less lucrative segment—for example, being the third-ranked country radio station rather than the first-ranked Urban Contemporary one—it will make the necessary format change. Rather than seeing an opportunity to fill the need for cultural programming, WGBH has concluded that its long-term future is better in NTI than in music, despite direct competition with WBUR.[74]

As can be seen by comparing both stations' schedules, (WBUR's in figure 20, WGBH's in table 22), their programming is remarkably similar.[75] The well-respected Eric Jackson has been on WGBH for more than thirty years after spending his early days on Boston college radio and playing jazz on the commercial station WILD. With WGBH's deemphasis of music, however, Jackson's Monday-to-Thursday-night slot for *Eric in the Evening* was converted to extra plays of American Public Media's *Marketplace* and NPR's *Morning Edition*, leaving only Friday, Saturday, and Sunday nights.[76]

Following the lead of commercial broadcasting, noncommercial stations are convinced that building loyal audiences today depends on embracing

FIG. 20. WBUR weekly schedule c. 2019. (https://www.wbur.org/radio/schedule)

principles of narrowcasting and that classical audiences do not want to hear jazz, jazz audiences do not want to hear classical, and news and information audiences don't want to hear music at all. This same principle, that music will alienate audience members that don't like the style, explains why the music acts now appear in the final segment of late-night network talk shows.

Under the care of the consultants and in keeping with now-accepted public radio practices, noncommercial broadcasters attempting to build and defend a substantial and loyal audience tend to conform to more rigid stylistic models.

TABLE 22. WGBH radio schedule, April 2020.

	Weekday	Saturday	Sunday
Midnight	As It Happens	Jazz Night in America	Jazz 24/7 from WGBH
1:00 a.m.	PRX Remix	Jazz 24/7 from WGBH	
3:00 a.m.	BBC World Service		
5:00 a.m.	Morning Edition	Latino USA	
6:00 a.m.		The Pulse	On Being
7:00 a.m.		Wait, Wait . . . Don't Tell Me	The *New Yorker* Radio Hour
8:00 a.m.		Weekend Edition Saturday	Weekend Edition Sunday
9:00 a.m.			
10:00 a.m.	1A	On The Media	Studio 360
11:00 a.m.	Boston Public Radio	Wait, Wait . . . Don't Tell Me	
12:00 p.m.		Innovation Hub	Living Lab radio
1:00 p.m.		This American Life	Reveal
2:00 p.m.	The Takeaway	Snap Judgment	The Moth Radio Hour
3:00 p.m.	The World	A Celtic Sojourn	Milk Street Studio
4:00 p.m.	All Things Considered		Travel with Rick Steves
5:00 p.m.			All Things Considered
6:00 p.m.	Marketplace	Live from Here with Chris Thile	Under the Radar with Calli Crossley
6:30 p.m.	All Things Considered		
7:00 p.m.	PBS NewsHour	Special Program	Selected Shorts
8:00 p.m.	The World	Says You	Arts and Ideas
9:00 p.m.	Eric in the Evening (Friday only, Radiolab, Boston Public Radio, other programs other nights)	Eric in the Evening	Eric in the Evening
10:00 p.m.			
11:00 p.m.			

An early step taken by the consultants and by the CPB was a comprehensive study of the public radio audience. The *Audience 88* study, authored by Thomas J. Thomas and Theresa R. Clifford, addressed three topics: enumerating audience composition in terms of numbers and types, devising strategies for building audiences, and targeting particular segments of the audience.

One of the important measurement concepts the report tries to familiarize its readers with is the distinction between "cume" (cumulative audience), which aggregates all the listeners who tune in to the station over the survey period, and average quarter hour, a measure of how many people are listening during an interval of fifteen minutes.[77] Radio consultants would come to stress that noncommercial stations did deceptively well with cume ratings because the listenership for each type of program (jazz, blues, alternative, news, folk) would be aggregated, as when a transit agency counts the number of passengers carried in a given month, as opposed to AQH, which is sensitive to listeners' tuning elsewhere after their type of program went off.

Audience 88 was mildly critical of business as usual in public radio (though subsequent reports would be even more direct in their prescribed remedies). For example, *Audience 88* chided stations for taking satisfaction in meeting the high-level goals espoused by their mission statements and was critical concerning a lack of objective metrics:

> For much of their history, public radio stations defined their mission in terms that were highly idealistic, broadly inclusive, frequently paternalistic, and often naive with respect to the opportunities and limits of radio broadcasting. Most stations' missions were, at bottom, only vague directives for actual operations, seldom translated into measurable standards suitable for performance evaluation. As audience researcher Tom Church put it, many stations could fulfill their mission without so much as a single person ever listening.
>
> This situation began to change in the early 1980's, influenced by audience research, stations' growing reliance on listeners' financial support, and practical experience.[78]

Given entrée to station management because of financially driven concerns, the *Audience 88* consulting team's focus on metrics fixes the managerial gaze on market issues: AQH is taken as linked to audience utility, and audience utility is taken as linked to memberships and pledges.

Consultants Thomas and Clifford suggested that, in the new reality of shrinking federal funding, stations needed to know what programming earned listeners, subscriptions, and underwriting revenue. "It was increasingly clear," they wrote, "that some forms of presentation encouraged listening while others did not; that some approaches to scheduling promoted listener loyalty while others turned away even ardent supporters; that some programs stimulated generous contributions while others were left begging."[79]

Audience 88 was loaded with listener data but acknowledged that the actions implied by these data would be painful with regard to mission: "To serve a niche, or market segment, effectively, a station, and public radio generally, must make choices about whom to serve. For many, that will be a difficult challenge."[80] The authors did not consider serving the public in general to be an appropriate course of action, but rather, thought public radio broadcasters should choose a niche, as highly formatted commercial radio was already doing.

The earthshaking finding of the *Audience 88* study was the conclusion that "information programming is public radio's biggest audience draw."[81] For the time being, Thomas and Clifford found it was a great advantage for stations to be strong in news and a single music type, that is, the news-classical, news-jazz, or news-AAA formats. Later reports would push back on this idea, and the WETA and WAMU schedules reflect the complete separation of news and music that is the trend in public radio today. An extreme example of the separation strategy is the programming at WNYC (all news and information) and its sister station WQXR (almost all classical music). The latter has one of the oldest call signs; it traces its origins to an AM band WQXR that began broadcasting in 1936 and from 1944 to 2009 was owned by the *New York Times*. WQXR-FM was an original FM station (with experimental operations that pre-date 1942) that always featured classical music. New York Public Radio acquired WQXR and its music library from the *New York Times* in a NBA-style three-way trade with Spanish-language broadcaster Univision that left Univision with the more powerful station (6 kW ERP, or effective radiated power) at 96.3 MHz and netted the *Times* cash.[82] New York Public Radio bought the new, weaker but affordable WQXR at 105.9 MHz (only 610 W ERP) for $11 million.[83] New York Public Radio then shifted all of its music programming from WNYC to WQXR, creating a music station and a news station. The shift left only the nightly *New Sounds* program on an otherwise all-NTI WNYC.

In October 2019 WNYC ignited a firestorm of opposition when it announced plans to cancel the long-running and eclectic *New Sounds*.[84] In its initial response the station admitted that music had little importance on WNYC: "'The decision to sunset New Sounds wasn't fueled solely by ratings,' Jennifer Houlihan Roussel, a spokeswoman for New York Public Radio, said in an email. The WNYC audience is overwhelmingly a news/talk audience, and we are consolidating music to Saturday nights to better serve that listenership.'"[85]

The Saturday New Standards Show, a great American songbook show, is the only other music program on WNYC, renamed and relocated after the suspension and firing of longtime host Jonathan Schwartz from his similar Sunday afternoon show.

Audience 88 offered a mixed opinion of jazz listeners, which it described as heavy radio users but those for whom "public radio gets only a portion of their attention."

> They are the least loyal listeners. They tune in to public radio the least number of times and the least number of days per week. When they do tune [in,] however, they listen for a while. Their average weekly time spent listening is more than classical listeners, but less than information listeners. *Jazz-dominant listeners are the least likely to be members.*
>
> Race is a significant factor. Compared to other formats, jazz listeners are more likely to be black. One of four jazz-dominant listeners is black; 40 percent of the blacks in the Audience 88 sample are jazz-dominant listeners.[86]

Note that in declaring jazz-dominant listeners "are more likely to be black," are "least likely to be members," and are the "least loyal listeners," Thomas and Clifford did not make recommendations that might result in programming that would encourage black listeners to become *more* loyal public radio listeners or would encourage more black listeners to be members. Rather than an effort to add new listeners to public radio, these recommendations were designed to more cloely bind existing NPR listeners to their stations. Rather than grow the cumulative audience, they would get listeners they already had to listen longer. *Audience 88* and many succeeding reports were silent on public radio's chronic diversity problems and possible solutions, though this issue was known at the time.

The report did explicitly make the following observation with sweeping consequences for public radio: Its data suggested that the diverse-appeal approach undercuts listener satisfaction and may reduce both the number of listeners and the level of listener support.[87]

A subsequent report, *Audience 2010*, released in 2006 by the Radio Research Consortium, was harsher still. Its thesis question, "Why has public radio's national audience momentum stalled?" was answered with a very public grading of the largest stations.[88] Using a curious military aviation metaphor, it stated that stations were either "climbers" (gaining audience), "cruisers" (maintaining audience), or "divers" (losing audience). It called out several of the nation's leading jazz stations: WPFW, steep diver; WBGO, steep diver; KKJZ, diver. A few others fared better: KJZZ, climber; KCSM, cruiser; KTSU, cruiser; WDCB, cruiser; WDUQ, cruiser. In a number of graphs it reported how programming changes had affected the audience trajectories of different programming cohorts. A major negative takeaway for jazz and music radio was that the "steep" climbers airing NTI (termed in the report N-I-E, for news, information, and entertainment) had almost completely shed their music programming. The most positive news for jazz and music was that the most recent success of music stations was enjoyed by those programming local rather than network music services. One might read that as supporting the reduction of NPR cultural programing.

Although Thomas and Clifford only recommended that public radio programmers stick to one style, others came along and applied this notion recursively, with the notion that if a single style was good, a predictable and narrow range within that style was better. After all, the term *jazz* refers to a wide range of music. (Recall the dilemma of the 1977 Washington, DC, jazz listener!) One can see this kind of distinction by sub-genre in the appeals of the news channels MSNBC, CNN, and Fox News. The result is the extension of the general trend of defining formats ever more narrowly to noncommercial radio.

Giovannoni called this move "congruent programming," in which the music of John Klemmer and of (pianist) Bill Evans are considered compatible on a sonic and textural basis, and that of Evans and fellow pianist Oscar Peterson, who have much more in common in musical terms, are not.[89] He asked radio programmers and DJs what principles guide their selections: "How about your music programming? Is it serving the listener or the musicologist? Are you programming for the mind or the ear. . . . Are your segues sensitive to musical texture? Do juxtaposed cuts match mood?"[90]

Giovannoni based this challenge on a CPB-financed study of whether New Age and jazz music could be combined in a single format. His interpretation of the findings was that it sometimes could, but it could not work in cases where the specific jazz selections were more "jarring" than the New Age music it was being paired with:

> Clearly, within formats populated by [Art] Blakey and [Oscar] Peterson, the answer is "no." This indicates one of two strategies: jazz programmers should either avoid this new music and keep on programming as they have been, or they should begin incorporating the new music into their playlist while concurrently culling tracks which do not have congruent appeals.[91]

To one who appreciates jazz, the conclusion that new age and jazz would be compatible in a music format is stunning, and for jazz fans, the idea of "culling" Art Blakey is appalling! More important than the suggestion of introducing new age or smooth jazz into jazz programming is Giovannoni's argument that if stations were programmed with the way listeners listen in mind, they would replace "existing 'genre-defined' programming with 'appeal-driven' programming," and that programmers should think less in musical-aesthetic terms and more in sonic terms.[92] Giovannoni seemed oblivious to the fact that jazz DJs are concerned with mix and pacing, that a sequence within a show that contains both "Bitches Brew" and "Flying Home" does require thought and planning. Indeed, there seems to be a basic contradiction at play. A jazz DJ might program a show as a jazz artist might create a set list—bright opening, ballad, triple-meter tune, blues, up-tempo closer—with an overall shape of musical energy, but Giovannoni's ideal programmers would favor a very gradual progression of mood and energy, maybe no change of mood or energy at all.

Although there are likely to be jazz listeners who sequence their listening his way, there are also listeners who play entire LPs or CDs from their collections with all the contrasts in style, tempo, and dynamics the artists and producers intended. Modern-day listeners will let their digital libraries sequence tracks in shuffle mode, clearly not conforming to principles of congruence. Finally, jazz tends to be quite conscious of the history of the music, and people will sometimes listen to a performer along with the performer's influential predecessors. It can be argued that jazz listeners, like any radio listeners, may change the station when they hear something they do not like, but it may be that a congruent theory of listening is unproven in the case of jazz.

While a CHR station (Contemporary Hits Radio, one of the many descendants of Top 40) might play a few punk or world music tracks, or an Urban

Contemporary station might play some hip hop or gospel tracks, there sometimes seems to be an extra level of agitation among fans if a jazz program plays "non-jazz" music. Serious jazz fans may be irritated to hear vocals by Sting or instrumental tracks by David Benoit mixed in with Gregory Porter, James Carter, and Keith Jarrett. Although this case can be overstated, by and large, radio formats are built around audience characteristics, rather than musical ones. In the example just given, the inclusion of music by Sting and Benoit would likely appeal to a wider audience, if they knew to listen for it; their exclusion would likely satisfy a smaller but intense core audience.

Both jazz and classical music are presented on radio as formats based on musical genre. Not only is this most unusual—commercial radio formats typically appeal to age cohorts by combining a blend of compatible musical styles with a scheme for the music and advertising's presentation—but genre-based formats bring along a veneer of authenticity not normally found in the presentation of music on the radio. The authority for determining genre boundaries is shared discursively among many parties. In his memoir of the days of free-form commercial radio Jim Ladd rather cynically distinguishes between research-driven formats and genres:

> Formats can be highly complex formulas usually based on "proven scientific principles" of demographics, call-out research, sales figures, telephone surveys, and something called "focus groups." . . . You will notice that I did not mention the word *music* in this definition of the format. Songs were thought of not as pieces of music, each with its own mood and message, but as product to which you the radio consumer would presumably respond.[93]

Ladd is describing commercial radio, where personnel perhaps feel more closely connected to record sales, concert attendance, music promotion, and the music industry as a whole than do noncommercial radio programmers, yet his descriptive critique of formats has some relevance to today's public radio. The trend of noncommercial radio formats to move closer in these aspects to those of commercial radio is simultaneously responsible in part for the long-term rise in public radio listenership and the increasing alarm of the old core of loyal listeners who seek alternatives to commercial radio heterodoxy. The public radio audience, which is by far the largest portion of the more general noncommercial audience, has grown dramatically over the years within the context of generally declining overall radio listenership. From an audience of two million listeners per week in the mid-1970s to twenty million per week in 1999, the weekly audience grew to about thirty-two million listeners 2011.[94] Put another way, public radio's share of all radio listeners grew from 5 percent in 1984 to 12 percent in 2003.[95]

Once critical to the mission of public radio, jazz, and music in general, have found themselves excluded more and more from its programming. Far from its peak in the 1980s, jazz has fallen almost into obscurity on many large noncommercial stations. Among stations that have made a strategic commitment to NTI, jazz has at worst—and far too frequently—been banished from the lineup and at best been made the silent partner in News-Jazz formats, relegated to non-core hours. As ironic as it is, this is a result of programming strategies and audience measurement techniques imported from commercial radio, the very thing that noncommercial radio aspires to differ from. It was always possible that the quest for a professional noncommercial radio sector would eventually lead to the adoption of commercial radio's practices; the 1983 NPR crisis opened the frightened office doors of countless public radio managers to the consultants who came knocking.

5

Don't Get Too Far Out

Programming Jazz on Noncommercial Radio

> Jazz police are looking through my folders
> Jazz police are talking to my niece
> Jazz police have got their final orders
> Jazzer, drop your axe, it's Jazz police!
> —Leonard Cohen

Like all art, jazz is marvelously adept at having multiple meanings. It is the music of revolt and of establishment values. It is anarchy and order, it is freedom and responsibility, it has rules and no rules, and it is black music and music for everyone. If it sounds good, it is good. Who is to say what is jazz and what is not? A ubiquitous yet poorly specified entity of great power and intimidation is known as "the jazz police?" For musicians, the jazz police are the scribes, "a cabal of jazz writers, reporters, and critics who influence, undermine, and control jazz musicians."[1] For radio programmers, the jazz police are everywhere: disapproving musicians, and irate and outspoken purist jazz fans who demand playlists of music to their liking, and in general, call for the exclusion of smooth jazz, instrumental R&B, and any music deemed to commercial.

With jazz enthusiasts determining noncommercial radio programming, albeit increasingly subject to managerial directions influenced by scientific prescriptions from public radio media consultants, commercial players such as record labels have limited influence on programming today compared to when jazz was on commercial radio. Tempting as it is to do so, we cannot attribute radio programming decisions solely to the jazz police. The range of musical styles on a given radio station depends mainly on a fuzzy combination of station finances, programmer tastes, and the ideological positioning of music by station ownership or management. If, as William Barlow observes, the "dialectical relationship between ideology and social constraints shapes the contours of community radio," then this dialectic shapes the contours of public radio stations as well.[2] In considering a station's ideological stance, it is helpful to consider what the station or owner declares publicly, in mission, vision, and value statements and in slogans, and to consider just what the sponsoring institution *is*; it is helpful to look at the larger mission and cultural worldview of the licensee. In short, it's what they say, but also what they do.

While there is a great deal of common repertoire that most jazz radio stations play, there are noticeable programming differences, which depend largely on their membership in the public sector/small budget category. The record industry, which now includes DIY artists, has in turn responded in a targeted manner, producing and distributing mainstream post-bop-styled jazz for the public radio sector, focusing the promotion of more adventurous and experimental recordings on smaller college and community noncommercial stations and internet music services and leaving smooth jazz and crossover material for commercial stations and black college radio.[3]

This chapter is primarily concerned with noncommercial radio and its interpretation of the jazz tradition. A fundamental ideological difference between conservative and progressive programmers concerns jazz's essential qualities and meaning; conservative programmers tend to stress the unique attributes and qualities of jazz, while progressive programmers tend to place jazz contextually in a spectrum of African American musical styles. Both value jazz as a "rare and valuable national American treasure," as proclaimed by H.R. 57 (1987), but for the former jazz is an object of art and for the latter jazz is art given purpose. Though race is not always the critical difference, the conservative and progressive programmers often have differing views of the centrality of blackness in jazz, with the former isolating jazz as a special American (black) music and the latter centering—or even de-centering—jazz as the apotheosis of the total body African American musical expression.

As important a determinant of programming choices is whether the station is engaged in the hustle for a suitably large audience, loyal subscriber-members, and underwriter support. Although I have distanced my use of *conservative* and *progressive* from their conventional political meanings, there is a resonance in that the conservative programming philosophy is more consistent with negating the political or ideological implications of jazz, positioning it as American music performed by Americans on American radio, while the progressive philosophy is inclined to resist this "arts for art's sake" stance, which disconnects jazz from its revolutionary political meaning.

Therefore, of the two types, progressive programmers tend to embrace the experimental, the scratchy low-fidelity, the hybrid, and the borderline commercial styles of jazz. A knowledgeable jazz programmer at a conservatively programmed station will, of course, appreciate early recordings by Louis Armstrong, Jelly Roll Morton, and Earl Hines but will be discouraged from playing them by management that is loathe to subject listeners' ears to surface noise and low-fidelity audio. Conservative jazz radio programming is greatly concerned with consistency of musical and sonic style. One conservative tendency is to have a consistent audio profile of the high-fidelity stereo recordings achieved from the 1950s onward, preferably recordings that never fully lose sight of the melody and music that respects tonality. Another is to feature music from a regular palette of acoustical musical timbres: brass and woodwinds, acoustic pianos, acoustic or electric bass, drum set, and guitar (with an amplified but natural sound) and to avoid the electronic sounds of jazz fusion, as well as aggressive funk grooves. Though it may seem confusing, this same mainstream music, that great body of post-bop jazz, also dominates progressive jazz programming. The progressive programmer may, however, be less concerned about smooth segues and more inclusive of jarring experimental music, extended tracks with long, elaborate improvised solos, older low-fi recordings, and for that matter, jazz that is closer to crossover with other popular genres. If this description seems somewhat directionless, it is, and is relatively freer from dogma concerning definitions of jazz.

Critics of the conservative view often take on Ken Burns's *Jazz*, the ten-hour film documentary aired on PBS in 2001 that has served as a lightning rod for discourse about jazz historiography. Billed as a history film, *Jazz* is already in a tough spot in connecting jazz's past to contemporary developments, but in locating "all worthy achievements in the past," it discards jazz's present, and in following the exhausted but durable trope of making great players into heroes the film neglects the communities that shaped jazz.[4] In consolidating its musical range around a core of mainstream styles, conservative jazz programming similarly embraces the nostalgic at the expense of the new—understand that this does not prohibit it from celebrating new artists and new releases, but it salutes that reigning order and resists engagement with current struggles, and it stifles voices that question whether this is the only correct way to play jazz.

Jazz is a music whose makers revere the old while celebrating the new. When questioned, the most innovative and experimental jazz artists will offer as favorites figures in the music going back many generations. All jazz programmers can be expected to play recordings by past greats and established artists, and in that regard can be expected to produce programming influenced by aesthetic impulses. Two essential differences distinguish the progressive from the conservative jazz broadcaster.[5] The progressive impulse is marked by a commitment to displaying the work of new artists and, more important, a variety of styles new and old. The second characteristic of progressive programming is the willingness to approach and cross the boundaries that set off who is and is not in jazz. In contrast, the conservative programmer reinforces the established jazz canon, and the new artists who are aired typically fit comfortably within the stylistic mainstream of that canon.

Music That Is Safe and Music on the Edge

What music is jazz and, perhaps more important, what music is *not* jazz has been a contentious issue since the music's early fans started to write about it in the 1920s. While the music of Cecil Taylor, Ornette Coleman, Oliver Lake, Muhal Richard Abrams, Geri Allen, Steve Coleman, and Peter Brötzmann has been accepted as jazz, these artists are almost totally absent from American jazz airwaves, and especially from public radio stations. There is still significant resistance in all quarters of jazz fandom, including listeners, writers, label owners, and established jazz musicians, to the experimental music traditions that began to emerge in the late 1950s. This experimental music is often edgy and uncomfortable. On the other end of the spectrum, and to a lesser extent, popular music hybrids such as acid jazz, jazz funk, jazz-rock, jazz fusion, and smooth jazz have also been refused admission, as indicated by the presence of the qualifier in each name. This music is safe from a tonal standpoint but considered by many to be too commercial.

What I hope to show is that while there is conservative and progressive programming, it is difficult to map music directly on to those terms. Some very progressive artists do achieve a degree of success on conservatively programmed stations. Musicians like Don Byron, whose thematic projects sometimes are heard, and Dave Douglass, who not only has a range of ensembles but has been a leader in using social media to connect with his audience despite the sometimes challenging nature of his music, are able to sometimes break through public radio's conservative guardrails and get played.

There are several possible ways to map jazz onto conservative and progressive positions, but it is difficult to do so using only musical attributes. The congruent programming approach discussed in Chapter 4 could be called sonically conservative; in it, listeners are not to be jostled by a sudden change to percussive music from mellow guitar grooves. But one could, from a library of smooth jazz—anathema to the jazz police—construct playlists heavy on greasy, soulful funk that would be welcomed on politically progressive community radio and college stations. It's not only the music.

One conservative-progressive discourse centered in the cultural politics of jazz that plays out openly on jazz radio concerns the inclusion or exclusion of jazz styles outside the post-bop mainstream. The boundaries described by Wynton Marsalis, artistic director of Jazz at Lincoln Center, and the principles behind this construction are seen as a "reference point" for what Herman Gray has labeled "the canonical project." The institutionality of the canonical view is central to understanding it. Though Marsalis has been seen as in concert with the cultural-political understanding of jazz as put forth by Albert Murray and Stanley Crouch, which in turn provided the ideological through line of Ken Burns's *Jazz*, Marsalis's struggle to bring respect to jazz finds significant common ground with Amiri Baraka as "an oppositional cultural strategy by African Americans engaged in struggles for institutional legitimacy and recognition."[6] In that struggle, which certainly did not originate with Marsalis but is traceable to the composing and presenting of large-scale jazz works by James P. Johnson, Duke Ellington, and Mary Lou Williams at institutional venues of prestige like Carnegie Hall and Town Hall, Marsalis has succeeded brilliantly.[7] The canonical school shut the jazz door behind them with a modernist embrace of virtuosity, structure, and standards and clear disdain for commercialism, a view that is completely compatible with a traditional and politically conservative black view of countering racial oppression and prejudice with unquestionable excellence, overachievement, a rejection of minstrel foolishness, and a disdain for sinful overindulgence in unearned pleasure. Of being "twice as good." Of being serious and businesslike. These values are also substructural pillars of the institutions—universities, performing arts centers, the Pulitzer Prize committee, public radio—from which jazz has been yearning for acknowledgment and acceptance.

Canonical conservatism sees different problems on either side of its protected slice of the jazz spectrum. Free jazz is chaos, Marsalis has said, and chaos is too much of an assault on middle-class values—the bourgeoisie of black struggle. Meanwhile, funk, soul, rock, and rap are too commercial to be respected as art (despite the embrace of hip hop by the academy) and often are seen as too concerned with short-term pleasure, a clear misreading of funk values. And canonical conservatives resent these commercial products' getting a ride on jazz's short cultural coattails. Gray writes, "In a rather ironic twist, Marsalis suggests that while commercialism contributes to the social diminution and loss of cultural respect and legitimacy for the music (in the eyes of some), popular music benefits, aesthetically and culturally, from its association with jazz."[8] I disagree with Gray there; it is hardly ironic. Jazz has been appropriated commercially and culturally in every era; in the twenties and thirties whites latched onto jazz as a revitalizing naturalistic tonic against encroaching modernism and the human destruction of a world war and a dehumanizing Great Depression; in the fifties it was an alternative to suburban conformity, the "grey flannel suit"; still later, jazz was a fine way to connect refinement and discriminating taste to consumerism—luxury automobiles, fine liquors, and expensive watches, all of which Marsalis himself has participated in marketing.

On the progressive side is the "jazz left," the musicians that trombonist and composer Frank Lacy calls "the Out Cats," a neat conflation of their predilection for playing "outside" music, their locus away from the mainstream resources that the canonical group controls, and their resistance to following the herd. Jazz projects that welcome experimentalism keep jazz moving, avoiding the tendency of canonical projects to in the words of Nathanial

Mackey, move jazz from a "verb" to a "noun." These progressive cultural projects emphasize "movement, innovation, and openness."[9] Gray writes:

> A cohort of Marsalis's contemporaries loosely constitutes what I refer to as the jazz left. Don Byron, Geri Allen, Steve Coleman, Gene Lake, Cassandra Wilson, Graham Haynes, Greg Osby, Kenny Garrett, James Carter, Terri Lynn Carrington, Vernon Reid, and Branford Marsalis draw liberally from a wide range of musical influences. These players expand and extend the very tradition that Marsalis and the canon makers at Lincoln Center want to formalize and protect from the contaminating influences of commercial culture and untutored tastes.[10]

It is a testament to the centrality of change and experimental practices in jazz that many of the above-named artists have achieved some level of acceptance on fairly conservative jazz radio stations, often through the love of the DJs and programmers. Yet a great number of stations would systematically avoid their music. Multi-instrumentalist Don Byron recognizes that his own envelope-pushing music and that of his allies barely exists in the canons of the jazz conservatives. In helping to create a festival of creative and overlooked artists at the Brooklyn Academy of Music in 1995, Byron explained, "I made the case that jazz's left half is being marginalized. It is being marginalized by people who present jazz in institutions, on the radio, in print and everybody knows that." He added, "Jazz is a two-headed monster," with a Democratic and a Republican side, and without the Democratic side, the beast dies."[11]

Within the discursive activity of sorting, categorizing, or labeling musical material considered jazz, it is possible to identify at least three impulses or motivations. The first is a curatorial impulse, and it maps very well onto the conservative activity of canonical projects such as Jazz at Lincoln Center. The curatorial impulse is to value the objects in the collection and acquire new objects that support or illuminate the ones already at hand. Although oppositional objects do enter the collection from time to time, adding such objects critiques the collection and calls into question its value and its truth. Often the oppositional objects serve to reassure the curators and users about their judgments. This impulse is well represented on public radio stations that play jazz.

It is the second impulse, the expansionist impulse, that is underrepresented in noncommercial jazz radio. It is the impulse to use the discursive categorizing activity to expand or grow the audience for jazz, to stretch what is allowed under the umbrella "jazz." The music industry embraces (and possibly subverts) this impulse for its own purposes when it creates such subgenres as smooth jazz and acid jazz and when it promotes the crossover projects of artists with jazz bona fides. Experimental musicians also embrace this impulse when they try to have their music included on jazz radio playlists and have their bands booked into jazz festivals and venues. The expansionist impulse is further underrepresented because it at heart embraces a commercial, market-driven virtue that would quickly derail the mission of noncommercial radio. While its consultants have indeed embraced the concept of expanding the jazz audience, they largely sanction only two paths: running away from startlingly innovative jazz or using congruent programming principles to guide music selection.

The third is the experimental impulse. It maps well onto the progressive activities that Gray associates with the jazz left. I contend that this impulse is merely to create new and interesting music, a perhaps too compact way of saying what Gray said; it wants to keep jazz moving. Not only making new music for the sake of novelty—along with imitation, one of the mother hooks of pop music—it is the truth of the new music's artistic vision that keeps jazz a verb.

Ironically, then, the two valuable sites for jazz radio in the expansionist and experimental modes are community and college radio, and this is another example of why one should be careful with the labels "progressive" and "conservative" for programming, because the wide, overlapping field of music is cherished by individuals and institutions all along the spectrum. There are canonical institutions where experimentalists such as Fred Ho, William Parker, and Frank Lacy can find adherents, and there are militant nationalists who have no need for "chaos." A strikingly anomalous case is college radio. With fewer budgetary pressures and student and volunteer staffs, the lack of concern with audience size seems to free college radio DJs to play whatever they are currently interested in, ranging from blues to jazz fusion to the Art Ensemble of Chicago. Among the radio stations of historically black colleges and universities some operate in the public radio mode and some in the college radio mode, but in general HBCU stations have most of the attributes of community stations.

Where the divergence between progressive and conservative jazz programming does seem to correlate well with station type is the programming of public and community radio stations, with the former tending to embrace the canonical project and the latter being somewhat more inclusive of the jazz left. Community radio's progressive credentials are jeopardized not by the inclusion of canonical music but by fiscal concerns. In fulfilling their mission, community stations sometimes reflect the caution that grassroots black organizations developed in the 1960s and 1970s in avoiding institutional funding. They have seen the influx of CPB and foundation funding ratchet stations away from the mission step by step. Similarly wary of institutional constraints but also determined to succeed without such resources, we find many of the musicians of the jazz left supporting each other in collectives such as the Association for the Advancement of Creative Musicians, the Vision Orchestra, and M-BASE to obtain some of the benefits without the creatively stifling weight of major institutions.[12]

Another confounding use of the categories "conservative" and "progressive" concerns smooth jazz. Also sometimes called "contemporary" jazz, "smooth jazz is a genre of pop music that is distinguished from the pop and rock mainstream by the de-centering of vocals and prominent use of traditional jazz instruments, such as the saxophone and keyboards, and continually adjusted to suit the perceived tastes of its targeted audience."[13] Smooth jazz has been called "progressive," "contemporary," or "modern" by some of its fans, mainly to distinguish it from what they consider the old-fashioned or traditional acoustic jazz forms, never mind that for mainstream fans, *traditional* evokes early New Orleans–style jazz. This additional dimension of confusing terminology is introduced here to disabuse the reader of the notion of conservative and progressive programming having exclusive ownership of any jazz style.

As valuable as these distinctions are, I find it more valuable, insofar as understanding jazz radio is concerned, to insist on a distinction between *conservative* and *progressive* not with regard to which styles are favored but with regard to how wide a range of styles is present. By this definition, commercial smooth jazz stations are conservative; while they claim for promotional purposes the legacies of Miles Davis, Sarah Vaughan, and Sonny Rollins, they play precious little of their music, and seldom does their programming deviate from typical smooth jazz styles.

Mission statements can give some insight into the ideological framing of jazz at many radio stations. Mission statements that use language describing jazz as "America's classical music" or "American art" tend to fit the conservative music profile and are often associated with professionally staffed stations affiliated with educational institutions. The simple insertion of "black" or "African American" into these phrases reframes the ideological claims of the slogans and pushes them in the oppositional direction. Radio stations whose mission statements emphasize that they provide access to underserved communities and voices with views rejected by mainstream politics tend to either remain silent on musical commentary or expressly invoke music as part of "the struggle." The latter tend to be student-run or community stations. In the case of community stations, jazz is often viewed as one among a range of oppositional musical styles including hip hop, blues, folk, jazz, and less commercial flavors of rock, a view quite compatible with Baraka's "changing same."[14] These stations tend to have little concern for uniform or consistent programming and leave the music selections largely in the hands of the program hosts, with progressive programming as the result.

The short-lived period of black liberation radio (discussed in Chapter 3) saw the exercise of this call for black unity and social justice through a broad embrace of black creative artists. This early idealism was reflected in the unifying WBLS roll call ("Dukes, & Counts, Kings (BB) and Queens (Aretha) . . .

Doo Wop & Funk & Rock & Blues & Soul & Jazz") and still finds voice in music heard on community radio such as Ursula Rucker's "Libation," aired on WOWD-LP, in which she shouts out and recognizes ancestors across the fields of literature, art, music, acting, politics, and social justice.

> Makers of music . . . But Not Just Music . . . Of Life. Art Blakey, John Coltrane, David "Honey-Boy" Edwards, Mahalia, Amália, Nina, Ella, Elvin Jones, Jimi Hendrix, Bob Nesta Marley, Weldon Irvine, Miles Davis, Scott Joplin, Billie Holiday, Marian Anderson, Marvin Gaye, Curtis Mayfield, Tupac, Biggie, Scott La Rock, Freaky Tah, ODB, Jam Master Jay, Tito Puente, Fela Kuti.[15]

Libation is a traditional African practice recognizing the loss of ancestors and yet their connectedness to our current lives. Though only the musical ancestors are cited in the edited quotation above, the inclusion of artists and liberation figures cements the relation between the spectrum of artistic acts with the performative act of seeking justice and freedom. The shout-out to the past is vital to the forward progress of jazz, where the new is built on the innovations and truths of the venerated ancestors and living elders. Whether constrained to be conservative or free to be progressive, and whether inclined to program conservatively or progressively, jazz programmers are usually facing conflicting impulses.

Programming Philosophies and Theories

Jazz radio programmers have much in common with other radio programmers. With an assigned amount of time to fill, they have to choose from a wide body of material while working under real or perceived constraints. Here the term *programmer* is being used generically to include anyone who has the autonomy or authority to select music, music programs, or music-related programs for broadcast. Depending on the organization, this independence of action resides with management, program producers, or DJ-hosts. Unlike music in television programs, stage productions, or films, where negotiating the "grand rights" fees for music can break budgets, the fees for broadcasting music on radio are covered by the "small rights" and are satisfied by the purchase of a blanket license from ASCAP, BMI, or Sesac. Hence for ordinary jazz radio broadcasting, the cost of using music is rarely a consideration.[16] Instead, programmers' constraints typically concern the station's overall format, the format, subject, or theme of a particular program, and the suitability of the body of recorded or live music available for broadcast.

The station format, if extant, may limit the style of music by avoiding "way out" free jazz or commercial-sounding smooth jazz or by discouraging long tracks (for example, those over six minutes) and thus eliminating extended improvised solos. For some stations, "way out" is any jazz performance that strays from a hummable melody. (Hummable by whom is a critical question for station management!) A format might discourage or encourage jazz organ, vocals, Latin jazz, or too many ballads. The format may dictate the manner of presentation, amount of speaking, and information—including discographic information—provided by the host. Old lo-fi recordings may be banned altogether. A given program may be in a time slot designed to serve a specific audience segment. For example, a big band and American Songbook program might be aimed at an older and not specifically jazz-loving audience in the early evening. Programs featuring early jazz or revivals of early styles often receive a similar treatment.

One can be pretty certain that jazz programmers or jazz DJs are enthusiastic fans and supporters of the genre, for there are certainly more lucrative areas in broadcasting than jazz. It seems likely that very few jazz DJs on noncommercial radio, unlike many from the commercial jazz radio era, are media professionals in the sense of actively pursuing non-jazz-related broadcasting positions.[17] Many DJs or hosts are themselves accomplished professional musicians such as drummers Jae Sinnett (WHRV-FM) and Kenny Washington, "the Jazz Maniac" (WBGO-FM), saxophonist Bob Parlocha, trumpeter Ray Vega (Vermont Public Radio), and of course the late piano greats Marian McPartland and Billy Taylor. Bassist Christian McBride has taken up Taylor's mantle and is heard often on public and satellite radio. Unique among spinners, the jazz DJ may be providing music from his or her own collection; a DJ's personal library may strongly reflect the DJ's own tastes; it may be deficient in new releases, or it could be comprised of mostly surefire audience favorites.

At many stations the program, music, or jazz director takes an active role in music selection. Despite the knowledge and taste of the on-air hosts, management has a number of tools that can be used to shape or constrain jazz programming, and these are not fundamentally different than those for other music formats. The music director at some stations may restrict the DJ to selections from the station's approved music library. At WBGO, for example, music director Gary Walker approves all music for the library, from which air personalities choose the records that fit into each structured hour.

Regarding more expensive programs such as live concerts, remotes, purchased syndicated music services, and feature programs with production costs, station management will be involved in the programming decisions and often express concerns about the program's musical content. Whatever the constraints, it is radio programmers who decide what music to play. The methods they use to make those decisions are varied. It can be useful to consider jazz (and other music) programmers as working through contending inclinations, impulses, allegiances, or forces that impact their approaches to music selection.[18]

Oppositional Pairs

Jazz programmers are constantly working within pairs of dialectic or binary oppositions. A well-known pair consists of a push and pull that contrasts the interests or directions set by the music industry with the interests of the audience. This *industry-audience* opposition is perhaps well understood in terms of popular music on commercial radio: The music industry seeks to promote new artists or musical styles, while the audience already has established favorites. The music industry has every incentive to promote new, lower-cost artists in place of some of the expensive or fading artists already on their rosters. The music programmer mediates between these industry efforts and the audience's interests. The programmer doesn't just sit between the two, arbitrating each party's interests; the programmer must also decide (consciously or subconsciously) whether allegiance, standing, and influence in the music industry is a career priority. For jazz programmers, influence in the music industry can mean close relationships with musicians, access to performing venues, and opportunities to "help" the jazz business.

Another opposition, *aesthetic-research*, pits the programmer's musical tastes against "scientific" audience research. The experienced jazz programmer has highly developed tastes and encyclopedic knowledge of the music but may have to choose music from a playlist determined by the surveyed findings of a test group. Some consultants assert the ability to extract musical elements that can be used to categorize new music as suited or unsuited for the station. It is possible to read into the aesthetic-research opposition one of the basic oppositions of noncommercial broadcasting—programming what the audience *should* or *needs to* hear versus what the audience *wants* to hear.[19] These two oppositions produce four "pure" programming philosophies: aesthetic, audience, research, and industry. Most often, though, programmers will function in some combination of them.

The Aesthetic Philosophy

In the aesthetic philosophy, already disparaged by the consultant David Giovannoni as the "musicologist" philosophy, programming decisions are based on the programmer's jazz knowledge and opinion of the value and importance of the music and musicians.[20] The aesthetic programmers exploit the expertise they have developed over the course of an extended and passionate engagement with music. Anyone might recognize that this appears to be a traditional jazz DJ trope, in which the DJ is educator, guide, advocate, and talent evaluator for the audience. With respect to jazz programming this philosophy does not necessarily favor a given music style because the programmer may prefer any style or have wide-ranging tastes. In chapter 1 we encountered DJs such as "Symphony" Sid Torin, who strongly favored the modernist music of bebop and acknowledged the greatness of earlier figures like Armstrong and Ellington but played them infrequently. The aesthetic philosophy would almost certainly find conflict with the congruent programming approach (discussed in Chapter 4), in which musical and performance elements such as form, surprise, harmonic ingenuity, and improvisatory brilliance may be secondary to sonic elements such as instrumentation, tempo, timbre, and vocal register.

Indeed, as they have tried to pilot their public radio jazz stations against unfavorable demographic headwinds, station managers and consultants alike have vilified the practice of relying on personal taste. Neal Sapper, an award-winning jazz record promoter, excoriated DJs who programmed according to their own preferences: "That's the attitude that's hurting jazz radio. People are programming for their own tastes. Sometimes it's their own elitist tastes [*sic*] that's limiting the ability to reach out and pull more people into the format. Too often they're programming for themselves and the people who work at the station."[21] Comments such as this blame programmer tastes for undercutting supposed gains attributable to carefully researched and managed formatting. It is probably not an accident that this accusation of elitism also lies at the heart of criticism of jazz in general.

The aesthetic philosophy—DJs playing what they like—has all but faded from commercial broadcasting, where scientific research, music industry considerations, music director–authored playlists, and rigid formatting are common practices inside radio's corporate model.[22] One of the attractive features of noncommercial radio is that it has been perceived as an alternative to the stale practices of commercial radio. The aesthetic programming philosophy can be easily found on community and college radio but less often on public radio, where it is constrained by management concerns about audience appeal such as format values, track length, variety, sonic compatibility, and playlist restrictions are likely to limit the range of music and artists played.

The Audience Philosophy

In abiding by the audience philosophy the programmer develops a surrogate empathy for the audience that "positions the programmer as a stand-in" for it.[23] It might be useful to think of a party DJ "reading the room" while crafting the music mix. For radio, the extreme example would be choosing music exclusively on the basis of audience requests. Totally by-request radio was found frequently in the early days of record-based music programming, as letters, postcards, and phone calls still had significant currency as audience research tools and because the practices of record promotion to radio DJs were just being developed.

This philosophy is one of several in which musicological knowledge is undesirable, in this case because it would create difference between programmer and listener. But in addition, audience programmers will trust their feeling for the listeners more than research or industry information. While this philosophy seems to be more appropriate to selecting the record mix for commercial radio (for example, in the black radio of my youth, smooth singing groups were somewhat more popular in Baltimore, while funk was more popular in DC) public radio consultants encourage just this type of "think like the audience" approach in urging programmers to adopt schedules, formats, and musical content that avoid abrupt changes in style during the broadcast day.

Former KXJZ station manager Carl Watanabe expressed wariness of programming based on the audience philosophy, especially an audience with jazz musicians:

> You've heard the old adage about how a radio host is supposed to be thinking of a person out there and speaking one-on-one? Well, a lot of times some jazz hosts envision a person who is another jazz musician like an Archie Shepp or Max Roach [who just dropped by]. They'll say to them, "I really dug your show, man." While it makes you feel good that a jazz giant dug your air shift, as a result you may play something a little out there or edgy, thinking that person is listening and you want to impress them rather than most of your listeners who are tuning in because they enjoy jazz.[24]

When music director Jon Norton described his process for selecting music at the former jazz and blues station WGLT, he sounded as if he was in step with the audience philosophy. "We have to pull in people who don't think they are jazz fans[,] who don't think they like jazz but when they hear our jazz because they can sing or hum along to it because it's melodic, they think 'I like that.'"[25] He is "not scientific," he added: "Not every song fits my definition; it's more of a gut feel." Norton, who dictates virtually every playlist for his air personalities, largely avoids music research, industry tips, and record reviews, preferring to listen for himself: "I trust my own gut."[26] Community radio, with its emphasis on access and local affairs, in fact embodies a radically different implementation of this philosophy through constant listener call-ins and community outreach. In community radio, each programmer is keeping in touch with the pulse of one of many of the station's audiences.

The Research Philosophy

The research philosophy involves the programmer's "being an informed consumer of 'scientific' and 'objective' information on the target demo[graphic]'s response to the station's programming."[27] In this philosophy, musicological tendencies are again completely rejected. Once more this strums a durable tension between ideas of broadcasting as service or as a business. Whether concerning network and local news operations or noncommercial broadcasting, the notion of "what the audience should hear is pitted against the view of what it wants to hear. The resulting philosophy is responsible for the large amount of time and pride of place that weather reporting receives on television newscasts as opposed to the city hall or school board beat.[28]

A veteran programmer described how research provides a blueprint for programming:

> "You get people in a room, you ask them what they want on the radio, and they tell you. Then you put it on, then you win." Audience research is valued because it maximizes the likelihood that only the most "viable" records are integrated into the station's music programming. Because as another programmer explained, "All the music is researched[,]" he can be assured that "these are the very best songs that we can be playing based on what listeners have told us. We stop playing songs that they have told us they are tired of." The "science" of music programming, according to this philosophy, is inherently conservative, "an enquiry into what is already being played, into what is already recognizable, into what the audience already likes about the station."[29]

In order for the process described above to work with current releases, research panels would need to meet frequently, but the increased frequency of meetings would potentially be worth the expense if the result were audience satisfaction. An alternative would be to use focus group responses to develop a set of sonic parameters that might be generalized so as to choose new music for the audience.

The research philosophy is potentially a powerful technique for jazz radio, since both the research methods and jazz programming can focus on jazz's back catalog. That is, like an oldies radio format, a lot of jazz radio is music from past years. Relatively few jazz programs feature only new music and, to the contrary, tradition and classics play a large role in many adventurous jazz programs. For an individual jazz station and perhaps any kind of music station, the cost of ongoing audience research testing might be prohibitive but, packaged as a service offered to like-minded stations, this kind of research can be priced at a figure that management can defend.

In public radio music programming, research is in the ascendency. The Giovannoni model of congruence has successfully promoted conservative programming on jazz stations around the country. With methodology borrowed from classical music stations, so-called modal music—not to be confused with the jazz term *modal*—principles have been used on jazz stations in the public radio sector. Actually, this conservative approach also affects community and college stations that use jazz programming services. A 1996 article in

Current described the process used by KPLU, one of the major jazz stations and provider of the overnight Jazz24 service, to collect modal data intended to retain NPR's loyal news listeners.[30] "When KPLU and [researcher George] Bailey brought 240 Seattle-area listeners into a room and played 120 selected jazz 'hooks' for them," wrote reporter Steve Behrens, "the testers of greatest interest were the ones who listen to NPR news." The research team found that listeners responded to music not along "musicological barriers" but according to sounds or moods. They found that listeners "distinguished just seven or eight modes" and they projected that KPLU would play "just two or three of those." From there, the researchers applied the modal categories to their jazz library, resulting in, as they say in both basketball and broadcasting, a shorter rotation, because they qualified music not by genre or composer "but by sound or modes (melody, tone, consistency between songs, etc.)" preferred by the focus group participants.[31]

The gospel of modal music has spread amid its apparent success. Several of the most prominent public sector jazz stations claimed success in increasing audiences using modal principles. "With its carefully honed 100 hours of jazz programming," KPLU showed impressive audience gains of 23 percent over the preceding five years and reached tenth place in its ratings market.[32] Scott Hanley, general manager of WDUQ in 2003 and once again at the helm of Pittsburgh's new jazz station WZUM, used the 1996 KPLU research data to claim dramatic audience growth, that is, until Duquesne University sold the station because of pressing financial needs. As argued above, the public radio stations are most likely to employ the conservative approach. Said Hanley,

> We decided to be a radio station first and a jazz radio station second. . . . If you believe that you are there to preserve jazz, then you act one way because you want it to be preserved and saved. I'm the GM of a leading NPR station and a[n] NPR board member, and I believe that jazz can actually grow its audience and become a much more important part of American cultural life. If I believe that, then I need to hold my station accountable for growing significantly in terms of its service to the public with jazz. That means I have to hold jazz accountable, my staff accountable[,] myself accountable it means that I can't let everyone do what they want to do without consequences.[33]

Surely Hanley was overstating his influence in trying to "hold jazz accountable." Jazz and jazz radio, though dependent, are not synonymous. But his statement reflects the tension between mission and market, and the pressure to meet the metrics facing public radio stations today.

Programmers using modal music research defend it against charges of homogenization by claiming that although different colleagues use the same research data, their stations sound different.[34] In 1999 the Sacramento station

KXPR (now KXJZ) was reported as using an automated library and programming application, MusicMaster, to manage its on-air playlists and minimize the impact of the host's taste on broadcast product.[35]

The Industry Philosophy

Despite the marginal commercial prospects for jazz, the industry philosophy is applicable to jazz radio as well. The corporate music industry has been conceptualized as a three-layer entity: the recorded music industry, the live music industry, and the music publishing industry.[36] Unlike the first two, music publishing today is a largely hidden activity, though it is the site of tremendous wealth generation and management. Many industry participants—publicists, agents, bookers, insurance brokers, lawyers—can be wrangled into one of these three areas, but others who are important yet harder to categorize are suggested by Andrew Dubber: music educators, musical instrument makers and sellers, music software producers, music therapists, arrangers, music library creators, database and meta-data managers, web designers, and IT specialists.[37]

There are structural relationships among jazz labels, presenters, promoters, artists, and the radio stations, though these are negligibly funded compared to pop music. The supply of new releases to radio stations is a clear and obvious example, but a network of personal and professional relationships permeates jazz culture. For instance, during interviews for this project the independent jazz record promoter Dick LaPalm (1927–2013) had a personal relationship with every jazz DJ who came up in conversation. LaPalm would arrange for DJs to meet performers backstage and deliver them for on-air appearances and photo opportunities. Further, jazz DJs look upon each other largely as colleagues rather than competitors and look at the music publicists who represent the hundreds of independently released jazz CDs each year as critical partners in jazz radio.

Programmers adhering to the industry philosophy see themselves as part of a greater music industry and their own activities as pivotal in breaking new artists and in being their early champions. These programmers value tips from industry insiders about new releases, as well as advice on how to interpret research data and music industry trends. They regard their relationships with music industry people as being of paramount importance. Most programmers do value their contacts in the music industry, see themselves as being in peer relationships with other broadcasters, and are aware that grooming these relationships helps their career prospects. The ideological distance between noncommercial radio and the larger music industry, however, serves to limit these close relationships in the world of jazz radio. For evidence of this ideological distance, one need only compare the minuscule presence of smooth jazz on noncommercial radio today—it mostly receives airplay in the context of the jazz–instrumental R&B spectrum on black college radio—with the omnipresence of fusion and soul jazz, despite the reservations of many jazz DJs, on commercial jazz radio in the 1970s.

Although noncommercial radio stations and individual jazz DJs depend on a complimentary supply of new releases and reissues, there seems to be little active courting of airplay by record labels in the style of record promotion in Pop, R&B, Country, and Indie music. New releases are advertised in jazz-oriented magazines, and music promoters make their artists available for interviews with program hosts, à la Dick LaPalm. Another factor inhibiting the adoption of the industry philosophy in music programming in general today is the proliferation of independent labels and artist-produced recordings. Rather than the small number of voices attempting to influence music consumption in the past, radio programmers now face a daunting number of new releases, many of which are DIY artist projects ranging from mediocre to top notch.

Philosophies in Conflict

For the programmer, the job can mean simultaneously negotiating the impulses just described. An aesthetic-research negotiation literally means mediating between one's own judgment of musical worthiness and audience research information. For the individual DJ, this may mean operating within a dialectic that pits the DJ's tastes against what is known (or assumed) about the audience's preferences. Of two DJs who like Cecil Taylor, for instance, one may be afraid the audience will find Taylor's music unpalatable, while another may be certain that the audience, if properly prepared, will hang in there. A student DJ may be on the air at WKCR (New York) during a Cecil Taylor festival, or a WBGO host may want to commemorate Taylor's birthday but be unable to find approved tracks in the library. In these last two cases, the aesthetic criteria and audience research have not been left to the individual but, rather, have been enforced by powers outside the programmer's control. WKCR is a station that is committed to playing experimental music and thus creates an aesthetic environment that does not discourage, and sometimes requires, the playing of such music. Its outlook assumes that its audience is willing to listen to adventurous music and has much less interest in research aimed at increasing the audience. On the other hand, WBGO's aesthetic boundaries are embodied in its approved library, its hourly format structure, and other procedures, all of which have been influenced by audience research. One way of considering the aesthetic-research axis is to think of the institutional position or ideology as shortening or lengthening one end or the other by placing a hard limit.

The venerated Felix Grant and the largely forgotten Harry Abraham were profiled in Chapter 2, but it is worth returning to them for remarks concerning their relationships with the audience and the music industry and on where they stood concerning their own tastes. As devoted jazz fans, both had a strong "musicological" sense of what was worth playing on their programs, and neither gave any evidence of paying attention to audience research data. And although both had extensive contact with the music industry contact—free records, PR information, publicist-arranged artists' interviews—their statements make clear that their own aesthetic judgment and knowledge of their audience had the most impact on their programming choices. Grant's concerns about his audience's and his station's limited appetite for jazz constrained his ability to follow his own aesthetic tastes in jazz. The music he liked was always in conflict with what he could get away with. Grant was careful to present music in such a way that the "non-jazz fan for the most part wouldn't really realize it was jazz."[38]

Abraham was aware that the audience on either end of his nightly overnight show was not a jazz audience. Therefore, he wrote, "The closest that you will come to hearing commercial music [on Abraham's program] is at the very beginning and very end of the program. These are transition periods, when that 'other' audience is at its peak."[39] Reflecting his aesthetics, a reference to "commercial music"—most likely pieces such as Chuck Mangione's "Feels So Good" or Grover Washington Jr.'s "Mister Magic"—was not a compliment from Abraham. He also demonstrated an industry orientation, though he showed more loyalty to the artists than to the record companies:

> I lean toward the current releases because those are the ones that most benefit the artist and are most representative of where he is at this moment. If I know Miles is coming to town and I play *Kind of Blue*, someone who is unfamiliar with his present garbage is going to be pissed. *Kind of Blue* is great music but it bears as much relevance to 1975 as the tooth fairy. I play it because it is good music, but aren't I better off playing Woody Shaw? Who needs the exposure more?[40]

With his tastes significantly less muted here, Abraham explains why he would rather play the current releases of Woody Shaw, whose music at that point was more to his liking anyway, than the past and therefore unrepresentative music of Miles Davis. Abraham saw himself as playing a part in both helping jazz artists succeed and in growing jazz audiences.

Returning to noncommercial radio, the programming philosophies of community and student-run college programmers, and their counterparts on public radio, could not stand in more stark relief. The free spirits of the former are almost completely free to follow their own aesthetic judgment, subject only to the limits of station policy. They operate without concern for ratings or continuity with adjacent radio programs. As a result, these programmers appear to operate according to the aesthetic philosophy with relatively little direct industry contact—there are still free CDs, but hosts are curious and inquisitive concerning new artists and new releases—and almost no concern for leaving the audience behind. There is some industry partnership however, beyond the distribution of music. Radio publicists (hired by the self-releasing artists) and the small labels that specialize in adventurous and experimental jazz recognize that college and community stations are more likely than public radio stations to play their music and, with limited means, work to create stronger relationships with those stations and the programmers there. Being significantly more structured, public radio has programmers who do not have the same latitude to air whatever music they want. Indeed, their format guidelines and approved playlists reflect significant underlying formal or informal research, at the same time maintaining a similarly cool partnership with an overlapping set of record companies that feature more mainstream music.

Veteran jazz broadcaster Maxx Myrick confirms most of the claims made above. Myrick was one of the pioneers of jazz programming on satellite radio, another highly formatted, narrowcast medium that attracts loyal audiences on a subscription basis. He made the following observation:

> I think the music that non-commercial/college radio stations play reflects the area and the personality of the presenters on those stations. It seems to me that a lot of times, the music played is a combination of music or artists that they are passionate about and music that record promoters/record labels send and "encourage" them to play. The trades/charts, i.e., *Jazz Week, Jazz Times, DownBeat* and *JazzIz* also play a role. In the case of Sirius XM, I believe there are other factors, like corporate oversight that requires justification of music added. That's just my two cents, when I created XM 70, I just played what I thought was great music and tried to play as much new music by current artists as possible. I'm told that this has changed since I left and the merger with Sirius. It is my understanding that the new Program Director has to deal with at least two layers of oversight involved in the decision-making process for choosing music for the channel. The Sr. VP is a rock guy, who has oversight of jazz, blues and classical and [the] Latin VP . . . has oversight of the jazz PD [program director].[41]

From Myrick's comments it can be seen that in highly structured organizations, significant bureaucratic policymaking and oversight are involved in radio programming. In such organizations research, corporate strategy, and industry alliances affect program content.

Jazz Radio Programming Is Also a Business

Having discussed programmers' philosophies, orientations, and limitations, it is useful to consider the range of jazz program types and programing opportunities on noncommercial radio. Jazz radio programming exists in many forms, ranging from the least structured—a radio DJ playing music without management input—to long-form features using the most sophisticated programming techniques. Below are several types of jazz programs.

- DJ programs that play recent releases and jazz classics; a general interest jazz show
- DJ programs that are based on subgenre themes: traditional jazz, vocals, piano music, big bands, jazz fusion, jazz from Brazil
- DJ programs that feature specific artists, locales, or collaborations as themes[42]
- Jazz education and history programs
- Profiles of major jazz figures, such as NPR's *Jazz Profiles* and the *Miles Davis Radio Project* (1991)
- Musician-hosted programs that include interviews with or music selected by guest jazz artists
- Regular shows by jazz presenting organizations, for example, a radio show by a local jazz society
- In-studio interviews or performances by jazz musicians on general interest programs, such as an appearance on NPR's *Fresh Air* or *Weekend Edition*, or on *A Prairie Home Companion*
- Feature stories on jazz musicians on general-interest programs
- Weekly performance series such as NPR's *Jazzset with Dee Dee Bridgewater* or *Jazz at Lincoln Center*
- Special marathon broadcast tributes to accomplished jazz artists, a specialty of WKCR (Columbia University, New York)
- Remotes, that is, broadcasts from normal live music venues such as clubs or concert stages
- Live coverage from jazz festivals, for example, the New Orleans Jazz and Heritage Festival, the Detroit Jazz Festival, and the Atlanta Jazz Festival

Any of these program types could appear on any kind of noncommercial radio station, though jazz programs exceeding one hour in length are seldom found on public radio. In addition, many types, even the most basic host-and-records show, could be offered by program producers to stations in other markets. More often, syndicated programs or those networked on an ad hoc basis usually feature a famed host—possibly an active musician like Christian McBride or a noted jazz authority—who presents interviews, conversation, or historical research, or offer "recorded live" music to other parts of the country. For example, the NPR program *Piano Jazz* (formerly *Marian McPartland's Piano Jazz* and produced by South Carolina Educational Television) features one-on-one interviews and performances, while *Jazz Night in America* (produced by Newark, New Jersey, jazz station WBGO and hosted by bassist Christian McBride) features edited performances recorded at various clubs and festivals. Many jazz radio stations augment their locally hosted music shows with these packaged national shows, often between 6 p.m. and 8 p.m. WBGO also produces the live NPR broadcast *Toast of the Nation*, which annually rings in the New Year across three U.S. time zones.

There are other program producers in addition to NPR-branded programming. PRX (formerly PRI, Public Radio International), perhaps best known for *This American Life*, offers *Jazz Happening Now*, a program concentrating on current performers and recent jazz releases, and *Jazz After Hours*, a four-hour late-night weekend record show aimed at stations needing automated overnight programming. *Jazz Happening Now* claims to be carried by forty-six U.S. radio stations. As PRI, from 1989 to 2015 it distributed *Riverwalk Jazz*, an unusual program that featured live performances of pre-1940s music by Jim Cullem's Riverwalk Jazz Band with notable guests such as Dick Hyman, Milt Hinton, and Clark Terry from The Landing, a club on San Antonio's historic Riverwalk. By featuring a live band, the program was able to overcome one (perceived) audience acceptance problem: scratchy low-fi pre-war recordings of early jazz music. Instead, the program featured meticulously recorded high-fidelity stereo audio. Selections by the band, with and without guests, were intercut with interview highlights from the featured guests. Though off the air, many of the *Riverwalk Jazz* programs are still available to listeners as two continuous streams from a Stanford University website.[43]

A quite active source of jazz programming, the African American Public Radio Consortium (AAPRC), was founded in 2000 with the goal of improving public radio's service to the African American community and other underserved communities. The AAPRC serves about eighty noncommercial radio stations including those of twenty-nine HBCUs. The following excerpt from its website relates the existing lack of public radio offerings serving the black community to the style of production and presentation dominating public radio today:

> We are partnering with producers, stations, hosts, artists, scholars, authors, business and civic leaders and more—to ramp up the volume of media content that increases ethnically diverse voices and culture in our industry.
>
> The Consortium is currently building a lineup of programs with public radio sensibilities and production values—that increases stations' ability to serve diverse audiences.[44]

In addition to its blues, gospel, reggae, and world music shows, the AAPRC offered eight jazz programs in 2020: *The Groove with Rufus Harrison* (KCEP-FM, Las Vegas), *Jazz in the New Millennium*, a new release-oriented program (WCLK-FM, Atlanta), *Return to the Source* with Douglas Turner (produced at Alabama A&M's WJAB-FM), *Café Jazz* with Gene Knight (WVAS-FM, produced at Alabama State University, Montgomery), *Cool Jazz Countdown*, highlighting the top ten jazz albums based on jazz charts, *Catch the Flo* with Marcus Johnson, *The Roots of Smooth* with Bobby Jackson, and *New Urban Jazz Lounge* with Bob Baldwin. Three other programs are categorized as Jazz and Soul including *The Soul of Jazz* with Jamal Ahmad (from Clark Atlanta University's WCLK-FM) and *The Wind Down*, hosted by Will Downing (Jackson State University's WJSU-FM). The AAPRC has also distributed dozens of specials concerning jazz and black music such as a profile of Sonny Rollins and tributes to NEA Jazz Masters.

Independent producers also offer jazz programs. Murray Street Productions presents *Jazz at Lincoln Center Radio*, *European Jazz Stage*, and other jazz-oriented programs among its offerings, produces webstreams for a variety of clients.[45]

One of the oldest business strategies in broadcasting is to export intellectual property, including programming and formats, created in one market to a different market for a fee. For the originating stations, these revenues help offset expenses and reduce financial pressures. The subscribing station gets a program that is compatible with its program objectives and mission, ostensibly at a lower cost than originating a program of its own. Several jazz audio streaming services provide programming on a twenty-four-hour basis (see table 23).[46] The future of this practice is somewhat in doubt because the internet makes even protected out-of-market radio programming available to resourceful listeners.

The best-known jazz program across America in recent years may have been the one hosted by the late Bob Parlocha (1938–2015), a saxophonist long associated with California jazz radio. The Chicago public radio station WFMT distributed Parlocha's program via the internet and satellite to as many as seventy radio stations.[47] Since his death, WFMT has produced its *Jazz Network* in-house, with hosts Dee Alexander, John Hill (a WBEE veteran), Dave Schwan, and Neil Tesser giving the service different voices. Such plug-and-play jazz

TABLE 23. Major jazz radio music services.

Provider	Programming Service	Year Started
Essential Public Media (formerly operated by WDUQ, Pittsburgh)	JazzWorks*	1996
PubRadio Network (former WDUQ programmers, WZUM)	PubMusic	2011
KNKX, formerly KPLU (Seattle/Tacoma, Washington)	Jazz24**	2008–2016
WFMT (Chicago)	WFMT Jazz Network	1997

* JazzWorks is now a legacy service with a few remaining clients.

** Jazz24 expired when Pacific Lutheran University sold KPLU to a community group that converted it to jazz station KNKX.

TABLE 24. Some popular jazz shows available on many stations.

Program	Provider/Syndicator
12th Street Jump	KCUR/PRX
Dream Farm Café	Dream Farm Radio
AfterGlow	WFIU/PRX
Jazz Night in America	WBGO/NPR
Jazz After Hours	PRX
Jazz Happening Now	PRX
Wood Warbler's JazzGrass Radio Show	PRX
Jazz in the New Millennium	AAPRC/KTSU
Soul of Jazz	AAPRC/WCLK
New Urban Jazz Lounge	AAPRC/WCLK

streams appeal to stations large and small. The Miami station WDNA-FM ("Jazz & Rhythm") used Parlocha's program in its overnight hours every broadcast day for a total of forty-two hours per week. Because listenership is lowest in the overnight hours, this tends to be the time for some of the most adventurous musical selections on many jazz radio stations, but Parlocha, offering audio to a diverse ad hoc network of stations, tended to avoid music that strays from the post-bop mainstream. Programming streams are also produced outside the station environment. Essential Public Media, which provides the stream *JazzWorks*, described by the broadcaster as "post-bop mainstream straight-ahead jazz," was the audio streaming service inherited by WYEP (Pittsburgh) when it purchased WDUQ from Duquesne University, while *PubMusic* is a streaming service started by disgruntled former WDUQ staffers who, until the recent launch of WZUM-FM (101.1)—returning jazz radio to Pittsburgh—were working independent of any radio station (table 24).[48]

A matrix of forces, impulses, and inclinations influences jazz programming. It is not surprising that the jazz heard on public radio tends toward compatibility with the value structure of the controlling institutions. The sum of these vectors tends to produce relatively conservative results so that post-bebop mainstream jazz is strongly favored over music considered experimental, such as free jazz, and music considered crossover, such as smooth jazz, jazz fusion, and acid jazz. There is sometimes more space for these less favored styles on college, HBCU, and community radio stations, and even public radio stations may make some accommodation for experimental music on their underappreciated HD radio subchannels. Jazz, however, is durable and resilient and capable of conveying multiple ideological meanings at once. No matter how conservatively or progressively programmed, it still carries the hopes and aspirations of its creators and listeners.

6

Jazz Is for Everybody

Missions, Precursors, Models, and Ownership

> It is an interesting fact that the ideals of the owners of a station are bound to creep in and be reflected in the output from that station. Water seeks its own level. Listeners, likewise, seek their own level.
> —Elmer Douglas

Assuming the license holder is actively engaged, noncommercial radio programming reflects, to a certain degree, the worldview of the license holder. In commercial broadcasting, profitability often trumps cultural preferences and political ideology. There, the ideology of the marketplace can result in programming, particularly for music, that may be personally repugnant to the station owner and senior management but satisfying in terms of financial performance. Noncommercial broadcasters, however, owe a more lasting allegiance to their mission although, over time, the mission can be undermined by financial imperatives. One exception is in college radio, where noncommercial programming commonly runs counter to licensee ideology, especially where the university holds the license but students and other volunteers run the station independent of university control and oversight.

In Chapter 4 the jazz programming policies of the largest noncommercial stations—generally public radio stations—were shown to be shaped by concerns about audience size and median age, demographics, pledge rates, listenership or utility measures, and the volume of underwriting. These large stations are captives in a recursive dance in which expensive national programming is deemed essential to achieving listenership and income targets, and the cost of that programming puts pressure on the station to achieve high listenership and income. In Chapter 5 jazz programmers' decisions were examined in relation to the perceived politics of the music, to the availability and use of audience research, and to the programmers' position relative to the audience, the jazz industry, and their own aesthetic judgement. Finally, in this chapter, the relation between jazz programming and radio stations' ideology, as often exemplified by their mission statements, is explored through a set of case studies.

Before the CPB was chartered, there was a bloc of educational radio stations that came to found the core of public radio, and it is worth considering the ideological range of the institutions that controlled these stations as reflected in their educational directions. National Public Radio founding father Bill Simmering's 1970 "mission statement" ended with the following: "The total service should be trustworthy, enhance intellectual development, expand knowledge, deepen aural esthetic enjoyment, increase the pleasure of living in a pluralistic society and result in a service to listeners which makes them more responsive, informed human beings and intelligent responsible citizens of their communities and the world."[1]

Enhancing intellectual development, expanding knowledge, and helping create a climate with responsive, informed human beings and intelligent, responsible citizens sounds an awful lot like the implied mission of most American universities (excepting, perhaps, "the pleasure of living in a pluralistic society"). But for institutions that would make this claim and those that would not, jazz could be supported on their radio stations because attitudes toward jazz and its treatment had evolved on campuses. As David Ake notes, since the 1960s "college music departments have emerged as among the most powerful forces shaping understandings of jazz in this country." Ake relates that their offerings of jazz history classes, the popularity of performance ensembles and improvisation courses, and the presence of visiting artists and artists-in-residence on these hallowed grounds has "unquestionably and drastically altered public perceptions of the genre."[2] I would add that the presentation of jazz on the universities' radio stations has extended that impact on the public beyond those campuses. One could further argue that the bulk of serious writing about jazz has moved from journalism to the academy.

Ake insightfully recognizes that all jazz is not equally welcome in the academy and gives the example of its embrace of John Coltrane's early music as a leader and its avoidance of his late music, at least in applied music departments. Ake notes, "The very arena that served to elevate jazz to the level of 'good music' also served to marginalize some of the music played as jazz in the outside world—that is, beyond the academy walls."[3] Some of those music's include free jazz, jazz fusion, smooth jazz, and funk.

While universities would see the embrace and avoidance strictly in terms of musical features—Coltrane's earlier music featured dazzling complexity and structural certainty that appeals to modernist pedagogues, whereas his late music loosened formal musical structures, disregarded tonal correctness, and featured timbral flexibility and expressiveness in ways Western music theory was ill-prepared to explain—Coltrane's late music also had features that were ideologically opposed to academia. For example, his embrace of collective improvisation, influenced by the free jazz musicians he admired, was counter to the individualism promoted throughout academic life, though it was in accord with black nationalist values of achieving social justice by means of collective and improvised action. And though Coltrane is such a central pillar of post-bop that none of his work can be totally ignored, the academy has snubbed musicians such as Albert Ayler and Sunny Murray.

While it seems safe to assume that a university would consider its professionally staffed radio station as an extension of its academic mission, a more concrete source of the philosophies of many noncommercial stations is their mission statements. The programming of jazz on noncommercial radio stations can be seen to mostly follow patterns correlated to whichever of five ownership or management models applies. The first two models, professionally staffed *university*-owned stations and professionally staffed *non-university* stations, comprise the public radio sector; these are the stations that typically have paid staffs and relatively large budgets. Using a pure term of convenience, the third model, student- or volunteer-staffed university-owned or-affiliated stations, are referred to as *college radio* to distinguish them from university radio. The remaining two types, *Pacifica Foundation* stations and independently licensed community radio stations share aspects of *community radio*, although the governance structure of Pacifica creates additional issues for music programming.

As might be expected, it is common for stations to problematize these distinctions. Many community stations call themselves "public radio" to emphasize the public that they serve and that supports them with funding. And almost all public and community radio stations will at some point describe themselves on the air as "listener supported." For jazz radio, the most significant complications are found at the news-jazz stations. Several of these stations have been licensed for decades to educational institutions, sometimes community colleges or boards of education, have only a handful of professional staffers, and mix eighteen or more hours of daily jazz with NPR's *Morning Edition* and *All Things Considered*. Such stations have volunteer hosts and can function more like community radio than public radio, despite their self-promotion.

Public radio stations may be licensed by independent non-for-profit corporations or foundations such as WETA (Greater Washington Educational Television Association, Inc.), WHYY (WHYY, Inc., Philadelphia), WGBH (WGBH Educational Foundation, Boston) or WBGO (Newark Public Radio, Inc.) or by similarly structured state broadcasting services such as WSCI (Charleston, South Carolina, Public Broadcasting). Public radio stations are frequently affiliated with private and public universities, colleges, or community colleges such as WGLT (Illinois State University), KCRW (Santa Monica College), WBJC (Baltimore Community College), WAMU (American

University), and WUOM (University of Michigan) or with state or municipal educational bodies such as WABE (Atlanta Board of Education). It is not unusual for an educational institution to divest its radio station, usually as an opportunity to close an institutional budget shortfall. In some cases, for instance, that of KPLU, the board of Pacific Lutheran University was convinced to sell the station, now (KNKX) to a community non-profit.[4]

In addition to the big public radio stations are community radio stations such as WRFG (Atlanta) and WDNA (Miami), operated by grass-roots organizations, and college radio stations that are licensed to or operated largely by students, such as WKCR (Columbia University) and WRCT (Carnegie Mellon University), any of which may occasionally run a national program on an à la carte basis. For example, WRCT airs the independently produced and syndicated *David Pakman Show* followed by *Democracy Now!* (originally a Pacifica program but independent since 2002) on weekdays at 7 a.m.

Finally, in a category of their own are the stations owned by the Pacifica Foundation including KFPA and KPFB (Berkley), WPFW (Washington, DC), and WBAI (New York) that mix local and satellite programming and combine aspects of the grass-roots community stations and the public broadcasters. Like community radio, Pacifica stations tailor their programming to their location, but like public radio, they have access to Pacifica network resources including *Democracy Now!*, *Hard Knock Radio*, and the *Pacifica Evening News* and the outstanding gavel-to-gavel coverage of congressional hearings, protest marches, demonstrations, and other live events of interest to progressive listeners. Pacifica has its own satellite distribution network, enabling spot news and interviews from locations served by its stations.

Any of the stations in these categories are likely to air classical or jazz music, as well as many other genres. For example, very few student-run stations will be formatted exclusively in one musical genre but, rather, will have music programs reflecting the tastes of individual show hosts; nor would these volunteer hosts normally have more than one time slot per week. College radio, perhaps best known as an incubator of indie rock and alternative music, has emerged over the past thirty years as the segment most open to experimental jazz, and the publicity managers at jazz labels that feature experimental music concentrate their efforts there rather than public-sector jazz stations, except for the specific DJs whom they know are receptive to this music.[5]

The remainder of this chapter is devoted to presenting examples of various types of noncommercial radio stations that feature jazz at the time of writing. It would be foolish to think that these stations capture the essential features of their types; every station has its own history and faces its own issues regarding financial challenges and survival. Probably the public radio stations appear the most uniform. The CPB qualification process is designed to encourage a nationwide standard of excellence. Though nothing lasts forever—there is no more Pan Am Airlines and the last Howard Johnson's closed in 2022—but the typical public radio licensees, universities and nonprofit foundations, tend toward the type of institutional structure that resists rapid change. Despite major budgeting issues, many public radio stations, especially those that mix daytime news with evening music, make an effort to produce a few hours of local content each day.

The stability of community radio seems to come from the deep commitment of its founders and staffers. Such stations experience irregular crises whose solutions require money—transmitter and studio equipment failures, threats to rented or donated studio and office space, costly new FCC regulations—as well as occasional personality battles over station control. And community stations are as varied as their communities. The establishment of low-power FM radio has brought a number of new community stations to the airwaves. Among the low-power FM stations that play jazz, some behave as community stations while others seem more like college radio, little concerned with community access and serving as the expressive voice of its owners or creators.

Public-Sector or CPB-Qualified Radio Stations

The largest noncommercial stations are the public radio stations, whose schedules tend to be dominated by national programming distributed by NPR, American Public Media, or Public Radio Exchange (PRX). Public radio stations tend to rank high in terms of operating budgets, professional staff size, and coverage area due to having the greatest effective radiated power.[6] They are also the largest in terms of listening audience. Because of the high quality of their programming and lack of commercial interruptions, in many markets the leading public radio station is in the top five or ten in ratings among all stations.

Almost without exception, these stations are CPB-qualified, meaning their governance, financial structure, and audience size meet the requirements set by the CPB for modest government support. Grants from the CPB may offset program acquisition costs (such as fees to air *All Things Considered* or *This American Life*) or program origination costs, or assist stations with improvements to technical facilities, fund community projects, or pay for professional services.[7] Because of the high cost of national programs, public radio stations tend to have multimillion-dollar budgets, extensive and regularly scheduled on-air fundraising, and professional on-air, operational, fundraising, and managerial staffs, supplemented by volunteers.

WBGO

Newark's WBGO is one of the leading jazz broadcasters in the United States, also reaching a worldwide audience on the Internet. Its location in the New York market gives it access to the musicians in what has traditionally been considered the world's largest and most important jazz community. The station is licensed to Newark Public Radio, Inc., and is a professionally staffed public-sector station unaffiliated with an educational institution, although its license was acquired via a friendly transaction from the Newark, New Jersey, Board of Education. WBGO's birth as a twenty-four-hour jazz station was directly tied to the 1980 demise of commercial station WRVR. The schedule consists almost entirely of jazz programming. Its daily fare consists overwhelmingly of DJs playing records. Monday through Friday there is a small block of nationally distributed jazz programs that air in the post-rush-hour period, 6:30 p.m. to 7:30 p.m., several of which are produced at WBGO, and a small strip of public affairs programs each day before the evening jazz programs. On occasion, it airs live jazz from its studios or from remote locations.

Among the larger public radio operations, WBGO has thirty-two full-time and eighteen part-time employees, along with approximately two hundred volunteers, 2017 operating revenues of $5 million, and operating expenses of $4.8 million.[8] By comparison, New York Public Radio, operator of WNYC and WQXR, a major producer (and purchaser) of national news, information, and cultural programs, is an order of magnitude larger than WBGO. The New York Public Radio stations had more than 450 employees and had operating revenues of $94.4 million and $94.7 million, respectively, in operating expenses in 2017.[9] (Another interesting point of comparison: WNYC/WQXR reported about $10 million in underwriting revenue compared to just $633,000 for WBGO.)

The mission statement of WBGO circa 2012 makes explicit reference to jazz but, relative to some other radio stations, this language makes few explanatory claims about why jazz is important:

> WBGO is a publicly-supported, cultural institution that champions jazz and presents news to a worldwide audience through radio, other technologies and events.
>
> Organizational values that guide WBGO in accomplishing its mission are:
> - A belief in the vibrancy and continuance of jazz as a cultural art form
> - Educational outreach is an important part of the station's programming
> - A diverse, open workplace that supports the development and enhancement of the staff's talents and skills
> - Listeners, members and the general public deserve to be treated with respect, quality service and information[10]

WBGO's current (2024) mission statement says even less about jazz:

> WBGO 88.3 FM / Newark Public Radio is a non-profit, publicly funded arts and cultural institution, dedicated to the curation, presentation, and

preservation of music created out of the African American experience. We are committed to providing our community with independently produced music programming and journalism for the purpose of public enrichment, entertainment, and insight.

WBGO accomplishes its mission through:

- Creating and distributing relevant audio, video, and editorial content that reflects honesty, complexity, and exceptional quality.
- Developing diverse and equitable platforms for presentation, discovery, and expression.
- Actively engaging with our audience and supporters to convey a dynamic representation of the communities in which we live and work.
- Providing a diverse and inclusive workplace with a foundation of integrity and equality.[11]

The station takes advantage of its location to present in-studio interviews, sponsor concerts and events in New Jersey and New York. Moreover, it uses its access to the New York jazz community to produce its own national programs such as *Live from Jazz at Lincoln Center*, *Jazzset*, and *Jazz from the Archives* (of the Institute for Jazz Studies).

Despite the quantity of jazz heard on WBGO, the station has been criticized for programming a narrow range of music, as was subconsciously indicated in its anniversary slogan, "25 Years, Straight Ahead." The station's presentation format was described in a 2004 *New York Times* article commemorating that anniversary:

> Under a system devised about a decade ago by the program director, Thurston Briscoe, and the music director, Gary Walker, WBGO sticks to a format that seldom ventures into the aurally demanding. Every hour, in almost unvarying sequence, hosts must begin with a "classic performance" like Miles Davis's "Solar," followed by a "power vocal" by one of a few well-known singers (Lena Horne, Natalie Cole, Carmen McRae), followed by a new recording, followed by a slightly older favorite (with a heavy emphasis on Latin jazz) and so on.[12]

In fact, a welcome change to that format was the requirement that the DJ include a Latin jazz selection in each hour.[13] The major narrowing of the WBGO format apparently took place after its first decade on the air (1980–1989). Before that, the station operated more informally, and its DJs had great discretion. Today WBGO not only is hesitant to program free or experimental music but also programs relatively little music recorded before 1940. Dan Morgenstern, former director of the Institute for Jazz Studies and a former WBGO program host, despairs that "listeners don't get to hear vintage

Billie Holiday, no Ellington from before the 1940's, no classic Lester Young with Count Basie."[14] Based on my own listening, Morgenstern overstates the case, but there is little music from before 1950 on WBGO. This bias against older music may be based on the fidelity and cleanliness of the recorded sound rather than on musical principles. Most of the older recordings have a noticeably low-fidelity sound compared to music recorded after about 1950. Public radio consultants have been promoting ideas of sonic consistency for a more than a decade, describing music more in terms of instrumentation, tempo, and mood than in terms of musical features, and WBGO, while not in agreement with some of their arguments about jazz, does appear to embrace a certain sonic standard.

Reluctance to program music that deviates from the dominant post-bop swing style is another matter. Oliver Lake, a member of the Association for the Advancement of Creative Musicians, expressed great surprise that on one occasion he actually heard a track from his CD *Cloth* on WBGO.[15] Yet the experimental pianist and composer Jason Moran identifies the weekly program *The Checkout* as a step forward.[16] Along with additional content on its own website, this program features new releases, live studio or on-location performances, and some experimental music. Josh Jackson's one-hour program/podcast is the one consistent show with a wider range of jazz music.

Like many public radio stations, but unusually for a jazz station, WBGO produces podcasts and web features, some from its on-air programs and others distributed from the website or by podcast apps. The WBGO podcasts, besides providing news, community affairs, and sports coverage, also present jazz features. In addition to *The Checkout*, *Jazz Night in America* and *Jazz United*, an interview show hosted by Nate Chinen and Greg Bryant, are available as podcasts.

KNKX

KNKX claims that it "delivers excellence in jazz, blues, and news with deep storytelling that inspires, informs, and connects our community."[17] Licensed to Tacoma, Washington, it is one of three NPR stations in Seattle (the others are KUOW-FM and KVTI-FM). Its budget of roughly $10 million is large for a jazz station, in part owing to the costs of acquiring national programs and producing the extensive local news coverage that gets integrated with the NPR network feed. It began service in 1966 as KPLU-FM, a student-run station that favored jazz and blues, evolving into a professional news-jazz public radio station. In 2016 its license holder, Pacific Lutheran University, announced plans to sell the station to NPR charter member KUOW, which had already completed the move to NTI (news, talk, and information) in 1992. (In 2021 the only music programs on KUOW were two hours of NPR's *World Café* on Saturday and the one-hour *Sound Opinions* from PRX on Sunday.) Fearing for the future of the jazz programming and locally produced news coverage that were the hallmarks of KPLU, a group led by its employees formed Pacific Public Media and raised $7 million to buy the station from Pacific Lutheran, averting the sale to KUOW. The new KNKX took on KPLU's fourteen news staffers, and its large budget supports almost fifty paid staff, including on-air hosts.

Typical of news-jazz stations, KNKX devotes a large portion of its schedule to non-jazz programs. On weekdays, like many West Coast stations, it carries *Morning Edition*, which it extends by airing live East Coast feeds as well as those intended for the Pacific time zone. To its credit, according to its 2021 schedule KNKX still has jazz programs in the midday hours between *Morning Edition* and *All Things Considered* and replays *Fresh Air* at 6 p.m. This contrasts with many news-jazz station schedules that favor nationally distributed public radio talk and discussion programs during the midday hours and limit jazz to evening hours. On weekends at KNKX, music programming takes over around noon.

The station's implementation and advocacy of modal, or audience research-based, programming when it was KPLU was discussed in Chapter 5. Although the modes driving the programming process are proprietary, KNKX does provide automatically updated playlists on its webpage, from which some inferences can be made about its programming rules, which seem to favor mainstream swinging groups featuring piano, guitar, and saxophone and jazz vocals instead of free jazz, jazz-funk, or new music that mixes some of these elements.[18] The station offers the Friday night *New Cool* program, hosted by Abe Besson, which features "21st century jazz inspired and informed by the sounds of today: hip-hop, & funk, Electronic music and punk rock," and *Grooveyard*, a mix of new and classic soul jazz and blues hosted by Stephanie Anne Johnson.[19] The station also devotes several hours each week to jazz connected to the local coverage area.

Overnight programming is efficiently provided by Jazz24, which is also offered to listeners as a separate web stream. This service is an example of an increasingly common practice wherein a radio station that offers several types of programming provides each type in a separate twenty-four-hour stream. For example, KCRW-FM (Santa Monica, CA) has a twenty-four-hour stream of its live on-air content, one of music from its signature *Morning Becomes Eclectic* program, and one consisting of all news. Jazz24 grew out of the forty-three-hundred-track jazz library produced by the modal programming process.[20] Although it is no longer a programming service sold to other jazz stations, Jazz24 is broadcast by a number of low-power FM stations around the country in addition to individual listeners.

Community Radio Stations

Community radio stations are often tied to progressive politics and social justice movements. Some have roots in the educational radio movement, but more often they emerged from the underground radio movement. That is, these radio stations, rather than representing a way of extending the educational mission beyond the walls of educational institutions or a means to make the performing arts accessible over the air, are seen by their founders and operators as means for social change. Fragile in regard to finances and dependent on volunteers, community stations generally foster political ideas unwelcome on mainstream radio. In the words of Robert Waterman McChesney, "Community radio is where one can go to get real criticism of corporate capitalism or U.S. foreign policy, or where one can go to get thorough discussion of the environment, which is impossible with NPR or commercial stations. The entertainment, too, tends to be far more eclectic than what can be found elsewhere on the dial."[21]

Community radio developed around the notion that people without economic and political power should nevertheless have access to the public airwaves. As Brandy Doyle writes, "What characterizes community radio stations in the US, as elsewhere, is a local, participatory approach to programming and often to the station's mission and governance as well. Community radio aims to include local voices and views not heard elsewhere in the media. Beyond that, not much is uniform."[22]

William Barlow notes that despite the specifics of location or audience, community stations value a doctrine of access while suffering severe constraints:

> Under the community radio umbrella there are both urban and rural progressive white stations, minority stations (Afro-American, Hispanic, Native American, multi-ethnic), college stations and even state-supported stations. . . . Regardless of their differences, however, all of the community-oriented radio stations in the US have two things in common: they share the same broadly defined ideological orientation and they face the same social constraints in their day-to-day operations. In addition to community involvement, their ideology champions progressive politics, alternative cultures and participatory democracy. Their common social constraints include government regulation, station financing, organization of resources, and operating in their respective environments, i.e., demographic markets.[23]

Typically, the community radio station's central goal is to give politically marginalized voices access to the airwaves. This desire results in musical programming with an often more easily identifiable ideological position. For example, many prominent political and social movements of the twentieth century were associated with a particular body of music. There were specific songs, styles, and artists connected with the temperance, suffrage, labor, anti-war, and civil rights movements. The "folk" aspects of folk, country, blues, bluegrass, and even jazz made these authentic musics of the people embraceable by progressives, socialists, and communists and emblematic of their causes. African American musical forms could be seen as oppositional to the prevailing racial policies, an argument made explicit by Amiri Baraka and Samuel Floyd.[24]

Washington, DC's WPFW is a Pacifica Foundation station operating in the manner of community radio. Its comingling of music and politics, typical of community radio but here specifically involving jazz, was described thus in a local news article:

> Music served a conscious-raising purpose. Talk shows were followed by jazz; many programs had hybrid formats. "The talk never stops and the music never ends" was how some programmers put it, according to [Tom] Porter, an early host at the station. Some of the music was headier and harder than the handful of other local jazz stations. Jazz was politics; politics was jazz. When Elvis Presley died a few months after WPFW went on the air, the station didn't air a tribute, "the explanation going that Elvis was a racist who stole his music from black people," the *Washington Post* reported at the time. WPFW's founders were five years into their struggle to get on the air when D.C. gained home rule in 1973, and their station shared the era's DNA. It was a station for a majority black city newly empowered to run itself; it was thoroughly ideological, coming just after the civil rights and anti-war generations; it was a station for black thought and black music and the highest intellectual aspirations of both; it was a space for ideas and anxieties—nutty ones, maybe, to the radio-dial wanderer—shut out of the mainstream.[25]

While the issues of Presley, race, authenticity, and theft are thoroughly muddled, the given rationale supports not only the notion of the ideological use of music but also the notion that an equally ideological statement can be created by the music that is not played. The intertwining of music and politics to such a degree that a radio program becomes difficult to label a talk show or a music show is typical of community radio, and strikingly atypical on public radio, where such comingling is limited mainly to political satire.

Finally, for those skeptical of concentrated corporate power and the domination of a market capital ideology on all aspects of life in the United States, to feature the music styles that manage to survive despite the disinterest of the music industry is to present an example of an alternative value system. Thus, it would appear that ideological differences between public and community radio stations are as clear as supporting the cultural hierarchy embodied in the education establishment or supporting the elevation of marginalized cultures.

In practice, the distinction between community radio and public radio can often be quite *in*distinct. Over time, some community radio stations have evolved into public stations. Pittsburgh's WYEP, for instance, began in 1975 as a threadbare community station with a focus on community access. It evolved into a CPB-qualified public radio station and grew prosperous enough to purchase the mostly jazz-formatted, professionally staffed WDUQ-FM and convert it into the public radio NTI station WESA. When community stations become more professionalized, the original mission of community access can be displaced by notions of community service; that is, the act of bringing programs not offered on other stations is considered a public service. Given the constant struggle within typical community stations to achieve a level of financial support sufficient to fund their barebones budgets, it is not surprising that they will sometimes seek to reform their very informal original management structures in order to keep from going under.

WRFG

Radio Free Georgia, Atlanta's WRFG-FM, is a good example of a community station that plays a significant amount of jazz. Broadcasting about forty hours of blues and jazz per week, the station airs programs that feature hip hop, soul, African, Caribbean, bluegrass, zydeco, Latin, Indian (Asian), and gospel, in addition to local, national, and international news. The founding of WRFG in 1973 was an attempt to create a radio station that reflected the activism and needs of the civil rights movement. Its founder, Student Nonviolent Coordinating Committee activist Fay Bellamy, told radio historian Brian Ward, "The interest was to start a nonprofit radio station which would allow movement people to have access to mass media, which we did not have at that time."[26]

As is not uncommon for community radio stations, the WRFG mission statement makes no mention of music but instead stresses community access, which the music programs represent:

> WRFG provides a voice for those who have been traditionally denied access to the broadcast media and the involvement of a broad base of community elements to guarantee that access. In the utilization of the Foundation's facilities and in its programs the following communities will receive first priority:
>
> 1. Those who continue to be denied free and open access to the broadcast media,
> 2. Those who suffer oppression or exploitation based upon class, race, sex, age or creed or sexual orientation.[27]

However, WRFG does call itself "your station for progressive information . . . and hand-picked music."[28]

According to its website, WRFG has a seventeen-member board of directors and a separate five-member community advisory board, with a permanent staff of only two: a station manager and an operations director. In turn, these two are guided by respective administration and operation committees formed of subsets of the board of directors and others. Typical of community radio stations, WRFG depends heavily on volunteers as on-air hosts and as off-air staff.

The eclectic program schedule reflects WRFG's commitment to access. Its weekday schedule begins with a four-hour blues show at 6 a.m. followed by two hours of "R&B from '50s to today's latest sounds."[29] After a noon-hour news and interview program, it airs Pacifica's hip hop talk show *Hard Knock Radio* and a program with world music, news, and commentary. In the hours from 4 p.m. to 8 p.m., before the daily folk and bluegrass hour, WRFG has programs dedicated to labor, women, health, African affairs, and youth. It would appear that jazz is limited to ten weeknight and eight weekend hours, but any of the public affairs programs might use music as part of the political discourse, as described by the producers of Tuesday afternoon's *Lambda Radio Report*:

> "Lambda Radio Report" is a radio news and entertainment magazine that keeps center WRFG's mission. We examine various social justice issues such as Poverty, discrimination and other Human Rights violations. Through commentaries, interviews, music and poetry we examine the issues of the day through the framework of intersectionality and Human Rights.[30]

Because the station has remained under the control of people committed to the community access ideal, even as different people have served on the board, WRFG has avoided the kind of mission-versus-market battles common to other stations. That does not preclude internal tensions resulting from differences in popularity and fundraising abilities. A 2003 *Atlanta Journal-Constitution* profile of the station made clear that though tensions exist, that the mission reigns:

> The station's anti-corporate, underdog philosophy is both its core strength and its weakness. There is constant tension between those who raise the most money, such as the relatively apolitical blues staff, and the social activists, whose public affairs shows attract far fewer listeners and very little money. But there's a richness of sound and opinion heard nowhere else on Atlanta radio. "We sometimes pick shows that have small audiences because we feel they're important," noted Joe Shifalo, a WRFG founder and a board member.[31]

As is the case in many community organizations, superior fundraising ability can result in the accumulation of power within the organization.

The range of jazz broadcast during those eighteen dedicated hours is quite broad. Each evening of Jazz to Soothe Your Soul, airing from 10 p.m. to midnight, has a different host or hosts. The subtitles of the programs are instructive in themselves (see table 25).

The continuing commitment to programming jazz on WRFG is all the more remarkable when considering Atlanta's importance as a center of hip hop and R&B music production, both well represented on the station schedule. In addition, the Atlanta radio market has a full-time jazz station in WCLK-FM, "The Jazzvoice of the City," licensed to Clark Atlanta University, a historically black college or university (HBCU).[32] Although WCLK has a racially diverse audience for its jazz programming, it also claims one of the nation's largest black noncommercial radio audiences. Atlanta is a majority African American city with a historically strong black middle class nurtured by the city's black colleges, which include Morehouse, Spellman, and Clark Atlanta University. The station's parent institution is part of a mature political insider tradition, just as WRFG represents more of an outsider position. Unlike WRFG, WCLK does not explicitly position jazz as part of overt left-progressive political activism. The WCLK mission statement echoes the historic mission of all HBCUs in being "dedicated to developing and providing professional quality multimedia and broadcast services that uplift, educate and inform the Atlanta community and worldwide audience," as well as the now-conventional position of cultural institutions regarding jazz—"to increase awareness of the significance of Jazz

TABLE 25. WRFG jazz programs, 2020.

	Program	Hosts	Description
Monday	Phases—Jazz on a Monday Night	Tawhiyda Tupac-el, Paul B. Williams	From available playlists, each program has a theme or featured artist. For example, shows have featured current Atlanta musicians. The three big band programs featured current big band releases, 1930s and '40s classics, and an all-Stan Kenton program.
Tuesday	Spectrum	James Ellison	No information available
Wednesday	Ellington, Monk, Trane and more . . .	Ralph Rice	No information available
Thursday	Ascension	John Derard	A show featuring music ranging from John Coltrane and Archie Shepp to Roy Hargrove and Terrance Blanchard
Friday	Last Stop on the 4 Train	Thomas Simmons	No information available
Saturday (a.m.)	Jazz Straight no Chaser	Lovell Hooks	Traditional jazz music, improvisational jazz music, interviews
Monday (overnight)	M.A.P.P.T.I.M.E.	Wanique Khemi, Tehuti Shabazz	Jazz music, metaphysical reasoning

M.A.P.P.T.I.M.E. = Meta-physical Answers and Personal/Political Truths Inside Musical Edutainment music as an American art form."[33] As is rather typical of HBCU radio, the range of jazz styles on WRFG runs from smooth jazz and R&B to almost all post-bop styles, but not much avant-garde music.

WDNA

A community radio station in Miami, Florida, WDNA, "Serious Jazz," is licensed to the Bascomb Memorial Broadcasting Foundation, whose sole purpose is to operate the station. Community radio stations tend to reflect the diversity of the community in which they are located, and WDNA is no exception. According to 2010 Census data, Miami-Dade County is 65 percent Hispanic, 17 percent black, 16 percent white, and 1.7 percent Asian; 51 percent of its residents are foreign-born, with 72 percent living in households where a language other than English is spoken.[34] More than other major urban areas, Miami's Hispanic community is itself quite diverse in terms of national origin. The countries producing the largest shares of Hispanic Miamians are Colombia with 4.6 percent, Cuba with 34.3 percent, the Dominican Republic with 2.3 percent, Honduras with 2.2 percent, Mexico with 2.1 percent, Nicaragua with 4.2 percent, and Puerto Rico with 3.7 percent.[35] While dominated by jazz, WDNA's music programming still reflects this diversity. According to (volunteer) General Manager Maggie Pelleyá, WDNA attracts an ethnically diverse audience "quite representative of the South Florida community."[36] (Pelleyá, who passed away in 2023, had guided the WDNA for more than forty years.) The weekday schedule includes a morning jazz program, *88 Jazz Place Morning*, whose music ranges from mainstream to soul jazz to the occasional avant-garde selection, plus Latin jazz and a bit of R&B. The 11 a.m. slot varies by day, with blues and oldies programs on some days and shows devoted to the jazz programs at the University of Miami and Florida International University on others. The Station features Latin jazz from noon to 3 p.m., a late afternoon drive-time jazz program similar to the morning mix, and another set of once-weekly programs in the 7 p.m. hour (the syndicated *Cool Jazz Countdown*, *Jazz Happening Now*, and Christian McBride's *Jazz Night in America*), *Cubaneando*, and *Jazz from the Hampton House*, a program featuring the music of artists who performed at the famed Miami venue for black entertainers. *Fusion Latina* airs weeknights from 8 p.m. to 11 p.m., with WFMT's internet distributed overnight show completing the broadcast day. On the weekends there are reggae, electronic, Indian, Brazilian, Afro Pop, and world music programs.

With no non-music programs on its schedule, WDNA is unique for a community radio station. Like other community stations, there is, however, sometimes a blurring of music and activism. It has been reported that the station can be a bit unpredictable—according to a local paper, "Tune in WDNA (FM 88.9) on a midweek afternoon and you may hear jazz, Latin soul music or poetry readings. Evenings, you may get reggae or an AIDS discussion."[37]

Sunday afternoons feature the weekly program in Urdu, the language of India and Pakistan. Before 1994 WDNA was a free-form community radio station playing a wide range of music including blues, gospel, acoustic, folk, and rock as well as jazz and Latin jazz.

The station's website states that its mission "is to provide quality public-centric music, arts, and cultural programming to the residents of South Florida and beyond. In an ever-changing radio landscape, WDNA remains committed to America's Classical Music, alternative voices, and the marriage of entertainment with enrichment." Because of the number of hours devoted to jazz and the wide range of jazz styles offered, it is considered by many as one of the nation's leading jazz radio stations.

Pacifica Foundation Stations

Marc Stern describes the Pacifica Radio Network (PRN) as "an alternative and highly politicized network of community radio stations and a national news service."[38] Matthew Lasar has reported that, with its long history of squabbles between the foundation and its stations, "Pacifica radio is widely regarded as something akin to the late Ottoman Empire of public broadcasting."[39] The PRN is wholly owned by the Pacifica Foundation, which was founded in 1946 as the brainchild of news reporter and conscientious objector Lewis Hill. Seeking to operate an AM radio station in Richmond, California, he instead was able to launch KPFA-FM in Berkeley in 1949.[40] Hill was a Gandhian pacifist, and through the Pacifica Foundation he and his colleagues hoped to further postwar peace by enabling communications between different peoples. From the beginning Pacifica, the number of whose stations would eventually grow to six (including KPFB [Berkeley], KPFK [Los Angeles], KPFT [Houston], WBAI [New York], and WPFW [Washington, DC]), operated under a non-hierarchical management model that while maximizing individual freedom minimized organizational discipline and cohesion and left it, again in Stern's words, "fractious," "internally contentious," and "prone to conflicts and confrontations."[41] As a result, Pacifica has undergone a series of internecine upheavals concerning local stations' issues as well as conflicts between the national board and local stations—particularly in the 1950s, again in the 1990s, and continuing today.[42] These struggles have affected local programming, as is currently the situation at WPFW and WBAI.

Pacifica's broadcast activities have three major components: the creation of national program content such as the newscast *Democracy Now!* and its celebrated gavel-to-gavel coverage of U.S. Supreme Court nomination hearings, a network infrastructure for the distribution of programs to its stations and others that subscribe to the distribution service, and the local programming content of its stations. Most of the Pacifica stations have a free-form programming model in which there is little attempt to create any kind of synergy between shows; an Irish folk music show may be preceded by a program dealing with personal computers and followed by opera or a blues program. The mix and focus of programming is unique to each station and is presumably relevant to the needs of the local community. For example, WPFW in Washington, DC, features a great deal of jazz programming, with hip-hop, Caribbean, African, and southern soul music featured in addition to news and public affairs. One lasting complaint about Pacifica stations, however, is that the programs tend to become sinecures, often running for decades until the host is unable or unwilling to continue, and little effort is made to keep the programming relevant or to appeal to a larger audience.

Founded in 1977, WPFW programmed more than one hundred hours of jazz per week until very recently. The station's slogan, "Jazz and Justice Radio," indicates the degree to which jazz is seen as political for the station. The high percentage of music on WPFW's program schedule stood out from those of other Pacifica stations that devoted a far greater share of the program day to public affairs. Defending the station from intra-Pacifica criticism, early 1990s station manager Leon Collins countered that jazz "is a more sophisticated form of social protest music. Jazz people are very political." It is not clear whether by "jazz people" Collins meant musicians, the audience, or both, but later in the same interview he also employed familiar language lauding jazz's uniqueness. "Jazz [is] the classical music of middle-class black America," said Collins, and the station was able to win the highly contested license in the DC market because through jazz, WPFW promised to serve "a sophisticated, upper-income, educated, and worldly" African American audience that fit "the elitist public radio concept."[43] Collins, while invoking language that lays claim to cultural standing ("classical music"), did so not in reference to universal or American values—in fact, it is significant that he didn't call jazz "America's classical music"—but to its specific appeal to "worldly," "sophisticated," and otherwise demographically desirable audience characteristics. His mention of "elitist public radio" seems to have less to do with WPFW's audience than to the way Pacifica successfully framed the station's proposed service model when applying to the FCC for its license.

Jazz is certainly not the only music heard on WPFW. Blues music has been programmed during the noon hour, and hip-hop and gospel music are also heard during the week. The programmers have long recognized that there are other groups within the black community and have addressed them with African and Caribbean music programs. For many years Saturday programming has heavily featured southern R&B, black oldies, and Latin jazz. Most of the WPFW music programs go beyond entertainment and present community announcements and take calls about issues of interest to the audience. The jazz playlists differ as well from those of most public radio stations. WPFW programmers often play longer tracks, air somewhat more adventurous and experimental music, particularly in the overnight programs, and juxtapose jazz selections with soul, R&B, or blues numbers. Jazz music with uplifting or spiritual themes, overtly political themes, titles, or lyrics, and combinations of music with spoken word are often heard on WPFW.

In early December 2012, general manager John Hughes abruptly announced sweeping proposed changes to the WPFW program schedule. The financial reasons for the changes were given in a news account: "'We have to stop the hemorrhaging,' said Tony Norman, chairman of the community board that oversees the station. 'We're losing money and audience. We have to make these changes.'"[44] The station's listening audience, which had peaked in the early 2000s, has decreased to about 150,000.[45] Furthermore, financial instabilities at Pacifica have stressed the WPFW budget (as well as the budgets of all of the Pacifica stations), which traditionally had been met by equal parts listener support, CPB funding (as a station serving a minority audience), and Pacifica grants. Although the station earns some income from its originated programs and from providing studio services in the nation's capital, Pacifica's bylaws forbid corporate underwriting. In a typical year, listener support provides about 80 percent of the station's income.[46]

The proposed (and at the time of writing partly implemented) changes conform to a familiar model: making WPFW largely a news and information radio station from 6 a.m. to 7 p.m. and leave jazz for non-peak listening hours. Some WPFW staffers and supporters were astonished to learn that much of the proposed daytime content would be familiar to NPR and PRX listeners: Cornell West and Tavis Smiley's *Smiley & West Show*, Michel Martin's *Tell Me More*, and *The Takeaway*, a PRX program once positioned as a *Morning Edition* alternative. The new schedule was announced on a Thursday, effective the following Monday. Many displaced show hosts were denied so much as a farewell. As Jonathan L. Fischer notes:

> The reshuffled programming grid, the volunteer hosts slowly learned, would largely separate nighttime music shows during the week from daytime talk programming—much of it syndicated from other stations around the country. Suddenly, D.C.'s community station would feature new shows from San Francisco, Los Angeles, New York—and most heretically, in the eyes of some stakeholders, from mainstream organizations like National Public Radio and Public Radio International.[47]

The resistance to this proposal was fierce. In the end, jazz did lose daytime hours on WPFW, but it retained the 3 p.m. to 5 p.m. weekday spot, and instead of standard public radio talk fare, programs that were locally produced, originated by Pacifica, and alternative filled the weekday morning schedule and the 5 p.m. to 7 p.m. news slot. Still, some have not recovered from the diminished emphasis on jazz at WPFW, nor from the manner of its implementation.

The motives behind the reduction in the amount and availability of jazz on WPFW embody the tension between mission and market. According to Fischer,

> To Hughes, who's led the nonprofit WPFW for nearly two years, the solution is running a station of musical obsessives and anti-establishmentarians more like a business—which means, in his telling, crafting a less jarring programming schedule that he hopes will bring a bigger audience and fill the station's coffers with more donations.[48]

Of course, the historical model of the noncommercial radio schedule was jarring, with blocks of widely differing programming in adjacent time periods. The station's previous daytime schedule alternated jazz, feminist programming, alternative health, and local political discussions. The changes are contentious not only because of the loss of favorite programs but because WPFW's shift signals conflict with three embedded values. First, The "Jazz and Justice" slogan overtly indicates the connection between the music and political expression during the station's history. Reducing the amount of jazz is seen by some in the community as a refutation of that connection. The sentiment of WPFW programmers was "the talk never stops and the music never ends"; "Jazz was politics; politics was jazz."[49] Second, although much of the proposed new daytime programming is either locally produced or comes from within Pacifica such as *Democracy Now!*, the importation of mainstream public radio programs is viewed with disdain in view of the station's commitment to provide access to disenfranchised voices. Third, WPFW has identified itself as a black and Latino radio station. The changes at WPFW have to be viewed in the greater context of gentrification in the District of Columbia. The station was founded when the District had a solid black majority. As an article written at the time stated, "To the dissenting programmers, the proposed schedule changes represent a betrayal of the station's mission as a progressive, even radical, alternative to mainstream radio and a preserver of jazz, one which particularly serves the D.C. area's black residents."[50]

A long-term influx of whites and Latinos has reduced the black majority in Washington DC to 50.7 percent.[51] As the political system has responded to these new demographic realities, there is a suspicion that WPFW is seeking financial stability on the model of the public radio stations that already serve the greater metropolitan area, exacerbating the existing tension between black WPFW and liberal white Pacifica. At WPFW, jazz has been seen as part of the political message of black radio.

As radio researchers, Lazarsfeld and Stanton pointed out in 1949, however, the industry—or in this case, the station—has to attract a large enough audience to stay alive.[52] For many years, WPFW has been trying to juggle its three overlapping audiences: the African American and multicultural audience, the jazz audience, and the liberal-progressive news and information audience. At best, the changes attempt to organize these audiences by time of day. The comments of a thoughtful listener perhaps make the case for a bit more professionalism while at the same time endorsing inclusive and diverse programming:

> WPFW is essential for the DC community. We simply must have the jazz and multi-cultural programming it provides. Also, it offers the unique voices of the local community in its commentary. However, the lack of practical information, such as local time, weather and traffic is often discouraging to listeners. If I really need to know the driving landscape/conditions during the morning and evening commutes, I can't listen to WPFW during those hours. Volunteerism and radicalism is great, even necessary, but professionalism and practicality are also necessary. Also—Put Jay Winter Nightwolf back on primetime. Native American interests should not be further marginalized.[53]

Only time will tell if WPFW is able to survive both the turmoil of Pacifica ownership and local demographic changes and retain its valuable jazz programming.

Student-Run College Radio

The college radio station has a long tradition in broadcasting. The University of Wisconsin's WHA is a broadcast pioneer that can trace its origin to the earliest experimental days of radio. By 1920 the university already had twenty years of experience operating a radio station. Typical of these early campus stations, WHA had a dual mission of providing technical and operational experience to students and providing a public service. For the university-affiliated noncommercial stations in the public radio sector, the educational and service mission assumed a greater priority than student training and participation. As has been shown, these CPB-qualified stations, including WHA and the Wisconsin Public Radio network, have gone the route of acquiring national programs and employing a professional staff.

The capital and operating costs of running a radio station are not insignificant, and many academic institutions have sold or abandoned their stations rather than ante up when faced with budget pressures. In several situations, universities faced with deficits have recognized that selling the license could help with financial needs.[54] Among jazz radio stations discussed in this volume, such deals include the sales of

- WDCU by the University of the District of Columbia (UDC) in 1997 to C-SPAN for $13 million[55]

- WDUQ by Duquesne University in 2011 to WYEP for $6 million[56]
- KPLU by Pacific Lutheran University in 2013 to Pacifica Public Media for $7 million[57]
- WSHA by Shaw University in 2018 to the Educational Media Foundation for $3.5 million[58]

An alternative to the professionally staffed university station is the college radio station staffed by students and volunteers. Many of these stations began as carrier-current AM stations, where unregulated radio signals of extremely limited range radiated from the electrical wiring in campus buildings. As these stations evolved, first into low-power FM—typically 10 watts—then into full-power stations, the tradition of student autonomy remained. In most cases the broadcast license holder is the university or board of trustees, but sometimes the student government organization is itself the licensee. (For example, the license for Georgia Tech's WREK-FM is held by the Radio Communications Board of Georgia Tech.) Tradition, formal, or informal agreements allow the students autonomy in operating the station, with the host school providing space and utilities.

When the university holds the license, the level of oversight can vary tremendously. At minimum, the university wants to avoid legal or litigious encumbrances, but it may also have concerns about the image presented by the programming, though most have learned that calling public attention to student-run stations will attract new listenership where there was very little to start with. In some cases, the political values of student programmers clash with those of university leaders, such as the case of Jesuit-run Georgetown University and its progressive/alternative rock station WGTB in the 1970s. The station was behaving far too much in the community radio mode in those turbulent times. It was the political conflict between WGTB and the university that led university president Timothy Healy to donate the station to UDC in 1979 (actually, he sold it for one dollar).[59] Student radio at Georgetown today takes place over closed-circuit and Internet broadcasting.

Crises and controversies aside, most college stations have a wide variety of music programs that typically represent the interests and taste of the program host and producers. The on- and off-air staff of a college station consists of student and non-student volunteers; usually no host is on the air more than once per week because of students' time constraints. Some college radio stations have formal training and internship programs, while at others radio veterans help the less experienced students with running a station. At a recent jazz radio conference, Malvin Massey, with WUMR-FM at the University of Memphis State since 1988, described a color-coded system he implemented to assist the less proficient student DJs with providing variety in music selections and to teach them jazz history.[60]

Complicating the university-college dichotomy are the HBCU radio stations. Some operate as public radio stations with aspects of community radio, and others resemble typical college stations with eccentric offerings. One critical difference for both types, compared to majority university and college stations, is the commitment to serve black audiences. According to various sources, there may be sixty or more black college radio stations; Hampton University's WHOV, founded in 1964, was the first HBCU-owned station. (Sadly, Shaw University's WSHA, founded in 1968, was sold in 2018.) Table 26, a confirmed list of thirty-three HBCU stations, gives an idea of how many such stations identify themselves with jazz.[61] Where music is concerned, these stations are operating in markets with either no other stations playing black music or with only one or two commercial stations doing so. In these cases, black college radio stations are usually determined to bridge the gaps in commercial programming, presenting R&B, hip hop, jazz, smooth jazz, gospel, blues, and sometimes politically oriented music in those communities. There are certainly several more HBCU operations using carrier current, internet streaming, or carriage on cable television systems than those using terrestrial radio.

Almost all of the HBCU radio stations have some jazz programming, usually including smooth and mainstream jazz, despite the slogan or format listing. For several of these stations, mainstream jazz is provided by the overnight jazz programming service from WFMT Chicago. Most of the HBCU stations are members of the AAPRC, and some originate consortium content. Almost all the stations listed as public radio or variety, and some of the others, have a serious commitment to news programming as well as music and carry *All Things Considered*, *Morning Edition*, or *Democracy Now!*

The embrace of jazz as a "rare and valuable national American treasure" is itself a dramatic turn for the HBCUs.[62] There was a historical unease with jazz in the classroom on the part of the "striving" black elites in the black colleges. For example, despite the entry of jazz education at the college level as early as 1942 at North Texas State, one could not obtain sanctioned instruction in jazz at HBCUs until the late 1960s. As late as 1975 a jazz concentration was available at only three of the southern HBCUs: Mississippi Valley State, Southern University (Baton Rouge), and North Carolina A&T.[63] In the late 1970s the author performed in the senior recital of Howard University's first jazz studies graduate, the late guitarist Noble Jolley. An additional reason for the late appearance of jazz education at the HBCUs could have been their traditional emphasis on training music educators.[64] Because jazz had yet to establish a place in the high schools until the 1960s, jazz may have been seen as irrelevant to the training of future teachers. This alone, however, cannot explain the devaluation of jazz at these schools. At the HBCUs, "pioneer jazz educators were faced with overcoming negative attitudes concerning jazz by administrators, educators, the

TABLE 26. HBCU radio stations.

Call sign, freq.	University affiliation	Station slogan	Station format[a]
WJAB-FM, 90.9	Alabama A&M University	Smooth Jazz and Cool Vocals	Jazz
WVAS-FM, 90.7	Alabama State University	The Jazz Giant	Jazz
WMWI-FM, 88.7	Miles College		College
KUAP-FM, 89.7	University of Arkansas at Pine Bluff	Smooth Jazz 89.7	Urban
WANM-FM, 90.5	Florida A&M University	The Flava Station[b]	Urban
WCLK-FM, 91.9	Clark Atlanta University	Atlanta's Jazz Station	Jazz
WHCJ-FM, 90.3	Savannah State University	Voice of Savannah State[c]	Variety
WKKC-FM, 88.3	Kennedy-King College	The New Sound of Soul	Urban
KGRM-FM, 91.5	Grambling University	Giving You Music and More[d]	Variety
WEAA-FM, 88.9	Morgan State University	Your Source for Cool Jazz and More: The Voice of the Community	Jazz
WESM-FM, 91.3	University of Maryland at Eastern Shore	Your Source of Jazz & Blues[e]	Jazz
WURC-FM, 88.1	Rust College	Rust College Public Radio	Public Radio
WVSD-FM, 91.7	Mississippi Valley State University	Voice of the Valley[f]	College
WJSU-FM, 88.5	Jackson State University	Jackson Mississippi's Source for News and Jazz	Jazz
WPRL-FM, 91.7	Alcorn State University	91.7, the Gold	Public Radio
KJLU-FM, 88.9	Lincoln University (Missouri)	Smooth Jazz 88.9	Jazz
WNCU-FM, 90.7	North Carolina Central University	Where Jazz Is Alive	Jazz
WRVS-FM, 89.9	Elizabeth City State University	89.9 ECSU[g]	Public Radio
WNAA-FM, 90.1	North Carolina A&T University	The Voice, 90.1	Variety
WSHA-FM, 88.9	Shaw University	sold 2018	Jazz
WSNC-FM, 90.5	Winston-Salem State University	Genuine Jazz	Jazz
WCSU-FM, 88.9	Central State University	Your Urban/Jazz Connection	Urban
WSSB-FM, 90.3	South Carolina State University	South Carolina's Jazz Station	Jazz
WFSK-FM, 88.1	Fisk University	Jazzie 88	Smooth jazz
KTSU-FM, 90.9	Texas Southern University	Your Community Station	Jazz
KPVU-FM, 91.3	Prairie View A&M University	The Original, 91.3 FM	Public Radio
WHOV-FM, 88.1	Hampton Institute	The Essence of Hampton University	Jazz
WNSB-FM, 91.1	Norfolk State University	Blazin' Hot 91.1	Hip Hop
WVST-FM, 91.3	Virginia State University	The Source	Variety
WRWS-LP, 99.1	Bethune-Cookman College	Daytona's Urban Jukebox	Urban
WASU-LP, 92.7	Albany State University	Real 92.7	Urban
WLCD-LP, 98.7	Lane College	The Dragon	College/Urban Oldies
WFVS-FM, 96.9	Fort Valley State University	Power Jamz 96.9	Variety

[a] In this table, Urban is short for Urban Contemporary.
[b] Format includes Gospel, R&B, and "Old School," Neo-Soul, Hip-Hop, Reggae, and Jazz.
[c] WHCJ plays a variety of musical styles including jazz, reggae, gospel, blues, hip hop, African, Latin, and alternative soul.
[d] Jazz is aired from 9 a.m. to 6 p.m. daily.
[e] Midday and evening jazz.
[f] "We bring you the best in jazz, inspirational music, and rhythm and blues."
[g] WRVS programs about twenty hours of jazz per week.

clergy, the lay public, and non-jazz musicians."[65] In fact, students and faculty alike were often cautioned in the strongest terms to stay away from jazz, caution they often did not heed; banned from playing jazz on campus, the same students might be hired privately to play at faculty parties.

Fortunately, jazz now has greater respect at all educational levels and among African American educators in music and the humanities, and this is reflected in the prominent place that jazz occupies today on black college radio.

WKCR

On April 30, 2024, Columbia University's WKCR-FM provided vital news reporting on the NYPD arrests on campus; in between eyewitness reports, it broadcast music by Jameel Moondoc, William Parker, and Hamid Drake. WKCR is a college radio station run mainly by students, alumni, and outside volunteers. It is known internationally for its jazz programming, especially since it has been available for many years as an internet stream. It is especially well known for its multi-hour (and sometimes multi-day) marathon broadcasts devoted to important jazz musicians, round-the-clock memorial broadcasts commemorating the deaths of major figures, and annual birthday broadcast marathons celebrating the careers of the likes of Duke Ellington, Charlie Parker, John Coltrane, and Lester Young. Several jazz shows, when not preempted by special broadcasts, appear daily on WKCR—*Daybreak Express*, *Bird Flight*, *Out to Lunch*, and *Jazz Alternatives*—sometimes with different hosts.[66] These four programs alone account for more than fifty hours of programming per week, and there are additional jazz programs on the weekend, including *Traditions in Swing*, which is devoted to jazz from the first half of the twentieth century. Most of the jazz programs feature a variety of styles, but there are exceptions. Phil Schaap's daily morning show *Bird Flight* was devoted exclusively to the recordings of Charlie Parker, while the rotating hosts of the noon hour's *Out to Lunch* sometimes play free jazz and experimental music. WKCR's current style of jazz programming dates to 1970:

> During the 1970s, the station took on its slogan and commitment to providing "The Alternative." WKCR strove to provide a home to music that was otherwise absent from the airwaves. In 1970, program director Tom Nesi appointed Jamie Katz as jazz director, who then recruited Phil Schaap and Sharif Abdus-Salaam, two programmers still broadcasting today. Within a year, 40 hours per week of airtime were devoted to jazz. The department featured both classic recordings and contemporary live performances, including a regular broadcast from the West End, which aired from 1977 to 1990.[67]

The station features Latin jazz, African music, bluegrass, and hip hop, but classical music (which tends toward twentieth- and twenty-first century works and early music) is the other major category of music on the program schedule.

The station's programming is approximately 35 percent jazz, 25 percent new music, and 20 percent classical music, with the remainder comprising ethnic and "American" music.[68] The station has a long-standing commitment to experimental music:

> The station also resolved to present new compositional and experimental music, establishing the New Music Department, which featured diverse composers and performers, such as Karlheinz Stockhausen, John Cage, and New York Downtown Scene pioneers John Zorn and Zeena Parkins. In 1987, Cage used WKCR's studio as his extended musical instrument. Station DJs passed him opera records from which he played random excerpts while manipulating all the other sound variables controllable from the studio.[69]

In contrast to public-sector WBGO, which also serves metropolitan New York, WKCR not only risks audience fatigue by playing a single artist for hours or days at a time, or playing all of the alternate takes of a Charlie Parker tune, but also will play older recordings—complete with limited fidelity—and avant-garde or experimental music. Its ability to program with such freedom, Travis Jackson surmised, "perhaps because it was less dependent on individual donors or commercial sponsors to stay on the air."[70]

Table 27 lists the day-long birthday celebrations that WKCR observes each year. For several of these musicians—Monk, Roach, Eldridge, Mingus, and Coleman—these broadcasts began while they were still alive, and some

TABLE 27. WKCR-FM Columbia University jazz birthday broadcasts.

Annual Observance	Honored Musician(s)
January 10	Max Roach (b. January 10, 1924; d. August 16, 2007)
January 30	Roy Eldridge (b. January 30, 1911; d. February 26, 1989)
March 9	Ornette Coleman (b. March 9, 1930; d. June 11, 2015)
March 10	Bix Beiderbecke (b. March 10, 1903; d. August 7, 1931)
April 7	Billie Holiday (b. April 7, 1915; d. July 17, 1959)
April 22	Charles Mingus (b. April 22, 1922; d. January 5, 1979)
April 29	Duke Ellington (April 29,1899; d. May 24, 1974)
July 4	Louis Armstrong (b. August 4, 1901; d. July 6, 1971)
August 4	Armstrong believed his birthday was July 4, 1900; WKCR celebrates both.
August 27–29	Lester Young (b. August 27, 1909; d. March 15, 1959) and Charlie Parker (b. August 29, 1920; d. March 12, 1955). WKCR plays Young until noon on August 28, then switches to Parker.
September 23	John Coltrane (b. September 23, 1926; d. July 17, 1967)
October 10	Thelonious Monk (b. October 10, 1917; d. February 17, 1982)
October 30	Clifford Brown (b. October 30, 1930; d. June 26, 1956)
November 21	Coleman Hawkins (b. November 21, 1904; d. May 19, 1969)

of them participated. In addition to the annual jazz birthdays, WKCR will preempt scheduled programming for memorial broadcasts celebrating the lives of important jazz figures shortly after their deaths. For instance, an all-day broadcast marking the death of drummer Jimmy Cobb was held on June 2, 2020. On several occasions, the rumored deaths of jazz musicians have been sadly confirmed by hearing their music being played nonstop on WKCR.

Besides the regularly scheduled birthdays and as-needed memorial broadcasts, the WKCR jazz department is known for its marathon broadcasts, which take as much time as needed to play every available recording of the featured musician. Although the marathons also have feature segments, perhaps on the theme of such as the fêted artist's recordings with another great, or rare recordings of alternate takes or bootlegs, the centerpiece of each marathon is the airing of all of the musician's work in chronological order. The first marathon featured the music of the late Albert Ayler in 1970. Though too many to list here, the marathons aired between 1985 and 1990 will give some idea of the stylistic range of the featured artists. The following is an excerpt from an interview where Phil Schaap, working from memory, recalled each marathon beginning with Ayler's in 1970.

> The third Lost Masters Festival, in May 1985, was Joe Smith, Lucky Thompson (the only living lost master), Booker Little, and Scott LaFaro. Summer '85 was Jack Teagarden. November of '85 was Jelly Roll Morton. Cannonball Adderley was May of '86. Summer '86 was Eddie Durham [he participated]. Rahsaan Roland Kirk was August of '86. Sun Ra was April of '87 [he participated], in conjunction with the New Music Department. Dizzy Gillespie was May of '87 [he participated]. Sidney Bechet was May of '88. Summer of '88 was the fourth Lost Masters Festival, with Big Sid Catlett, Ma Rainey, Billy Strayhorn and Serge Chaloff. Fats Waller was May of '89. Art Blakey was November of '89 [he participated]. May of '90 was Ella Fitzgerald and Lionel Hampton [he participated].[71]

The amazing range of music, from Morton, Bechet, and Teagarden to Little, Kirk, and Sun Ra, not to mention the important but overlooked musicians Chaloff, Durham, and LaFaro illustrates not only the unusual value of WKCR to jazz listeners in New York and around the world, but also how the station is run counter to radio programming conventions. The dedication of immense blocks of time to these musicians is completely out of step with endorsed public radio practices. From the standpoint of variety, spending three hours listening to the master and alternate takes of two months of Lucky Thompson's recording sessions would be, to many listeners, monotonous. On a personal note, turning every radio in the house to WKCR and immersing myself in the music of Rahsaan Roland Kirk for more than a week in 1986 was a life-changing experience.

The death of six-time Grammy winner Phil Schaap (1951–2021) leaves many listeners concerned about the future of jazz on the station. Although there have been many stalwart jazz presenters besides Schaap on WKCR including Sharif Abdus-Salaam and Ted Panken, within the delicate balance of power between current students, alumni, outside volunteers, and the station's nine standing departments, it is thought that Schaap was an energetic and compelling voice for jazz.[72]

KTSU

Texas Southern University is an HBCU located in Houston, and its KTSU-FM is a leading noncommercial radio station. Among its multiracial listenership is one of the nation's largest black audiences.[73] As with most HBCU stations, the range of its jazz programming extends not so much in the direction of experimental music but toward funk, R&B, and smooth jazz. For example, rather than play a percussive and angular original Thelonious Monk recording of "Evidence," one might instead hear a version featuring mellow guitar and strings. As the Houstonian Jason Moran described the KTSU of the 1990s, "Houston had a great jazz station . . . it wasn't as wild as 'KCR [New York's WKCR], but was the Southern, black version of 'KCR and they played a wide spectrum."[74] Indeed the station's slogan is "Jazz in all its colors, and a whole lot more." Its programming was succinctly described in a 2002 *Houston Press* article declaring it the city's best radio station:

> "Jazz in All Its Colors" is the motto of Texas Southern University's radio voice, and they live up to those fine words. Not many stations can boast a palette quite like KTSU's rainbow of gospel, jazz (Latin and Anglo), hip-hop, blues, zydeco, R&B, oldies, soul and reggae. There are also the commentaries, profiles and historical reminiscences of Frank Torry, a walking, talking compendium of all things African-American in Houston. Props also go out to the station for allowing the still-running Kidz Jamm on the air way back in 1983, when mainstream radio outlets were insisting that rap was just a fad. KTSU knew better than those folks then, and when it comes to running a quality radio station, they still do.[75]

KTSU drastically increased the amount of jazz it programmed per week when the University of Houston's KUHF-FM moved to fill the classical music void when the commercial classical station abandoned the format in 1987. The station adopted a proprietary and protective posture concerning jazz. The management team at the time was quoted in a news article describing the jazz programming as ranging "from the acoustic mainstream of the '50s and '60s to more contemporary sounds," as being "firmly committed to jazz as the central focus of their programming." Further, "there is so much in terms of the art form of jazz that needs to be preserved, since it is America's gift to the world . . . we need to be the guardians, to preserve its past and to promote its future."[76] Though the station claimed that it programmed the widest possible range of jazz, there were complaints that it didn't play enough traditional jazz, classic jazz, or new music.

Low-Power FM: Once Again, Still Here

Over the course of the past fifteen years there has been a boom in low-power FM (LPFM) radio stations. In 2005, the first year the FCC reported a separate tally for them, there were 498 LPFM stations. By 2016 there were more than 1,500, their share growing in that time from one-fifth to three-eighths of all noncommercial FMs. In 2020 the FCC reported that there were 4,172 educational FM stations and 2,159 LPFM stations. By these measures, and particularly in view of the explosive growth of LPFMs, the battle for low-power stations that was waged by community broadcasting advocates must be considered a success. However, the procedure for resolving low-power license requests has resulted in a great number of these stations' being used to form ad hoc networks. Low-power LPFMs stations have become a welcome but underappreciated addition to the noncommercial jazz radio world.

Though the current era of low-power radio dates to the 2000 ruling by the FCC that established the service, it has a prehistory reflecting reciprocal opposition with established broadcasters from the commercial and the noncommercial sectors. The FCC issued the first FM Class D licenses in 1948 with the goal of encouraging more educational institutions to use the reserved 88 to 92 MHz educational band. Class D stations were originally limited to 10 watts of transmitter power and, though restricted in their geographical reach, could be operated very inexpensively. Many of these early low-power stations were operated under the guise of high school and college student training labs.

This changed with the Public Broadcasting Act of 1967. The radio advocates who managed to scotch tape "radio" into what had been drafted as a public television bill also hoped to create a professional and nationwide educational radio service. This put the notions of what was "educational" into conflict: Was it mistake-prone and clunky-sounding radio that trained student broadcasters or professional-sounding radio bringing education and culture to listeners? In the view of advocates of the latter, the Class D stations were occupying valuable noncommercial spectrum assignments. With a goal of forcing the Class D stations to improve or go away, the CPB, acting on behalf of the professional camp, petitioned the FCC in 1972 to eliminate stations that did not have at least 100 watts of effective radiated power. The FCC would issue such a ruling in 1978. Much to their dismay, many stations, including my own WRCT-FM (Carnegie Mellon University), successfully made the jump to the new power levels.

The idea of low-power radio did not perish, however. An important factor in the eventual re-establishment of a low-power service was the steady yet shifty presence of illegal broadcasters, so-called pirate radio stations operating without a license and in defiance of the FCC enforcement efforts. Ironically, FCC chairman William Kennard, who in his previous role as FCC general counsel had led an aggressive campaign to silence the pirates, acknowledged that illegal broadcasters and their near decade of civil disobedience had played a large role in the eventual victory by LPFM advocates. Christopher Lucas interprets the African American Kennard's support as intending to create "an alternative radio industry" with space for minority ownership of commercial low-power radio stations.[77]

But the LPFM that came through the rulemaking and legislative process was limited to noncommercial broadcasting, thus protecting the incumbent commercial industry from new competition. Low-power FM was strongly supported by the community radio movement. With a clear focus on and commitment to community access to the public airwaves, advocates saw low-power radio as a way to broaden participation in radio and a counter to the narrowing of programming content, especially the de-emphasis on music and local content, that had been gripping public radio.

Simply shaping the regulatory, legislative, and litigative contest over low-power radio as a battle between commercial and noncommercial interests would be a misleading simplification. In this fight, the public and commercial radio stations at times shared similarly establishment viewpoints. The National Association of Broadcasters, the trade organization of commercial broadcasting, and NPR joined forces to oppose the establishment of low-power stations and, failing that, to limit the number that would be permitted. In support of LPFM was a strained mix of bedfellows in "a coalition of alternative media activists allied with fundamentalist churches and conservative groups."[78]

With both the commercial and the public radio sectors opposed to LPFM and citing concerns about interference, it took a congressional mandate to prod the FCC to find a workable technical basis for establishing a new low-power FM service that did not interfere with existing service. As with the old Class D stations, only noncommercial operation is allowed, and transmitter power is limited to 100 watts. But LPFM stations can operate on any FM channel assignment that meets the guidelines to prevent interference with existing stations; they are not limited to the noncommercial band. This relaxed interference protocol requires the stations to avoid interference only with full-power stations assigned to the same frequency—these will be separated by a significant distance—and the stations on the immediately adjacent frequencies.

For religious and conservative interests, participation in the low-power coalition paid off. In 2016 Pew Research published a survey that demonstrated the strength of religious broadcasters in LPFM. Five radio formats accounted for 70 percent of all LPFMs. Variety programming accounted for 31 percent, with religious stations combining for 39 percent— Religion (23 percent), Christian (7 percent), Religious music (5 percent), and Spanish/Religious (4 percent).[79]

With more than twenty-four hundred stations, many offering a variety of musical programming, it is exceedingly difficult to enumerate the number of stations playing jazz. A quick search at the invaluable radio-locator.com website produced a list of nineteen LPFM stations that gave jazz (or smooth jazz) as their format in 2020 (see table 28).

A thorough review of the database at the website lpfmdatabase.com produced forty-four jazz stations (table 29) as well as the following interesting statistics.[80] Religious, Christian, and Spanish Religious stations combined to account for 931, or 45 percent, of all LPFM stations. Although the FCC limited ownership to one station per licensee, 108 stations broadcast the Seventh-day Adventist Church's Three Angels Broadcasting Network, and another 121 stations broadcast the Catholic Church's EWTN (Eternal Word Television Network) radio programs. These two networks have evaded the goal of stimulating diversity in programming, one intention of authorizing low-power stations. Overall, the stripping of commercial stations from the final

TABLE 28. Jazz and smooth jazz low-power FM stations, April 2020.

Call Sign	Frequency	City	Format
KAJI	95.3 LPFM	Palm Desert, CA	Jazz
KBJZ	94.1 LPFM	Juneau, AK	Jazz
KMFO	98.1 LPFM	Tulsa, OK	Jazz
KOJH	104.7 LPFM	Kansas City, MO	Jazz
KVNM	101.1 LPFM	Veguita, NM	Jazz
WCRX	102.1 LPFM	Columbus, OH	Jazz
WETF	105.7 LPFM	South Bend, IN	Jazz
WJSK	101.1 LPFM	Bartlett, NH	Jazz
WJZP	107.9 LPFM	Portland, ME	Jazz
WQJC	107.9 LPFM	Quincy, IL	Jazz
WSAX	98.5 LPFM	Columbus, OH	Jazz
WXHQ	105.9 LPFM	Newport, RI	Jazz
KCYI	97.7 LPFM	Oklahoma City, OK	Smooth Jazz
KJZT	90.1 LPFM	Tulsa, OK	Smooth Jazz
KRWV	99.3 LPFM	Gold Canyon, AZ	Smooth Jazz
KWBR	105.7 LPFM	Saint George, UT	Smooth Jazz
WJZK	97.3 LPFM	Fort Walton Beach, FL	Smooth Jazz
WNOZ	95.3 LPFM	New Orleans, LA	Smooth Jazz
WTTZ	93.5 LPFM	Baltimore, MD	Smooth Jazz

Source: The Low-Power FM Database, lpfmdatabase.com, April 2020.

TABLE 29. Radio Locator list of jazz and smooth jazz LPFM stations, April 2020.

Call Sign	Frequency	Licensee	City	Format
WUMO-LP	94.5	AframSouth	Montgomery, AL	Urban Gospel/Jazz
WTUS-LP	103.3	Tuscaloosa City Board of Education	Tuscaloosa, AL	Travelers Info/Smooth Jazz
KBJZ-LP	94.1	Gastineau Broadcasting Corp.	Juneau, AK	Jazz/Blues
KRWV-LP	99.3	Gold Canyon Public Radio, Inc.	Gold Canyon, AZ	Smooth Jazz/Variety/Pacifica
KHOX-LP	106.7	Waxman Educational Corp.	Walnut Ridge, AR	Jazz
KFGD-LP	92.5	Fig Garden Police Protection District	Fresno, CA	Jazz/Classical
KAJI-LP	95.3	American Jazz Institute	Palm Desert, CA	Jazz
KJBU-LP	99.3	The Community Advocacy Coalition of Ventura County	Oxnard, CA	Urban/Smooth Jazz stream
KVCB-LP	100.9	Vacaville Christian Schools	Vacaville, CA	Jazz/Variety (HD)
WJZK-LP	97.3	Bayshore Community Broadcasting Corp.	Ft. Walton Beach, FL	Smooth Jazz
WASU-LP	92.7	Albany State University	Albany, GA	R&B/Jazz
KDKI-LP	103.9	Tamarack Community Broadcasting, Inc.	Twin Falls, ID	Jazz/Swing/Big Band
WLBM-LP	105.7	Blues & Soul, Inc.	Danville, IL	R&B/Blues/Jazz/Gospel
WQJC-LP	107.9	Quincy Not For Profit Jazz Corp.	Quincy, IL	Jazz
WETF-LP	105.7	Latino Task Force for Education, Inc.	South Bend, IN	Jazz
WNOZ-LP	95.3	M&M Community Development, Inc. New Orleans Branch	New Orleans, LA	Smooth Jazz
WJZP-LP	107.9	All Inclusive, Inc.	Portland, ME	Urban/Jazz
WTTZ-LP	93.5	State Of Maryland, MDOT, Maryland Transit Administration	Baltimore, MD	Traffic Info/Smooth Jazz (stream)
WMVK-LP	107.3	State Of Maryland, MDOT, Maryland Transit Administration	Perryville, MD	Traffic Info/Smooth Jazz//WTTZ-LP
WFAH-LP	102.1	Greater Flint Arts Council	Flint, MI	Jazz
WKIU-LP	94.7	Tupelo 2000, Inc.	Tupelo, MS	Gospel/Jazz
KWPQ-LP	103.3	Willow's Wood Community Network	Springfield, MO	Blues/Jazz
KOJH-LP	104.7	Mutual Musicians Foundation, Inc.	Kansas City, MO	R&B/Jazz
KXZI-LP	101.9	The Cross Works Ministries	Kalispell, MT	Jazz/Blues/Folk/Bluegrass
WJSK-LP	101.1	The Bartlett-Jackson Community Broadcasters Association	Bartlett, NH	Jazz
WUPC-LP	102.3	Radio Alerta	Arrowhead Village, NJ	Smooth Jazz/Soft AC
KVNM-LP	101.1	Idea Ministries	Veguita, NM	Jazz/Urban Gospel
WYLT-LP	100.3	Action Community Television, Inc.	Rocky Mount, NC	R&B/Smooth Jazz
WDFC-LP	101.7	CUMC Radio LLC	Greensboro, NC	Classical/Smooth Jazz
WEOM-LP	103.1	World Evangelistic Outreach Ministries, Inc.	Thomasville, NC	Gospel/Jazz/Urban

(continued)

TABLE 29 (continued)

Call Sign	Frequency	Licensee	City	Format
WBWH-LP	96.1	Bluffton College	Bluffton, OH	Smooth Jazz/Variety (TuneIn)
WSAX-LP	98.5	SEMM Foundation	Columbus, OH	Smooth Jazz
KJZT-LP	90.1	Tulsa Community Radio, Inc.	Tulsa, OK	Smooth Jazz
KCYI-LP	97.7	Edwards Broadcasting	Oklahoma City, OK	Smooth Jazz
KMFO-LP	98.1	Oklahoma Jazz Hall of Fame, Inc.	Tulsa, OK	Jazz
WLCD-LP	98.7	Lane College	Jackson, TN	Blues/Oldies/Jazz (stream)
WPTP-LP	100.1	Alton Park Development Corp.	Chattanooga, TN	Smooth Jazz/Urban Gospel (Live365)
WQJZ-LP	103.9	Stones River Community Media Alliance	Murfreesboro, TN	Jazz/Blues/Easy Listening
KKVI-LP	98.3	Gospel American Network	Greenville, TX	Urban Gospel/Jazz (stream)
KYBS-LP	99.9	Balch Springs Radio De La Comunidad	Balch Springs, TX	Urban Gospel/Jazz
KCGF-LP	100.5	Sunday Morning Glory Radio, Inc.	San Angelo, TX	Urban Gospel/R&B/Smooth Jazz
KJZX-LP	101.9	Third Coast Activist Resource Center	Austin, TX	Jazz
KWSP-LP	104.9	Home Town Communications, Inc.	Kerrville, TX	Soft AC/Jazz
KWBR-LP	105.7	Association of Community Resources and News (A.C.O.R.N.)	St. George, UT	Smooth Jazz

Source: Www.radio-locator.com, April 2020.

LPFM system has failed to make a dent in the centralization of commercial radio, and the one-by-one license approval process, oblivious to other license applications, has allowed coordinated conservative and religious groups to use the system to create alternative national networks. Lucas, perhaps overgeneralizing, remarked, "Kennard's rezoning project, intended to increase minority ownership in broadcasting, had been transformed into the familiar noncommercial roster of churches, schools, and municipalities."[81]

Jazz has benefited from LPFM, but it is not clear whether jazz fans know to listen for it. Besides the 44 jazz stations, in April 2020 lpfmdatabase.com listed another 619 stations—30 percent of the total—described as "Variety," many of which at least have a jazz program or two. Given Kennard's intent and the ultimate share taken up by various formats, one would have to conclude that for jazz and music programming, LPFM has, disappointingly, been hijacked though not totally voided.

The existence of these LPFM stations broadcasting jazz of some type is nonetheless encouraging for jazz listeners and musicians. Despite their small coverage areas, many low-power stations are also streaming their programming on the internet; moreover, the database list is misleading in that many hours of jazz are being broadcast every day on other low-power stations. It is useful to look at a few such stations to find examples of jazz programming.

WOWD-LP

The creation of WOWD-LP was spearheaded by veteran NPR journalist Marika Partridge, a Takoma Park, Maryland, resident who became aware that a round of low-power applications was soon to be considered (in 2011) by the FCC. Though the license application for LPFMs is free, the engineering and legal work required to complete a successful application can be a significant expense. By means of concerts, T-shirt sales, and an Indiegogo campaign, more than $65,000 was raised for the application process and for use in building the studio.

The story of WOWD-LP's licensing process illustrates how the FCC transferred much of the cost of fact-finding to the applicants. Their recruitment of good engineers and lawyers, along with solid political connections, proved decisive in getting the license. A *Washington Post* article related that

> the brain trust proved decisive in the unforgiving FCC process, which relies on competing license seekers to rat out the mistakes in each other's applications.
>
> One by one, Takoma-based lawyer Michael Richards combed the documents filed by three other finalists for the same frequency, 94.3. The group persuaded the Maryland Highway Department, which wanted to beam traffic updates from a College Park antenna, to drop out after finding a mistake in its proposed tower location.
>
> "I basically went with the message that there was a tremendous application coming from my constituents in District 20 and that there appeared to be a problem with their own application and asked if they would consider stepping aside," said state Sen. Jamie B. Raskin (D-Montgomery), a Takoma Park resident.
>
> Richards next notified the FCC of a flaw in the nonprofit status of another finalist, a group related to the D.C. jazz club HR-57. And in the case of the Washington Peace Center, which had sponsored an application on behalf of the Latino Media Collective, he found that a key document had been signed not by an officer of the center, as required by the FCC, but by the office manager.
>
> It was enough. In January 2015, the FCC announced that the other two were disqualified and Takoma Radio had won the license.[82]

Though not true of all low-power stations, WOWD-LP is built around the access model familiar from community radio: "If you've got a good idea for a show, we want to hear it."[83]

In addition to WOWD-LP's clearly labeled jazz shows (shown in table 30)—Thursday's *Jazz Now* and *In the Jazz Kitchen* and Saturday's *This! Music*—by

TABLE 30. Sample WOWD-LP program schedule.

	Sun 7/23	Mon 7/24	Tue 7/25	Wed 7/26	Thu 7/27	Fri 7/28	Sat 7/29
8:00 a.m.	The Melody Divas	Ride with Clyde the DJ Driver	Tuesday Morning Mix (Steve)	My Tiny Morning Show (Bob Boilen)	Coffee and Classics (Carson)	Ballads in the Morning (Marika, Heater, Severn, Clay)	Robin's Radio Show
9:00 a.m.	Forbidden Alliance (Robbie White)			TIZITZ with Tebabu			Lost Treasures (DJ Bookish, DJ Mackie
10:00 a.m.		Afropop Worldwide	Check in Time (Marika)	Borderlines! (Bobby [sdiki], Lady Myrrh, Milo)	Jazz Now (Ed Smith)	WOWD Music Library	This! Music (Bobby [sdiki], Clay)
11:00 a.m.		Hi-Fi Diner (Lis)					
12:00 p.m.	Sunday Midday (Sarah B)	The Beat Lounge (DJ Adam)	Rock n Roll Rabbit Hole (Scott, Walter)	We Are Takoma/ Somos Takoma			
1:00 p.m.	Talk of Takoma (Eric Bond)			Afrobeat Orbit (DJ Eme)	Bienvenido al Tango (Phil, Maxfield)		RootsRockReggae (Ebony)
2:00 p.m.		Guitar Arcade (Patrick)	WOWD Music Library	What Year Is This? (Brandon Wetherbee)			
3:00 p.m.	WOWD Music Library			Afropop Worldwide	Hot Sauce Lounge (DJ Special Sauce)		Makings of Modern Music (Nic & Otto)
4:00 p.m.		Circles (Steve Lorber)	Epic City (Carolivia Herron)	DC Music with Bryan & John	Music Matinee (DJ total)	Walking on the Moon	Roadside Attraction (Brian McGuire)
5:00 p.m.	The Musical Traditions Encounter (Steve)		Sugar and Spice (Mabel, Bella)		Rudie-Patootie Rae	The Weekly (Shomari, DJ Ali)	
6:00 p.m.		High-n-Low (DJ Urbanova)	Blues Hall of Fame (Big Boy Little, Steve)	Classical American Dipthongs (Bruce)	Capital Doom (Et, Ty)	The Groove Line (T Willy Will)	Roots and Wings Radio Hour (Becky, Chris)
7:00 p.m.	Takoma Cabaret (Peter, Mauren)	Como la Flor (Valentina)			Indie Penchant (Sara)	Vientos de Latinoamérica (Luis Ayala)	

	The Sound of Soul with D'Nicole	What's up Next (The Previously Unknown Legend)	Bayou Boogie (Michael)	The Soul Sonic Show (Alpha Betts, DJ Mezkla)		The Infinite Number of Monkeys Program	Divino Maravilhoso (DJ D'Emcee, Matt Hooke)
8:00 p.m.							
9:00 p.m.		Monday Evenings with the WOWD Library			In the Jazz Kitchen (Bill Simmons, Michael Simmons)		
10:00 p.m.	A Little Me Time (Dianne Be)		Mood Music (Amy, Brad)	Wednesday Night "Meg"		Block Period (The Block Period Crew)	Horas Rockeras (Ratan Rockero, Lobo)
11:00 p.m.	The Flex (Mary, Jose, Awad)	DMV Underground (Cardo)	WOWD Music Library		Red Panda Radio (Red Panda)	Old Kids on the Block (Hunter, Lia)	
12:00 a.m.			WOWD Overnight Music Library	WOWD Overnight Music Library		WOWD Overnight Music Library	WOWD Overnight Music Library
1:00 a.m.	WOWD Overnight Music Library	WOWD Overnight Music Library	WOWD Overnight Music Library		WOWD Overnight Music Library		
2:00 a.m.							
3:00 a.m.							
4:00 a.m.							
5:00 a.m.							
6:00 a.m.							
7:00 a.m.							

Source: WOWD-LP, Takoma Park, MD, July 23–29, 2023, Progam Schedule, wowd.org.

clicking on the interactive schedule one finds jazz played in a number of programs. For the week shown, these include most of the *WWOD Music Library* slots (most likely automated programming set up by Partridge and music director Michael Phillips), *Hi-Fi Diner*, *Wednesday Night "Meg,"* and Friday's *Infinite Number of Monkeys Program*—a free-form program with the slogan "An infinite number of monkeys with an infinite number of turntables will eventually play your favorite record. The math says you should tune in."[84]

The *This! Music* show is emblematic of the potential of low-power radio to play music that would have difficulty finding a place on larger radio stations. The website describes it as a program that plays "free jazz and other music that is entirely improvised. No standards, no standard repertoire."[85] The show's playlist for April 11, 2020, included the following artists: Lisa Sokolov, Geri Allen, Charlie Haden, Paul Motian, Myra Melford, Linda Sharrock, Eric Watson, William Parker, and Yuko Fujiyama. Not one of these recordings was on a major or jazz major label.

WSFM-LP

Promoted as AshevilleFM, WSFM-LP is a community-oriented low-power station that mixes local and national news (Pacifica's *Democracy Now!*) and talk with music. Its programming serves to amplify the underrepresented voices of the Asheville, North Carolina, community through announcements, on-air interviews, and underwriting.[86] As with many stations, it is partly successful from the point of view of diversity; the station has program hosts of color, but apparently there is only one person of color among the management team and board of directors.

The bulk of the station's music programming is varied and presented mainly in a free-form style. Some insight into the adventurousness of the jazz programming is indicated in table 31, a jazz Top Ten published on AshevilleFM.org by station jazz director Jonathan Price (host of *Tenor to Tabla*).[87]

TABLE 31. AshevilleFM Jazz Top Ten, March 17, 2020.

1. Firecracker Jazz Band, Return to the Twenties (CUPI IONIAN)
2. Angel Bat Dawid, The Oracle (INTERNATIONAL ANTHEM)
3. Rent Romus' Lords of Outland, 25 Years Under the Mountain (EDGETONE)
4. Enrico Fazio Critical Mass, Wabi Sabi (LEO)
5. Matthew Shipp, Invisible Light, Live São Paulo (HAT HUT)
6. Jaimie Branch, Fly or Die II: Bird Dogs of Paradise (INTERNATIONAL ANTHEM)
7. Vijay Iyer and Craig Taborn, The Transitory Poems (ECM)
8. Pat Metheny, From This Place (NONESUCH)
9. Whit Dickey Tao Quartets, Peace Planet/Box of Light (AUM FIDELITY)
10. Frode Gjerstad, Fred Lonberg-Holm, and Matthew Shipp, Season of Sadness (ILUSO)

TABLE 32. AshevilleFM schedule, week of April 12, 2020 (jazz programming in bold).

	Sunday	Monday	Tuesday	Wednesday	Thursday	Friday	Saturday
12:00 a.m.	Wiggle Room	Democracy Now!	Democracy Now!	Democracy Now!	Democracy Now!	Democracy Now!	Melody in Mayhem
1:00 a.m.		Early Morning Music Rotation	Early Morning Music Rotation	Early Morning Music Rotation	Early Morning Music Rotation	Early Morning Music Rotation	
2:00 a.m.	Early Morning Music Rotation						Early Morning Music Rotation
3:00 a.m.							
4:00 a.m.							
5:00 a.m.							
6:00 a.m.	Morning Music Rotation	Morning Music Rotation	Morning Music Rotation	Morning Music Rotation	Morning Music Rotation	Morning Music Rotation	Morning Music Rotation
7:00 a.m.		La Neta News—Monday	La Neta News—Tuesday	La Neta News—Wednesday	La Neta News—Thursday	La Neta News—Friday	
8:00 a.m.	Come on in My Kitchen	Guided Meditation	Positive Vibes	Guided Meditation	Guided Meditation	Guided Meditation	Radio Active Kids
9:00 a.m.	2000 Years of Radio	Dreamers and Doers		CV19 Update—Wednesday	9 'n the Mornin'	CV19 Update—Friday	
10:00 a.m.		Democracy Now!	Democracy Now!	Democracy Now!	Democracy Now!	Democracy Now!	Loose Fit
11:00 a.m.		Living Well	Lucid	Cesspool of Sin	Daddypops	In the Box	
12:00 p.m.	Electro Retro	Life out of Tunes	Short Circuit	Not Your Mother's Tongue	Closer to the Edge	Deep Cuts	Brown Mountain Lights
1:00 p.m.							
2:00 p.m.	The Final Straw Radio		Beyond the Realm of Comprehension	Musical Migrations			Scores for You and Yours
3:00 p.m.	Onward Through the Fog	Songs for Friends			Riffin'	The Good, the Bad, and the Ugly	Steve Sax Syndrome
4:00 p.m.							
5:00 p.m.	WordPlay				Slumber Party	Too Dark for Disney	Slay the Mic
6:00 p.m.	Morning Mixtape	The Fusion Forest	La Neta—Martes	6 p.m. News Hour	La Neta—Jueves		
7:00 p.m.				Let There Be Rock		Mental Notes	
8:00 p.m.	Rebellious Jukebox	Ecstatic Listening	The UnCola		The Mothership Slight Return	. . . And the Address	Stank Free Radio
9:00 p.m.							
10:00 p.m.	The Horses' Mouth with Bowditch	Ritmo Kultural	Evening Music Rotation	Flytrap	OM		Bye All Means Necessary
11:00 p.m.	Evening Music Rotation					Melody in Mayhem	

Source: https://www.ashevillefm.org/schedule/, accessed July 25, 2023.

WETF-LP

The final example of an LPFM is WETF-LP in South Bend, Indiana, a twenty-four-hour jazz station that mixes local programs, many featuring local musicians in performance or via their recordings, with nationally available jazz programming. Large blocks of time when no volunteers would be available are occupied by jazz programs from the WFMT (Chicago) jazz service distributed by PRX, from WFIU (Bloomington, Indiana), or from stations affiliated with the New England Public Radio network (WFCR and WICN). Some of the imported NEPR programs are carried live, whereas the WFMT program is provided to stations in repeating program blocks.[88]

The driving force behind WETF-LP appears to be Eliud Villanueva, an experienced radio hand who helped apply for and construct both this station, "The Jazz Station," and WSBL-LP, "Radio Sabor Latino." The latter station is licensed to the League of United Latin American Citizens South Bend Council 5001, Inc., a 501(c)(3) organization that is affiliated with another nonprofit, the Latino Task Force for Education, which hold the license for WETF-LP.[89]

The South Bend LULAC chapter instituted a fundraising program to provide scholarships, and the low-power radio stations came to be a part of this effort. In the 1990s South Bend lost its only Latinx radio programming, the one-hour show that Villanueva had taken over from his mentor Ramon Rodriguez. They set out to replace it. According to radiosaborlatino.com,

> Mr. Villanueva and Mr. Rodriguez had researched starting a radio station, just to find out that it was an extremely expensive proposition. By coincidence, a few months later, Mr. Villanueva read an article in the South Bend Tribune announcing that the FCC had approved a rule that would allow Not-for-Profit organizations to apply for a new type of FM radio stations (Low Power stations). At the time Mr. Villanueva was, and still is, an active member of LULAC Council 5001. He proposed to the directors to apply for one of these stations[;] according to him it would make it easier to raise funds for the main purpose of the group, college scholarships. After their approval, he filed all the documentation necessary[;] in April 2001 LULAC Council 5001 was granted a construction permit for a radio station to broadcast at 98.1 MHz FM.[90]

Despite the need for broadcast equipment and construction labor, Villanueva managed to launch both stations. Having personally met those needs, Villanueva and the WETF board dedicated the second station to jazz with a mission to "Preserve, Promote, Perpetuate and Present Jazz as America's original art form."[91]

The construction permit had an expiration date of October 12, 2002. The fact that the date was the original Columbus Day was seen by some as a good omen for a Hispanic endeavor.

TABLE 33. Partial lineup of local programs on WETF-LP.

Program	Host	Description
Front Row Seat	Eliud Villanueva	Recordings of live performances
Collector's Choice	Mike Finnerty or Brent Banulis	No information given
Open Mike	Eliud Villanueva	Recordings of local (and South Bend) live performances
Shaving Your Eyebrows	Paul McEldowney	Music of the future. Paul searches for the latest avant-garde music recordings and plays them for us, giving details about the artists and the music itself.
The Latest	Eliud Villanueva	New releases.
The Vocalists		No information given
This Is the Gig	Stephen and Mary Merriman	Featuring music and live interviews with touring national and international jazz artists performing at Playhouse, interviews with artists of the community, and discussion of the art of jazz and jazz in our community

TABLE 34. WETF-LP's "Shaving Your Eyebrows" sample playlist, October 3, 2018.

Artist	Track	Album
Derek Bailey/David Holland	"Improvised Piece III"	Improvisations for Cello and Guitar
Jan Garbarek Quartet	"Beast of Kommodo"	Afric Pepperbird
Sun Ra	"And This Is My Beloved"	Bad and Beautiful
Evan Parket/Anthony Braxton/Derek Bailey	"Za'id"	Company 2
Markus Stockhausen/Simon Stockhausen/Jo Thönes	"Aparis"	Aparis
Mark Isham/Art Lande	"The Melancholy of Departure"	We Begin
Emanative	"Planet B"	Planet B
Palm Unit	"The Creator Has a Masterplan"	Hommage à Jef Gilson
Khan Jamal	"Infinity"	Infinity
Terry Riley/Don Cherry	Excerpt	Live Köln 23.2.1975

Conclusions

The prospects for the future of jazz on noncommercial radio are threatened not by competing music, nor directly by a withdrawal of aesthetic support by the institutions involved in noncommercial broadcasting, but by financial pressures. Reductions in CPB support for cultural programming on public radio, and recurring fears that an ideologically opposed Congress will "zero out" such support entirely, have motivated stations to adopt audience research methodology from commercial radio with the hope of capturing more paying members and reaping more underwriting revenue. Audience research has identified the classical and jazz music audiences as affluent and loyal but aging, while identifying the news, talk, and information audience as even more affluent, even more prone to contribute, and somewhat younger. In addition, NTIs programming attracts corporate underwriting—corporations like having their names heard by the decision makers who listen to shows like *Marketplace* each evening—which provides an additional measure of fiscal stability. Ironically, the affluent and highly educated noncommercial radio listener has the attention span and interest to invest in long-form programming, which noncommercial radio's networks and programming consortiums excel at producing, even as such programs are among the most expensive. The result is that noncommercial radio stations have, for survival and in consideration of their futures, followed the money to news, talk, and information and away from music.

Even stations that have stuck with music programming, either because of the strength of their cultural mission or because they operate in a market where some other noncommercial station has already grabbed the NTI role, have "professionalized" their operations according to the dominant audience research strategies in an attempt to hold audience and increase the number of subscribers. This has led to a much narrower range of music programming, "lite classical" in the case of classical and "jazz that swings" or mainstream, post-bop, nondissonant, and mostly mellow jazz. Listener-challenging experimental jazz (including 1940s bebop), free jazz, and surprisingly, the pre-high-fidelity music of Duke Ellington, Billie Holiday, and Louis Armstrong are likely to be heard only on community radio or college stations with student and volunteer staffs, because those stations are less likely to be as concerned about audience size.

Jazz radio is losing its place of importance with musicians as well, both in terms of the value musicians derive from listening to the radio and in their perception of the value of airplay on their own careers. Musicians creating experimental music are dubious of receiving exposure on the larger public radio stations but grateful for the occasional DJ there and on community and college radio who will play their music. Musicians are cognizant of the limited range of musical styles being played on noncommercial radio and either tailor their music to fit the prevailing formats or bypass radio altogether.

Finally, record labels find that there is little they can do to promote music outside the prevailing styles on jazz radio today. In the era of jazz on commercial radio, the common goal of commerce intersected with an appreciative enthusiasm for the music on the part of deejays, promoters, and record labels. Radio played a major role in the acceptance of bebop, cool jazz, hard bop, soul jazz, and jazz fusion. While a number of programmers had reservations about some of these styles, in their shared commercial environment, record sales, audience ratings, and advertising revenue as the markers of success and professional achievement competed with musical preference, of course not always happily. Jazz's residency on noncommercial radio means that vision of commercial success is not a deeply shared value. The jazz programming heard today is shaped by largely conservative aesthetic principles, as a baseline determined by the ideological position of the license holder concerning jazz, but further constrained by conventional wisdom in audience research that stresses a consistent sonic approach to music that discourages innovation and diversity in jazz on the radio.

Postscript
Jazz Radio Present and Future

As the 1960s became the 1970s, jazz was at a crossroads. In the eyes of a generation of black commercial radio owners and station managers coming into power, jazz was a crown jewel of African American culture, but it that could not stand up to the mass appeal of soul, funk, and disco. Public radio was taking off and, desperately needing to demonstrate that it could provide cultural value where commercial radio had failed, brought jazz aboard.

With a few miraculous exceptions, jazz is no longer found on commercial radio. Even its reprobate cousin smooth jazz, with its heavy soul and funk grooves, has become increasingly hard to find.[1] Jazz was a staple of network-era commercial radio, but it gradually faded with the postwar rise of R&B, rock and roll, and soul. Jazz, now considered a listener's music, thrived during the exciting upswing of noncommercial and public radio in the 1970s and 1980s but is now greatly at risk there, supplanted to a great extent by news and information programming. The ascent and decline of jazz began in the 1950s. Increasing respect for its artistic significance and cultural value was accompanied by its fading commercial fortunes.

Beginning with MTV, music radio has faced a flock of serious competitors that have eroded its dominance as a site of music listening and as the place where careers were launched and hits were "broken." The synergistic postwar partnership between records and radio has lost much of its potency. Rather than responding to these challenges with creative programming, the radio industry innovated cost-efficient management practices and used its lobbying power to obliterate restrictions on ownership. The resulting concentration and consolidation in media markets limited competition and stabilized advertising rate cards but failed to heal ailing music radio.

As the competing flock reached cruising altitude, noncommercial radio—founded by radio lovers stymied by commercial radio's stagnant formulas—was nearing its own peak as a place of innovative programming. Its last wave of new programming ideas, exemplified by *This American Life* (1995), *Studio 360* (2000–2020), *On Being* (2001–2022), *Radiolab* (2002), the *TED Radio Hour* (2012), and *Bullseye with Jesse Thorn* (2000)[2] all responded to the call for increased news and information programming and pushed public radio away from music and in the direction of time-insensitive podcasts.[3] One can easily see that podcasts are radio's (broadly defined) incarnation of the on-demand programming model that has taken over subscription television viewing.

Radio was once the most vibrant connection, other than live performances, between jazz musicians and jazz fans. It was a shared experience, hosted by trusted and familiar DJs and valued by all members of the jazz community. It is difficult to imagine a return to prominence for radio or for jazz on radio. However, internet streams and new listening models such as podcasts, while unable to match the mass appeal of the 50,000-watt radio stations of the past, provide means for jazz music makers to continue to reach jazz listeners. As for noncommercial radio, jazz will remain as long as its ideological meanings contribute to the mission.

Disruptions and Fluidity of Function

The march of time has shown that seemingly durable media institutions will eventually encounter competition and the threat of bypass. The evening network TV newscasts killed afternoon newspapers, cable TV news eroded the utility of the national weekly news magazines, and the internet forced a restructuring of even the strongest of the remaining morning newspapers, thus severing the thing the customers most wanted (the news) from the thing supporting the cost of newsgathering (paid advertising, not the paper's price). Cable television shrank the seemingly invulnerable broadcast TV networks, then Netflix changed from snail-mailing DVDs to streaming movies and producing original content, leading to cable cord-cutting. The film industry had fought to distinguish itself from television, then came to accommodate television, and lately began to explore on-demand distribution models (see the COVID-19 pandemic).

Often technology, such as the wide availability of internet at decent rates, enabled these disruptions.[4] Well-established and profitable media products and industries based on entrenched business models have been damaged, displaced, or destroyed by new models, more often than not enabled by new technologies. Tim Wu categorizes these technology-based innovations as either sustaining or disruptive, the latter when the technology threatens to displace existing products or services, the former when they improve them without displacement.[5] Disruptive technologies can be harnessed by the threatened industry, as when the radio networks nimbly shifted to become television networks. By exploiting their popularity with viewers, holding firm to their network affiliate relationships, and producing local news and sports programs, local television stations survived cable TV by fighting to be included in cable lineups. Now with cable itself suffering from cord-cutting, local stations have found that their over-the-air, and now digital, operations are a business advantage. Yet television still disrupted the radio industry by commandeering its mass audience and taking with it its national advertising. Radio responded by using formatted music as inexpensive programming with which to attract local audiences. Today, radio stations with music formats are threatened by new media: peer-to-peer file sharing, music on YouTube, internet music services, and the internet streams of competing radio stations from around the world.

The coexistence of digital TV broadcasting, cable TV, and internet video delivery exemplifies the public's indifference to underlying delivery methods. Will consumers care about the details of music delivery? Not according to some industry figures, who see only "forms of audio. The only difference really is how you access them—and it's a minor difference."[6] That is, ease of access (connecting to a music source that uses the internet is at least as easy as tuning a radio ever was) and music quality (listeners get the music they want, presented in a way they are satisfied with) will answer that question.

In 2017 my undergraduate students at the University of Pittsburgh conducted radio use surveys across several generations of listeners. A striking finding was that few of the students or their peers had a clear view of what radio was. That is, although most of their actual over-the-air radio listening is done in the car, many respondents used *radio* to describe a number of listening experiences, often referring to streaming services such as Spotify, Deezer, Apple Music, or Tidal. The automobile is the one remaining stronghold for terrestrial radio listening, and even there, smartphones threaten to displace it, using cell service internet and Bluetooth or wired connection to allow streaming services to be heard in the car rather than AM, FM, or Sirius XM.

The merging of radio into unspecified audio and the progression from watching "what's on TV tonight" to binge-watching Netflix or Hulu illustrates the fluidity of such terms as radio and TV and underlines the notion that service concepts can have lives distinct from their original technological platforms. Are these examples any more dramatic than whether phone calls use the public switched telephony network or voice-over-internet protocol or, for that matter, involve a "telephone" or use a device identified as a phone? For some time, a number of devices and practices have been becoming functions, and the common understanding of many functions and practices is being revised. These include

- Radio (function). The use of wireless electromagnetic technology to distribute programming. Traditional radio and television met all three requirements of the broadcast paradigm described below: geographical reach, simultaneous delivery, and programmed content. The 2017 University of Pittsburgh student survey participants described a lot of things as radio, including streaming service playlists.

- Radio (device). Listening has moved from specific devices designed to receive radio signals to general and specialized computing devices that can support audio but, significantly, cannot directly receive AM, FM, or digital broadcast signals. The smartphone, laptop, and desktop computer have displaced the audio sound system for all but the most dedicated young audiophiles. When tiring of listening via earbuds, users can switch to more comfortable headphones or speakers that are either wired or connected wirelessly. Indeed, smart speakers are rapidly becoming an important vehicle for home listening, playing radio station streams when directed but probably more often used in conjunction with a streaming music services and playlists.[7]
- Listening (practice). It turns out that a simultaneous listening audience was more important to the broadcaster than to the listener, but streaming services have revamped methods of advertising from bulk to targeted. Music listening has evolved from a shared to a private experience. Part of the trend was miniaturization of components, but between the pocket transistor radio, the Walkman, and later the iPod and smartphone, was social listening via the loudspeakers of the component stereo and the boom box.
- Programming (practice). There may continue to be innovation in programming—for example, podcasting has evolved as a platform that supports a wide range of program formats, including serialized fiction and nonfiction, as well as music. Meanwhile, podcasting has had a reciprocal influence on radio programming. But does music programming continue to have an essential value to listeners?[8] The relative popularity of music podcasts would indicate that there is.
- Gatekeeping (function). Several of the traditional gatekeeping bottlenecks have been bypassed by DIY recording and internet distribution. But the listener's time is still limited. For this reason, time, programming, the final component of the broadcast paradigm, must remain of value to listeners, although it seems self-evident that a listener having easy-to-navigate self-programming options will have a low tolerance for programmed content that fails to maintain their interest.
- Music itself in the form of songs and recordings, fixed items backed by intellectual property laws. Sampling, mashups, remixes, and other user processes have already challenged the meaning of songs, compositions, and recordings.

Beyond Radio

With jazz radio, and the decline of radio as a cultural force, in mind, I keep returning to questions about the continuing value of radio-like audio. It might be helpful to think about three aspects of broadcast radio, what I call the broadcast paradigm: geographical reach, simultaneous consumption (or parallel delivery), and programmed content.[9]

Digital media and evolving modes of purchasing, receiving, and listening to audio will affect jazz radio and the descendants of jazz radio. It is the third requirement of the paradigm, programmed content, that interests me most in speculating about the future. In broadcasting, the programming function—determining what is on and not on—is a key site of gatekeeping, and, dating back to the early twentieth-century song pluggers, money has always been showered on these major decision points. Legal, semi-legal, illegal, ethical, and unethical resources have been applied at this point in radio, and naturally most of those resources spent on pop music.

More specifically, is programming of enough value to listeners for someone, perhaps listeners, perhaps someone else, to pay for it, either directly or indirectly? As we observe the way people listen to the new radio—Spotify, Tidal, and so on—the answer seems to be: yes? Recent studies indicate that streaming users are, on average, listening for 2.5 hours per day, dividing that listening fairly equally between, in the case of Spotify, user-generated playlists, Spotify-generated playlists, and listening to tracks suggested by Spotify algorithms, and that two-thirds of listeners aged sixteen to forty discover new music through online playlists.[10]

The streaming services have created a presence at a critical point on the path between music producers and consumers. Record labels pay to have prominently placed playlists on streaming services, with Spotify and major labels owning most of the popular playlists and indie labels owning a lesser amount.[11] Influencers are being paid to create playlists, and some influencers are creating reputations that carry weight with listeners and the music industry. Clearly influencers are open to, well, influence. Although it constitutes a small fraction of overall radio programming, some general trends in radio will most likely hold true for jazz as well. It is worth considering whether the restructured culture industry and aestheticians will find the means and motivation to re-establish in new media the types of mediated influence that they have exercised in current and past broadcasting models.

In the United States, at least, radio, though still a great source of revenue, is by many measures in decline as a cultural force.[12]

Buy or Rent?

Old-school music fans can still purchase digital music downloads or actual physical CDs, and the real O.G.s can join forces with the new audiophile hipsters and enjoy the resurgent boom in LPs. But since 2005, streaming music has overtaken all forms of owning music.[13] And streaming is displacing terrestrial radio as the primary mode of listening. Although users are not listening simultaneously as in a true broadcast, social media platforms like YouTube allow listeners and viewers to share thoughts with others about music.

The Recording Industry Association of America (RIAA) reported that for the fifth consecutive year, despite COVID-19–related tour cancellations and other disruptions, total revenues from recorded music grew to $12.2 billion in 2020. The outright purchase of music in the form of vinyl records, CDs, and permanent digital downloads constituted only 15 percent of all revenue, with streaming accounting for 83 percent. Discounting inflation, the $12 billion in recording industry income for 2020, based largely on non-ownership listening, has nearly replaced the revenue based entirely on physical product, which amounted to $15 billion in 1998.[14] Most streaming revenue is from subscriptions and ad revenues, but about 10 percent, or $1.2 billion, comes from "digital and customized digital radio"—Pandora, SiriusXM, and internet radio. Digital radio revenue grew by 3.9 percent in 2020, but far less robustly than did the overall streaming category at 13.4 percent.[15] This is perhaps good news for radio-type music listening.

Given the vitality of these new media offerings and the financial advantages of a fee-based business model, one might once again ask why the broadcast model persists. When it comes to radio itself, recent Nielsen data find adults (eighteen and over) listening to radio, on average, a bit more than one hour per day.[16] The broadcast industry maintains that in 2017, 270 million Americans, or 93 percent, listened to terrestrial radio at least once each week.[17] It is also possible that a portion of the additional 3.5 to 4 hours they spend engaged with computer, phone, or tablet internet service involves listening to music or radio-like services. Put another way, one can understand that radio will continue to exist as a legacy enterprise for the foreseeable future, but why are alternative models that embody some or all features of the broadcast model continuing to be launched?

The workings of streaming services' algorithmic playlists are nebulous and opaque; they analyze user plays, skips, and finishes to determine the popularity of songs on lesser playlists before promoting the most successful to more prominent lists. The algorithms are closely held trade secrets, but because they are confidential, they could be rigged to favor preferred "partners." Spotify has made public statements denouncing playlist payola and asserting that is not tolerated, but there are more subtle forms of influence. But equally opaque and nebulous are the playlists developed by music critics and influencers. Major labels own several lists to ensure that their products get enough plays to advance. Fortunately, at the extreme, as has always been the case with payola, the self-limiting mechanism of tilting the machine is that too many underserved plugs will result in an unenjoyable listening experience.

Satellite Radio, Station- and Internet-Only Streams, and Podcasts

Besides the structured playlists of streaming music services, jazz fans can look forward to some other options for a programmed jazz listening experience. The initial proposal for U.S. satellite radio in 1990 offered great promise and a wide range of music, comedy, news, and sports channels on a subscription basis. Satellite radio is an expensive and technologically complex way to distribute radio programming that nonetheless is simple for its customers to use and difficult for direct competitors to breach. The nearly universal availability of the internet has made it easy for program providers, including actual and faux jazz radio stations, to reach listeners around the world at little cost and with little technical knowledge. Finally, podcasts (audio programs downloadable from a website), which take structural cues from radio production but can be listened to on an on-demand basis, can be tailored to topics of narrow interest such as jazz.

SiriusXM has the advantage of nearly nationwide coverage; jazz fans on long drives no longer need to hunt for a noncommercial station to tune into for the next fifty miles. But the outlook is decidedly mixed for jazz on satellite radio. The 2008 merger of Sirius and XM came after an expensive talent war that left plenty of corporate debt. Jazz, classical, country, and hip hop channels were among the interesting offerings eliminated. The losses included "Beyond Jazz" (progressive jazz), "Águla" (regional Mexican), "the Rhyme" (early hip hop), "Fuego" (reggae and Hispanic), and "Ngoma" (African music).[18] The diversity promised when these services launched has been a victim of narrow operating margins resulting from high-priced on-air talent and costly sports program rights.

Currently SiriusXM offers its thirty-one million subscribers one full-time jazz channel, "Real Jazz," a title certain to differentiate it from the neighboring "Watercolors," which features smooth and "contemporary" jazz.[19] "Real Jazz," on channel 67, is listed as "classic jazz, the original American art form. Hear the masters who pioneered the music and the new artists who continue the tradition into the 21st century." The slogan is totally consistent with public radio's representation and presentation of jazz as American exceptionalism, and its jazz programming is similar in range to that of a typical public radio station. At least one other channel might appeal to jazz fans: "Seriously Sinatra" is a channel devoted to Sinatra and singers of what's called "the great American songbook." In addition to shows playing recordings, recorded concerts and interviews hosted by noted Philadelphia bassist Christian McBride are regular features on "Real Jazz," while another regular program is hosted by producer and bassist (and bass clarinetist) Marcus Miller. Miller's program is one of the channel's most eclectic. Sadly, despite the capability to easily offer additional jazz channels over SiriusXM.com, which allows internet music streams beyond the fixed capacity of the satellite broadcasting system, the only other options are the additional smooth jazz channel "Instrumental Contemporary Jazz" and such seasonal offerings as the jazz Christmas channel and (since 2023) the annual March offering of the "Women in Jazz" channel in celebration of Women's History Month.

One thing working in favor of jazz radio, at least in the near term, is the proliferation of streaming radio or radio-like broadcasts. While the internet can deliver individual content to users, it can also very efficiently deliver simultaneous (nearly—if we don't quibble over a few hundred milliseconds) to a worldwide audience. As we saw in the first few paragraphs of this book, there is concern that the management of WBGO is paying more attention to its worldwide streaming audience than to the local audience served by its 88.3 MHz transmitter. The internet has provided a miracle: The ability to listen to a radio station from anywhere has been a dream of DXers for more than a century.[20]

However, the global reach of the internet also puts all these radio stations into real or imagined competition with one another. For this reason, Nielsen Audio (formerly Arbitron) tracks and provides ratings should they exceed a threshold for six types of "radio" stations: AM, FM, HD-multicast channels, and internet streams of each of those three. One reason Nielsen does this is to account for the different advertising that may be sold on each platform.[21] It is unclear whether this competition will in the long run result in fewer jazz stations or will strengthen them all. So far, FM HD channels have been a technical success that has struggled to find listeners. Like the old FM analog subcarrier channels, HD has been a good place for a public radio NTI station to bury its jazz and music programming. In the car, few drivers seem aware of the HD option or how to select the channels. But on a radio station's website or an aggregator's menu, the alternative HD services look less like an afterthought.

The internet streaming aggregator radio.net lists more than a thousand internet jazz radio streams. Table 35 shows the first ten that came up on a given day in 2021.

Although the term was coined by in 2004 by BBC and *Guardian* journalist Ben Hammersley, the podcast had its beginning when audio enthusiasts realized they could download radio episodes and even record live internet streams as mp3 files for later offline listening.[22] Podcasting seems to answer the needs of African Americans to some extent. Thirty-four percent of U.S. adults are nonwhite, yet 41 percent of podcast listeners aged eighteen or older are nonwhite. The numbers of Asian American and African American podcast listeners exceed their share of the U.S. population each over listening by 2 percent, and Hispanics by 3 percent.[23] National Public Radio is just one of the public radio program producers that is becoming strongly involved in podcasting. There are jazz podcasts representing all the program types discussed in Chapter 5 and more, as there are also podcasts aimed at musicians wishing to improve their playing techniques and business practices, podcasts devoted to jazz education, and podcasts related to the music business.

TABLE 35. Sample list of internet jazz streams.

Stream name	Origin	Programming
First 10 jazz streams listed at radio.net		
Radio Swiss Jazz	Berne, Switzerland	Blues, Jazz, Chillout
DeutschlandFunk	Cologne, Germany	Classical, Jazz
FIP	Paris, France	Jazz, World, Film and Musical
Whisperings Solo Piano Radio	Eugene, OR	Classical, Jazz
The Jazz Groove--West	San Francisco, CA	Jazz
Smooth Jazz Florida	Cocoa Beach, FL	Jazz
101 Smooth Jazz Mellow Mix	London, UK	Chillout, Jazz, Easy Listening
TSF Jazz	Paris, France	
Smooth Jazz Tampa Bay	Tampa Bay, FL	Funk, Jazz
Sublime FM	Ultrecht, Netherlands	Jazz
Last 5 of 1,167 jazz streams		
Imunique365	Detroit, MI	Soul, R&B, Funk, Jazz
The Mellow Guitar Place	United States	Jazz, Easy Listening, Blues
The Jazz Guitar Place	United States	Jazz Instrumental
Jazz Music Radio	Germany	Jazz
CFOU 89.1 FM	Trois-Rivières, Canada	Pop, Jazz, Alternative, Electro

Streaming and Jazz Musicians

Streaming may hold promise for jazz listeners, but the musicians find themselves severely undercompensated, especially in comparison to the old system of physical record sales, that is, once musicians forced record companies to be accountable. Unlike radio and television broadcasting, leading performers earn royalties from streaming but do so at rates far below those paid to composers and publishers.[24]

The NEA Jazz Master Maria Schneider, an award-winning composer for jazz orchestra—that is, recordings with high session costs—told the music writer Stuart Nicholson just how poorly the system works for her and other professional musicians. For Schneider, the problems begin with her, not a record label, shouldering the costs of the recording. Her production costs can run to the tens of thousands of dollars with little hope of recovering a significant fraction from streaming. Whereas CD sales paid her perhaps 15 percent to 20 percent of the purchase price of label issues, the fixed rate of fractional cents per play are exactly the same for her as for the "kid who makes a record in his bedroom." She related,

> We're all being paid the same, I'm not allowed in that system to figure out my costs, figure out the size of my market—if you were selling clothes,

or selling food or selling shoes, lampshades or doorknobs, anybody who manufactures things has a cost for design, for materials, for manufacturing and distribution and knows the size of their audience. So if you're a small company making chi-chi lampshades you're going to charge a fortune for them, but if you're selling them in a discount store or a place like Ikea, you're charging much less for it. But in music we can't do that, we're all the same.[25]

In other words, for the number of plays typical for jazz, streaming revenue cannot hope to replace the proceeds from physical copies or purchased digital downloads. Jazz musicians will have to look at audio streaming as promoting their live performances and building their reputations and fan bases.

During the Coronavirus pandemic, jazz musicians and venues explored video streaming for pay as a way to reach audiences unable to see the music in person. Well before the 2019 pandemic the New York jazz club Smalls, under the ownership of Spike Wilner, had been one of the leaders in streaming performances on a subscription basis. One reason for Wilner's success is that his strong relationships with the Smalls's performing musicians have created some level of trust with regard to intellectual property concerns. The pandemic brought about a rash of virtual performances, lectures, chats, and teaching viewed on the internet and as in-club performances have resumed, the lasting impact of the virtual experience is likely to continue.

The Future of Jazz on the Web Depends on the Future of the Web

Many of the current and future directions discussed here relating to jazz radio are dependent on the current business model of internet availability and access. Monopolistic control of the internet transport layer or control over access to the internet could put many of these services at risk. The future of net neutrality is a concern. One principle of net neutrality is that both large internet backbone carriers and the internet service providers that link users, large and small, to the internet treat all data packets the same. It is recognized that the internet service providers or backbone carriers could generate additional revenue by charging different amounts for certain kinds of services (for example, offering ultra-low-latency video and audio at a higher price), by favoring the traffic of a customer paying a premium for preferred treatment, or by favoring the traffic of its own affiliated businesses. Net neutrality as law was repealed by a 2017 FCC ruling and affirmed by subsequent court decisions. Various states including California have passed net neutrality legislation, and court challenges to the FCC's authority to override state bills relating to net neutrality have yet to be settled. And it seems certain that future changes in administrations will result in attempts to reverse the net neutrality rules once again.

Much early commentary on so-called new media reverberated with optimistic proclamations about the democratizing benefits of the internet. The internet and new media have undermined some industry practices but reinforced others. For something as financially inconspicuous as jazz, the internet does offer amazing possibilities to connect musicians and listeners without the absolute interference of gatekeepers. Much of the cost of this new and developing infrastructure has already been shifted from record companies and radio stations to musicians and listeners, and costs will continue to shift.

Nicholas Garnham notes that networks, "essentially collaborative social institutions," offer opportunities for control and rewards. According to him, media products (music, movies, television programs) have characteristics of public goods—consumption by one person does not "limit or inhibit" another's—and that one way to protect revenue flows is to erect artificial barriers or "box offices" to convert public goods into private ones.[26] He continues,

> This question of barriers or bottlenecks where the product flows and thus the financial flows through the system can be controlled and exploited brings us to the issue of networks. The media are primarily distribution networks, not units of production. The media have been largely defined in terms of, and constructed around, technologies of reproduction and the systems of distribution based upon them. . . . Network economics is all about sharing resources rather than about exchanging discrete, substitutable, and therefore competitive, products or services. A network optimizes its value when everyone is connected, and it can be used by anyone to connect to anyone.[27]

Garnham raises a troubling notion about extending models of classical networks to new media. The traditional idea that a network has maximum value when it has maximum connectivity and low transactional costs (the ideology of a classical network) conflicts with the developing idea that one possible new media endgame is to erect subscription barriers to content, precisely because media goods can move so freely over new media networks.

John Hartley and colleagues are among many who caution against unbridled optimism concerning the brave new world of new media:

> New media technologies such as digital broadcasting, pay-per-view and the Internet are seen as challenging the gatekeeping role. But this may prove to be a utopian assumption. Certainly with the Internet, search engines can be understood as digital gatekeepers. Performing the role of deciding what information is relevant to your query, search engines may not be bound by personal ideologies, yet they are a product of the structural and organizational procedures of the provider who supplies them.[28]

These observations, made in 2002, presaged current controversies in social media, where the warnings about search engines, information vetting, and structural and organizational procedures have been realized and exceeded.

One optimistic assessment that is faltering, for jazz musicians at least, is Chris Anderson's notion of "long tail" economics, which theorizes that inventories of durable but slow-selling "classics" will have respectable aggregate sales relative to current chart-toppers and blockbusters.[29] This model sounds suspiciously like our familiar jazz re-issue labels, but there are real differences. The efficacy of the long tail is predicated on a number of features including maintaining broad product offerings with low inventory costs. Such constraints serve music well, particularly music stored and distributed digitally. Advocates of the long-tail approach maintain that there is little need to identify hits or outstanding music because if it is all available, in the long run the winners will be found, and the cost of maintaining all the rest of the music is negligible. A critical feature of the long-tail model is, however, missing: The consumer and industry shift from the purchase of music, either on physical media or as user-hosted downloads, to streaming content has reduced the artist's share of transactions dramatically.[30]

It seems that the broadcast paradigm—simultaneous presentation to a dispersed audience of programmed content—has relevance in the new media environment. What seems at first glance to be the least critical of the three components, simultaneous consumption, may hold a key for understanding not only the decline of the importance of radio but also recent shifts in the political climate of the United States as well. Although the use of computers and digital technology to produce and store video and audio has had a great impact, it is the replacement of real-time $1:n$ (where n is a very large number of receivers) networks with virtual-path, connect-on-demand IP networks—the internet—that has so deeply restructured communication, including listening to music. This is because in a world with only $1:n$ networks, owning such a network or renting it to parties wanting to be the "1" was a position of great advantage. These networks are expensive to build and operate, and alternative paths to the desired customers are scarce. Obtaining access to them required money, and the political economy concerning access to such networks may have contributed to a certain enforced civility.

One way to summarize these arguments about the relation of jazz and radio is to think about it as a problem of the utilization and control of scarce resources and the reconciliation of competing market, aesthetic, and ideological influences on the allocation of those resources. In radio's earliest days, the resources—a frequency assignment, capital and operating funds, and radio technology itself—were extremely scarce, and access was tightly controlled by a few individuals and corporations. Jazz was sonically compatible with early radio technology and ideologically compatible with the discourse of modernity and primitivity embodied in radio itself. As network radio developed, highbrow culture had the capital to demand representation, but America's unspoken ideology of market economics, as usual, trumped cultural capital, and high culture took a limited role. Music was being created in venues all over the country, but as Garnham points out, it is "cultural distribution, not cultural production that is the key locus of power and profit."[31]

Conclusion

After the emergence of television in the 1950s, radio was reorganized along the lines of a new, post-network business model, and despite the increased availability of the resources (namely, more radio stations) jazz lost out to new music genres that enjoyed greater popularity. Eventually, another reorganization created a sheltered noncommercial market that valued cultural capital. By this time, jazz had enough to qualify for a significant place in broadcasting, but budget pressures and audience research methods adopted from commercial radio began to squeeze out music of all types. Finally, the internet challenged the concept of scarcity of distribution channels. Without the need to allocate a scarce resource, how do culture industries exercise the controls that benefited them in the paradigm of scarcity? Perhaps this is possible only if doing so can provide a synergistic and tangible benefit to the public.

Once a rejuvenating place of refuge, public radio became, in its own ways, as rigid in its thinking about music as commercial radio since, from the 1990s on, stations that used to offer a wide range of news and cultural programming came to focus on a single thing. For jazz fans, the concerns about noncommercial radio have become less about what jazz gets aired than about whether any gets aired at all. A brief period in the 1970s was an exciting time in radio when diversity of voices resulted in the presentation of diverse styles. That was an incomparable period when the contestation of a wide range of styles took place on jazz-formatted commercial and on jazz-friendly noncommercial stations.

Public radio stations playing jazz today have largely reached a consensus around "melodic" jazz with the hope it will please, and more important, not displease, contributing audience members. Hence most jazz on public radio is compressed into a narrow range of mainstream post-bop styles. Little by way of experimental music that challenges the conventions of tonality, tempo, timbre, or structure, nor commercially tinged music that mixes R&B, hip hop, and rock, is welcome on public jazz radio. And neither are scratchy old lo-fi recordings from the 1920s and 1930s. The remaining place where a broad range of jazz is found is on community radio and college radio, and there, jazz is being presented in its greatest diversity with the knowledge that jazz has revolutionary meanings.

But radio is changing, the way listeners listen to music is changing, and jazz is changing, despite its challenges on public radio. The internet has created new possibilities for distributing music and for connecting with listeners. Examining the current state of jazz within the internet-based music network today suggests that jazz is unlikely to gain any status relative to popular music but has many opportunities to avoid gatekeepers and reach music fans, despite gatekeeping's having a value-added benefit to jazz musicians and listeners. Jazz will continue to change; its meanings will continue to be fluid and multivalent, and though it will never regain the level of popularity it had in the 1930s, jazz will continue to be influential, affecting other music styles and training popular musicians.

All jazz, conservative and progressive, will benefit from the open internet of long-tail economics and user-initiated selection of music. Wide access to the internet by content providers will ensure that jazz beyond the post-bop mainstream will be available for those looking for it. There is little reason, however, to expect a renaissance of high-profile jazz programming. Creative music will continue to suffer on programmed channels, thus making it harder to gain new followers. It is likely that jazz from the progressive school will continue to suffer so long as jazz is on entities seeking popularity. Because it is not popular, the process of learning about jazz and sharing knowledge will continue to be a part of its enjoyment.

Even as the internet presents opportunities for musicians to reach audiences with a minimum of intervention by gatekeepers, a flood of product and diminishing audience time for music listening creates challenges for artists. Among the emerging opportunities for musicians trying to build a fan base are the analytical tools made available by the two-way connections of internet delivery. If they reach listeners over the internet, their opportunities to collect audience research information are magnified, much in the way streaming services include IP addresses, subscriber information, and connection details—especially "drops," or disconnects that represent listener referenda on new music. The capabilities of the technology (internet) to provide connection and session data (analytics) are potential resources for jazz musicians to use in extending their audiences. Whether or not the permanent ownership of music products will rebound via some technology, access to analytics concerning one's own intellectual property is valuable. Access to and ownership of the aggregated analytics concerning a class of IP are power.

Jazz continues to change, but so do our notions and models of radio and listening. The postwar history of jazz radio has demonstrated that jazz is at a disadvantage on social networks that require or demand popularity. Still, jazz has dedicated fans who will seek it out wherever it is available, and it has adherents who will make it available to listeners, one way or another, at great personal sacrifice.

APPENDIX A

Notable Jazz Disc Jockeys

Dick LaPalm (1928–2013) was an independent record promoter. For many years he was closely associated with Nat Cole. He was a wonderful senior figure from a past day of record promotion who loved to share information with researchers. LaPalm provided this list of DJs in 2012.

DJ	Station(s) most associated with	City
Influential		
Mort Fega	WEVD	New York
"Symphony" Sid Torin	WADO	New York
Sid McCoy	WCFL	Chicago
Dick Buckley	WNIB, WBEZ	Chicago
Felix Grant	WWDC, WMAL	Washington, DC
Dick Martin	WWL	New Orleans
Chuck Niles	KBCA	Los Angeles
Rick Holmes	KBCA	Los Angeles
Harvey Huston	WPEN	Philadelphia
Doug Arthur	WCAU	Philadelphia
Norm Nathan	WHDH	Boston
Bill Marlowe	WBZ	Boston
Jim Rockwell	WKMH	Detroit
Ed Love	WCHD, WDET	Detroit
Jim Lowe	WRR	Dallas
Leo Chears	KWK, WSIE	St. Louis
Pat Henry	KJAZ	San Francisco
Oscar Treadwell	WNOP	Cincinnati
Bill Currie	WBT	Charlotte

DJ	Station(s) most associated with	City
Important		
Al "Jazzbeaux" Collins	WNEW	New York
Ed Beach	WRVR	New York
Allan Grant	WABC-FM	New York
Fred Robbins	WOV	New York
Holmes Daddy-O Daylie	WAIT	Chicago
Marty Faye	WAAF	Chicago
Yvonne Daniels	WSDM, WCFL	Chicago
Bob Perkins	WHYY, WRTI	Philadelphia
Sid Mark	WHAT	Philadelphia
Joel Dorn	WHAT	Philadelphia
Bob Murphy	WJBK	Detroit
John McClellan	WCOP	Boston
Tony Cennamo	WBUR	Boston
Alex "Sleepy" Stein	KNOB	Los Angeles
Jim Gosa	KBCA	Los Angeles
Gene Norman	KLAC	Los Angeles
Willis Conover	WWDC, VOA	Washington, DC
Bill Mayhugh	WMAL	Washington, DC
Paul Anthony	WRC	Washington, DC
Harley Brinsfield	WBAL	Baltimore
John Hardy	KFRC	San Francisco
Jerry Dean	KJAZ	San Francisco
Herb Wong	KJAZ	San Francisco
China Valles	WTMI	Miami
Tony Mowod	WDUQ-FM	Pittsburgh
Phil Brooks	WKPA	Pittsburgh
Ronnie Barrett	WDOK	Cleveland
Dave Hawthorne	WDOK	Cleveland
Tom Brown	WHK	Cleveland
Ray Allen	WCUY-FM	Cleveland
Ray Scott	WNOP	Cincinnati
Leo Underhill	WCKY	Cincinnati
Leigh Kamman	MN Public Radio	
Al Gourrier	WYLD	New Orleans
Spider Burks	KXLW	St. Louis
Jim Bolen	KWK	St. Louis

DJ	Station(s) most associated with	City
Joe Rico	WEBR	Buffalo
Carroll Hardy	WEBR	Buffalo
Phil McKellar	CBC	Toronto
Herb Lance	WERD	Atlanta
H. Johnson	WABE	Atlanta
Tom Mercein	WTMJ	Milwaukee
Ron Cuzner	WFMR	Milwaukee
Bill Ardis	WHAM	Rochester, NY
Harry Abraham	WHAM	Rochester, NY
Gene Amole	KVOD	Denver
Wes Bowen	KSL, KUER	Salt Lake City
Ed Horne	WLOK	Memphis
Henry Wailes	WCVE	Richmond, VA

APPENDIX B

Jazz Radio Stations circa 2020

On radio-locator.com, sixty-three stations self-reported as jazz radio. An additional seventeen stations self-reported as smooth jazz.[1] Of the smooth jazz stations, two were AM stations, eight were using commercial FM frequencies at full power, 6 were LPFMs, and only one (WFSK, Fisk University, Nashville, Tennessee) was a full-power station in the noncommercial band. Of the jazz stations, three were AM stations, three operated at full power on commercial frequencies, and ten were LPFM stations.

Stations KKJZ (Long Beach, California), WBGO (Newark, New Jersey), and WDNA (Miami, Florida) had the most website visits originated by the radio-locator.com links. Similarly, KKJZ, KUVO (Denver, Colorado), and KNTU (McKinney, Texas) had the most internet listening sessions originating from radio-locator's links.

Thirteen jazz stations were licensed to HBCUs, including the smooth jazz station at Fisk University.

These are certainly not all the radio stations broadcasting jazz in the United States. Hundreds more stations have at least one jazz program. The self-reported listing in radio-locator.com cannot be assumed to be 100 percent accurate as to station programming.

Call Sign	Frequency	City	Affiliation/Owner	Format
KAJI (LPFM)	95.3 LPFM	Palm Desert, CA	American Jazz Institute	Jazz
KBEM	88.5 FM	Minneapolis, MN	Minneapolis Public Schools	Jazz
KBJZ (LPFM)	94.1 LPFM	Juneau, AK	Gastineau Broadcasting Corp.	Jazz
KBSK	89.9 FM	McCall, ID	Boise State University	Jazz
KCCB	1260 AM	Corning, AR	Shields-Atkins Broadcasting	Jazz

Call Sign	Frequency	City	Affiliation/Owner	Format
KCCK	88.3 FM	Cedar Rapids, IA	Kirkwood Community College	Jazz
KCSM	91.1 FM	San Mateo, CA	College of San Mateo	Jazz
KEWU	89.5 FM	Cheney, WA	Eastern Washington University	Jazz
KJEM	89.9 FM	Pullman, WA	Washington State University	Jazz
KJLU	88.9 FM	Jefferson City, MO	Lincoln University	Jazz
KJZC	90.5 FM	Chadron, NE	Chadron State College	Jazz
KJZP	90.1 FM	Prescott, AZ	En Familia, Inc.	Jazz
KJZX (LPFM)	89.1 LPFM	Austin, TX	Jazz ATX	Jazz
KKJZ	88.1 FM	Long Beach, CA	California State University atLong Beach	Jazz
KLGE	94.1 FM	Hydesville, CA	Lost Coast Communications	Jazz
KMFO (LPFM)	98.1 LPFM	Tulsa, OK	Oklahoma Jazz Hall of Fame, Inc.	Jazz
KMHD	89.1 FM	Gresham, OR	Mt. Hood Community College	Jazz
~~KNTU[a]~~	~~88.1 FM~~	~~McKinney, TX~~	~~University of North Texas~~	~~Jazz~~
KOJH (LPFM)	104.7 LPFM	Kansas City, MO	Mutual Musicians Foundation	Jazz
KRTU	91.7 FM	San Antonio, TX	Trinity University	Jazz
KSDS	88.3 FM	San Diego, CA	San Diego City College	Jazz
KTSU	90.9 FM	Houston, TX	Texas Southern University	Jazz
KUNV	91.5 FM	Las Vegas, NV	University of Nevada at Las Vegas	Jazz
KUVO	89.3 FM	Denver, CO	Rocky Mountain Public Media	Jazz
KUWL	90.1 FM	Laramie, WY	University of Wyoming	Jazz
~~KVJZ~~	~~88.5 FM~~	~~Vail, CO~~	~~Rocky Mountain Public Media~~	~~Jazz~~
KVNM (LPFM)	101.1 LPFM	Veguita, NM	Idea Ministries	Jazz
KVSF	101.5 FM	Pecos, NM	Hutton Broadcasting	Jazz
WAJH	91.1 FM	Birmingham, AL	Alabama Jazz Hall of Fame	Jazz
WBGO	88.3 FM	Newark, NJ	Newark Public Radio	Jazz
WBRH	90.3 FM	Baton Rouge, LA	Baton Rouge Magnet High School	Jazz
WCLK	91.9 FM	Atlanta, GA	Clark Atlanta University	Jazz
~~WCRX (LPFM)~~	~~102.1 LPFM~~	~~Columbus, OH~~	~~Bexley Public Radio Foundation~~	~~Jazz~~
WDCB	90.9 FM	Glen Ellyn, IL	College of DuPage	Jazz
WDNA	88.9 FM	Miami, FL	Bascomb Memorial Broadcasting Foundation	Jazz

Call Sign	Frequency	City	Affiliation/Owner	Format
WDPS	89.5 FM	Dayton, OH	Dayton City Schools	Jazz
WEAA	88.9 FM	Baltimore, MD	Morgan State University	Jazz
WESM	91.3 FM	Princess Anne, MD	University of Maryland atEastern Shore	Jazz
WETF (LPFM)	105.7 LPFM	South Bend, IN	Latino Task Force for Education	Jazz
WGMC	90.1 FM	Greece, NY	Greece Central School District	Jazz
WHOV	88.1 FM	Hampton, VA	Hampton University	Jazz
WICN	90.5 FM	Worcester, MA	WICN Public Broadcasting	Jazz
WJAB	90.9 FM	Huntsville, AL	Alabama A&M University	Jazz
~~WJSK (LPFM)~~	~~101.1 LPFM~~	~~Bartlett, NH~~	~~Bartlett-Jackson Community Broadcasters Assn.~~	~~Jazz~~
WJSU	88.5 FM	Jackson, MS	Jackson State University	Jazz
WJZP (LPFM)	107.9 LPFM	Portland, ME	All Inclusive, Inc.	Jazz
~~WJZR[b]~~	~~105.9 FM~~	~~Rochester, NY~~	~~North Coast Radio~~	~~Jazz~~
WJZZ	88.1 FM	Montgomery, NY	Hudson Valley Public Radio	Jazz
WNCU	90.7 FM	Durham, NC	North Carolina Central University	Jazz
WPUT	90.1 FM	North Salem, NY	Foothill Public Radio	Jazz
WQJC (LPFM)	107.9 LPFM	Quincy, IL	Quincy Not for Profit Jazz Corporation	Jazz
WRTE	90.7 FM	Chicago, IL	Chicago Public Media	Jazz
WRTI	89.3 FM	Coatesville, PA	Temple University	Jazz
WSAX (LPFM)	98.5 LPFM	Columbus, OH	Columbus Jazz Alliance	Jazz
WSIE	88.7 FM	Edwardsville, IL	Southern Illinois University at Edwardsville	Jazz
WSNC	90.5 FM	Winston-Salem, NC	Winston-Salem State University	Jazz
WSSB	90.3 FM	Orangeburg, SC	South Carolina State University	Jazz
WUCF	89.9 FM	Orlando, FL	University of Central Florida	Jazz
WVAS	90.7 FM	Montgomery, AL	Alabama State University	Jazz
WVID	90.3 FM	Anasco, PR	Centro Colegial Cristiano, Inc.	Jazz
WWOZ	90.7 FM	New Orleans, LA	Friends of WWOZ	Jazz
WXHQ (LPFM)	105.9 LPFM	Newport, RI	Newport Musical Arts Association	Jazz
WXTS	88.3 FM	Toledo, OH	Toledo Public Schools	Jazz
WZBR	1410 AM	Dedham, MA	Langer Broadcasting Group	Jazz
WZUM	1550 AM	Braddock, PA	Pittsburgh Public Media	Jazz

Call Sign	Frequency	City	Affiliation/Owner	Format
WZUM	88.1 FM	Bethany, WV	Pittsburgh Public Media	Jazz
KAJZ	106.5 FM	Granite Shoals, TX	Bryan King (owner)	Smooth Jazz
KCYI (LPFM)	97.7 LPFM	Oklahoma City, OK	Edwards Broadcasting	Smooth Jazz
~~KJZT (LPFM)~~	~~90.1 LPFM~~	~~Tulsa, OK~~	~~Tulsa Community Radio~~	~~Smooth Jazz~~
KOAZ	1510 AM	Isleta, NM	Vanguard Media	Smooth Jazz
KORJ	97.7 FM	Butte Falls, OR	Threshold Communications	Smooth Jazz
KRWV (LPFM)	99.3 LPFM	Gold Canyon, AZ	Gold Canyon Public Radio	Smooth Jazz
KSFE	96.7 FM	Grants, NM	Vanguard Media	Smooth Jazz
KTCE	92.1 FM	Payson, UT	Moenkopi Communications	Smooth Jazz
KWBR (LPFM)	105.7 LPFM	Saint George, UT	Association of Community Resources and News	Smooth Jazz
WAEG	92.3 FM	Evans, GA	Perry Broadcasting of Augusta	Smooth Jazz
WEIB	106.3 FM	Northampton, MA	Cutting Edge Broadcasting	Smooth Jazz
WFSK	88.1 FM	Nashville, TN	Fisk University	Smooth Jazz
WJZA	1310 AM	Decatur, GA	Davis Broadcasting of Atlanta	Smooth Jazz
WJZK (LPFM)	97.3 LPFM	Fort Walton Beach, FL	Bayshore Community Broadcasting Corp.	Smooth Jazz
WNOZ (LPFM)	95.3 LPFM	New Orleans, LA	M&M Community Development, Inc., New Orleans Branch	Smooth Jazz
WNSY	100.1 FM	Talking Rock, GA	Davis Broadcasting of Atlanta	Smooth Jazz
WSBZ	106.3 FM	Miramar Beach, FL	Carter Broadcasting	Smooth Jazz
WTTZ (LPFM)	93.5 LPFM	Baltimore, MD	State of Maryland, Maryland Dept. of Transportation	Smooth Jazz

Source: Compiled from the www.radio-locator.com database.

Strikethough indicates stations that are no longer on the air.

[a] This station switched to Alternative in July 2022.

[b] This station ended jazz programming on July 10, 2022. Jazz was heard there since 1993. https://radioinsight.com/headlines/232445/wjzrs-jazz-programming-comes-to-an-end/.

Notes

Introduction

1. Karl Ottenhoff, "WBGO to Embrace Change, Cling to Its Roots as It Enters a New Chapter, New CEO Says," guest editorial, *Newark Star Ledger*, February 10, 2020. https://www.nj.com/opinion/2020/02/no-fruit-without-roots-so-wbgo-will-keep-theirs-as-it-enters-a-new-chapter-new-ceo-says.html.

2. Genesis 2:20.

3. The Ramsey Lewis Trio recording of "The in Crowd" reached #5 on the Billboard Hot 100 in October 1965, as had Stan Getz and Astrud Gilberto's "Girl from Ipanema" the previous year. "The Pink Panther Theme" peaked at #10 in May 1964. Kenny Ball and His Jazzmen had a #2 Hot 100 hit with "Midnight in Moscow," a version of a popular 1950s Soviet song.

4. These are the Billboard Top 100 and Black chart peaks for each: "Mercy, Mercy, Mercy" (11, 2), "The Sidewinder" (81), "Killer Joe" (74), and "Chameleon" (42, 18). *Billboard* chart data are from individual issues archived at worldradiohistory.com. All future references to *Billboard* charts are from this website.

5. Jae Sinnett, Facebook.com post, August 14, 2020, https://www.facebook.com/jae.sinnett/posts/pfbid0YggawaGar453xutGnYex96Z7×7NHBtdEiQZZRhCtG6NqwkakaquAyTgWvA5prGNhl.

6. In another Facebook.com post (June 13, 2021) Jae Sinnett related his experience of having three top-ranked jazz radio releases but selling few units. According to Sinnett, independent releases typically sell from 150 to 1,000 copies from online physical retailers and that label releases might reach 3,500. In his view, only established stars such as Pat Metheny or Herbie Hancock can sell 10,000 or more, and that is based more on the listeners' history with the artists than on hearing and admiring the new records.

7. Paul M. Hirsch, "Processing Fads and Fashions: An Organization-Set Analysis of Cultural Industry Systems," *American Journal of Sociology* 77, no. 4 (1972): 639–59.

8. While 175,000 is a big number for jazz, as of March 2024, Billie Eilish had more than forty-nine million subscribers. "Billie Eilish," https://www.youtube.com/channel/UCiGm_E4ZwYSHV3bcW1pnSeQ; "Emmet Cohen," https://www.youtube.com/channel/UCuKBb-0F0qT_deSpMLsFRA.

9. Radio scholars such as Robert Waterman McChesney, Michele Hilmes, and Jason Loviglio, along with culture industry thinkers like Antonio Gramsci and Theodor Adorno, have centered their work on the struggle between commercial interests and cultural elites for control of or at least access to the airwaves. Others, such as Clifford John Doerksen, see the audience as playing a central role by giving presumptive consent to the business-oriented ideology of twentieth-century America. Michele Hilmes, *Radio Voices: American Broadcasting, 1922–1952* (Minneapolis: University

of Minnesota Press, 1997); Michele Hilmes and Jason Loviglio, *Radio Reader: Essays in the Cultural History of Radio* (New York: Routledge, 2002); Robert Waterman McChesney, *Rich Media, Poor Democracy: Communication Politics in Dubious Times* (Urbana: University of Illinois Press, 1999). T. W. Adorno, "A Social Critique of Radio Music," *Kenyon Review* 18, no. 3/4 (1996): 229–35; Clifford John Doerksen, *American Babel: Rogue Radio Broadcasters of the Jazz Age* (Philadelphia: University of Pennsylvania Press, 2005); Elena Razlogova, *The Listener's Voice: Early Radio and the American Public* (Philadelphia: University of Pennsylvania Press, 2011); Susan J. Douglas, *Listening In: Radio and the American Imagination, from Amos 'N' Andy and Edward R. Murrow to Wolfman Jack and Howard Stern* (New York: Times Books, 1999).

10. Barbara D. Savage, *Broadcasting Freedom: Radio, War, and the Politics of Race, 1938–1948* (Chapel Hill: University of North Carolina Press), 1999; William Barlow, *Voice Over: the Making of Black Radio* (Philadelphia: Temple University Press, 1999); Brian Ward, *Radio and the Struggle for Civil Rights in the South* (Gainesville: University Press of Florida, 2004); Louis Cantor, *Wheelin' on Beale: How WDIA-Memphis Became the Nation's First All-Black Radio Station and Created the Sound That Changed America* (New York: Pharos, 1992); Ryan Ellett, *Encyclopedia of Black Radio in the United States, 1921–1955* (Jefferson, NC: McFarland, 2012).

11. The FCC, an independent federal regulatory agency directly overseen by Congress, was preceded by the Federal Radio Commission (FRC), established by the Radio Act of 1927. Prior to the founding of the FRC, radio matters not handled by the military were under the supervision and regulation of the Department of Commerce.

12. Edward Brooke III, a Republican from Massachusetts, served in the U.S. Senate for two terms, from 1967 to 1979.

13. Black musicians did appear on sponsored broadcasts, but many more appearances were on "sustaining" shows. *Sustaining* was a euphemism. A network wanted nothing more than to have a sponsor take on a show and remove those airtime minutes from the sustaining inventory. However, as a public relations gambit, the networks frequently boasted about their sustaining shows, which did account for a large share of their high culture programming.

14. Actually, in the 1930s Guy Lombardo was quite popular with Harlem listeners. Ricky Riccardi, *Heart Full of Rhythm: The Big Band Years of Louis Armstrong* (New York: Oxford University Press, 2020), 37.

15. Terry Eagleton, *The Ideology of the Aesthetic* (Cambridge, MA: Blackwell, 1990), 7.

16. Gennari, for example, considers how these ideological positions are discoverable in the discourse about jazz criticism and the critique of Ellington's extended works. John Gennari, "Jazz Criticism: Its Development and Ideologies," *Black American Literature Forum* 25, no. 3 (1991): 449–523.

17. Ingrid T. Monson, *Freedom Sounds: Civil Rights Calls out to Jazz and Africa* (New York: Oxford University Press, 2007), 71.

18. Michael Judge, "Jazz Was His Earliest Muse," *Wall Street Journal*, February 22, 2011.

19. John F. Szwed, "Blue Nippon: Authenticating Jazz in Japan by E. Taylor Atkins," *Journal of Japanese Studies* 29, no. 1 (2003): 223.

20. Lisa Davenport, *Jazz Diplomacy: Promoting America in the Cold War Era* (Jackson: University Press of Mississippi, 2009), 12.

21. Davenport, *Jazz Diplomacy*, 5. Many writers have discussed interactions between jazz and cold war ideologies. Of particular interest are Penny M. Von Eschen, *Satchmo Blows up the World: Jazz Ambassadors Play the Cold War* (Cambridge, MA: Harvard University Press, 2004); Monson, *Freedom Sounds*; Uta G. Poiger, *Jazz, Rock, and Rebels: Cold War Politics and American Culture in a Divided Germany* (Berkeley: University of California Press, 2000); Christian G. Appy, *Cold War Constructions: The Political Culture of United States Imperialism, 1945–1966* (Amherst: University of Massachusetts Press, 2000); and Terence Ripmaster, *Willis Conover: Broadcasting Jazz to the World* (n.p.: iUniverse, 2007).

22. Lerone Bennett Jr., "The Soul of Jazz," *Ebony*, December 1961, 114.

23. Tynan is quoted in Bennett Jr., "The Soul of Jazz," 116.

24. Pierre Bourdieu, *Distinction: A Social Critique of the Judgement of Taste* (Cambridge, MA: Harvard University Press, 1984), 21.

25. Travis A. Jackson, *Blowin' the Blues Away: Performance and Meaning on the New York Jazz Scene* (Berkeley: University of California Press, 2012), 5.

26. The full quote: "The tremendous burden of sociology which Jones would place upon this body of music is enough to give even the blues the blues." Ralph Ellison, "Blues People," in *Shadow and Act* (New York: Random House, 1964), 249.

27. Albert Murray and Robert Bone Collection (Columbia University Libraries), *The Blue Devils of Nada: A Contemporary American Approach to Aesthetic Statement* (New York: Pantheon, 1996).

28. John A. Kouwenhoven, "What's 'American' About America," in *The Jazz Cadence of American Culture*, ed. Robert G. O'Meally (New York: Columbia University Press, 1998), 128–29.

29. Eric Lott, "Bebop's Politics of Style," in *Jazz Among the Discourses*, ed. Krin Gabbard (Durham, NC: Duke University Press, 1995), 246.

30. Lott, "Bebop's Politics of Style," 248.

31. Christopher H. Sterling and John M. Kittross, *Stay Tuned: A History of American Broadcasting* (Mahwah, NJ: Lawrence Erlbaum, 2002).

32. Eric W. Rothenbuhler and Tom McCourt, "Radio Redefines Itself, 1947–1962," in *Radio Reader: Essays in the Cultural History of Radio*, ed. Michele Hilmes and Jason Loviglio (New York: Routledge, 2002), 367.

33. Philip K. Eberly, *Music in the Air: America's Changing Tastes in Popular Music, 1920–1980* (New York: Hastings House, 1982).

34. See Ken Vail, *Duke's Diary*, 2 vols. (Lanham, MD: Scarecrow, 2002); Klaus Stratemann, *Duke Ellington: Day by Day and Film by Film* (Copenhagen: JazzMedia ApS, 1992); Chadwick Jenkins, "A Question of Containment: Duke Ellington and Early Radio," *American Music* 26, no. 4 (2008): 415–41; William Randle Jr., "Black Entertainers on Radio, 1920–1930," *Black Perspective in Music* 5, no. 1 (1977): 67–74; Henry T. Sampson, *Swingin' on the Ether Waves: A Chronological History of African Americans in Radio and Television Broadcasting, 1925–1955*, 2 vols. (Lanham, MD: Scarecrow, 2005); Noah Arceneaux, "Blackface Broadcasting in the Early Days of Radio," *Journal of Radio Studies* 12, no. 1 (2005): 61–73; Court Carney, *Cuttin' Up: How Early Jazz Got America's Ear* (Lawrence: University Press of Kansas, 2009).

35. The intersection of jazz and politics has been a vibrant area of study. Notable works include Monson, *Freedom Sounds*; Davenport, *Jazz Diplomacy*; Von Eschen, *Satchmo Blows up the World*; and Scott Knowles DeVeaux, *The Birth of Bebop: A Social and Musical History* (Berkeley: University of California Press, 1997).

36. One exception is chapter 4 in Lopes (2002), which considers the role of influential DJs in promoting the developing bebop style. Paul Douglas Lopes, *The Rise of a Jazz Art World* (Cambridge: Cambridge University Press, 2002).

37. Marcello Sorce Keller, "Musicologists and the Radio: A Short List of Questions, Problems, and Issues," in *Talk About Radio: Towards a Social History of Radio (Zur Sozialgeschichte Des Radios)*, ed. Theo Mäusli (Zurich: Chronos, 1999), 116.

38. Mark Katz, *Capturing Sound: How Technology Has Changed Music* (Berkeley: University of California Press, 2004); Jonathan Sterne, *The Audible Past: Cultural Origins of Sound Reproduction* (Durham, NC: Duke University Press, 2003); Timothy Dean Taylor, Mark Katz, and Tony Grajeda, *Music, Sound, and Technology in America: A Documentary History of Early Phonograph, Cinema, and Radio* (Durham, NC: Duke University Press, 2012); Alexander G. Weheliye, *Phonographies: Grooves in Sonic Afro-Modernity* (Durham, NC: Duke University Press, 2005); Paul D. Greene and Thomas Porcello, *Wired for Sound: Engineering and Technologies in Sonic Cultures* (Middletown, CT: Wesleyan University Press, 2005); Timothy Dean Taylor, *The Sounds of Capitalism: Advertising, Music, and the Conquest of Culture* (Chicago: University of Chicago Press, 2012).

39. Warren R. Pinckney, "Jazz in Barbados," *American Music* 12, no. 1 (1994): 62.

40. Elijah Wald, *How the Beatles Destroyed Rock 'N' Roll: An Alternative History of American Popular Music* (Oxford: Oxford University Press, 2009), 92–93.

41. Tim J. Anderson, *Making Easy Listening: Material Culture and Postwar American Recording* (Minneapolis: University of Minnesota Press, 2006), xix.

42. For example, the top-rated program of the 1940–1941 radio season, the NBC Red network's *Jack Benny Program*, airing Sunday nights at 7:00 p.m., garnered an average 30.8 rating. In 1940 each rating point equaled 285,000 homes (the 28.5 million radio homes were estimated to cover 81.1 percent of U.S. homes). So the Benny program was heard in about 8.78 million homes. Jim Ramsburg, *Network Radio Ratings, 1932–1953: A History of Prime Time Programs Through the Ratings of Nielsen, Crossley, and Hooper* (Jefferson, NC: McFarland, 2012), 98.

43. In 1932 William Cardinal O'Connell pronounced crooning a "degenerate form of singing" and asserted that "no true American would practice this base art." Taylor, Katz, and Grajeda, *Music, Sound, and Technology*, 319.

44. Wald, *How the Beatles Destroyed Rock 'N' Roll*, 95.

45. This is always the case in a 1:n branching network where n is a large number. The cost of operating a branch should be less than the revenue earned using that branch, and the capital costs associated with the branch must be recoverable in a reasonable time period. How, then, could a record company afford to send a truck to a store when the cost of the truck run is $75 if it isn't reasonably sure it will get more than $75 in sales from that truck? For a multi-client delivery service, called a distributor, however, that truck could carry $1,000 of potential sales product or more for the $75 cost. In turn, it charges the record company an amount that is more in line with the expected record sales, but it does this for all the other clients whose product is on the truck as well.

46. John Hartley et al., *Communication, Cultural and Media Studies: The Key Concepts*, 3rd ed. (London: Routledge, 2002), 95.

47. "Policing the Music Air: Everyone Wants No Self-Payola," *Billboard*, December 29, 1945, 13.

48. Nancy Sinatra, "Radio Free America," *New York Times*, August 3, 2009, https://www.nytimes.com/2009/08/04/opinion/04sinatra.html.

49. Fabian Holt, *Genre in Popular Music* (Chicago: University of Chicago Press, 2007), 106–7.

50. Lisa Hamel, "Old Hand at Jazz," *New York Times*, April 27, 1958.

51. "Core Values of Jazz Formats," abridged report, Walrus Research, Spring 2004. https://walrusresearch.com/__static/91e74f33a2cf7a59a8aa56b3a10e6d09/core-values-jazz-stations.pdf?dl=1.

52. Ted Hendrickson, "It's the Audience, Stupid: Jazz Radio 2003," *CMJ*, October 20, 2003, 13.

53. There were always more position wanted ads than person wanted ads regarding jazz specialists.

54. Lopes, Rise of a Jazz Art World, 170.

55. A list of important and influential DJs as ranked by record publicist Dick LaPalm is provided in appendix B.

56. Should one doubt the ability of black radio to transmit clandestine messages, in 1970 a rival for WOOK's license charged that radio preachers were using Bible verses to promote play on certain illegal numbers: "And, then He came back on Wednesday and bless so beautifully with Psalm 71 and 9. Just a straight pathway for you [read: play 719]." Robert J. Samuelson, "Broadcasts Linked to Numbers," *Washington Post*, 3 July 1970, B5.

57. James C. Scott, *Domination and the Arts of Resistance: Hidden Transcripts* (New Haven: Yale University Press, 1990).

58. Brian Ward, *Radio and the Struggle for Civil Rights in the South* (Gainesville: University Press of Florida, 2004), 204.

59. A commonly held understanding of social media influencers is as follows: A social media influencer is a user on social media who has established credibility in a specific industry. Such a user has access to a large audience and can persuade others by virtue of authenticity and reach.

60. Gilbert Williams, "The Black Disc Jockey as a Cultural Hero," *Popular Music and Society* 10, no. 3 (1986): 82.

61. Dick LaPalm, telephone interview by the author, November 9, 2012.

62. Creed Taylor, interview with Marc Myers, pt. 6, July 15, 2008, https://www.jazzwax.com/2008/07/interview-cre-1.html.

63. Davie Ake has written about this at the borders of jazz and rhythm and blues, but more generally writers such as Frith have also considered it. David Andrew Ake, *Jazz Cultures* (Berkeley: University of California Press, 2002); Simon Frith, *Performing Rites: On the Value of Popular Music* (Oxford: Oxford University Press, 1996).

64. Nadine Cohodas, *Princess Noire: The Tumultuous Reign of Nina Simone* (New York: Pantheon, 2010), 368.

65. Brian D. Holland and Earl Klugh, "Earl Klugh Interview: Guitars, George Benson, and Naked Guitar," *Guitar International*, https://web.archive.org/web/20151222110942/http://guitarinternational.com/2010/12/21/earl-klugh-talks-guitars-george-benson-and-naked-guitar/.

66. Bernard Gendron, *Between Montmartre and the Mudd Club: Popular Music and the Avant-Garde* (Chicago: University of Chicago Press, 2002), 126.

67. It should come as no surprise that musicians who play commercial music loathe the implication of classical music's being called "legit," or legitimate.

68. One can see an analog in how it took the popularity of "hot" to create the need for the "sweet" label to describe an exnominated performance aesthetic, similar to the way "whiteness" was formed in relation to blackness.

69. Christopher Wilkinson, "Sweet Dance Music," in *Grove Music Online*, 2015, https://www-oxfordmusiconline-com.pitt.idm.oclc.org/grovemusic/view/10.1093/gmo/9781561592630.001.0001/omo-9781561592630-e-1002276633.

70. Eric Thacker, "Hot (i)," in *Grove Music Online*, 2002, https://www-oxfordmusiconline-com.pitt.idm.oclc.org/grovemusic/view/10.1093/gmo/9781561592630.001.0001/omo-9781561592630-e-2000208300.

71. Patrick Lawrence Burke, *Come in and Hear the Truth: Jazz and Race on 52nd Street* (Chicago: University of Chicago Press, 2008).

72. Bill Smith, "Bring Back Those Big Bands! Two Philadelphia Disc Jockeys Produce an Amazing Series of Four-Hour Shows," *Metronome*, August 1954, 21.

73. Gendron, *Between Montmartre and the Mudd Club*, 128–29.

74. Lopes, *Rise of a Jazz Art World*.

75. Lopes, *Rise of a Jazz Art World*, 213.

76. Keir Keightley, "Music for Middlebrows: Defining the Easy Listening Era, 1946–1966," *American Music* 26, no. 3 (Spring 2008): 315–16.

77. I like to describe free jazz as loosening the constraints of conventional music making in any or all of four aspects: (1) freeing the music from the hierarchy of tonality, (2) freeing instrumental timbre and techniques from "correct" practices and using timbre as a primary means of expression, (3) freeing the performance from aspects of form and structural organization, and (4) freeing the performance from the regularity of pulse or meter. All four of these aspects have become permanent fixtures in post-bop mainstream jazz performances; it is only a matter of degree and of how many appear simultaneously!

78. Charles D. Carson, "'Bridging the Gap': Creed Taylor, Grover Washington, Jr., and the Crossover Roots of Smooth Jazz," *Black Music Research Journal* 28, no. 1 (Spring 2008): 2.

79. Carson, "Bridging the Gap," 3.

80. Some argue that smooth jazz is dead as measured by radio ratings and the dwindling number of smooth jazz stations. However, there is still a market for smooth jazz records, and of particular interest to me as a performer, a healthy live performance market for smooth jazz bands playing for black audiences aged forty-five and older. David Adler, "Crossing Over: Is Smooth Jazz Dead?" *JazzTimes*, October 22, 2019, https://jazztimes.com/features/columns/crossing-over-is-smooth-jazz-dead/; Bobby Owsinski, "Is Smooth Jazz Dead or Is It Just Bad Data?," Hypebot, July 14, 2015, https://www.hypebot.com/hypebot/2015/07/is-smooth-jazz-dead.html.

Chapter 1. Jazz Here and Jazz There

1. A 1948 *Billboard* report claimed that in houses with radio and television sets, the televisions were getting "3 times as much play" as the radios. "TV Sets in Use 3–1 over AM," *Billboard*, July 24, 1948, 12.

2. Bruce Lenthall, "Critical Reception: Public Intellectuals Decry Depression-Era Radio, Mass Culture, and Modern America," in *Radio Reader: Essays in the Cultural History of Radio*, ed. Michele Hilmes and Jason Loviglio (New York: Routledge, 2002), 53.

3. The great film composer Bernard Herrmann started by composing for CBS, including work for Orson Welles's Mercury Theatre Company of the Air.

4. Alexander Russo, "Defensive Transcriptions: Radio Networks, Sound-on-Disc Recording, and the Meaning of Live Broadcasting," *Velvet Light Trap* no. 54 (2004): 6; Michael J. Socolow, "To Network a Nation: NBC, CBS, and the Development of National Network Radio in the United States, 1925–1950" (PhD diss., Georgetown University, 2001).

5. National Broadcasting Company, *Broadcast Advertising: A Study of the Radio Medium*, vol.1: *The Fourth Dimension of Radio Advertising* (New York: National Broadcasting Company, 1929), 27.

6. Radio stations are assigned an operating frequency by the FCC. In the earliest days of radio, wavelength, inversely proportional to frequency, was used more often because early receiver designs focused on length of antenna. A four-hundred-meter assignment implied precise operation at 750 kHz, but in practice, a band of frequencies from 710 to 790 kHz would be considered four-hundred-meter operation. Soon, more precision and stability could be achieved, and the same span would be considered as nine separate AM channels.

7. In 1921 the Department of Commerce established two wavelengths for the "broadcast service." It allocated 360 meters for stations broadcasting news, lectures, concerts, ballgames, and the like. Crop reports and weather information, of vital interest to farmers, were to be broadcast on 485 meters. It was not expected that a station providing both services would rapidly switch between wavelengths, but rather, that it would schedule different broadcast day segments for each service. In 1922 the Class B service, assigned to 400 meters, was introduced. Thomas H. White, "Building the Broadcast Band," http://earlyradiohistory.us/buildbcb.htm#complexities.

8. United States Department of Commerce, "Radio Service Bulletin" no. 125, August 31, 1927,

9. Just try to imagine a radio broadcast with a stuffy announcement before each selection—"This is a recorded musical selection."

9. United States Department of Commerce, "Radio Service Bulletin" no. 139, October 31, 1928, 15.

10. United States Department of Commerce, "Radio Service Bulletin" no. 139, October 31, 1928, 15.

11. Russo, "Defensive Transcriptions," 4–17.

12. Socolow, "To Network a Nation," 84.

13. "75% of All Radio Stations on Discs," *Variety*, December 24, 1930, 58.

14. Martin Block seems to have had the early press advantage, being in New York, and many early sources, including the Wikipedia entry for KFWB (https://en.wikipedia.org/wiki/KFWB), credit him with Make-Believe Ballroom. Other sources credit Jarvis with creating the concept and being the first to put it on the air, where its popularity led to multiple versions by stations in other U.S. radio markets. In 1992 Bob Weiss, who was mentored by Jarvis, told Laurence W. Etling, "I was always very perturbed to see Martin Block taking the credit . . . when in fact he was a sponger. He did not create or originate, he imitated. . . . When I went back East, I heard Martin Block and I said, 'Oh, God, he doesn't hold a candle to Al.' . . . This was Al's show, and he just took it and copied it exactly." Laurence W. Etling, "Al Jarvis: Pioneer Disc Jockey," *Popular Music and Society* 23, no. 3 (1999): 41–52.

15. This creating of an imaginary where one medium imitated another was nothing new; Duke Ellington re-created the aura of a live show and broadcast from the Cotton Club with the 1929 studio recording *A Nite at the Cotton Club*, complete with phony announcer patter from his manager Irving Mills. Nor was the live imaginary a passing fad. Years later, both Julian "Cannonball" Adderley's *Mercy, Mercy Mercy! Live at "The Club"* (1967) and *Charles Mingus Presents Charles Mingus* (1960) would masquerade as LPs recorded in front of a live audience. Even the Temptations offered a single, "I Can't Get Next to You" (1969), with its opening also sampled to begin "Psychedelic Shack" (1970), in which songwriter-producer Norman Whitfield used wildly enthusiastic party sounds to create an imagined live performance space.

16. Al Jarvis, "The Disc Jockey," *Billboard*, April 25, 1953, 39.

17. William Barlow, *Voice Over: The Making of Black Radio* (Philadelphia: Temple University Press, 1999), 51.

18. Barlow, *Voice Over*, 55.

19. Barlow, *Voice Over*, 57.

20. Michael Streissguth, "Jack L. Cooper," in *Biographical Encyclopedia of Radio*, ed. Christopher H. Sterling (London: Routledge, 2013), 68–69.

21. Barlow, *Voice Over*, 57.

22. Barlow, *Voice Over*, 57.

23. It also illustrates that WSAI did not promote a DJ or host for its "records" show. *Radio Dial*, 7 August 1931, 6.

24. Clifford John Doerksen, *American Babel: Rogue Radio Broadcasters of the Jazz Age* (Philadelphia: University of Pennsylvania Press, 2005).

25. There are two kinds of stations on a broadcast network: owned and operated stations, which are owned by the network corporation, and affiliates, which are independently owned and carry network programming according to a business arrangement.

26. The station moved from Brooklyn, New York, to the Washington, DC, area in 1927 and was renamed WJSV in 1929 after James S. Vance, publisher of the *Fellowship Forum*, an anti-Catholic newspaper, who was said to be a high-ranking Ku Klux Klan official. Vance described his objectives to the *New York Times* thus: While featuring old-fashioned songs and hymns, weekly sermons, and lectures about agriculture, he said, "It will be our main object to 'pierce' the ether frequently with talks on pure patriotism by some outstanding American. We shall undertake to give instructions in civil government as it applies to our own country and in comparison with that of other nations." Mark Jones, "The Klan Leaves Its Mark on Washington's Airwaves," Boundary Stones: WETA's Local History Website, January 13. 2015, https://boundarystones.weta.org/2015/01/13/klan-leaves-its-mark-washingtons-airwaves.

27. "Say It with Music Marks Trend," *DownBeat*, June 15, 1942, 12–13.

28. "Disc Jockeys Air Phenomenon: Many Media Are Used but the Show Is Its Own Best Promotion," *Sponsor*, September 2, 1949, 77.

29. "Disc Jockeys Air Phenomenon," 36; "FCC Roundup," *Broadcasting and Telecasting*, September 5, 1949, 87.

30. Barlow, *Voice Over*, 58.

31. "Platters Sell Broadcasting," *Billboard*, December 29, 1945, 13.

32. The same is true for songs and records played on local radio, only smaller amounts of royalties are earned.

33. Tim J. Anderson, *Making Easy Listening: Material Culture and Postwar American Recording* (Minneapolis: University of Minnesota Press, 2006), xix.

34. "Songs with Most Radio Plugs," *Billboard*, January 7, 1939, 10.

35. *Billboard* has long featured a number of charts. For example, "It's Been a Long, Long Time" (at #5) and "It Might as Well Be Spring" (at #6) were both on the January 19, 1946, Honor Roll of Hits. "It Might as Well Be Spring" was also posted in a list of songs from popular films, in this case *Too Young to Know* (Warner Brothers, released December 1, 1945). The songs were also on the sheet music sales chart at numbers 6 and 8, respectively. A separate and alphabetical Music Popularity Chart listed both of the songs as remaining six weeks on the list of songs with the "greatest radio audiences," while yet another chart, Records Most-Played on the Air, indicated that the version of "It's Been a Long, Long Time" by Bing Crosby and the Les Paul Trio had been number 8 the previous week and the one by Harry James had been number 7 at the same time. As for "It Might as Well Be Spring," both Dick Haymes's and Sammy Kaye's versions made the chart. A new entry on the record chart at number 14, "Come to Baby, Do" was represented by Les Brown, the King Cole Trio, Jimmy Dorsey, and Duke Ellington. Listeners were even less discriminating when it came to juke box plays; "It Might as Well Be Spring" had versions by Kaye (#4) and Haymes (#10), and "It's Been a Long, Long Time" had versions by James (#8), Crosby (#9), and Charlie Spivak (#11) earning jukebox plays.

36. These are all so wonderful. The 1938 version by Chu Berry and His Little Jazz Ensemble featured Roy Eldridge (tp), Chu Berry (ts), Clyde Hart (p), Danny Baker (g), Artie Shapiro (b), and Sid Catlett (ds). Django Reinhardt's 1938 version had Larry Adler (harmonica), Stéphane Grappelli (p), Reinhardt, Joseph Reinhardt, and Eugène Vées (g), and Roger Grasset (b), and Coleman Hawkins and His Orchestra (1939) featured Hawkins (ts), Tommy Lindsay, Joe Guy (tp), Earl Hardy (tbn), Jackie Fields, Eustis More (as), Gene Rodgers (p), William Oscar Smith (b), and Arthur Herbert (d).

37. Heath Lowrance, "How the Great Depression Gave America the Blues," *History*, September 2008, https://sites.google.com/site/thegreatdepressionblues/.

38. Milt Gabler, "Reminiscences of Milton Gabler: Oral History, 1959." Columbia University Libraries, Columbia Center for Oral History. https://oralhistoryportal.library.columbia.edu/document.php?id=ldpd_4076824, 11–12. This account seems plausible considering that there were numerous record-pressing plants located between Camden, New Jersey, and Bridgeport, Connecticut.

39. In *Honkers and Shouters*, Arnold Shaw described Grant as an early R&B singer using Nat Cole as a model and as "a sepia crooner with blues inflection and a black sound." Arnold Shaw, *Honkers and Shouters: The Golden Years of Rhythm and Blues* (New York: Macmillan, 1978), 91.

40. Ellington had been a consistent hit maker in the 1940s but had his last hit in 1948 with "Don't Be So Mean to Baby" featuring Al Hibbler's vocals. Many of these hitmaking jazz artists had their last black music chart hits in this era, including Lionel Hampton (1950), Billy Eckstine (1952, except for a Quincy Jones hit in 1972), and Count Basie (1956 and a 1968 comeback hit).

41. Aaron J. Johnson, "A Date with the Duke: Ellington on Radio," *Musical Quarterly* 96, no. 3/4 (2013): 369–405.

42. Nightingale Gordon, *WNEW: Where the Melody Lingers On* (New York: Nightingale Gordon, 1984).

43. Any live event originating outside the radio or television studio or production center is a remote. Today's technologies include optical fiber cables, satellite and microwave links, and the internet. Radio broadcasts of sporting events may still use circuit-based remote wires.

44. Suraya Mohamed, "Toast of the Nation 2020: The Jazz Collective Edition," https://www.npr.org/2019/12/26/787762117/toast-of-the-nation-2020-the-jazz-collective-edition.

45. Scott DeVeaux, "The Emergence of the Jazz Concert, 1935–1945," *American Music* 7, no. 1 (1989): 6–29.

46. DeVeaux, "The Emergence of the Jazz Concert," 11.

47. *Rhythm and blues* started to replace *race music* in the 1940s. A succession of coded terms such as *sepia* and *ebony* marked the public negotiation of African American otherness with the classification schemes of commercial enterprise. Race records had included not only blues but also black show tunes, calypso, novelty songs, ragtime, and black swing—pretty much anything secular. *Pop music* has always been equally poorly defined. In this book it is the general, undifferentiated top-selling music. In terms of aesthetics, from the 1940s on, pop music favored slick production values—strings, horns, woodwinds, effects, percussion used for exotica rather than groove, vocal arrangements and choruses—over raw and bare-bones presentations. Rather than engage in the art-versus-commerce debate that usually surrounds pop music descriptions, I embrace Bill Lamb's notion that "pop music has usually been identified as the music and the musical styles that are accessible to the broadest audience." Bill Lamb, "What Is Pop Music? The Definition from the 1950s to Today," liveaboutdotcom, September 29, 2018, https://www.liveabout.com/what-is-pop-music-3246980.

48. Because of the phenomenon of atmospheric skip, AM radio stations can interfere with one another at great distances at night. Clear channels are AM frequency assignments that have only a single station, at high power, assigned to them. A clear channel station can be heard in scores of states during the overnight hours, and they charge advertisers accordingly.

49. The song "11:60 PM" is one of the records that demonstrates the pre-1950s stature of big band vocalists. Kallen's full vocal chorus is buried behind a long intro, a band half-chorus, and James's own trumpet solo, and was tucked in before the shout chorus and ending. There were exceptions, but many band singers had yet to throw off the yoke of the big band leaders.

50. A *Dave Garroway Show* episode from June 9, 1950, can be heard at otrcat.com. It's a thirty-minute music and comedy program that begins with his theme "Sentimental Journey" and features Mel Tormé as his guest. https://www.otrcat.com/p/dave-garroway-show.

51. Sid McCoy, interview with Sonja Williams, June 19, 1995, Archives of African American Music and Culture, Indiana University.

52. Christopher H. Sterling and Michael C. Keith, "Sounds of Change: A History of FM Broadcasting in America," *Journal of Popular Music Studies* 21, no. 3 (2009): 137.

53. "Disk Jockey: Air Phenomenon," *Sponsor*, August 29, 1949, 28–29.

54. Jack Kerouac, *On the Road* (New York: Penguin, 1991), 247.

55. There was FM broadcasting in 1947, but not much. And there were not many FM radio receivers to be had then, either. Dan Morgenstern, interview with Hank Hehmsoth, https://www.youtube.com/watch?v=oC52vJePQy4. Video no longer available.

56. Morgenstern, interview.

57. Morgenstern, interview.

58. "Vox Jox: A National Accounting of Disk Jockey Activities," *Billboard*, June 19, 1948, 23.

59. Gilbert Williams, "The Black Disc Jockey as a Cultural Hero," *Popular Music and Society* 10, no. 3 (1986): 81.

60. Arnold Passman, *The Deejays* (New York: MacMillan, 1971), 67.

61. Morgenstern interview. Stan Kenton was often attacked by jazz critics and musicians for his overly orchestrated productions. Dizzy Gillespie, who rarely put down anyone publicly, blasted Kenton in Art Taylor, *Notes and Tones: Musician-to-Musician Interviews*, expanded ed. (New York: Da Capo, 1993), 126–27.

62. Miles Davis and Quincy Troupe, *Miles: The Autobiography* (New York: Simon and Schuster, 1989), 157–60.

63. Lisa Hamel, "Old Hand at Jazz," *New York Times*, April 27, 1958.

64. Rusty Hassan, "Jazz Radio in Washington, DC," in *DC Jazz: Stories of Jazz Music in Washington, DC*, ed. Maurice Jackson and Blair A. Ruble (Washington: Georgetown University Press, 2018), 91.

65. "Disk Jockey Page," *Metronome*, June 1960, 43.

66. Mixing jazz and comedy is largely a lost art today, but it was a fairly common program practice on all-jazz radio stations reflecting the way both were presented in nightclubs. In a famous anecdote, Bill Cosby, opening for John Coltrane, did a spot-on impression of Coltrane only to be joined note for note by the saxophonist.

67. Mort Fega was profiled in the April 1957 "Television and Radio" column by Dan Morgenstern, "Mort Fega: DJ with Soul," *Metronome*, July 1961, 18, and in "Disc Jockey Page," *Metronome*, June 1960, 43.

68. "Disc Jockey Page."

69. Carter Harmon, "Jazz at Midnight Pays Its Own Way," *New York Times*, February 1, 1948.

70. "Fred Robbins Is Dead; Radio and TV Host, 73," *New York Times*, June 25, 1992.

71. Jose Fritz, "The 1280 Club," *Arcane Radio Trivia*, December 2008, http://tenwatts.blogspot.com/2008/12/1280-club.html. Once at 1280 kHz, WADO was able to operate as a Class B station with 50,000 watts in the day and 7,200 watts at night. Since the 1960s it has been a Spanish-language station.

72. Robin D. G. Kelley, *Thelonious Monk: The Life and Times of an American Original* (New York: Free Press, 2009), 130.

73. Ashlee Christensen, "Amplify: Mary Dee Dudley," HerStry (blog), December 19, 2019, https://herstryblg.com/amplify/2019/12/19/amplify-mary-dee-dudley.

74. "Mary Dee Dudley," Pittsburgh Music History, https://sites.google.com/site/pittsburghmusichistory/pittsburgh-music-story/radio/mary-dee-dudley. An air survey attributed to Mary Dee giving some indication of the range of Dee's selections in January 1950 was posted on January 28, 2024, on the ARSA Survey Collection website. Her top ten artists were (1) Erroll Garner ("Skylark"), (2) Teresa Brewer ("Music, Music, Music"), (3) Patti Page ("With My Eyes Wide Open I'm Dreaming"), (4) Freddie Mitchell ("Air Mail Boogie"), (5) Doc Sausage and His Mad Lads ("Rag Mop"), (6) Little Miss Cornshucks ("Keep Your Hand on Your Heart"), (7) Ruth Brown ("Love Me Baby"), (8) Harry Belafonte ("They Didn't Believe Me"), (9) Nellie Lutcher ("Glad Rag Doll"), (10) Little Willie Littlefield ("The Moon Is Risin'), http://las-solanas.com/arsa/survey.php?sv=169311. By comparison, a July 30, 1955, survey attributed to Dee had this top ten: (1) The Platters ("Only You and You Alone"), (2) Count Basie and His Orchestra ("Every Day"), (3) The Crew Cuts ("A Story Untold"), (4) Clyde McPhatter ("Hot Ziggity"), (5) Wild Bill Davis Trio ("Land of Dreams"), (6) Ray Charles ("This Little Girl of Mine"), (7) Sammy Davis Jr. ("That Old Black Magic"), (8) Patti Page ("Piddly Patter Patter"), (9) The Five Keys ("Don't You Know I Love You"), (10) The Danderliers ("Shu-Wop"), http://las-solanas.com/arsa/survey.php?sv=93126.

75. Continuity directors' duties usually include supervising and screening on-air content to ensure that it meets station and legal policies, assigning copy and script writers, and sometimes performing music licensing duties such as logging musical selections or managing selections to minimize rights payments. Marks's obituary is found at https://www.findagrave.com/memorial/188266106/betty-lou-marks.

76. Barbara Hodgkins, "Jumping Jockey: Pittsburgh's Bettelou Purvis Is a Jazz Trumpeter's Daughter," *Metronome*, June 1951, 24.

77. Hodgkins, "Jumping Jockey."

78. "Jazz Diary," *Playback*, September 1949, 17.

79. Both of these surveys come from a large collection on the Airheads Radio Survey Archive, http://www.las-solanas.com/arsa/.

80. Tadd Dameron's compositions include several jazz favorites: "Hot House," "Our Delight," "Good Bait," "If You Could See Me Now," "Lady Bird," and "On a Misty Night."

81. "Platter Spinner Patter: All About Disk Jockeys," *Cash Box*, June 28, 1952, 31.

82. On July 3, 1951, the *Pittsburgh Press* reported that Bettelou Purvis had $200 stolen from her purse while working at WPGH. Perhaps she moved back and forth between Pittsburgh and New York. In 1957 Purvis filed suit to declare her missing father dead. She died in Fort Lauderdale, Florida in 1976. https://www.findagrave.com/memorial/188266106/betty-lou-marks.

83. Joel Rose, "Hal Jackson Was Pioneering Voice in Black Radio," https://www.npr.org/2012/05/24/153634905/hal-jackson-was-pioneering-voice-in-black-radio.

84. Marc Fisher, "Hal Jackson," *Washington Post*, May 24, 2012, https://www.washingtonpost.com/local/obituaries/hal-jackson-black-radio-pioneer-and-civil-rights-activist-dies-at-96/2012/05/24/gJQAQScMoU_story.html?utm_term=.affdd24d1bb5.

85. Marc Fisher, *Something in the Air: Radio, Rock, and the Revolution That Shaped a Generation* (New York: Random House, 2007).

86. Fisher, "Hal Jackson."

87. Mel Watkins, "Hal Jackson, 96, New York Broadcaster Who Broke Racial Barriers in Radio, Dies," *New York Times*, 24 May 2012.

88. Hal Jackson and James Haskins, *The House That Jack Built: My Life Story as a Trailblazer in Broadcasting and Entertainment* (New York: Amistad, 2001), 103–5.

89. Jackson and Haskins, *The House That Jack Built*, 57.

90. Watkins, "Hal Jackson."

91. "The Forgotten 15,000,000," *Sponsor*, 24 October 1949, 54.

92. "Joe Adams interview on KOWL," National Visionary Leadership Project, https://youtu.be/n43n510C4jg.

93. Hunter Hancock, interview with Lex Gillespie, January 20, 1995, Archives of African American Music and Culture, Indiana University.

94. Hunter Hancock, "Huntin' with Hunter: The Story of the West Coast's First R&B Disc Jockey" (exclusive for the Doo-Wop Society of Southern California), http://www.electricearl.com/dws/hunter.html.

95. Tom Reed, *The Black Music History of Los Angeles, Its Roots: 50 Years in Black Music: A Classical Pictorial History of Los Angeles Black Music of the 20's, 30's, 40's, 50's and 60's; Photographic Essays That Define the People, the Artistry and Their Contributions to the Wonderful World of Entertainment* (Los Angeles: Black Accent on L.A. Press, 1992).

96. In college I shared a ride from Pittsburgh to my home in Washington, DC, with a college friend and his mother. When I told her that I played jazz, she didn't hesitate to tell me that it was "hard core junkie music." It was a pleasant trip.

97. Norman Mailer, Jean Malaquais, and Ned Polsky, *The White Negro* (San Francisco: City Lights, 1957).

98. Ellison is quoted in Louis Menard, "It Took a Village: How the *Voice* Changed Journalism," *New Yorker*, January 5, 2009.

99. Advertisement, "A Market All of Its Own," *Broadcasting*, July 24, 1944, 52. Perhaps reproducing here the list from the ad will make more clear what WLIB did play: "'The popular classics with a blend of the modern'—familiar light classic and classic melody, opera, operetta, musical comedy and motion picture tunes, soft-sweet ballads of today and yesterday, Gypsy music, choral groups, Gilbert and Sullivan and Latin-American rhythms."

100. The ad appeared in *Broadcasting*, February 16, 1948, 35.

101. James Howe, "Duplication," *Broadcasting*, June 7 1948, 62.

102. Harley's sandwich shop, which advertised on the 1:30–2:30 a.m. jazz show, continued to advertise on late night jazz programs for decades! "Those Riches in the Indies," *Broadcasting Telecasting*, January 26, 1953, 81; Jacques Kelly, "Original Harley and His Harley Original," *Baltimore Sun*, April 23, 1993, https://www.baltimoresun.com/news/bs-xpm-1993-04-23-1993113083-story.html.

103. Robert Hilson Jr., "Hulbert, 'Bald Prince' of Radio, Dies: Black Pioneer Brought City New Sound in '50s," *Baltimore Sun*, December 25, 1996.

104. Advertisement, *Broadcasting Telecasting*, October 1, 1956, 59.

105. Advertisement, *Broadcasting Telecasting*, October 1, 1956, 105.

Chapter 2. Independent Contractors

1. *Broadcasting Yearbook 1942* (Washington, DC: Broadcasting Publications, 1942), 11; *Radio Annual 1942*, ed. Jack Alicoate (New York: Radio Daily, 1942), 207; *Radio Annual 1947*, ed. Jack Alicoate (New York: Radio Daily, 1947), 77; *Broadcasting*, September 19, 1955, 51.

2. William Barlow, *Voice Over: The Making of Black Radio* (Philadelphia: Temple University Press, 1999), 124.

3. Barlow, *Voice Over*, 122.

4. Broadcast engineers refer to the entire audio or video path from source (such as microphone, turntable, or camera) to transmitter as the "air chain."

5. Marc Fisher, *Something in the Air: Radio, Rock, and the Revolution That Shaped a Generation* (New York: Random House), 204.

6. Barlow, *Voice Over*, 133–75.

7. For eight years (1985–1993) Joyner, "The Fly Jock," physically commuted daily between his morning show in Dallas and his afternoon show in Chicago. *Destination Freedom* (1948–1950) was a biographical black history program produced by NBC station WMAQ in conjunction with the *Chicago Defender*. The episodes were written by Richard Durham, and among the many voices heard on its broadcasts were Hugh Downs, Vernon Jarrett, Oscar Brown Jr., and Studs Terkel. (In 1948 Jarrett and Brown created *Negro Newsfront*, the nation's first black daily radio news program [https://www.thehistorymakers.org/biography/vernon-jarrett-39].) Later episodes produced after a fractious departure by Durham in 1950 shifted from an emphasis on black history to generalized American patriotism.

8. Barlow, *Voice Over*, 98; Robert Pruter, *Doowop: The Chicago Scene* (Urbana: University of Illinois Press, 1996), 222.

9. Barlow, *Voice Over*, 99.

10. Sid McCoy, interview with Sonja Williams, June 19, 1995, Archives of African American Music and Culture, Indiana University.

11. Herb Kent, interview with Sonja Williams, March 29, 1995, Archives of African American Music and Culture, Indiana University.

12. Barlow, *Voice Over*, 100.

13. Barlow, *Voice Over*, 100.

14. Pruter, *Doowop*, 222.

15. Pruter, *Doowop*, 224.

16. Jon Thurber, "David 'Fathead' Newman, Jazz Saxophonist," *Los Angeles Times*, January 30, 2009.

17. Norman W. Spaulding, "History of Black Oriented Radio in Chicago, 1929–1963" (PhD diss., University of Illinois at Urbana-Champaign, 1981), 164–65.

18. Elena, Razlogova, *The Listener's Voice: Early Radio and the American Public* (Philadelphia: University of Pennsylvania Press, 2011), 141.

19. Barlow, *Voice Over*, 1.

20. Barlow, *Voice Over*, 104.

21. Gilbert Williams, "The Black Disc Jockey as a Cultural Hero," *Popular Music and Society* 10, no. 3 (1986): 81.

22. Barbara Savage's *Broadcasting Freedom* recovers the history of serious network and large-city programming supported by the government to enlist black support for the war, programming that was skillfully hijacked by ambitious and opportunistic race progressives to not only reach black audiences but to present positive images countering *Amos 'n' Andy* to the white audience, as well. Barbara Savage, *Broadcasting Freedom: Radio, War, and the Politics of Race, 1938–1948*, Chapel Hill: University of North Carolina Press, 1999.

23. During Sid McCoy's employment, WCFL was a sort of a general, anything-but-rock-and-roll station, WGES was a black appeal station, and KGIL mixed news, talk, and big band music.

24. McCoy interview.

25. McCoy interview.

26. Dan Kening, "Overnighters to Remember," *Chicago Tribune*, March 15, 1992.

27. Kening, "Overnighters to Remember."

28. Tex Gathings (1928–2020) would become the production manager at WOOK-TV when United Broadcasting established the UHF station after a lengthy process in 1962. Gathings was the producer of the legendary *Teenarama Dance Party* (1963–1970), a black record and dance program patterned after *American Bandstand*. Gathings's love of jazz may be the reason Lionel Hampton was signed as the original WOOK-TV music director.

29. Williams, "Black Disc Jockey," 123.

30. Mark R. Smith, "A Broadcasting Beacon: WANN Radio, from 'The Other' Annapolis to the Smithsonian," *What's Up?* February 5, 2016, https://whatsupmag.com/culture/broadcasting-beacon-wann-radio-the-other-annapolis-smithsonian/.

31. Shernay Williams, "The Legendary 'Little Willie' Adams, Dead at 97," *Baltimore Afro American*, June 30, 2011.

32. Ronald J. Stephens, "Carr and Sparrow's Beach, Annapolis, Maryland (1926–1974)," BlackPast.org (2014), https://www.blackpast.org/african-american-history/carr-and-sparrow-s-beach-annapolis-maryland-1926-1974/.

33. Roger Catlin, "How Radio DJ Hoppy Adams Powered His 50,000 Watt Annapolis Station into a Mighty Influence," *Smithsonian*, June 16, 2015, https://www.smithsonianmag.com/smithsonian-institution/dj-hoppy-adams-radio-annapolis-station-influence-segregated-america-180955594/.

34. Adams's noontime show was heard personally by the author circa 1982–1984.

35. For example, in 2022, considering black radio alone, one can find classic hip hop, Quiet Storm, Rhythmic Adult Contemporary, Rhythmic Contemporary, Rhythmic Oldies, Urban Contemporary, Urban Adult Contemporary, and classic soul. Often the distinction between two similar-sounding formats is whether hip hop is included or excluded.

36. Hoyt Curtin (1922–2000) led a company that created jazz-inflected scores for *The Flintstones, The Jetsons, Top Cat,* and *Johnny Quest*.

37. Charles Nanry, *American Music: From Storyville to Woodstock* (New Brunswick, NJ: Transaction, distributed by E. P. Dutton, 1972), 2.

38. Nat King Cole, *Let's Face the Music!* arranged and conducted by Billy May, Capitol Records, W-2008 (1964); Frank Sinatra, *Sinatra-Basie: An Historical Musical First*, Reprise Records R-1008 (1961).

39. My own early professional music experiences were with such bands backing Gladys Knight and the Pips and Aretha Franklin.

40. "Jazz Takes a Blow, Chicago Radio Switches to 'Rock'," *Jet*, April 6, 1967, 55.

41. Ben Burdeen, program director of WSDM-FM, quoted in Paul Zakaras, "Chicago Disk Experts Stress Importance of Jazz Promotion," *Billboard*, July 16, 1966, 36.

42. One clever alternative to the weekend exile was the sponsored short feature show, in which a two- or three-minute burst of information is sandwiched between or around sponsors' ads. Neil Chayet's *Looking at the Law*, for example, ran for forty-one years over Boston's WBZ and nationally on CBS radio affiliates.

43. Zenitha Prince, "Baltimore Radio Dj Icon 'Sir Johnny O' Dies at 70," *Baltimore Afro American*, November 1, 2013, https://www.afro.com/baltimore-radio-dj-icon-sir-johnny-o-dies-at-70/.

44. *Broadcasting*, December 30, 1957, and December 29, 1969.

45. Christopher H. Sterling and Michael C. Keith, "Sounds of Change: A History of FM Broadcasting in America," *Journal of Popular Music Studies* 21, no. 3 (2009): 237. This makes logical sense, too. The educational part of the FM band is 20 percent of the total FM spectrum. Given that more of the educational broadcasters are operating at lower power, a little over 20 percent can be accommodated. This explosion in station growth before the year 2000 has brought more than two thousand low-power FM (LPFM) stations into the noncommercial radio totals.

46. Ken Ringle, "The Great Equalizer: Felix Grant's Jazz Program Helped Bring the City Together," *Washington Post*, October 13, 1993.

47. Ringle, "The Great Equalizer."

48. Keir Keightley, "'Turn It Down!' She Shrieked: Gender, Domestic Space, and High Fidelity, 1948–59," *Popular Music* 15, no. 2 (1996): 149–77.

49. "Why Hi-Fi," *Metronome*, April 1954, 4.

50. These data are from Sterling and Keith, "Sounds of Change," 238.

51. Christopher H. Sterling and John M. Kittross, *Stay Tuned: A History of American Broadcasting* (Mahwah, NJ: Lawrence Erlbaum, 2002), 236.

52. Michael C. Keith, "Turn On . . . Tune In: The Rise and Demise of Commercial Underground Radio," in *Radio Reader: Essays in the Cultural History of Radio*, ed. Michele Hilmes and Jason Loviglio (New York: Routledge, 2002), 392.

53. Fisher, *Something in the Air*, 164.

54. Fisher, *Something in the Air*, 166.

55. House of Representatives, Ninety-third Congress, Second Session, on H.R. 8266, H.R. 14619, and S. 585 . . . July 22, 1974, "All-Channel Radio: Hearing Before the Subcommittee on Communications and Power of the Committee on Interstate and Foreign Commerce" (Washington, DC: Government Printing Office), December 31, 1974.

56. Sterling and Keith, "Sounds of Change," 129–33.

57. "The Aging Audience," Walrus Research, Spring 2009, https://blatherwatch.blogs.com/files/aging_public_radio_audience_-_walrus_research.pdf.

58. Kim Simpson, *Early '70s Radio: The American Format Revolution* (New York: Continuum, 2011), 120.

59. The decade from 1970 to 1980 was a critical time for the creation of radio formats. Top 40 led to Contemporary Hits Radio (CHR), and AOR splintered into Classic Rock, Modern Rock, Active Rock, and others. Middle of the Road would produce soft rock as well.

60. The times shown in this table are not running times in the program but, rather, running times on the aircheck tape. Like many airchecks, this tape was probably paused and started in real time to record Daylie at the expense of the records.

61. Daddy-O Daylie was WGRT's jazz DJ, but Richard Steele, then a soul/R&B DJ, would later become a venerated jazz DJ on public radio station WBEZ-FM in Chicago.

62. A survey chart for WGRT is available. See the ARSA radio survey website, http://www.las-solanas.com/arsa/surveys_item.php?sv=64412.

63. "Hassle over Daddy-O Radio Time Resolved," *Chicago Daily Defender*, February 6, 1971, 1; "Daddy-O Daylie Show Returns to WGRT," *Chicago Daily Defender*, February 8, 1971, 10; "Huddle over Daddy-O Cut," *Chicago Daily Defender*, February 2, 1971, 3. One of my favorite etymologies of slang is *rap*. These days its strongest connotation is with hip hop vocals, but in my youth, rap had two diametrically opposed meanings. In one, to rap meant to speak from the heart in a genuine and earnest manner. People would hold rap sessions where troubled youth could speak freely, and singers like Isaac Hayes would include a several-minute-long rap in a song such as "By the Time I Get to Phoenix." But also, a young man's rap described his ability to talk smoothly with the ladies, and earnestness had little to do with that skill!

64. "Leaders Back Daddy-O in Hassle," *Chicago Daily Defender*, February 1, 1971, 1.

65. AM radio signals can travel hundreds or thousands of miles at night via a phenomenon known as ionospheric skip, whereby medium-wave radio waves headed skyward encounter an ionized region above the earth's atmosphere that reflects the signal back towards the earth. By the 1920s national authorities from around the world agreed to allocate broadcast frequency assignments and transmitter power in order to alleviate interference between stations. In North America, a number of AM frequencies are designated as clear channels and are divided between countries according to international agreements. The stations broadcasting on a clear channel can easily cover half of the continental United States. *Broadcasting and Cable Yearbook 2009* (New Providence, NJ: Bowker, 2009), C42–3.

66. Letter from Harry Abraham to Paul Baker obtained from http://www.jazzhouse.org/nlib/index.php3?read=baker1.

67. Letter from Harry Abraham to Paul Baker.

Chapter 3. Jazz Around the Clock

1. For example, companies looking to advertise their products nationally do not purchase ads in individual markets themselves; instead, local stations make deals with national "reps" who handle nationwide ad purchases.

2. Color scan of a brochure aimed at potential KJAZZ advertisers (undated), http://www.timhodges.net/SPIRIT/ Accessed 11 October 2011.

3. Color scan of a brochure aimed at potential KJAZZ advertisers (undated), http://www.timhodges.net/SPIRIT/ Accessed 11 October 2011.

4. "KNOB (FM) Sets All-Jazz Format," *Broadcasting*, September 2, 1957, 96; "KNOB Turns on All-Jazz Format," *Broadcasting*, March 24, 1958, 98.

5. Lee Zhito, "LP Programming," *Billboard*, March 27, 1961, 8.

6. "For the Record: Station Authorizations, Applications," *Broadcasting*, May 9, 1961, 101.

7. WAZZ was to take *Sleepy's Hollow*, *El Dormido*, *Jazz International*, and *Jazz Goes to Church*. "Music as Written," *Billboard*, January 9, 1961, 53; "Pitt Snares KNOB Jazz," *Billboard*, August 14, 1961, 24.

8. "FM 'Turns on' Happy Sponsors," *Broadcasting*, July 31, 1967, 104.

9. Eliot Tiegel, "KNOB, WNOP . . . And All That Jazz," *Billboard*, March 27, 1965, 56.

10. Eliot Tiegel, "Jazz Beat. Broadcast Scene: Summing Up," *Billboard*, June 18, 1966, 22, 26.

11. Tom Schnabel, "KBCA-FM 105.1: A Slice of L.A. Radio History," KCRW Music News, January 2, 2017, https://www.kcrw.com/music/articles/kbca-105-1-fm-a-slice-of-l-a-radio-history.

12. Schnabel, "KBCA-FM 105.1: A Slice of L.A. Radio History."

13. Zan Stewart, "Jazz Notes: KKJZ's Format Change Spells the End of an Era," *Los Angeles Times*, September 21, 1990, F22.

14. It is worth noticing the tune at the top of the survey, "The Swinging Shepherd Blues." It was originally by Moe Kauffman, but this version by noted jazz and R&B bassist and arranger Johnny Pate was a jazz hit covered by many artists including Ella Fitzgerald, Herbie Mann, and Natalie Cole. "Swinging Shepherd" was a catchy jazz flute feature that had crossover appeal. Pate is also well known for arrangements for Curtis Mayfield and for his scoring the films *Shaft in Africa* and *Shaft's Big Score*.

15. Earl Paige, "WAAF: Stock in Yards & Jazz," *Billboard*, November 19, 1966, 36.

16. The source of the names of jazz artists the host typically played is found in Paige, "WAAF," 44.

17. An aircheck of a Sunday Daddy-O Daylie show from 1972 can be found https://archive.org/details/wgrt-daddy-o-daylie-jazz-padio-6-25-72 and is described in table 11, in Chapter 2.

18. See http://www.phillyradioarchives.com. It was also reported that jazz programming on WHAT increased from fifteen to eighteen hours in 1959. "Fanfare: Single-Minded Schedule," *Broadcasting*, March 9, 1959, 130; Tiegel, "Jazz Beat. Broadcast Scene: Summing Up," 26.

19. Tiegel, "Jazz Beat. Broadcast Scene: Summing Up," 29.

20. Tiegel, "Jazz Beat. Broadcast Scene: Summing Up," 26.

21. Lewis B. Cullman, Can't Take It with You: The Art of Making and Giving Money (Hoboken, NJ: Wiley, 2004), 17.

22. Fred Ferretti, "The White Captivity of Black Radio," *Columbia Journalism Review* 9, no. 2 (1970): 35–36.

23. "WBEE-AM Jazz Station Celebrates 46th Year," *Chicago Defender*, October 8, 2001, 16; Earl Calloway, "WBEE radio to Broadcast African American Music," *Chicago Defender*, March 17, 1990, 65.

24. Charles Sherrell, remarks found at http://www.broadcasturban.net/jazz, accessed September 11, 2011, but no longer available.

25. Charles Sherrell, interview by Sonya D. Williams, Archives of African American Music and Culture, Indiana University, March 28, 1995.

26. Robert Feder, "With Sale of Jazz Station, WBEE Owner Calls It Quits," *Chicago Sun-Times*, May 2, 2003, 63.

27. "WBEE-AM Jazz Station Celebrates 46th Year," 16.

28. Corey Hall, "Untitled," *Chicago Weekend*, December 13, 2001, 3.

29. Ibid.

30. Patricia Walker, "The Chicago Station with All Those Girls," *Chicago Tribune*, March 16, 1969, A6.

31. Ray Brack, "Record Promotion Men Speakers for WSDM, Chi Stereo Station," *Billboard*, March 12, 1966, 22, 26.

32. Cheryl Lavin, "Linda Ellerbee," *Chicago Tribune*, July 30, 2000, https://www.chicagotribune.com/news/ct-xpm-2000-07-30-0007300441-story.html.
33. Earl Paige, "WSDM-FM Reshapes to Jazzrock Style," *Billboard*, April 3, 1971, 43.
34. Paige, "WSDM-FM Reshapes to Jazzrock Style," 42.
35. Paige, "WSDM-FM Reshapes to Jazzrock Style," 42.
36. Burdeen is quoted in Paige, "WSDM-FM Reshapes to Jazzrock Style," 42–43.
37. *Billboard*, January 1965, 23, 36. The magazine described the "rapid response ratings" thus: "not a popularity poll, the ratings are strictly on the comparative ability of the stations and air personalities to influence their listeners to purchase the singles and albums played on the air."
38. United States National Advisory Commission on Civil Disorders, *Report of the National Advisory Commission on Civil Disorders* (Washington, DC: U.S. Government Printing Office, 1968), 20.
39. In 1970 the Race Relations Information Center of Nashville listed nine black-owned or partly black-owned radio stations: KPRS, Kansas City; WCHB and WCHD-FM, Detroit; KWK, St. Louis; WEBB, Baltimore; WJBE, Knoxville; and WRDW, Augusta, Georgia (the preceding three owned by James Brown); WHOV-FM, Hampton, Virginia (owned by the Hampton Institute); and WSHA-FM, Raleigh, North Carolina (owned by Shaw University; since sold). The February 9, 1969, issue of *Advertising Age* listed seven more stations owned at least in part by African Americans: WGPR, Detroit; WMPP, Chicago; WEUP, Huntsville; WTLC-FM, Indianapolis; WORV, Hattiesburg, Mississippi; WWWS-FM, Saginaw; and WVOE, Chadbourn, North Carolina. The first black-owned station, WERD in Atlanta, had been sold to white owners. Ferretti, "White Captivity of Black Radio," 36–37.
40. William Barlow, *Voice Over: The Making of Black Radio* (Philadelphia: Temple University Press, 1999), 233. Two factors led to the WTOP-FM gift. First, the station was the underused stepchild of very successful WTOP-AM, one of the nation's first all-news stations. Second, the *Washington Post* was coming under scrutiny because of new regulations that limited cross-ownership of media properties within a single market. That was then. Now there are no such limits, and group owners such as Clear Channel radio own more than a dozen stations in certain markets.
41. Billy Taylor and Teresa L. Reed, *The Jazz Life of Dr. Billy Taylor* (Bloomington: Indiana University Press, 2013), 175.
42. Claude Hall, "Jazz Sales Spurting in New York Thanks to Airplay by WLIB-FM," *Billboard*, April 23, 1966, 24.
43. Barlow, *Voice Over*, 230.
44. Theodis Ealey, Soul Patrol Newsletter, http://soul-patrol.com/newsletter/in/view1.php?id=976.
45. Barlow, *Voice Over*, 234.
46. Nelson George, *The Death of Rhythm & Blues*, (New York: Pantheon, 1988), 130.
47. Kim Simpson, *Early '70s Radio: The American Format Revolution* (New York: Continuum, 2011), 151.
48. Barlow, *Voice Over*, 235.
49. Marc Fisher, *Something in the Air: Radio, Rock, and the Revolution That Shaped a Generation* (New York: Random House, 2007), 205.
50. Barlow, *Voice Over*, 237.
51. Hollie I. West, "It's All in the Format: Black Radio," *Washington Post*, January 28, 1973, L1.
52. Fisher, *Something in the Air*, 206.
53. Fisher, *Something in the Air*, 207.
54. Barlow, *Voice Over*, 241.
55. Timothy B. Tyson, *Radio Free Dixie: Robert F. Williams and the Roots of Black Power* (Chapel Hill: University of North Carolina Press, 1999), 285.
56. Tyson, *Radio Free Dixie*, 287.
57. Tyson, *Radio Free Dixie*, 288.
58. Several nonprofit institutions managed to obtain commercial-band FM frequency assignments because at the time of their acquisition, FM stations were not very valuable. Over the years many of these stations have been either been sold by cash-strapped owners (New York's WNYC-FM, although the foundation that bought WNYC from the city later bought the commercial

station WQXR-FM from the *New York Times*) or been operated commercially (Howard University's WHUR-FM, which was a divestment gift to the university from the *Washington Post*).

59. ARSA (Airheads Radio SurveyArchive) collection of radio surveys, http://las-solanas.com/arsa/index.php. The 1975, 1977, and 1978 surveys are by Gary Pfeifer, and the1979 survey is by Paul Haney.

60. Charles Mitchell, "Why It's So Hard to Find Jazz on the Radio," *Jazz*, Spring 1980, 52.

61. Recollection of Batt Johnson at http://www.wrvrlives.org, a site that is no longer available. See https://www.archive.org/web/20160306072458/http://wrvrlives.org.

62. Doug Hall, "N.Y. Jazz Community Irate on Losing Its Only Jazz Station," *Billboard*, September 20, 1980, 20.

63. Will Layman, "How Did the 1970s Wean Young Jazz Fans, Part Two: Soul Jazz 'Makin' It Real,'" Big Butter and Egg Man (blog), http://bigbutterandeggman.blogspot.com/2010/08/how-did-1970s-wean-young-jazz-fans-part.html.

64. WRVRLives.com is no longer available. The Internet Archive site may provide an idea of its content: https://www.archive.org/web/20160306072458/http://wrvrlives.org.

65. Leonard Feather, "Crossover Albums," *Billboard*, February 8, 1975, 25.

66. Feather, "Crossover Albums," 25. In the battle between jazz and jazz fusion, purists found even the acoustic soul jazz hits of Blue Note preferable to electric guitars and sythesizers.

67. Feather, "Crossover Albums," 25.

68. Gary Giddins, "Hit or Miss," *New York*, January 16, 1978, 69.

69. For instance, CBS was spending $8 million to $10 million per year for so-called independent promotion men. Such promotion not only pushed their product but squeezed out independent competitors. The entire industry was spending perhaps $40 million. In 1985 the record industry was spending at least 20 percent of its pretax profits on this type of promotion. Fredric Dannen, *Hit Men: Power Brokers and Fast Money Inside the Music Business* (New York: Times Books, 1990), 13–15.

70. Giddins, "Hit or Miss."

71. Giddins, "Hit or Miss."

72. *Broadcasting and Cable Yearbook*, 1974, 1975, 1978 (Sol Taishoff, ed.), and 1981. Unil 1991 it was published by Broadcasting Publications, Washington, DC; from 1992 to 2010 by R. R. Bowker, New Providence, NJ. The *Yearbook* ceased publication after the 2010 edition, but under a new publisher (Grey House) was relaunched as the *Complete Television, Radio & Cable Industry Directory* in 2013. The 2017 edition lists approximately three hundred jazz stations but does not distinguish between commercial and noncommercial stations. Unfortunately, a cursory examination of the list reveals entries such as WNYC (New York) that has no consistent jazz programming.

Part II. Jazz on Noncommercial Radio

1. Ralph Engelman, *Public Radio and Television in America: A Political History* (Thousand Oaks, CA: Sage, 1996); Hugh Richard Slotten, *Radio's Hidden Voice: The Origins of Public Broadcasting in the United States* (Urbana: University of Illinois Press, 2009); Jack W. Mitchell, *Listener Supported: The Culture and History of Public Radio* (Westport, CT: Praeger, 2005); Marc J. Stern, "The Battle for Pacifica," *Journal of Popular Culture* 38, no. 6 (2005): 1069–87; Matthew Lasar, *Pacifica Radio: The Rise of an Alternative Network* (Philadelphia: Temple University Press, 1999); Janey Gordon, *Community Radio in the Twenty-First Century* (New York: Lang, 2012).

Chapter 4. Paradise Found, Paradise Lost

1. According to the 1987 *Broadcasting and Cable Yearbook*, about 250 stations claimed a jazz format for at least twenty hours per week, of which about 85 percent were noncommercial. Perhaps another 400 stations reported playing jazz regularly, but less than twenty hours per week. Twenty hours per week could be accomplished with one or two weekday jazz shows. *Broadcasting and Cable Yearbook 1987 (*Washington, DC: Broadcasting Publications, 1987).

2. Both 33-1/3 rpm LPs and 45 rpm singles used the postwar microgroove technology, but they had different backers. The 45 had been developed by RCA in 1949, whereas the LP came out of CBS Laboratories in 1948. The LP was seen as a medium suited to the longer durations of classical music

but also allowed ten to twelve short popular records to be collected on a single disc as opposed to the notebook collection of 78 rpm records that had been sold as "albums." The longer duration of LPs also suited extended-length jazz performances.

3. Jack W. Mitchell, "Lead Us Not into Temptation: American Public Radio in a World of Infinite Possibilities," in *Radio Reader: Essays in the Cultural History of Radio*, ed. Michele Hilmes and Jason Loviglio (New York: Routledge, 2002), 406.

4. Tom Thomas, with others, "Roundtable: The Future of Jazz Radio," with Ed Gordon. National Public Radio, August 10, 2006, https://www.npr.org/templates/story/story.php?storyId=5633331.

5. Adding to the confusion about how many stations there are, the Arbitron report counted some station internet streams and some station HD streams. Arbitron, *Public Radio Today 2012: How America Listens to Radio* (New York: Arbitron, 2012); "Broadcast Stations Totals as of June 30, 2012," FCC News Release, http://fjallfoss.fcc.gov/edocs_public/attachmatch/DOC-315231A1.pdf.

6. Such counts are endlessly frustrating. The count of sixty-three that I give here is flawed in that Columbia University's WKCR is not one of the self-reported jazz stations, even as it offers well in excess of fifty hours of jazz programming per week.

7. A few hundred more stations, with a similar proportion of commercial to noncommercial stations, broadcast fewer than twenty hours of jazz per week. These figures reflected slight declines from 2009 data, with two fewer noncommercial stations playing jazz, and nine fewer stations overall. *Broadcasting and Cable Yearbook 2009* (New Providence, NJ: Bowker, 2009), D-737–9.

8. The station totals are from the FCC, www.fcc.gov/media/broadcast-station-totals.

9. Eric W. Rothenbuhler, "Commercial Radio and Popular Music: Processes of Selection and Factors of Influence," in *Popular Music and Communication*, ed. James Lull (Newbury Park, CA: Sage, 1987), 83.

10. John Merli, "As Personal Income Grows, So Does Listening," *Broadcasting*, May 18, 1998, 42.

11. Arbitron, *Public Radio Today 2012*, 23.

12. David Giovannoni, Thomas J. Thomas, and Theresa R. Clifford, "Public Radio Programming Strategies: A Report on the Programming Stations Broadcast and the People They Seek to Serve" (Washington, DC: Corporation for Public Broadcasting, 1992), 43.

13. "The Aging Audience," Walrus Research, Spring 2009, 6, https://blatherwatch.blogs.com/files/aging_public_radio_audience_-_walrus_research.pdf.

14. Susan K. Sell, "Revenge of the 'Nerds': Collective Action Against Intellectual Property Maximalism in the Global Information Age," *International Studies Review* 15, no. 1 (2013): 67–85.

15. Walrus Research and AudiGraphics, *Audience 2010 Interim Report 6: Losing Our Grip* (Olney, MD: Radio Research Consortium, 2006).

16. Tom McCourt, *Conflicting Communication Interests in America: The Case of National Public Radio* (Westport, CT: Praeger, 1999), 155.

17. McCourt, *Conflicting Communication Interests in America*, 133.

18. National Public Radio, *2017 Annual Report*, https://media.npr.org/documents/about/annualreports/2017_Annual_Report.pdf.

19. John Mark Dempsey, "A More Inclusive Public Service: Can NPR Serve All of America?" in *Radio's Second Century: Past, Present, and Future Perspectives*, ed. John Allen Hendricks (New Brunswick, NJ: Rutgers University Press, 2020), 163.

20. To name a few: *On the Media, Radiolab, Ask Me Another*, WYNC (New York), *1A*, WAMU (Washington, DC), *On Point, Here and Now, Only a Game*, WBUR (Boston), and *Fresh Air*, WHYY (Philadelphia).

21. This observation was made by WAMU listener Kurt Schroeder in a letter to the editor (*Washington Post*, June 15, 2018), https://www.washingtonpost.com/opinions/the-departure-of-hot-jazz-throws-cold-water-on-public-radio/2018/06/15/5fc3cb06-6fe8-11e8-b4d8-eaf78d4c544c_story.html. To be fair, one national program heard on WAMU is its own *1A*. And *Hot Jazz Saturday Night* has thankfully been returned to the WAMU lineup since then.

22. Schroeder, letter to the editor, *Washington Post*, June 15, 2018.

23. "Sterling Yates: Mad Man of Music and Many Voices," Pittsburgh Music Story: Radio website, https://sites.google.com/view/pittsburghmusichistory/pittsburgh-music-story/radio/sterling-yates; Ron Weiskind, "Life with Father: The Steigerwalds Break the Mold," *Pittsburgh Post-Gazette Magazine*, June 14, 1988, 11.

24. The author fondly recalls his father listening to a favorite church broadcast on Sundays from Laurel, Maryland, daytimer WLMD followed by an afternoon polka broadcast.

25. WQED ran *Jazz Decades* on Saturday nights, a rare exception to its classical and news format of the 1970s. This program, hosted by Ray Smith, had a venerable history. It began in 1958 on WKOX (105.7) in Framingham, Massachusetts. Smith took the program to WGBH (Boston) in 1972 when WKOX changed format. WGBH, which itself has withdrawn from jazz programming, described *Jazz Decades* as featuring "traditional jazz, big band, and swing from the 20th century and earlier, including recordings from as early as 1890. Host Ray Smith has been the voice of Jazz Decades for more than 30 years, culling his programs from the more than 90,000 titles in his personal collection." Jose Fritz, "Jazz Decades," *Arcane Radio Trivia* (2012), https://tenwatts.blogspot.com/2012/04/jazz-decades.html.

26. See https://www.wesa.fm.

27. After a partial return on WYZR-FM in 2014, full-time jazz radio returned to Pittsburgh with Pittsburgh Public Media's launch of stations WZUM-AM (2016), WZUM-FM (2016), and FM repeater W266CV-FM (2017) under the leadership of Chuck Leavens, Scott Hanley, and Todd Staley.

28. Julia Cook, "WYEP Marks 40 Years as 'the Station That Refused to Die,'" *Pittsburgh City Paper*, June 25, 2014.

29. Hollie I. West, "Smooth Sounds: The Rising (Air) Waves of Jazz," *Washington Post*, November 29, 1977, B9.

30. West, "Smooth Sounds."

31. Jeffery Yorke, "Jazz Spots on the Radio Dial," *Washington Post*, August 22, 1986, weekend section, 9.

32. Yorke, "Jazz Spots on the Radio Dial."

33. Ed Wiley III, "Short-Circuiting College Airwaves—Radio Station WCDU-FM [sic] and Radio Stations at College Campuses," *Diverse (Issues in Higher Education)* (2007), http://diverseeducation.com/article/8310/.

34. Marc Fisher, Something in the Air: Radio, Rock, and the Revolution That Shaped a Generation (New York: Random House, 2007), 172.

35. It is true that there are exceptions like the AAA format or the eclectic music programming of KCRW.

36. Christopher H. Sterling and Michael C. Keith, "Sounds of Change: A History of FM Broadcasting in America," *Journal of Popular Music Studies* 21, no. 3 (2009): 149.

37. John Witherspoon et al., *A History of Public Broadcasting* (Washington, DC: Current, 2000), 99.

38. Drew Lindsay, "Has Success Spoiled NPR?," *Washingtonian*, March 1, 2007.

39. Arbitron, *Public Radio Today 2012*; Arbitron, *Public Radio Today: How America Listens to Public Radio Stations: 2005 Edition* (New York: Arbitron, 2005).

40. Walrus Research and AudiGraphics, *Audience 2010 Interim Report 6*.

41. For the WBFO schedule, see https://news.wbfo.org/schedule/week.

42. *Buffalo/Toronto Jazz Report*, December 1978, 14.

43. At least two well-received recordings came from *Jazz Alive*: Sarah Vaughan Live at Rosy's, recorded May 31, 1978, and released in 2016, and *Jaco Pastorius: Truth, Liberty & Soul Live in NYC*, recorded June 27, 1982, and released in 2017.

44. Ralph Engelman, *Public Radio and Television in America: A Political History* (Thousand Oaks, CA: Sage, 1996), 86.

45. Engelman, *Public Radio and Television in America*, 87–88.

46. "CPB, NPR, WRTI: Connecting the Dots to Understand Public Radio Funding," wrti.org, https://www.wrti.org/post/cpb-npr-wrti-connecting-dots-understand-public-radio-funding.

47. Engelman, *Public Radio and Television*, 92–93.

48. Engelman, *Public Radio and Television*, 93.

49. Jesse Walker, "With Friends Like These: Why Community Radio Does Not Need the Corporation for Public Broadcasting," in *Cato Policy Analysis 277* (Washington, DC: Cato Institute, 1997), n.p.

50. Though public spending on broadcasting has conservative opponents, it also has conservative supporters who either appreciate the quality programming that results or at least are aware of its popularity and utility with their constituents who support it.

51. Richard Harrington, "NPR Seeks New Funds: Will Approach Private Sector for More Aid," *Washington Post*, November 12, 1981, C1.

52. The Congressional Budget Office Glossary of Terms defines *forward funding* as follows: "The provision of budget authority that becomes available for obligation in the last quarter of a fiscal year and remains available during the following fiscal year. Forward funding typically finances ongoing education grant programs. Compare with advance appropriation, obligation delay, and unobligated balances." https://www.cbo.gov/sites/default/files/cbofiles/attachments/glossary.pdf.

53. Jack W. Mitchell, *Listener Supported: The Culture and History of Public Radio* (Westport, CT: Praeger, 2005), 102.

54. Harrington, "NPR Seeks New Funds."

55. Harrington, "NPR Seeks New Funds," C6.

56. When the author was a radio technician in 1975, such announcements were limited to the name and location of the underwriter. This policy was relaxed to allow a one-line slogan to be appended, as in "Midnight Jazz is underwritten by Pete's Pizza. When you get the munchies, think Pete's!" Current noncommercial underwriting announcements are pretty much indistinguishable from commercial advertisements.

57. Phil McCombs and Jacqueline Trescott, "NPR: The Dream Failed," *Washington Post*, August 16, 1983, B11.

58. Phil McCombs and Jacqueline Trescott, "NPR: Camelot in Crisis," *Washington Post*, August 15, 1983, C1.

59. McCombs and Trescott, "NPR: Camelot in Crisis," C4.

60. Jacqueline Trescott, "Mankiewicz to Leave NPR amid Financial Crunch," *Washington Post*, April 20, 1983, A1; Engelman, *Public Radio and Television*, 103.

61. National Public Radio IRS Form 990 2015, https://projects.propublica.org/nonprofits/organizations/520907625.

62. Trescott, "Mankiewicz to Leave NPR," A15.

63. J. Mitchell, *Listener Supported*, 101.

64. Joshua Clark Davis and Seth Kotch, "Media and the Movement: Activist Community Radio in the American South" (2015), http://www.flowjournal.org/2015/05/media-and-the-movement/.

65. Davis and Kotch, "Media and the Movement."

66. Thanks to longtime jazz host Rusty Hassan for providing a program guide from which this table was re-created.

67. Lindsay, "Has Success Spoiled NPR?"

68. David Giovannoni and George Bailey, "Appeal and Public Radio's Music" (Washington, DC: Corporation for Public Broadcasting, 1988), 3.

69. Giovannoni and Bailey, "Appeal and Public Radio's Music."

70. Witherspoon et al., History of Public Broadcasting, 97–98.

71. The daypart is an industry-standard division of the radio day into discrete audience segments. Not only are ratings examined by daypart, but dayparts are used to schedule different types of commercials. The standard divisions are as follows: (1) Morning drive: 6:00 a.m. to 10:00 a.m.; (2) Daytime: 10:00 a.m. to 3:00 p.m.; (3) Afternoon drive: 3:00 p.m. to 7:00 p.m.; (4) Nighttime: 7:00 p.m. to 12:00 p.m.; (5) Overnight: 12:00 p.m. to 6:00 a.m.

72. David Duff, "In Life, Music Has a Special Place. It Should in Radio," *Current*, December 17, 2007 (emphasis added).

73. Nat Hentoff, "Jazz Revolution Vs. Radio Station Slashing Jazz," *JazzEd*, September 2012, http://www.jazzedmagazine.com/3097/articles/guest-editorial/jazz-revolution-vs-radio-station-slashing-jazz/.

74. And that competition is quite direct at times. Both stations air *Morning Edition* and *All Things Considered* starting at the same time.

75. For the WGBH schedule, see https://www.wgbh.org/schedule?type=radio&channel=89.7+WGBH.

76. Galen Moore, "WGBH to Cancel Eric in the Evening, Weeknights," *Boston Buisness Journal*, June 21, 2012, https://www.bizjournals.com/boston/blog/mass_roundup/2012/06/wgbh-eric-in-the-evening.html.

77. Thomas J. Thomas and Theresa R. Clifford, *Audience 88: Issues and Implications* (Washington, DC: Corporation for Public Broadcasting, 1988), 7–8, ARAnet Public Radio Research.

78. Thomas and Clifford, *Audience 88*, 27.

79. Thomas and Clifford, *Audience 88*, 27.

80. Thomas and Clifford, *Audience 88*, 29.

81. Thomas and Clifford, *Audience 88*, 10. *Audience 88* defined *Jazz dominant listener* as "a person who listens to jazz programming more than any other format and who listens to an hour or less per week of either information programming or classical music. Jazz-dominant listeners comprise 10 percent of public radio's weekly audience" (8).

82. Felix Gillette, "The *New York Times* Sells WQXR for $45 Million; WNYC Will Take over Classical Music Station," *New York Observer*, July 14, 2009.

83. The reduced power and possible interference with other stations diminished WQXR's potential audience from seventeen million to fourteen million people. Author's calculations based on data from WQXR: https://www.wqxr.org/about/tuning_in/.

84. John Schaefer had hosted the program for more than thirty-seven years on the station. A fierce protest by listeners and the New York music community led WNYC to reverse the decision and retain the program. Michael Cooper, "WNYC Is Dropping 'New Sounds' After 37 Years. Musicians Are Mourning," *New York Times*, October 11, 2019; Michael Cooper, "A Musical Revolt Succeeds: WNYC, in a Reversal, Keeps 'New Sounds,'" *New York Times*, October 21, 2019.

85. Cooper, "WNYC Is Dropping 'New Sounds.'"

86. Thomas and Clifford, *Audience 88*, 12 (emphasis added).

87. Thomas and Clifford, *Audience 88*, 25.

88. Walrus Research and AudiGraphics, "Audience 2010: Reinvigorating Public Radio's Public Service and Public Support," *Interim Report 7* (Olney, MD: Radio Research Consortium, 2006).

89. Giovannoni and Bailey, *Appeal and Public Radio's Music*, 22.

90. Giovannoni and Bailey, *Appeal and Public Radio's Music*, 23.

91. Giovannoni and Bailey, *Appeal and Public Radio's Music*, 93.

92. Giovannoni and Bailey, *Appeal and Public Radio's Music*, 26.

93. Jim Ladd, *Radio Waves: Life and Revolution on the FM Dial* (New York: St. Martin's, 1991), 47.

94. J. Mitchell, "Lead Us Not into Temptation"; Arbitron, *Public Radio Today 2012*.

95. Walrus Research and AudiGraphics, *Audience 2010 Interim Report*.

Chapter 5. Don't Get Too Far Out

1. Eugene Holley Jr., "Profiling the Jazz Police," *new music usa*, no. 28 (May 2014), https://nmbx.newmusicusa.org/profiling-the-jazz-police/.

2. William Barlow, "Community Radio in the US: The Struggle for a Democratic Medium," *Media, Culture, and Society* 10 (1988): 83.

3. I hope this doesn't give the impression that black college or HBCU radio is only interested in smooth jazz. Far from it, because smooth jazz can be considered instrumental R&B, most HBCUs include smooth jazz in the range of music they air, which often includes hip hop, funk, mainstream jazz, and gospel.

4. George Lipsitz, *Footsteps in the Dark: The Hidden Histories of Popular Music* (Minneapolis: University of Minnesota Press, 2007), 82.

5. It is worth noting that opportunities to get on radio are uncommon, and at times, progressive programmers find themselves working under conservative programming constraints.

6. Herman Gray, *Cultural Moves: African Americans and the Politics of Representation*, American Crossroads (Berkeley: University of California Press, 2005), 34.

7. John Louis Howland, *Ellington Uptown: Duke Ellington, James P. Johnson, and the Birth of Concert Jazz* (Ann Arbor: University of Michigan Press, 2009); Tammy L. Kernodle, *Soul on Soul: The Life and Music of Mary Lou Williams* (Boston: Northeastern University Press, 2004).

8. Gray, *Cultural Moves*, 39.
9. Gray, *Cultural Moves*, 52.
10. Gray, *Cultural Moves*, 54.
11. Peter Watrous, "Brooklyn Academy Finds Room for the Outsiders of Jazz," *New York Times*, October 12, 1995, C22.
12. Fear of institutional strings makes for a great topic. Most of the organizations cited pre-date Jazz at Lincoln Center. Clearly the series has been a wildly successful accomplishment. For decades jazz musicians have attempted to get a taste of the institutional support afforded to classical music. After the success of Marsalis and his team, the question is now, can we engage these institutions without being tied up by the "strings"?
13. Scott Knowles DeVeaux and National Endowment for the Arts, "Jazz in America: Who's Listening?" (Carson, CA: Seven Locks, 1995).
14. Imamu Amiri Baraka (LeRoi Jones), *Black Music* (New York: Morrow, 1968), 180–211.
15. Ursula Rucker, "Libations," from the CD *Ma'at Mama*, Studio !K7 !K7194CD, Germany, 2006.
16. However, for a newer medium, podcasts, this is not the case. Podcasters are subject to surprisingly large royalty fees relative to the revenue most podcasts can generate.
17. Yet some are professional broadcasters who love jazz. For example, Bill Daughtry can sometimes be heard on WBGO even though his main gig is as a sportscaster and sports talk host on New York C news and sports stations.
18. Jarl A. Ahlkvist, "Programming Philosophies and the Rationalization of Music Radio," *Media, Culture, and Society* 23, no. 3 (2001): 339–58.
19. Charles Edward Hamilton Jr., "The Interaction Between Selected Public Radio Stations and Their Communities: A Study of Station Missions, Audiences, Programming and Funding" (PhD diss., University of Maryland, 1994), 46–64.
20. David Giovannoni and George Bailey, "Appeal and Public Radio's Music" (Washington, DC: Corporation for Public Broadcasting, 1988).
21. Neal Sapper was reported as making these comments at an industry gathering. Sapper was responding to WBGO's longtime program director Thurston Briscoe, who asserted that public radio could learn from commercial radio's audience testing and research methods and that stations needed to move away from relying on the musical tastes of DJs and programmers. Keith Zimmerman and Kent Zimmerman, "The Jazz Roundtable Tackles the New Realities of Jazz Radio," *Gavin Report*, March, 28, 1997, 32.
22. The relative freedom of black DJs to choose their own music until the late 1970s left them vulnerable to payola charges and investigation. Black DJs had a freer hand because the white managers and owners who dominated black-appeal radio beginning in the late 1940s recognized their limits regarding evaluating records and appealing to black audiences.
23. Ahlkvist, "Programming Philosophies," 347–48.
24. Keith Zimmerman and Kent Zimmerman, "Sacramento Gets Jazz CPR—Capital Jazz Radio," *Gavin Report*, July 26, 1999, 52.
25. WGLT program director Jon Norton, telephone interview with the author, November 12, 2012.
26. Norton interview with the author.
27. Ahlkvist, "Programming Philosophies," 348.
28. In fact, the way local television newscasts have been organized reflects considerable research. In the '70s, weather only led newscasts when extreme weather was expected. Today, after the top or breaking stories are teased, the weather is presented during the first programming block, often appearing three or more times in a thirty-five-minute telecast.
29. Graeme Turner, "Who Killed the Radio Star? The Death of Teen Radio in Australia," in *Rock and Popular Music: Politics, Policies, Institutions*, ed. Tony Bennett et al. (London: Routledge, 1993), 150.
30. Steve Behrens, "Jazzcasters Try Music Testing to Pick Cuts," *Current*, September 2, 1996, https://current.org/1996/09/jazzcasters-try-music-testing-to-pick-cuts/.
31. Ted Hendrickson, "It's the Audience, Stupid: Jazz Radio 2003," *CMJ*, October 2003, 12.
32. Hendrickson, "It's the Audience, Stupid," 12.

33. Hendrickson, "It's the Audience, Stupid," 12.

34. Zimmerman and Zimmerman, "Sacramento Gets Jazz CPR," 52.

35. In 1991 Capital Public Radio (now CapRadio) added KXJZ (88.9) as a jazz and news station to its operation of KXPR (90.5), its classical station. In 2006 KXPR and KXJZ exchanged frequencies and now KXJZ is now an NPR news station and KXPR is a classical music station. Both offer some jazz programming on the weekends.

36. Patrik Wikström, *The Music Industry: Music in the Cloud*, Digital Media and Society Series (Cambridge, UK: Polity, 2009).

37. Andrew Dubber, *Radio in the Digital Age* (Cambridge, UK: Polity, 2013), 81.

38. Ken Ringle, "The Great Equalizer: Felix Grant's Jazz Program Helped Bring the City Together," *Washington Post*, October 13, 1993.

39. Letter from Harry Abraham to Paul Baker, http://www.jazzhouse.org/nlib/index.php3?read=baker1.

40. Letter from Harry Abraham to Paul Baker.

41. Maxx Myrick, pers. comm., December 11, 2009.

42. For forty years Phil Schaap (WKCR-FM, New York) hosted *Bird Flight*, a program devoted to the recordings of Charlie Parker that aired each weekday morning.

43. *Riverwalk Jazz* programs can be heard at https://riverwalkjazz.stanford.edu/.

44. African American Public Radio Consortium, https://aaprc.org/.

45. Public radio program providers National Public Radio, Public Radio International, and Murray Street Productions are found, respectively, at www.npr.org, www.pri.org, and www.murraystreet.com.

46. Mike Janssen, "Two More Feeds Syndicate Jazz to Public Radio," *Current*, October 3, 2011.

47. The (former) Jazz with Bob Parlocha website was http://www.jazzwithbobparlocha.com/listen/index.html. Fortunately, there is another website dedicated to Parlocha complete with an archive of programs from 2012 to 2016, the "Jazz with Bob Parlocha Archives," http://jazzstreams.org/JwBP/JwBP-index.php.

48. Janssen, "Two More Feeds."

Chapter 6. Jazz Is for Everybody

1. Jack W. Mitchell, Listener Supported: The Culture and History of Public Radio (Westport, CT: Praeger, 2005), 55–56.

2. David Andrew Ake, *Jazz Cultures* (Berkeley: University of California Press, 2002), 112.

3. Ake, *Jazz Cultures*, 112.

4. When a jazz station goes up for sale, the local jazz community's fears are well-founded. Consider the loss of WDCU to C-SPAN Radio in Washington, DC, and of WDUQ to news, talk, and information station WESA in Pittsburgh.

5. Yulan Wang, pers. comm., December 3, 2012.

6. Effective radiated power takes into account transmitter power, antenna height, and antenna gain, where antenna gain is the dB ratio of the performance of a specific antenna design to that of a reference antenna such as a dipole or an isotropic radiator.

7. The ability to use federal funding to pay NPR fees has been threatened by some in Congress. WGLT 2011 Annual Report, https://www.wglt.org/transparency-and-public-files#annualreports.

8. WBGO IRS 990 filing 2017. https://www.guidestar.org.

9. WNYC IRS 990 filing 2018. https://www.guidestar.org. WNYC operates three stations: WNYC-FM, WNYC-AM, and WQXR-FM. The last is the home of WNYC's classical music programs.

10. The station's 2012 mission statement can be found at http://web.archive.org/web/20130731002714/http://www.wbgo.org/about/mission.

11. The current mission statement is found at https://www.wbgo.org/wbgo-mission-vision-core-values.

12. David Corcoran, "25 Years, Straight Ahead: A Radio Success Story," *New York Times*, April 25, 2004.

13. Chris Washburne, pers. comm., n.d.

14. Corcoran, "25 Years, Straight Ahead."
15. Oliver Lake, private conversation, n.d.
16. Jason Moran, pers. comm., October 19, 2012.
17. KNKX Pacific Public Media IRS Form 990, 2018.
18. Though it would be difficult to search the KNKX database systematically using the website interface, some random searches seldom turned up the following: late-career Coltrane, electric Miles Davis, Kamasi Washington, Geri Allen, Pharoah Sanders, Vijay Iyer, Jason Moran, Tyshawn Sorey, Steve Coleman, or Muhal Richard Abrams.
19. The schedule is found at https://www.knkx.org/schedule.
20. One commenter appreciates the Jazz24 mix, writing, 'When "Planet Jazz" suddenly popped up at KUOW I put in about 20 hours critically listening to what is obviously the intended 'competition' to JAZZ24. I found it to be more of one person's preference in jazz rather than matching the community preference as JAZZ24 does. The mix is more harsh and much less well balanced to my ear. It was not something I would enjoy listening to." Tyler Falk, "Future of KPLU's Popular Jazz Stream Hinges on Fundraising Campaign," *Current*, May 9, 2016.
21. Robert Waterman McChesney, *Blowing the Roof off the Twenty-First Century: Media, Politics, and the Struggle for Post-Capitalist Democracy* (New York: Monthly Review Press, 2014), 177–78.
22. Brandy Doyle, "LPFM's First Decade: Community Radio, Small-Time Broadcasters and Network Syndication," in *Community Radio in the Twenty-First Century*, ed. Janey Gordon (Oxford: Peter Lang, 2012), 42.
23. William Barlow, "Community Radio in the US: The Struggle for a Democratic Medium," *Media, Culture, and Society* 10 (1988): 83.
24. Imamu Amiri Baraka, *Black Music* (New York: Morrow, 1968); Samuel A. Floyd, *The Power of Black Music: Interpreting Its History from Africa to the United States* (New York: Oxford University Press, 1995). The notion of the "changing same" seems consistent with the constantly subversive nature of blues, jazz, soul, and R&B, which one can always read as opposing the status quo. Hip hop has given a new spin to this opposition. Though some of the music is clearly bringing attention to social injustice, a significant part of hip hop culture is obsessed with financial success and demanding access to corporate wealth.
25. Jonathan L. Fischer, "The Airing of Grievances: Can WPFW Modernize While Remaining D.C.'s 'Jazz and Justice' Station?" *Washington City Paper*, December 14, 2012, http://www.washingtoncitypaper.com/articles/43566/the-airing-of-grievances-can-wpfw-modernize-while-remaining-dcs/.
26. Brian Ward, *Radio and the Struggle for Civil Rights in the South* (Gainesville: University Press of Florida, 2004), 334.
27. Mission statement, WRFG-FM, http://wrfg.org/mission.asps.
28. This statement is found at https://wrfg.org/donate/.
29. The program schedule can be seen at http://wrfg.org/schedule/asp.
30. Program schedule, http://wrfg.org/schedule/asp.
31. Rodney Ho, "Shoestring Radio: Scrappy Independent Station WRFG Celebrates 30 Years of Providing a 'Voice for the Voiceless'," *Atlanta Journal-Constitution*, April 30, 2003.
32. Most HBCUs were founded during the fifty years following the U.S. civil war for the purpose of providing higher education to African Americans, who were overwhelmingly excluded from white institutions. There are both public and private HBCUs.
33. WCLK's mission statement is found at http://www.wclk.com/.
34. The census data are from http://quickfacts.census.gov/qfd/states/12/12086.html.
35. U.S. Census Bureau, Decennial Census 2000 and 2010. Miami-Dade County, Department of Planning and Zoning 2011, http://www.miamidade.gov/business/library/reports/data-flash-hispanics-origin.pdf.
36. Judith Hudson, "Talk Radio: Maggie Pelleya Discovers Inspiration, Changes at WDNA," *Caribbean Today*, September 1, 2011.
37. Pat Curry, "On the Radio: WDNA Spells Diversity with Music, Readings," *Fort Lauderdale Sun Sentinel*, June 18,1992.
38. Marc J. Stern, "The Battle for Pacifica," *Journal of Popular Culture* 38, no. 6 (2005): 1069.

39. Matthew Lasar, "Is Pacifica Radio Worth Saving?" *Nation*, February 11, 2015, https://www.thenation.com/article/archive/pacifica-radio-worth-saving/.
40. Jesse Walker, *Rebels on the Air: An Alternative History of Radio in America* (New York: New York University Press, 2001), 48.
41. Stern, "Battle for Pacifica," 1075.
42. Matthew Lasar, *Pacifica Radio: The Rise of an Alternative Network* (Philadephia: Temple University Press, 1999); Jeff Land, *Active Radio: Pacifica's Brash Experiment* (Minneapolis: University of Minnesota Press, 1999).
43. Charles Edward Hamilton Jr., "The Interaction Between Selected Public Radio Stations and Their Communities: A Study of Station Missions, Audiences, Programming and Funding" (PhD diss., University of Maryland, 1994), 158.
44. Paul Farhi, "WPFW-FM Will Undergo Radical Change to a More Mainstream Lineup of Programming," *Washington Post*, December 1, 2012.
45. Fischer, "Airing of Grievances."
46. Based on figures from the 2001, 2012, and 2021 editions of Pacifica Foundation, "Financial Statements and Independent Auditor's Report." Available on the WPFW website, https://wpfwfm.org/radio/about-us/financials.
47. Fischer, "Airing of Grievances."
48. Fischer, "Airing of Grievances."
49. Fischer, "Airing of Grievances."
50. Fischer, "Airing of Grievances."
51. "District of Columbia Quickfacts," http://quickfacts.census.gov/qfd/states/11000.html.
52. Paul F. Lazarsfeld and Frank Stanton, *Communications Research, 1948–1949* (New York: Harper and Brothers, 1949), xiv.
53. The online comments of listener "Connie M., Concerned Listener" to Fischer, "Airing of Grievances."
54. Regarding the sale of WDUQ, see Chris Young, "Mugged: The Deal for WDUQ Could Leave Employees and Jazz Fans Feeling Robbed," *Pittsburgh City Paper*, February 24, 2011, http://www.pghcitypaper.com/pittsburgh/mugged-the-deal-for-wduq-could-leave-employees-and-jazz-fans-feeling-robbed/Content?oid=1381015. With respect to the sale of WDCU, see "C-Span Moves to Radio. WDCU-FM Disappears: Public Affairs Format to Replace Jazz at Washington Station," *Baltimore Sun*, August 15, 1997.
55. Valerie Strauss, "C-SPAN Buys Radio Station from UDC," *Washington Post*, August 14, 1997.
56. Karen Everhart, "In Pittsburgh, a Broker Turns Operator: Jazz Station WDUQ Sold to Public Radio Captial and Local Partner," *Current*, January 24, 2011.
57. Fortunately, KPLU is still a news-jazz radio station.
58. Brooke Cain, "The Sale Price of Shaw University's WSHA Radio Station Is Revealed in FCC Filing," *Raleigh News & Observer*, May 2, 2018, https://www.newsobserver.com/news/local/article210275599.html. Shaw University has plans for the station to continue operation as an internet-only service.
59. Guy Raz, "Radio Free Georgetown: The Hippies Who Ran Georgetown University's WGTB Plugged the Viet Cong, Gay Liberation, and Abortion Rights on the Jesuits' Dime. Who Did They Think They Were?" *Washington City Paper*, January 29, 1999.
60. Malvin Massey, remarks during a panel titled "Selecting and Scheduling Music" at JazzWeek2019 in San Jose, California, August 8, 2019.
61. Several sources were used to compile this list including radio-locator.com and https://tenwatts.blogspot.com/2006/10/historically-black-fm.html, in addition to websites for individual stations.
62. This language is from the landmark 1987 Resolution of the 100th Congress, H.Con.Res.57, "A concurrent resolution expressing the sense of Congress respecting the designation of jazz as a rare and valuable national American treasure," introduced by Representative John Conyers of Michigan.
63. London G. Branch, "Jazz Education at Black Colleges and Universities" (PhD diss., Southern Illinois University, 1975), 103–5.
64. George Lewis, private conversation, December 6, 2006.
65. Branch, "Jazz Education," 16.

66. The exception is the late Phil Schaap's (1951–2021) *Bird Flight*, which continues to air every weekday from 8:20 a.m. to 9:30 a.m.
67. The full history is at http://www.studentaffairs.columbia.edu/wkcr/history.
68. Phil Schaap, interview by Evan Spring, October 5, 1992, https://www.cc-seas.columbia.edu/wkcr/content/phil-schaap-interview.
69. Schaap interview.
70. Travis Jackson, *Blowin' the Blues Away: Performance and Meaning on the New York Jazz Scene* (Berkeley: University of California Press, 2012), 80.
71. Schapp interview.
72. The following departments vie for airtime and studio resources at WKCR: American, Arts, Classical, In All Languages, Jazz, Latin, New Music, News, and Sports. https://www.cc-seas.columbia.edu/wkcr/departments.
73. David Giovannoni, Thomas J. Thomas, Theresa R. Clifford "Public Radio's Service to African Americans: Findings from the Public Radio Programming Strategies Project" (Washington, DC: Corporation for Public Broadcasting, 1995).
74. Moran, pers. comm., October 19, 2012.
75. "Best Radio Station: KTSU-FM/90.9," *Houston Press*, October 26, 2002, http://ezproxy.cul.columbia.edu/login?url=http://search.proquest.com/docview/367691736?accountid=10226.12/31/2012.
76. Rick Mitchell, "KTSU Radio Keeps Jazz Tradition Alive: Devoted Staff Plays Music in All Its Colors," *Houston Chronicle*, June 3, 1990, http://ezproxy.cul.columbia.edu/login?url=http://search.proquest.com/docview/295633087?accountid=10226.
77. Christopher Lucas, "Cultural Policy, the Public Sphere, and the Struggle to Define Low-Power FM Radio," *Journal of Radio Studies* 13, no. 1 (2006): 61.
78. Lucas, "Cultural Policy," 51.
79. Nancy Vogt, "Number of U.S. Low-Power FM Radio Stations Has Nearly Doubled Since 2014," Pew Research Center (September 19, 2016), https://www.pewresearch.org/fact-tank/2016/09/19/number-of-u-s-low-power-fm-radio-stations-has-nearly-doubled-since-2014/.
80. Station information is from LPFMDatabase.com.
81. Lucas, "Cultural Policy," 62.
82. Steve Hendrix, "A Station Is Born: Inside the High-Risk, Low-Watt, Quirky World of Community Radio," *Washington Post*, August 5, 2016.
83. Hendrix, "A Station Is Born."
84. The WOWD-LP schedule for week of April 12, 2020, is taken from https://takomaradio.org/schedule.
85. WOWD-LP schedule, https://takomaradio.org/schedule.
86. For more on WSFM-LP, see https://www.ashevillefm.org/schedule/.
87. Asheville FM 103.3 WSFM-LP Top Play Charts, posted March 17, 2020, https://www.ashevillefm.org/post/asheville-fm-1033-wsfm-lp-top-play-charts-march-8-14-2020/.
88. This information is taken from https://wetfthejazzstation.org/weekly-schedule.
89. Licensing information is from the 2018 IRS Form 990, South Bend Council 5001, Guidestar.com.
90. This history of WSBL-LP is excerpted from www.radiosaborlatino.com/about.
91. https://jazzradiowetf.org/. The WETF mission statement was available on an earlier, now defunct web address.

Postscript

1. As commercially oriented as smooth jazz is, its failure as a radio format seems to imply more about ad buyers' perception of smooth jazz listeners than it does about ratings.
2. *Bullseye* is a great example of an innovative college radio program (started in 2000 as *The Sound of Young America*) that began to reach a larger audience as a podcast, which facilitated its greater distribution on public radio, first by PRI and later by NPR.
3. It is worth mentioning *All Songs Considered* (2000), a podcast that some stations broadcast on a regular basis.

4. The definition of *decent* changes with time, but the wide availability of 10 MB download rates to homes was enough to put a business model with streaming compressed video into play.

5. Tim Wu, *The Master Switch: The Rise and Fall of Information Empires* (New York: Knopf, 2010), 20.

6. John Allen Hendricks, *Radio's Second Century: Past, Present, and Future Perspectives* (New Brunswick, NJ: Rutgers University Press, 2020), 4–5.

7. In late 2022 Amazon leaked information relating to reduced development support for its smart speakers. Amazon's disappointment stemmed from the lack of revenue-generating transactions using the smart speakers such as ordering merchandise, in favor of non-revenue-generating actions such as playing internet radio or requesting local weather.

8. Music-related podcasts enjoy strong ratings (as a percent of all podcast listening) at home (28 percent), in transit (25 percent), and at work (23 percent) News and comedy are the top performers. Of podcast genres that attract more men than women, music podcasts have one of the slightest differences (53 percent to 48 percent) as opposed to both sports and technology (80/20). For African American listeners, the top five podcast genres in 2020 were music, health and fitness, religion, kids and family, and government. "Podcasting Today: Insights for Podcast Advertisers," Nielsen, February 2021, https://www.nielsen.com›insights›2022›podcasting-today.

9. One peril of studying radio is its diminishing centrality in our daily media experience. The broadcast paradigm is useful in evaluating the relevance of radio studies to other services. For example, from 1985 to 2001 a basic cable channel called "The Box" broadcast music videos on demand by 900 number, that is, paid viewer requests. "The Box" seemed nationwide but was really a server-driven franchise seen in more than 150 different markets. It did have unique and simultaneous coverage within each affiliate market. For passive viewers, the content appeared programmed, and in fact, it was; the selections were made by viewers willing to spend $2 to see a video. "The Box" both met and failed the last condition of the broadcast paradigm.

10. These figures are taken from https://www.businessofapps.com/data/spotify-statistics/.

11. Symphonic Blog (author), "How to Get on Spotify's User-Generated Playlists," *Hypebot*, September 11, 2018, https://www.hypebot.com/hypebot/2018/09/how-to-get-on-spotifys-user-generated-playlists.html.

12. The largest radio company, iHeartRadio (formerly Clear Channel Broadcasting, Inc.) went private in 2008 and is now a subsidiary of Bain Capital, LLC along with Clear Channel Outdoor Holdings (an outdoor advertisement business). The combination, Clear Channel Media Holdings, Inc., had revenues of $ 6.246 billion in 2012 according to "CC Media Holdings, Inc. Revenue, Credit Rating, and Other Financial Data," https://www.netcials.com/financial-revenue-history-usa/1400891-cc.media-holdings-inc/. According to the company's 2012 SEC 10-K filing, about half of that, more than $3 billion, came from radio-related activities, producing almost $1 billion in operating income. In 2014 CC Media Holdings was rebranded iHeartMedia, Inc., and Clear Channel Communications, Inc., became iHeartMedia Inc. http://edgar.secdatabase.com/1389/73970813000003/filing-main.htm.

13. According to RIAA data, 2016 was the year when streaming revenue passed digital and physical sales. https://www.riaa.com/u-s-sales-database/.

14. It's too bad that, adjusted for inflation, the 1998 U.S. revenue approached $25 billion (in 2020 dollars). Also, it is unclear how much U.S. recorded music revenue is outside the RIAA.

15. Joshua P. Friedlander, "Year-end 2020 RIAA Revenue Statistics," https://www.riaa.com/reports/2020-year-end-music-industry-revenue-report/.

16. "The Nielsen Total Audience Report, March 2021," https://bnqdigital.com/2021/03/26/the-nielsen-total-audience-report-advertising-across-todays-media/.

17. Ninety-three percent of all adults listen to radio at least once a week. "Audio Today 2018: How American Listens," https://www.nielsen.com/insights/2018/how-america-listens-the-american-audio-landscape/.

18. Andrew Dubber, *Radio in the Digital Age* (Cambridge, UK: Polity, 2013), 94.

19. SiriusXM's first quarter 2021 report information is found at https://www.prnewswire.com/news-releases/siriusxm-reports-first-quarter-2021-results-301278518.html.

20. The practice known as DXing is listening to distant radio stations over the air. The nighttime propagation properties of AM radio make it ideal for distant listening just as FM is not. I

used to listen to Harry Abraham's *Best of All Possible Worlds* jazz show from WHAM in Rochester, New York, as I got off work at 1 a.m. at WGTS-FM in Takoma Park, MD. I listened to WBBM (Chicago) the night Harold Washington was elected the first black mayor of that city from my bedroom in Baltimore. My personal DX record was listening to KOA (Denver) on my car radio in Atlanta, Georgia, in 1981.

21. Although radio stations may also court advertisers with the prospect of internet-enabled reach, agreements are made with streaming aggregators such as Tune-in, radio.net, and Audacity that allow them to insert their own ads into the stations' program streams. The radio stations get internet streaming, the aggregators provide infrastructure and placement of stations on a widely distributed app, and the inserted ads are the aggregators' revenue source.

22. I was one of those enthusiasts. Among the early shows I recorded was *It's Only a Game* from WBUR, *Schickele Mix* (I have 38 of the 199 programs in my computer), *Whadya Know with Michael Feldman* from Minnesota Public Radio, and *The Bama Hour* from WPFW.

23. "Podcasting Today—February 2021," https://www.nielsen.com/insights/2021/podcasting-today-2-2/.

24. One study estimates the following artist payouts for one million song plays: Spotify, $3,000–$6,000, Amazon Music, $5,000, Apple Music, $5,000–$5,500, Google Play, $12,000, Pandora, $1,400, YouTube, $1,700. Cathy Applefeld Olson, "Are Music Streaming Companies Finally Ready to Change the Way They Pay Artists?" *Forbes*, March 3, 2021, https://www.forbes.com/sites/cathyolson/2021/03/03/are-music-streaming-companies-finally-ready-to-change-the-way-they-pay-artists/?sh=1cc516ac72f6.

25. Stuart Nicholson, "Maria Schneider Interview: 'I'm not interested in everybody in the world listening to my music for free, I can't exist that way,'" *jazzwise*, September 15, 2020, https://www.jazzwise.com/features/article/maria-schneider-interview-i-m-not-interested-in-everybody-in-the-world-listening-to-my-music-for-free-i-can-t-exist-that-way?fbclid=IwAR0mPMWR3BjjB7noOHzqqZYOFbkCPR72f6ATM3IISMXJhNcTlyDYiIU7UOc#.X2T6juHBTmM.facebook.

26. Nicholas Garnham, *Emancipation, the Media, and Modernity: Arguments About the Media and Social Theory* (Oxford: Oxford University Press, 2000), 58.

27. Garnham, *Emancipation, the Media, and Modernity*, 59.

28. John Hartley et al., Communication, Cultural and Media Studies: The Key Concepts (London: Routledge, 2002), 94–95.

29. Chris Anderson, *The Long Tail: Why the Future of Business Is Selling Less of More* (New York: Hyperion, 2008).

30. An artist who is retaining $0.20 per digital download is earning perhaps only $0.003 per stream.

31. Nicholas Garnham, "Public Policy and the Cultural Industries," in *Capitalism and Communication: Global Culture and the Economics of Information*, ed. Nicholas Garnham and Fred Inglis (London: Sage, 1990), 31.

Appendix B

1. Data from radio-locator.com, accessed 14 April 2020, edited and updated 7 July 2021.

Bibliography

"75% of All Radio Stations on Discs." *Variety*, December 24, 1930, 58.
Adler, David. "Crossing Over: Is Smooth Jazz Dead?" *JazzTimes*, October 22, 2019.
Adorno, T. W. "A Social Critique of Radio Music." *Kenyon Review* 18, no. 3/4 (1996): 229–35.
Ahlkvist, Jarl A. "Programming Philosophies and the Rationalization of Music Radio." *Media, Culture, and Society* 23, no. 3 (May 1, 2001): 339–58.
Ake, David Andrew. *Jazz Cultures*. Berkeley: University of California Press, 2002.
Anderson, Chris. *The Long Tail: Why the Future of Business Is Selling Less of More*. New York: Hyperion, 2008.
Anderson, Tim J. *Making Easy Listening: Material Culture and Postwar American Recording*. Minneapolis: University of Minnesota Press, 2006.
Appy, Christian G. *Cold War Constructions: The Political Culture of United States Imperialism, 1945–1966*. Amherst: University of Massachusetts Press, 2000.
Arceneaux, Noah. "Blackface Broadcasting in the Early Days of Radio." *Journal of Radio Studies* 12, no. 1 (2005): 61–73.
Baraka, Amiri [LeRoi Jones]. *Black Music*. New York: Morrow, 1968.
Baraka, Amiri [LeRoi Jones]. *Blues People: Negro Music in White America*. New York: Morrow, 1963.
Barlow, William. "Community Radio in the US: The Struggle for a Democratic Medium." *Media, Culture, and Society* 10 (1988): 81–105.
Barlow, William. *Voice Over: The Making of Black Radio*. Philadelphia: Temple University Press, 1999.
Behrens, Steve. "Jazzcasters Try Music Testing to Pick Cuts." *Current*, September 2, 1996.
Bennett, Lerone, Jr. "The Soul of Jazz." *Ebony*, December 1961.
Bourdieu, Pierre. *Distinction: A Social Critique of the Judgement of Taste*. Cambridge, MA: Harvard University Press, 1984.
Brack, Ray. "Record Promotion Men Speakers for WSDM, Chi Stereo Station." *Billboard*, March 12, 1966, 22, 26.
Branch, London G. "Jazz Education at Black Colleges and Universities." PhD diss., Southern Illinois University, 1975.
Burke, Patrick Lawrence. *Come in and Hear the Truth: Jazz and Race on 52nd Street*. Chicago: University of Chicago Press, 2008.
Cantor, Louis. *Wheelin' on Beale: How WDIA-Memphis Became the Nation's First All-Black Radio Station and Created the Sound That Changed America*. New York: Pharos, 1992.
Carney, Court. *Cuttin' Up: How Early Jazz Got America's Ear*. Lawrence: University Press of Kansas, 2009.
Carson, Charles D. "'Bridging the Gap': Creed Taylor, Grover Washington, Jr., and the Crossover Roots of Smooth Jazz." *Black Music Research Journal* 28, no. 1 (Spring 2008): 1–15.

Catlin, Roger. "How Radio DJ Hoppy Adams Powered His 50,000 Watt Annapolis Station into a Mighty Influence." *Smithsonian*, June 16, 2015. https://smithsonianmag.com/smithsonian-institution/dj/hoppy-adams-radio-annapolis-station-influence-segregated-america-180955594/.

Christensen, Ashlee. "Amplify: Mary Dee Dudley." *HerStry* (2019). Published electronically December 19. https://herstryblg.com/amplify/2019/12/19/amplify-mary-dee-dudley.

Cohodas, Nadine. *Princess Noire: The Tumultuous Reign of Nina Simone*. New York: Pantheon, 2010.

Cullman, Lewis B. *Can't Take It with You: The Art of Making and Giving Money*. Hoboken, NJ: Wiley, 2004.

Dannen, Fredric. *Hit Men: Power Brokers and Fast Money Inside the Music Business*. New York: Times Books, 1990.

Davenport, Lisa. *Jazz Diplomacy: Promoting America in the Cold War Era*. Jackson: University Press of Mississippi, 2009.

Davis, Joshua Clark, and Seth Kotch. "Media and the Movement: Activist Community Radio in the American South." (2015). Published electronically February 19. http://www.flowjournal.org/2015/05/media-and-the-movement/.

Davis, Miles, and Quincy Troupe. *Miles: The Autobiography*. New York: Simon and Schuster, 1989.

Dempsey, John Mark. "A More Inclusive Public Service: Can NPR Serve All of America?" In *Radio's Second Century: Past, Present, and Future Perspectives*, edited by John Allen Hendricks, 154–72. New Brunswick, NJ: Rutgers University Press, 2020.

DeVeaux, Scott Knowles. *The Birth of Bebop: A Social and Musical History*. Berkeley: University of California Press, 1997.

DeVeaux, Scott Knowles. "The Emergence of the Jazz Concert, 1935–1945." *American Music* 7, no. 1 (1989): 6–29.

DeVeaux, Scott Knowles, and National Endowment for the Arts. "Jazz in America: Who's Listening?" Carson, CA: Seven Locks, 1995.

"Disc Jockeys Air Phenomenon: Many Media Are Used But the Show Is Its Own Best Promotion." *Sponsor*, September 2, 1949, 36–37, 75–77.

"Disk Jockey: Air Phenomenon." *Sponsor*, August 29, 1949, 28–29, 44, 46–48.

"Disk Jockey Page." *Metronome*, June 1960, 43.

Doerksen, Clifford John. *American Babel: Rogue Radio Broadcasters of the Jazz Age*. Philadelphia: University of Pennsylvania Press, 2005.

Douglas, Elmer. "Lines from a Listener." In Chicago Tribune *Picture Book of Radio*, 65–74. Chicago: Chicago Tribune, 1928.

Douglas, Susan J. *Listening In: Radio and the American Imagination, from Amos 'N' Andy and Edward R. Murrow to Wolfman Jack and Howard Stern*. New York: Times Books, 1999.

Doyle, Brandy. "LPFM's First Decade: Community Radio, Small-Time Broadcasters and Network Syndication." In *Community Radio in the Twenty-First Century*, edited by Janey Gordon, 33–54. Oxford: Lang, 2012.

Dubber, Andrew. *Radio in the Digital Age*. Cambridge, UK: Polity, 2013.

Duff, David. "In Life, Music Has a Special Place. It Should in Radio." *Current*, December 17, 2007.

Eagleton, Terry. *The Ideology of the Aesthetic*. Cambridge, UK: Blackwell, 1990.

Eberly, Philip K. *Music in the Air: America's Changing Tastes in Popular Music, 1920–1980*. New York: Hastings House, 1982.

Ellett, Ryan. *Encyclopedia of Black Radio in the United States, 1921–1955*. Jefferson, NC: McFarland, 2012.

Ellison, Ralph. "Blues People." In *Shadow and Act*, 247–58. New York: Random House, 1964.

Engelman, Ralph. *Public Radio and Television in America: A Political History*. Thousand Oaks, CA: Sage, 1996.

Etling, Laurence W. "Al Jarvis: Pioneer Disc Jockey." *Popular Music and Society* 23, no. 3 (1999): 41–52.

"Fanfare: Single-Minded Schedule." *Broadcasting*, March 9, 1959, 128.

"FCC Roundup." *Broadcasting and Telecasting*, September 5, 1949, 87.

Feather, Leonard. "Crossover Albums." *Billboard*, February 8, 1975, 25–30.

Ferretti, Fred. "The White Captivity of Black Radio." *Columbia Journalism Review* 9, no. 2 (1970): 35–39.

Fisher, Marc. *Something in the Air: Radio, Rock, and the Revolution That Shaped a Generation.* New York: Random House, 2007.
Floyd, Samuel A. *The Power of Black Music: Interpreting Its History from Africa to the United States.* New York: Oxford University Press, 1995.
"FM 'Turns on' Happy Sponsors." *Broadcasting*, July 31, 1967, 100 (Special Report: FM).
"For the Record: Station Authorizations, Applications." *Broadcasting*, May 9, 1960, 101.
"The Forgotten 15,000,000: Part II." *Sponsor*, October 24, 1949, 30–31, 42, 44, 53–54.
Frith, Simon. *Performing Rites: On the Value of Popular Music.* Oxford: Oxford University Press, 1996.
Fritz, Jose. "The 1280 Club." *Arcane Radio Trivia* (2008). Published electronically, December 4. http://tenwatts.blogspot.com/2008/12/1280-club.html.
Fritz, Jose. "Jazz Decades." *Arcane Radio Trivia* (2012). Published electronically April 2. https://tenwatts.blogspot.com/2012/04/jazz-decades.html.
Garnham, Nicholas. *Emancipation, the Media, and Modernity: Arguments About the Media and Social Theory.* Oxford: Oxford University Press, 2000.
Garnham, Nicholas. "Public Policy and the Cultural Industries." In *Capitalism and Communication: Global Culture and the Economics of Information*, edited by Nicholas Garnham and Fred Inglis, 154–69. London: Sage, 1990.
Gendron, Bernard. *Between Montmartre and the Mudd Club: Popular Music and the Avant-Garde.* Chicago: University of Chicago Press, 2002.
Gennari, John. "Jazz Criticism: Its Development and Ideologies." *Black American Literature Forum* 25, no. 3 (1991): 449–523.
George, Nelson. *The Death of Rhythm & Blues.* New York: Pantheon, 1988.
Giddins, Gary. "Hit or Miss." *New York*, January 16, 1978, 69–71.
Gordon, Janey. *Community Radio in the Twenty-First Century.* New York: Lang, 2012.
Gordon, Nightingale. *WNEW: Where the Melody Lingers On.* New York: Nightingale Gordon, 1984.
Gray, Herman. *Cultural Moves: African Americans and the Politics of Representation.* Berkeley: University of California Press, 2005.
Greene, Paul D., and Thomas Porcello. *Wired for Sound: Engineering and Technologies in Sonic Cultures.* Middletown, CT: Wesleyan University Press, 2005.
Hall, Claude. "Jazz Sales Spurting in New York Thanks to Airplay by WLIB-FM." *Billboard*, April 23, 1966, 24.
Hall, Corey. "Untitled." *Chicago Weekend*, December 13, 2001.
Hamilton, Charles Edward, Jr. "The Interaction Between Selected Public Radio Stations and Their Communities: A Study of Station Missions, Audiences, Programming and Funding." PhD diss., University of Maryland, 1994.
Hartley, John, Martin Montgomery, Ellie Rennie, and Marc Brennan. *Communication, Cultural and Media Studies: The Key Concepts.* London: Routledge, 2002.
Hassan, Rusty. "Jazz Radio in Washington, DC." In *DC Jazz: Stories of Jazz Music in Washington, DC*, edited by Maurice Jackson and Blair A. Ruble, 91–106. Washington, DC: Georgetown University Press, 2018.
Hendricks, John Allen. *Radio's Second Century: Past, Present, and Future Perspectives.* New Brunswick, NJ: Rutgers University Press, 2020.
Hendrickson, Ted. "It's the Audience, Stupid: Jazz Radio 2003." *CMJ*, October 20, 2003, 12–13.
Hentoff, Nat. "Jazz Revolution Vs. Radio Station Slashing Jazz." *JazzEd*, September 2012, 40–42.
Hilmes, Michele. *Radio Voices: American Broadcasting, 1922–1952.* Minneapolis: University of Minnesota Press, 1997.
Hilmes, Michele, and Jason Loviglio. *Radio Reader: Essays in the Cultural History of Radio.* New York: Routledge, 2002.
Hirsch, Paul M. "Processing Fads and Fashions: An Organization-Set Analysis of Cultural Industry Systems." *American Journal of Sociology* 77, no. 4 (1972): 639–59.
Hodgkins, Barbara. "Jumping Jockey: Pittsburgh's Bettelou Purvis Is a Jazz Trumpeter's Daughter." *Metronome*, June 1951, 24.
Holley, Eugene, Jr. "Profiling the Jazz Police." *new music usa*, no. 28 (May 2014). https://nmbx.newmusicusa.org/profiling-the-jazz-police/.
Holt, Fabian. *Genre in Popular Music.* Chicago: University of Chicago Press, 2007.

Howe, James. "Duplication." *Broadcasting*, June 7, 1948, 62.
Howland, John Louis. *Ellington Uptown: Duke Ellington, James P. Johnson, and the Birth of Concert Jazz*. Ann Arbor: University of Michigan Press, 2009.
Jackson, Hal, and James Haskins. *The House That Jack Built: My Life Story as a Trailblazer in Broadcasting and Entertainment*. New York: Amistad, 2001.
Jackson, Travis A. *Blowin' the Blues Away: Performance and Meaning on the New York Jazz Scene*. Berkeley: University of California Press, 2012.
Janssen, Mike. "Two More Feeds Syndicate Jazz to Public Radio." *Current*, October 3, 2011.
Jarvis, Al. "The Disc Jockey." *Billboard*, April 25, 1953, 39.
"Jazz Takes a Blow, Chicago Radio Switches to 'Rock.'" *Jet*, April 6, 1967.
Jenkins, Chadwick. "A Question of Containment: Duke Ellington and Early Radio." *American Music* 26, no. 4 (2008): 415.
Johnson, Aaron J. "A Date with the Duke: Ellington on Radio." *Musical Quarterly* 96, no. 3/4 (2013): 369–405.
Katz, Mark. *Capturing Sound: How Technology Has Changed Music*. Berkeley: University of California Press, 2004.
Keightley, Keir. "Music for Middlebrows: Defining the Easy Listening Era, 1946–1966." *American Music* 26, no. 3 (Fall 2008): 309–35.
Keightley, Keir. "'Turn It Down!' She Shrieked: Gender, Domestic Space, and High Fidelity, 1948–59." *Popular Music* 15, no. 2 (1996): 149–77.
Keith, Michael C. "Turn On . . . Tune In: The Rise and Demise of Commercial Underground Radio." In *Radio Reader: Essays in the Cultural History of Radio*, edited by Michele Hilmes and Jason Loviglio, 389–404. New York: Routledge, 2002.
Keller, Marcello Sorce. "Musicologists and the Radio: A Short List of Questions, Problems, and Issues." In *Talk About Radio: Towards a Social History of Radio = Zur Sozialgeschichte Des Radios*, edited by Theo Mäusli, 115–26. Zurich: Chronos, 1999.
Kelley, Robin D. G. *Thelonious Monk: The Life and Times of an American Original*. New York: Free Press, 2009.
Kernodle, Tammy L. *Soul on Soul: The Life and Music of Mary Lou Williams*. Boston: Northeastern University Press, 2004.
Kerouac, Jack. *On the Road*. New York: Penguin, 1991.
"KNOB (FM) Sets All-Jazz Format." *Broadcasting*, September 2, 1957, 96.
"KNOB Turns on All-Jazz Format." *Broadcasting*, March 24, 1958, 98.
Kouwenhoven, John A. "What's 'American' About America." In *The Jazz Cadence of American Culture*, edited by Robert G. O'Meally, 123–36. New York: Columbia University Press, 1998.
Ladd, Jim. *Radio Waves: Life and Revolution on the FM Dial*. New York: St. Martin's, 1991.
Lamb, Bill. "What Is Pop Music? The Definition from the 1950s to Today." liveaboutdotcom (2018), https://www.liveabout.com/what-is-pop-music-3246980. Published electronically September 29.
Land, Jeff. *Active Radio: Pacifica's Brash Experiment*. Minneapolis: University of Minnesota Press, 1999.
Lasar, Matthew. "Is Pacifica Radio Worth Saving?" *Nation*, February 11, 2015. https://www.thenation.com/article/archive/pacifica-radio-worth-saving/.
Lasar, Matthew. *Pacifica Radio: The Rise of an Alternative Network*. Philadelphia: Temple University Press, 1999.
Lazarsfeld, Paul F., and Frank Stanton. *Communications Research, 1948–1949*. New York: Harper and Brothers, 1949.
Lenthall, Bruce. "Critical Reception: Public Intellectuals Decry Depression-Era Radio, Mass Culture, and Modern Ameirca." In *Radio Reader: Essays in the Cultural History of Radio*, edited by Michele Hilmes and Jason Loviglio, 41–62. New York: Routledge, 2002.
Lipsitz, George. *Footsteps in the Dark: The Hidden Histories of Popular Music*. Minneapolis: University of Minnesota Press, 2007.
Lopes, Paul Douglas. *The Rise of a Jazz Art World*. Cambridge: Cambridge University Press, 2002.
Lott, Eric. "Bebop's Politics of Style." In *Jazz Among the Discourses*, edited by Krin Gabbard, 243–55. Durham, NC: Duke University Press, 1995.

Lowrance, Heath. "How the Great Depression Gave America the Blues." *History*, September 2008. https://sites.google.com/site/thegreatdepressionblues/.
Lucas, Christopher. "Cultural Policy, the Public Sphere, and the Struggle to Define Low-Power FM Radio." *Journal of Radio Studies* 13, no. 1 (2006): 51–67.
Mailer, Norman, Jean Malaquais, and Ned Polsky. *The White Negro*. San Francisco: City Lights, 1957.
"Mary Dee Dudley." *Pittsburgh Music History*. https://sites.google.com/site/pittsburghmusichistory/pittsburgh-music-story/radio/mary-dee-dudley.
McChesney, Robert Waterman. *Blowing the Roof off the Twenty-First Century: Media, Politics, and the Struggle for Post-Capitalist Democracy*. New York: Monthly Review Press, 2014.
McChesney, Robert Waterman. *Rich Media, Poor Democracy: Communication Politics in Dubious Times*. Urbana: University of Illinois Press, 1999.
McCourt, Tom. *Conflicting Communication Interests in America: The Case of National Public Radio*. London: Praeger, 1999.
Menard, Louis. "It Took a Village: How the *Voice* Changed Journalism." *New Yorker*, January 5, 2009, 36–45.
Merli, John. "As Personal Income Grows, So Does Listening." *Broadcasting*, May 18, 1998, 42.
Mitchell, Charles. "Why It's So Hard to Find Jazz on the Radio." *Jazz*, Spring 1980, 48–54, 56–57.
Mitchell, Jack W. "Lead Us Not into Temptation: American Public Radio in a World of Infinite Possibilities." In *Radio Reader: Essays in the Cultural History of Radio*, edited by Michele Hilmes and Jason Loviglio, 405–22. New York: Routledge, 2002.
Mitchell, Jack W. *Listener Supported: The Culture and History of Public Radio*. Westport, CT: Praeger, 2005.
Mohamed, Suraya. "Toast of the Nation 2020: The Jazz Collective Edition." https://www.npr.org/2019/12/26/787762117/toast-of-the-nation-2020-the-jazz-collective-edition.
Monson, Ingrid T. *Freedom Sounds: Civil Rights Calls out to Jazz and Africa*. New York: Oxford University Press, 2007.
Moore, Galen. "WGBH to Cancel Eric in the Evening, Weeknights." *Boston Business Journal*, June 21, 2012.
Murray, Albert, and Robert Bone Collection (Columbia University Libraries). *The Blue Devils of Nada: A Contemporary American Approach to Aesthetic Statement*. New York: Pantheon, 1996.
"Music as Written." *Billboard*, January 9, 1961, 5, 53.
Nanry, Charles. *American Music: From Storyville to Woodstock*. New Brunswick, NJ: Transaction Books; dist. by E. P. Dutton, 1972.
National Broadcasting Company. *Broadcast Advertising: A Study of the Radio Medium*, vol.1: *The Fourth Dimension of Radio Advertising*. New York: National Broadcasting Company, 1929.
Owsinski, Bobby. "Is Smooth Jazz Dead or Is It Just Bad Data?" Hypebot, July 14, 2015. https://www.hypebot.com/hypebot/2015/07/is-smooth-jazz-dead.html.
Paige, Earl. "WAAF: Stock in Yards & Jazz." *Billboard*, November 19, 1966, 36, 42.
Paige, Earl. "WSDM-FM Reshapes to Jazzrock Style." *Billboard*, April 3, 1971, 42–43.
Passman, Arnold. *The Deejays*. New York: Macmillan, 1971.
Pinckney, Warren R. "Jazz in Barbados." *American Music* 12, no. 1 (1994): 58–87.
"Pitt Snares KNOB Jazz." *Billboard*, August 14, 1961, 24, 52.
"Platter Spinner Patter: All About Disk Jockeys." *Cash Box*, June 28, 1952, 31.
"Platters Sell Broadcasting." *Billboard*, December 29, 1945, 13.
Poiger, Uta G. *Jazz, Rock, and Rebels: Cold War Politics and American Culture in a Divided Germany*. Berkeley: University of California Press, 2000.
"Policing the Music Air: Everyone Wants No Self-Payola." *Billboard*, December 29, 1945, 13.
Pruter, Robert. *Doowop: The Chicago Scene*. Music in American Life. Urbana: University of Illinois Press, 1996.
Ramsburg, Jim. *Network Radio Ratings, 1932–1953: A History of Prime Time Programs Through the Ratings of Nielsen, Crossley, and Hooper*. Jefferson, NC: McFarland, 2012.
Randle, William, Jr. "Black Entertainers on Radio, 1920–1930." *Black Perspective in Music* 5, no. 1 (1977): 67–74.
Razlogova, Elena. *The Listener's Voice: Early Radio and the American Public*. Philadelphia: University of Pennsylvania Press, 2011.

Reed, Tom. *The Black Music History of Los Angeles—Its Roots: 50 Years in Black Music; A Classical Pictorial History of Los Angeles Black Music of the 20's, 30's, 40's, 50's and 60's; Photographic Essays That Define the People, the Artistry and Their Contributions to the Wonderful World of Entertainment.* Los Angeles: Black Accent on L.A., 1992.

Riccardi, Ricky. *Heart Full of Rhythm: The Big Band Years of Louis Armstrong.* New York: Oxford University Press, 2020.

Ripmaster, Terence. *Willis Conover: Broadcasting Jazz to the World.* n.p.: iUniverse, 2007.

Rose, Joel. "Hal Jackson Was Pioneering Voice in Black Radio." https://www.npr.org/2012/05/24/153634905/hal-jackson-was-pioneering-voice-in-black-radio.

Rothenbuhler, Eric W. "Commercial Radio and Popular Music: Processes of Selection and Factors of Influence." In *Popular Music and Communication*, edited by James Lull, 78–95. Newbury Park, CA: Sage, 1987.

Rothenbuhler, Eric W., and Tom McCourt. "Radio Redefines Itself, 1947–1962." In *Radio Reader: Essays in the Cultural History of Radio*, edited by Michele Hilmes and Jason Loviglio, 367–87. New York: Routledge, 2002.

Russo, Alexander. "Defensive Transcriptions: Radio Networks, Sound-on-Disc Recording, and the Meaning of Live Broadcasting." *Velvert Light Trap*, no. 54 (Fall 2004): 4–17.

Sampson, Henry T. *Swingin' on the Ether Waves: A Chronological History of African Americans in Radio and Television Broadcasting, 1925–1955.* 2 vols. Lanham, MD: Scarecrow, 2005.

Savage, Barbara. *Broadcasting Freedom: Radio, War, and the Politics of Race, 1938–1948.* Chapel Hill: University of North Carolina Press, 1999.

"Say It with Music Marks Trend." *DownBeat*, June 15, 1942, 12–13.

Scott, James C. *Domination and the Arts of Resistance: Hidden Transcripts.* New Haven: Yale University Press, 1990.

Sell, Susan K. "Revenge of the 'Nerds': Collective Action Against Intellectual Property Maximalism in the Global Information Age." *International Studies Review* 15, no. 1 (2013): 67–85.

Shaw, Arnold. *Honkers and Shouters: The Golden Years of Rhythm and Blues.* New York: Macmillan, 1978.

Simpson, Kim. *Early '70s Radio: The American Format Revolution.* New York: Continuum, 2011.

Slotten, Hugh Richard. *Radio's Hidden Voice: The Origins of Public Broadcasting in the United States.* Urbana: University of Illinois Press, 2009.

Smith, Bill. "Bring Back Those Big Bands! Two Philadelphia Disc Jockeys Produce an Amazing Series of Four-Hour Shows." *Metronome*, August 1954, 21–22.

Smith, Mark R. "A Broadcasting Beacon: WANN Radio, from 'The Other' Annapolis to the Smithsonian," *What's Up?* February 5, 2016. https://whatsupmag.com/culture/broadcasting-beacon-wann-radio-the-other-annapolis-smithsonian/.

Socolow, Michael J. "To Network a Nation: NBC, CBS, and the Development of National Network Radio in the United States, 1925–1950." PhD diss., Georgetown University, 2001.

"Songs with Most Radio Plugs." *Billboard*, January 7, 1939, 10.

Spaulding, Norman W. "History of Black Oriented Radio in Chicago 1929–1963." PhD diss., University of Illinois at Urbana-Champaign, 1981.

Stavitsky, Alan G. "From Pedagogic to Public: The Development of U.S. Public Radio's Audience-Centered Strategies—WOSU, WHA, and WNYC, 1930–1987." PhD thesis, Ohio State University, 1990.

Stephens, Ronald J. "Carr and Sparrow's Beach, Annapolis, Maryland (1926–1974)." BlackPast.org (2014). Published electronically April 23. https://www.blackpast.org/african-american-history/carr-and-sparrow-s-beach-annapolis-maryland-1926-1974/.

Sterling, Christopher H., and Michael C. Keith. "Sounds of Change: A History of FM Broadcasting in America." *Journal of Popular Music Studies* 21, no. 3 (2009): 324.

Sterling, Christopher H., and John M. Kittross. *Stay Tuned: A History of American Broadcasting.* Mahwah, NJ: Erlbaum, 2002.

Stern, Marc J. "The Battle for Pacifica." *Journal of Popular Culture* 38, no. 6 (2005): 1069–87.

Sterne, Jonathan. *The Audible Past: Cultural Origins of Sound Reproduction.* Durham, NC: Duke University Press, 2003.

Stratemann, Klaus. *Duke Ellington: Day by Day and Film by Film.* Copenhagen: JazzMedia ApS, 1992.
Streissguth, Michael. "Jack L. Cooper." In *Biographical Dictionary of Radio*, edited by Christopher H. Sterling, 68–69. London: Routledge, 2013.
Szwed, John F. "*Blue Nippon: Authenticating Jazz in Japan* by E. Taylor Atkins." *Journal of Japanese Studies* 29, no. 1 (Winter 2003): 222–25.
Taylor, Art. *Notes and Tones: Musician-to-Musician Interviews.* Expanded ed. New York: Da Capo, 1993.
Taylor, Billy, and Teresa L. Reed. *The Jazz Life of Dr. Billy Taylor.* Bloomington: Indiana University Press, 2013.
Taylor, Timothy Dean. *The Sounds of Capitalism: Advertising, Music, and the Conquest of Culture.* Chicago: University of Chicago Press, 2012.
Taylor, Timothy Dean, Mark Katz, and Tony Grajeda. *Music, Sound, and Technology in America: A Documentary History of Early Phonograph, Cinema, and Radio.* Durham, NC: Duke University Press, 2012.
Thacker, Eric. "Hot (i)." In *Grove Music Online*, 2003. https://www-oxfordmusiconline-com.pitt.idm.oclc.org/grovemusic/view/10.1093/gmo/9781561592630.001.0001/omo-9781561592630-e-2000208300.
Tiegel, Eliot. "Jazz Beat. Broadcast Scene: Summing Up." *Billboard*, June 18,1966, 22, 26.
Tiegel, Eliot. "KNOB, WNOP . . . And All That Jazz." *Billboard*, March 27, 1965, 56, 64.
Turner, Graeme. "Who Killed the Radio Star? The Death of Teen Radio in Australia." In *Rock and Popular Music: Politics, Policies, Institutions*, edited by Tony Bennett, Simon Frith, Lawrence Grossberg, John Shepard and Graeme Turner, 142–55. London: Routledge, 1993.
Tyson, Timothy B. *Radio Free Dixie: Robert F. Williams and the Roots of Black Power.* Chapel Hill: University of North Carolina Press, 1999.
United States National Advisory Commission on Civil Disorders. *Report of the National Advisory Commission on Civil Disorders.* Washington, DC: U.S. Government Printing Office, 1968.
Vail, Ken. *Duke's Diary.* 2 vols. Lanham, MD: Scarecrow, 2002.
Vogt, Nancy. "Number of U.S. Low-Power FM Radio Stations Has Nearly Doubled Since 2014." (2016). Published electronically September 19. https://www.pewresearch.org/fact-tank/2016/09/19/number-of-u-s-low-power-fm-radio-stations-has-nearly-doubled-since-2014/.
Von Eschen, Penny M. *Satchmo Blows Up the World: Jazz Ambassadors Play the Cold War.* Cambridge, MA: Harvard University Press, 2004.
"Vox Jox: A National Accounting of Disk Jockey Activities." *Billboard*, June 19, 1948, 23.
Wald, Elijah. *How the Beatles Destroyed Rock 'N' Roll: An Alternative History of American Popular Music.* Oxford: Oxford University Press, 2009.
Walker, Jesse. *Rebels on the Air: An Alternative History of Radio in America.* New York: New York University Press, 2001.
Walker, Jesse. "With Friends Like These: Why Community Radio Does Not Need the Corporation for Public Broadcasting." *Cato Policy Analysis 277.* Washington, DC: Cato Institute, July 24, 1997.
Ward, Brian. *Radio and the Struggle for Civil Rights in the South.* Gainesville: University Press of Florida, 2004.
Weheliye, Alexander G. *Phonographies: Grooves in Sonic Afro-Modernity.* Durham, NC: Duke University Press, 2005.
White, Thomas H. "Building the Broadcast Band." June 7, 2008. http://earlyradiohistory.us/buildbcb.htm#complexities.
"Why Hi-Fi." *Metronome*, April 1954, 13.
Wikström, Patrik. *The Music Industry: Music in the Cloud.* Cambridge, UK: Polity, 2009.
Wiley III, Ed. "Short-Circuiting College Airwaves—Radio Station WCDU-FM [sic] and Radio Stations at College Campuses." *Diverse (Issues in Higher Education)* (2007). Published electronically July 12. http://diverseeducation.com/article/8310/.
Wilkinson, Christopher. "Sweet Dance Music." In *Grove Music Online*, 2015. https://www-oxfordmusiconline-com.pitt.idm.oclc.org/grovemusic/view/10.1093/gmo/9781561592630.001.0001/omo-9781561592630-e-1002276633.

Williams, Gilbert. "The Black Disc Jockey as a Cultural Hero." *Popular Music and Society* 10, no. 3 (1986): 79–90.
Witherspoon, John, Roselle Kovitz, Robert K. Avery, Alan G. Stavitsky, Steve Behrens, J. J. Yore, and Richard Barbieri. *A History of Public Broadcasting*. Washington, DC: Current, 2000.
Wu, Tim. *The Master Switch: The Rise and Fall of Information Empires*. New York: Knopf, 2010.
Zakaras, Paul. "Chicago Disk Experts Stress Importance of Jazz Promotion." *Billboard*, July 16, 1966, 36.
Zhito, Lee. "LP Programming." *Billboard*, March 27, 1961, 8.
Zimmerman, Keith, and Kent Zimmerman. "Sacramento Gets Jazz CPR—Capital Jazz Radio." *Gavin Report*, July 26, 1999, 52.

Interviews

Benson, Al. Archives of African American Music and Culture, Indiana University.
Gabler, Milt. "Reminiscences of Milton Gabler: Oral History, 1959." Columbia University Libraries, Columbia Center for Oral History. https://oralhistoryportal.library.columbia.edu/document.php?id=ldpd_4076824.
Hancock, Hunter. Interview with Lex Gillespie, January 20, 1995. Archives of African American Music and Culture, Indiana University.
Hassan, Rusty. Telephone interview with the author, n.d.
Holland, Brian D., and Earl Klugh. "Earl Klugh Interview: Guitars, George Benson, and Naked Guitar." *Guitar International*. https://web.archive.org/web/20151222110942/http://guitarinternational.com/2010/12/21/earl-klugh-talks-guitars-george-benson-and-naked-guitar/.
"Joe Adams interview on KOWL." National Visionary Leadership Project, https://youtu.be/n43n510C4jg.
Kent, Herb. Interview with Sonja Williams, March 29, 1995. Archives of African American Music and Culture, Indiana University.
LaPalm, Dick. Telephone interview with the author, November 19, 2012.
McCoy, Sid. Interview with Sonja Williams, June 19, 1995. Archives of African American Music and Culture, Indiana University.
Morgenstern, Dan. Interview with Hank Hehmsoth. https://www.youtube.com/watch?v=oC52vJePQy4.
Norton, Jon. Telephone interview with the author, November 12, 2012.
Schaap, Phil. https://www.cc-seas.columbia.edu/wkcr/content/phil-schaap-interview.
Sherrell, Charles. Interview with Sonya D. Williams, March 28, 1995. Archives of African American Music and Culture, Indiana University.
Taylor, Creed. Interview with Marc Myers, pt. 6, July 15, 2008. https://www.jazzwax.com/2008/07/interview-cre-1.html.
Thomas, Thomas, with others. "Roundtable: The Future of Jazz Radio," with Ed Gordon. National Public Radio, August 10, 2006, transcript. https://www.npr.org/templates/story/story.php?storyId=5633331.

Industry Reports

"The Aging Audience." Walrus Research, Spring 2009. https://blatherwatch.blogs.com›files›aging_public_radio_audience_-_walrus_research.pdf.
The Airheads Radio Survey Archive, a collection of radio surveys. http://las-solanas.com/arsa/index.php.
Arbitron. *Public Radio Today: How America Listens to Public Radio Stations; 2005 Edition*. New York: Arbitron Inc., 2005.
Arbitron. *Public Radio Today 2012: How America Listens to Radio*. New York: Arbitron, 2012.
Broadcasting Yearbook 1942. Washington, DC: Broadcasting Publications, 1942.
Broadcasting and Cable Yearbook 1974. Edited by Sol Taishoff. Washington, DC: Broadcasting Publications, 1974.

Broadcasting and Cable Yearbook 1975. Edited by Sol Taishoff. Washington, DC: Broadcasting Publications, 1975.
Broadcasting and Cable Yearbook 1978. Edited by Sol Taishoff. Washington, DC: Broadcasting Publications, 1978.
Broadcasting and Cable Yearbook 1981. Washington, DC: Broadcasting Publications, 1981.
Broadcasting and Cable Yearbook 2009. New Providence, NJ: Bowker, 2009.
"Core Values of Jazz Formats," abridged report, Walrus Research, Spring 2004. https://walrusresearch .com›__static›91e74f33a2cf7a59a8aa56b3a10e6d09›core-values-jazz-stations.pdf?dl=1.
Giovannoni, David, and George Bailey. "Appeal and Public Radio's Music." Washington, DC: Corporation for Public Broadcasting, 1988.
Giovannoni, David, Thomas J. Thomas, and Theresa R. Clifford. "Public Radio Programming Strategies: A Report on the Programming Stations Broadcast and the People They Seek to Serve." Washington, DC: Corporation for Public Broadcasting, 1992.
National Public Radio. *2017 Annual Report*. https://media.npr.org/documents/about/annual reports/2017_Annual_Report.pdf.
Public Radio Today 2012: How America Listens to Radio. "Broadcast Stations Totals as of June 30, 2012," FCC News Release. http://fjallfoss.fcc.gov/edocs_public/attachmatch/DOC-315231A1 .pdf.
Radio Annual 1942. Edited by Jack Alicoate. New York: Radio Daily, 1942.
Radio Annual 1947. Edited by Jack Alicoate. New York: Radio Daily, 1947.
Radio Research Consortium. *Audience 2010: Reinvigorating Public Radio's Public Service & Public Support*. Interim Report 7. Olney, MD: Walrus Research/AudiGraphics, Inc., for the Radio Research Consortium. May 16, 2006.
Thomas, Thomas J., and Theresa R. Clifford, *Audience 88: Issues and Implications*. Washington, DC: Corporation for Public Broadcasting, 1988. ARAnet Public Radio Research.
Thomas, Thomas J., Theresa R. Clifford, and David Giovannoni. "Public Radio's Service to African Americans: Findings from the Public Radio Programming Strategies Project." Washington, DC: Corporation for Public Broadcasting, 1995.
Walrus Research and AudiGraphics, *Audience 2010 Interim Report 6: Losing Our Grip*. Olney, MD: Radio Research Consortium, 2006.
Walrus Research and AudiGraphics. "Audience 2010: Reinvigorating Public Radio's Public Service and Public Support." Interim Report 7 (Olney, MD: Radio Research Consortium, 2006).

Index

Abbott, Robert Sengstacke, 73–74
ABC: ABC/Impulse, 130; ABC-Paramount, 25–26; WJZ (New York) as flagship, 41, 56, 64–65
Abdus-Salaam, Sharif, 216, 219
Abraham, Harry, 91, 106, 186–87
Abrams, Muhal Richard, 173
acid jazz, 15, 173, 175, 192. *See also* crossover jazz
Adams, Charles "Hoppy," 23, 81–84
Adams, Joe, 66, 110
Adams, William L. "Little Willie," 81–82
Adderley, Cannonball, 4, 11–12
advertising, commercial radio and, 39, 42, 76, 80, 116, 119, 124, 127–29
aesthetic philosophy of programming, 10, 180–81, 187–88
African American(s): black-owned broadcasting companies and radio stations, 66, 71, 105, 113, 115, 121, 127, 271n39 (*see also* Inner City Broadcasting Company; WLIB AM/FM); as DJs (*see* African American DJs); early voicelessness in federal policy matters, 8; Great Migration, 9, 73–74, 121; as listeners (*see* African American listeners); as musicians (*see* African American musicians); nature and origins of jazz music and, 9, 12, 28–29. *See also* civil rights movement; Jim Crow
African American DJs: Charles "Hoppy" Adams, 23, 81–84; Joe Adams, 66, 110; William L. "Little Willie" Adams, 81–82; Al Benson (Arthur Bernard Leaner), 66, 73, 74–77, 78, 79; in Chicago, 73–84; control of playlists, 76–77, 277n22; Jack L. Cooper, 39–40, 42, 64, 73–75, 77; Yvonne Daniels, 51, 77, 79, 86, 117;

Daddy-O Daylie (Holmes Bailey), 51, 77–78, 101–5, 112, 113, 269nn61–63; Mary Dee Dudley (Mary Elizabeth Goode), 59–62, 79, 265n74; influence on African American consumption of jazz, 24–25; Hal Jackson, 23, 64–66; Herb Kent "The Cool Gent," 75; Martha Jean the Queen, 72; Sid McCoy, 51, 75, 77, 78–79, 86
African American listeners: advertising sales and, 39, 42, 76, 80, 116, 119, 124, 127–29; black progressive radio and jazz, 119–26; influence of African American DJs on consumption of jazz, 24–25; as jazz-dominant listeners, 165–66, 276n81; music in social politics of aspiration and, 75; in the New York City area, 54; programming aimed at, 3 (*see also* Black Appeal/Negro Appeal format); research studies on, 7
African American musicians: black bands as guest attractions via remote broadcasts, 36; de facto segregation policies, 8, 258n13; in radio orchestras, 36, 258n13. *See also names of specific musicians*
African American Public Radio Consortium (AAPRC), 190–91, 214
Ahmad, Jamal, 191
Ake, David, 194
Alexander, Dee, 191
Allen, Geri, 173
Allen, Steve, 51
Allen, William "Hoss," 77
The All-Negro Hour (WSBC, Chicago), 40
Altschul, Barry, 130
American Federation of Musicians (AFM), 29, 36
American Public Media, 161, 197

American Public Radio, 153
American Songbook, 85, 179, 241
Amos, Kevin, 143–44
Amos 'n' Andy (blackface program), 38, 40
AM radio: AM/FM distribution of radio stations (1955), 71, 109; jazz as active, subliminal component of, 85. *See also* commercial radio
Anderson, Tim, 19
Anthony, Paul, 144
AOR (album-oriented rock) format, 59, 97, 99, 100, 119, 120, 142, 207, 269n59
Apple Music, 237
Arbitron data (formerly Nielsen), 112, 116, 138, 242
A&R (artist and repertoire) men, 6, 78
Armstrong, Edwin, 98–99
Armstrong, Louis, 9, 20, 42, 55, 68, 75, 130, 171–72, 181, 232
Art Ensemble of Chicago, 176
ASCAP (American Society of Composers, Authors, and Publishers), 40, 46, 178
Association for the Advancement of Creative Musicians, 21–22, 176, 200
Atlantic Records, 86, 97
Atlas, Ralph, 105, 113
AT&T Long Lines, 36–38, 47–49
Audience 88 study (Thomas and Clifford), 163–66
Audience 2010 report (Radio Research Consortium), 166
audience philosophy of programming, 180, 181–82
audience research/modal data: Arbitron data (formerly Nielsen), 112, 116, 138, 242; data analytics, 248; focus groups and, 168, 183, 184; Nielsen data (now Arbitron), 240, 242; for noncommercial radio, 2, 138, 147–48, 160, 164, 180–82, 186–87, 193–94, 201, 231–33, 247; University of Pittsburgh student survey (2017), 237–38
Austin, Patti, 130
average quarter hour (AQH), 160, 163, 164
Ayler, Albert, 195, 218

backselling, 21
Bacon, Paul, 58
Bailey, George, 184
Bailey, Holmes, 77
Baker, Chet, 68
Baldwin, Bob, 191
Ball, Kenny, 4
bandleaders: as DJs, 51–52, 79, 112; as gatekeepers, 26, 42, 44; live remotes and, 36–39, 49–51, 54, 56, 64–65, 82–84, 111; payola and, 21

Banks, Dolly and William, 114
Baraka, Imamu Amiri (Leroi Jones), 14, 15, 125, 173–74, 177, 203
Barlow, William "Bill," 7, 40, 73, 74, 75, 77, 123, 170–71, 202
Basie, Count, 8, 17, 28, 29, 47, 82, 85, 117, 199–200
Beach, Ed, 129, 131
beat culture, 53–57
Beatles, 117, 134
bebop and bop: black militancy and, 14–15, 29; Daddy-O Daylie (Holmes Bailey) as DJ and, 77–78; end of network era in radio and, 29–30; Mort Fega as DJ and, 56–57; hard bop and, 11–12, 15, 31, 232; "moldy figs" vs. "modernists," 29; as new style, 53, 76; origins of, 8, 11–12, 29–30; popular music vs., 30–31; post-bop styles of, 15, 28, 31, 171–73, 192, 195, 200, 207, 232, 247, 248; Bettelou Purvis (Marks) as DJ and music director, 56, 62–64; Fred Robbins (Fred Rubin) as DJ and, 57–59; Symphony Sid Torin (Sidney Tarnopol) as DJ and, 53–57, 181
Bee, Tommy, 112
Beech, Ed, 56
Behrens, Steve, 184
Bellamy, Fay, 204
Bennett, Lerone, Jr., 12
Benoit, David, 168
Bensky, Larry, 160
Benson, Al (Arthur Bernard Leaner), 66, 73, 74–77, 78, 79
Benton, Brook, 86
Berry, Chu, 44–45
Besson, Abe, 201
big band music. *See* swing
Billboard, 110, 114, 127–29; disk jockey vs. network model of programming, 42; Honor Roll of Hits, 43–44, 263n35; non-jazz readership, 130; rapid response ratings, 120–21, 271n37; R&B LP chart, 86, 87–90; Songs with Most Radio Plugs, 44; Top 100/Hot 100, 8–9, 25, 42–43, 90, 94; Top Record Sales, 44–45, 47
Birdland (New York), 54, 56, 64–65
Black Appeal/Negro Appeal format: African American musical styles and, 171; black progressive radio and jazz, 119–26; confluence of styles on, 85–86; ethnic programming and, 57–58; format "churn" and, 119–20; Harlem Hit Parade, 44, 47; jive/hip street language of DJs and, 25, 26, 40, 56–58, 65, 68–69, 70, 74, 77, 123; multiple meanings of black music, 22; origins and growth of, 71–73, 79; Quiet

Storm formats, 126; United Broadcasting and, 79–80, 115; WANN (Annapolis), 23, 64, 80–84; WBEE (Harvey, IL), 40, 74, 113, 114–17, 119; white-owned stations and, 86, 115, 121, 122, 127, 131; WNJR (Newark), 64–65, 115. *See also* African American DJs
black arts movement, 12–14, 121
black church music and gospel: first DJs and, 40; Gospel format, 60, 85, 215, 223, 224; in the Negro folk idiom, 12; soul jazz and, 13, 31
blackface, 38, 40
black liberation radio, 121–26, 133, 177–78
black pride movement, 13
black urban style. *See* rhythm and blues (R&B)
Blakey, Art, 63, 80, 167
Blesh, Rudi, 54
Block, Martin, 39–40, 46, 65, 262n14
block time arrangements, 42
blogging, 6, 7, 24, 57–58, 122–23
Blue Network (NBC stations), 37, 41, 95
Blue Note Records, 53, 58, 97, 130
blues: Chicago DJs and, 75, 76; decline of jazz radio and, 85; gospel music and, 12; soul jazz and, 12, 31
Blum, Larry, 80–81
Blum, Morris, 80, 82
BMI, 178
Booker T & the MGs, 13
bossa nova, 16
Bourdieu, Pierre, 13
Bracken, James, 74
Brighter Side of Darkness, 86
Briscoe, Thurston, 199
British Broadcasting Corporation (BBC), 144, 149, 153, 242
Broadcasting Freedom (Savage), 7, 267n22
Broadcasting Yearbook, 91–93
Broadcast Music, Inc., 40
broadcast paradigm, 237–39, 246
brokered-time model, 40, 42, 74, 79, 116–17, 120n
Brötzmann, Peter, 173
Brown, James, 67, 85
Brown, Oscar, Jr., 56, 112
Brown, Ruth, 8
Brubeck, Dave, 47
Bryant, Bobby, 4
Bryant, Greg, 200
Bryant, Ray, 8–9
Buckley, Dick, 112–13
Burdeen, Bert, 117–19
Burns, Ken, 172, 173–74
Byron, Don, 173, 175

Calloway, Cab, 8, 36, 62, 95
Cantor, Louis, 7
Capitol Records, 55
Carn, Doug and Jean, 126
Carnegie Commission, 152
Carnegie Corporation of New York, 150
Carnegie Hall (New York), 133, 174
Carr's Beach (Chesapeake Bay) concerts, 81–84
Carson, Charles, 32
Carter, James, 168
Carter, Vivian, 74
cartoons: jazz music used with, 85; *Zippy the Pinhead*, 53, 54
Cash Box (magazine), 43
Castro, Fidel, 125
Cavalcade of Jazz (1945–1958), 67
CBS, 37, 41, 54
CBS Records, 129
CDs, 6, 20, 167, 185, 187–88, 239–40, 243. *See also* records and recordings
Chanticleer Broadcasting, 69–70
Charles, Ray, 4, 12, 13, 31, 47, 66, 76, 85, 86
Chedwick, George "Porky," 77
Chess, Leonard, 113
Chess, Phil, 113
Chess records, 78, 86, 113
Chicago Public Radio, 21–22
Chinen, Nate, 200
CHR (Contemporary Hits Radio) format, 167–68, 269n59
Church, Tom, 137, 160, 164
civil rights movement, 7, 9, 29, 90, 121, 123, 202–3, 204; black church in, 13; DJs and, 25; lack of black radio ownership and, 115. *See also* Jim Crow
classical music, 5, 84–85, 99–100; black conservatory-trained musicians, 12; exclusion from noncommercial programming, 168–69; FM radio and, 97, 109; jazz as America's classical music, 11, 127, 177, 209; noncommercial radio and, 141–42, 157–58, 159; Second Viennese school, 12. *See also* noncommercial radio
Clear Channel (now iHeart Radio), 21, 271n40, 282n12
Clifford, Theresa R., 163–66
Clinton, Larry, 29
Cobb, Jimmy, 218
Cobb, Joe, 78
Cohen, Emmett, 7
Cohen, Leonard, 170
Cole, Nat "King," 4, 25, 29, 47, 65, 67, 85, 86
Coleman, Ornette, 10, 125, 173
Coleman, Steve, 173

Index   297

college radio, 5, 212–20; college music departments and, 194–95, 207, 214–16; financial supports for, 147; HBCU radio stations, 176, 190, 206–7, 214–16, 219–20, 279n32; as incubator of indie rock and alternative music, 196; jazz programming by, 141–42, 196; KTSU-FM (Texas Southern University), 219–20; licensing of stations, 196, 213; nature of, 195, 196, 213; professionally staffed university-owned stations vs., 195, 212–13; sales of licenses, 146, 191, 212–13, 214, 280n54; WKCR-FM (Columbia University), 216–19. *See also* experimental/"outside" jazz; low-power FM
Collins, Leon, 209
Coltrane, John, 12, 15, 111, 112, 122, 127, 194–95
Columbia, 131
commercial radio, 33–134, 232–33; advertising and, 39, 42, 76, 80, 116, 119, 124, 127–29; age of network radio (1927–1946), 22, 35; all-jazz pioneers, 4, 108–19; AM stations in the 1960s, 84–96; audience size and characteristics, 147; decline of jazz on, 5, 16, 32, 47, 75, 79, 85–89, 91–96, 126–34, 235, 261n80; early DJs and recorded music, 39–42; FM explosion 1960s to 1970s and, 86, 96–99; formats (*see* radio formats); frequency assignments, 124, 126–27, 271–72n58; highbrow/lowbrow distinction on networks, 41; hit records vs. hit songs, 42–45; jazz move to noncommercial stations, 132–34; jazz station list (circa 2020), 253–56; live remotes, 36–39, 49–51, 54, 56, 64–65, 82–84, 111; network formation in the 1920s, 8; omnibus/variety programming, 4, 36–39, 41, 50–51, 69, 72, 85, 139; partnership between radio and records, 45–47; postwar decline of radio networks, 3, 15–16, 19, 35–36, 45, 91–93, 235–36; profit maximization and, 9–10, 139, 147, 161, 202, 203; radio station identification spots, 9, 24; record playing and network radio stations, 18–20, 36–39; research-driven formats and genres, 168; tactics used in noncommercial radio, 161–62; transcription programs, 36, 38–39, 46, 49–50, 52, 58, 59; underground/progressive radio movement and, 99–101
Commodore music label, 46
Commodore Music Shop (New York), 46
Communications Act (1934), 8
community radio, 202–12; activism and, 204, 205, 207–8; central goal of, 202–3; ideological use of music and, 202–3; as independently licensed radio stations, 195; jazz as music of resistance on, 15; jazz programming by, 141–42; licensing of stations, 196–97; low-power FM and (*see* low-power FM); nature of, 202; ownership/management models, 195; Pacifica Foundation profile, 208–12 (*see also* Pacifica Radio Network); professionalization of, 151; public radio vs., 154–56, 195, 204 (*see also* public radio); stability of, 197; WDNA-FM (Miami), 207–8; WRFG-FM (Radio Free Georgia, Atlanta), 204–7
Condon, Eddie, 29
Conover, Willis, 41
conservative programming, 171–78; conservative vs. progressive camps and, 10, 15, 22, 171–78, 248; critics of, 172; mainstream styles in, 15, 21–22, 23; nature of, 15, 171–72
"contemporary" jazz. *See* smooth/contemporary jazz
Cooke, Sam, 13, 125
cool jazz, 12, 15, 31, 190–91, 207, 232
Cooper, Jack L., 39–40, 42, 64, 73–75, 77
Cooper, Trudy, 40
Cordell, Lucky, 75
Cornelius, Don, 78
Corporation for Public Broadcasting (CPB), 136, 150–54; *Audience 88* study, 163–66; budget/qualification standards for radio stations, 140, 146–47, 150–51, 154, 176, 196–201, 210, 212, 231–32; creation and funding of National Public Radio (1970), 141–42, 147–48, 152, 153, 194; creation of (1967), 135, 141–42, 150; low-power FM radio and, 220; Public Broadcasting Act (1967) and, 135, 150, 220
Correll, Charles, 38
Cosby, Bill, 78
Cotton Club (New York), 20, 47–48, 54, 262n15
Country and Western/Country format, 42, 52, 85, 93, 107, 112, 127, 128
COVID-19 pandemic, 1, 236, 240, 244
Crocker, Frankie, 122–23
Crosby, Bing, 47
cross-media conglomerates, 38, 45–47
crossover jazz, 4, 8–9, 13, 15, 32, 90, 106, 129–33, 171, 172, 192
Crouch, Stanley, 173–74
Crystal, Billy, 46
C-SPAN (Cable Satellite Public Affairs Network), 146, 212
Cuban Communism, 125–26
Cugat, Xavier, 64
Cullem, Jim, 190
Curtin, Hoyt, 85

298 Index

Daley, Joe, 130
Dameron, Tadd, 63
Daniels, Billy, 79
Daniels, Yvonne, 51, 77, 79, 86, 117
Davenport, Lisa, 11
Davis, Miles, 22, 23, 31, 56, 63, 117, 122, 127, 177, 187
Dawkins, Ernest, 21
Dawson, William, 74
Daylie, Daddy-O (Holmes Bailey), 51, 77–78, 101–5, 112, 113, 269nn61–63
dayparts, 91, 275n71
Dee Dudley, Mary (Mary Elizabeth Goode), 59–62, 79, 265n74
Deezer, 237
DeVeaux, Scott, 49
Dial label, 53
disco music, 19
Dixieland jazz, 4, 27–28, 29, 130
DIY releases/radio, 6, 142, 171, 186, 238
DJs, 22–26, 39–42, 51–67; African Americans as (*see* African American DJs); automated programming systems vs, 51, 228; celebrity DJs, 51–52; control of playlists/programming, 22–24, 45, 46, 52–59, 73–77, 79, 94–96, 97, 106–7, 117, 132 (*see also* programmers and programming; programming philosophies and theories); decline of air personality importance, 51; first DJs and recorded music, 39–48; growth and extent of use (1949), 41–42; jazz DJs on non-jazz commercial stations, 101–7; jazz DJ tributes by year, 55; jazz specialists, 23–24; jive/hip street language and, 25, 26, 40, 56–58, 65, 67–70, 74, 77, 123; list of notable jazz DJs, 249–51 (*see also names of specific DJs*); payola and, 21, 45, 55, 58, 69, 240, 272n69, 277n22; personal libraries of, 95, 179; pre-format jazz DJs, 51–67; presentation styles, 23, 26, 53; professional musicians as, 51–52, 79, 112, 179; women as (*see* women DJs)
D'Lugoff, Art, 127–29
Doggett, Bill, 82
Dolphy, Eric, 12
Donahue, Tom, 100
Dorsey, Jimmy, 29
Dorsey, Thomas A., 12
Dorsey, Tommy, 29, 51–52, 66
Douglas, Elmer, 193
Douglass, Dave, 173
Dowd, Tom, 97
DownBeat (magazine), 21–22, 91–93
Downing, Will, 191
Doyle, Brandy, 202
Dubber, Andrew, 185

DuBois, W. E. B., 13
Duff, David, 137, 160–61
DVDs, 236
DXing, 242, 282–83n20

Eagleton, Terry, 9–10
early jazz, 15, 18, 27–29, 179, 190
earplugs/earbuds, 94, 238
Eastman, John, 110
Eastwood, Clint, 10–11
Easy Listening/Good Music format, 5, 8, 19, 30, 51, 68–69, 84–85, 93, 94, 97, 109
Eaton Richard, 65, 79
Eberhardt, Pam, 117
Eberly, Phil, 16
Eckstine, Billy, 63, 65
Educational Media Foundation, 213
educational radio: educational television funding and, 150–51; FM bands reserved for educational/noncommercial use (1945), 135, 136, 138, 149–50; ownership/management models, 195; Public Broadcasting Act (1967) and, 135, 150, 220; reorganization of, 141–42. *See also* college radio; low-power FM; public radio
Edwards, Oliver, 40
Eldridge, Roy, 44–45
Electronics Industry of America, 98
Ellerbee, Linda, 117
Ellett, Ryan, 7
Ellington, Duke, 8, 14, 17, 27, 29, 75, 174; as celebrity DJ, 51–52; Cotton Club (New York) and, 20, 47–48, 54, 262n15; Jim Crow and, 40; station identification by, 24
Ellison, Ralph, 14, 68
Encyclopedia of Black Radio in the United States (Ellett), 7
Engelman, Ralph, 150–51
ERP (effective radiated power), 165
Essential Public Media, 192
ethnic programming, 56–58, 71–73, 121–22, 202, 216–17; foreign-language broadcasting and, 7; frequency assignment and, 40, 57, 72–73; Latinx radio programming, 230–31; omnibus/variety model and, 85; rhythm & blues as, 57–58; Sirius XM and loss of programs, 241. *See also* Black Appeal/Negro Appeal format; Gospel format
Evans, Bill, 166
Evans, Gil, 31
Evans, Sam, 75–76
experimental/"outside" jazz, 7, 21–22, 124, 171–76, 192, 196, 199–200, 232, 247; DIY releases/radio, 6, 142, 171, 186, 238. *See also* college radio; community radio; progressive programming

Index   299

Faith, Percy, 30
Fax, Jesse, 124
Feather, Leonard, 29, 130, 132
Federal Communications Commission. *See* U.S. Federal Communications Commission (FCC)
Federal Radio Commission (FRC), 37–38, 258n11, 262n7
Fega, Mort, 56–57
Ferguson, Bert, 72
Ferguson, Maynard, 56
Field, Ken, 161
Fields, Joe, 129, 132–33
Fields, Sam, 112
Fischer, Jonathan L., 210, 211
Fisher, Marc, 99, 121
Fitzgerald, Ella, 29, 47, 82, 84
Floyd, Samuel, 203
FM radio: AM/FM distribution of radio stations (1955), 71, 109; explosion in 1960s to 1970s, 86, 96–99; first FM Class D licenses (1948), 220, 221; FM bands reserved for educational/noncommercial use (1945), 3, 5, 135, 136, 138, 149–50; FM broadcasting launch, 5, 35, 69, 96; FM HD channels, 242; FM receiver market penetration, 98, 99; origins and growth of, 5, 35, 69, 86, 96–99; public radio growth and, 16, 19. *See also* low-power FM; noncommercial radio
Ford, Frank, 70
Ford Foundation, 150
The Forward (newspaper), 56
Frankenheimer, John, 66
Franklin, Aretha, 123
free-form/underground/progressive radio, 4, 5, 15, 99, 143, 168, 208–9
free jazz (the New Thing), 107, 134, 174, 178–79, 192, 194–95, 199, 201, 216, 228, 232; critics of, 22; limited acceptance with jazz audiences, 31; nature of, 261n77; origins of, 31; in progressive programming, 15
frequency assignment: AM bandwidth and, 94, 106, 269n63; for clear-channel stations, 106; commercial frequencies, 124, 126–27, 271–72n58; ethnic programming and, 40, 57, 72–73; FCC role in, 262n6; of jazz radio stations circa 2020, 253–55; music genre and, 97. *See also* low-power FM
Fritz, Jose, 57
Fuller, Gil, 63
funk, 12, 31, 85, 107, 133, 134, 172–74, 182, 201

Gabler, Milt, 46
Garner, Errol, 29

Garnham, Nicholas, 245
Garroway, Dave, 51, 77, 78
gatekeepers, 20–22; backselling and, 21; bandleaders as, 26, 42, 44; complaints about, 21–22; new media and lack of, 238, 245, 248; payola and, 21, 45, 55, 58, 69, 240, 272n69, 277n22; role and power of, 6, 20–21; song pluggers and, 21, 44, 239; station library and format restrictions, 2, 6, 179, 186, 188; types of, 6, 20–21 (*see also* DJs; programmers and programming; radio station managers; record promoters)
Gathings, Tex, 79, 268n28
Gaye, Marvin, 123
Gendron, Bernard, 27
George, Nelson, 123
Getz, Stan, 47, 56
Giddins, Gary, 130–32
Gillespie, Dizzy, 47, 63, 65, 82, 83, 127
Giovanni, Nikki, 122
Giovannoni, David, 160, 166–67, 180–81, 183
Godfrey, Arthur, 41, 51
Golson, Benny, 4
Goode, Mal, 60
Goodman, Benny, 29, 69–70
Gordon, Dexter, 63
Gordon, Phil (Dr. Jive), 122
Gosden, Freeman, 38
Gospel format, 60, 85, 215, 223, 224
gospel music. *See* black church music and gospel
Gradeja, Tony, 18
Grant, Cecil, 47
Grant, Felix, 23, 24, 95–96, 101, 145–46, 186–87
Granz, Norman, 49, 50
Gray, Glen, 29
Gray, Herman, 173, 174, 176
Great Depression, 46, 174
Greater New York Broadcasting Corporation, 57–58
Great Migration, 9, 73–74, 121
Green, Al, 86
Greene, Paul D., 18
Guevara, Che, 125

Hammersley, Ben, 242
Hampton, Lionel, 8, 47, 82
Hancock, Herbie, 4, 124, 130
Hancock, Hunter, 66–67
Hanley, Scott, 184
hard bop, 11–12, 15, 31, 232
Harlem Hit Parade, 44, 47
Harmon, Carter, 57, 58
Harper, Walt, 79, 80
Harris, Wynonie, 66

Harry James Orchestra, 51
Hartley, John, 245–46
Hassan, Rusty, 56
Hawkins, Coleman, 44–45, 47
Hawkins, Erskine, 8
Hayes, Isaac, 77–78, 86, 123
Haynes, Roy, 23
HBCU (Historically Black College and University) radio stations, 176, 190, 206–7, 214–16, 219–20, 279n32
Healy, Timothy, 213
Heath, Jimmy, 68
Hefflin, Leon, Sr., 67
Hentoff, Nat, 161
Herman, Woody, 29
Herron, Michael, 126
Herschel (Andrew Venezie), 142
hi-fi audio culture, 4, 5, 19, 96, 97–100
Hill, John, 191
Hill, Lewis, 208
Hines, Earl, 8, 36, 171–72
Hinz, Robert C., 150–51
hip hop, 27, 67–68, 174
Ho, Fred, 176
Hofstadter, Richard, 14
Holiday, Billie, 29, 65, 68, 82, 104, 199–200, 232
Holland, Dave, 130
Holmes, Richard "Groove," 11–12, 90, 122
Holt, Fabian, 21
Horne, Lena, 64
Hot Jazz Saturday Night, 141, 145, 157–58, 273n21
"hot" music styles, 11, 26, 28, 50, 70, 261n68
housing boom/home ownership, 94, 96
Howe, James L., 69–70
Howlin' Wolf (Chester Arthur Burnett), 12
Hughes, John, 210, 211
Hughes, Langston, 125
Hulbert, "Hot Rod," 70
Husing, Ted, 54

iHeart Radio (formerly Clear Channel), 21, 271n40, 282n12
Impulse label, 90
industry-audience opposition in programming, 180
Inner City Broadcasting Company, 66, 68, 127
Institute for Jazz Studies, 199
internet: analytical tools and, 248; democratizing benefits of, 245–46; DIY releases/radio and, 6, 142, 171, 186, 238; future of jazz on the web and, 244–47; "long tail" economics and, 246, 248; net neutrality and, 244; new radio/streaming services

and, 7, 191–92, 216–19, 236, 237, 239–40, 242–44, 283n21; new technologies and, 236–39; podcasts and web features, 184, 191, 200, 201, 236–38, 241, 242, 282n8; scarcity of distribution channels and, 247. *See also* new media; social media

Jackson, Bobby, 191
Jackson, Brian, 49, 77–78
Jackson, Eric, 161
Jackson, Hal, 23, 64–66
Jackson, Jesse, 105–6
Jackson, Josh, 200
Jackson, Mahalia, 12
Jackson, Michael, 67
Jackson, Millie, 86
Jackson, Travis, 13
Jackson, Willis "Gator," 122
Jackson 5, 86
James, Etta, 4
Jarreau, Al, 124
Jarrett, Keith, 168
Jarvis, Al, 39–40, 66, 262n14
Jazz (2001 PBS documentary), 172, 173–74
Jazz24 programming, 184, 201, 279n20
Jazz at Lincoln Center (New York), 49, 173, 175, 189, 191, 199, 277n12
Jazz at the Philharmonic series, 49, 50
Jazz Diplomacy (Davenport), 11
jazz fusion, 126, 127, 172, 176, 189, 192, 194, 232; jazz-funk, 15, 16, 173, 201; jazz-rock, 16, 31, 107, 129–30, 134, 173; nature of, 31. *See also* crossover jazz
Jazzmobile (New York), 122
jazz music, 26–32; as active, subliminal component of AM radio, 85; as America's classical music, 11, 127, 177, 209; anti-jazz (Tynan) and, 12–13; arrival on noncommercial radio in the 1970s, 5–6, 15, 16; black classical music and, 9, 27; buy versus rent decision and, 239–40; conservative vs. progressive discourse, 10, 15, 22, 171–78, 248; criticism of, 129–32; decline in mass radio appeal, 5, 16, 32, 47, 75, 79, 85–89, 91–93, 126–34, 235; early resistance to, 67–70; as film music, 85; general-interest and black press coverage of, 24; iconic jazz figures on jazz radio, 44, 47; identity distinct from popular music, 9, 29–30; ideology and, 9–18; "jazz," as term, 26–27; jazz specialty shows, 66; move from commercial to noncommercial radio, 91–96; as music of black resistance, 14–15; musicology and, 13, 17–18, 28, 32, 49; nature and origins of, 9, 12, 28–29; Negro folk idioms and, 12; parties of radio-delivered music and, 13;

Index   301

jazz music (*continued*): in politics of jazz radio, 15, 17, 21–22, 25; pop music vocal style and, 47, 62–63; as "rare and valuable national American treasure," 133, 171, 214, 219–20, 280n62; recognition as an art form by U.S. educational institutions, 142; styles of (*see* jazz music styles); syncopated music styles and, 18–19; on television, 28, 85, 122; tension over nature vs. meaning of, 2–3. *See also* jazz radio

jazz music styles, 7, 27–32; acid jazz, 15, 173, 175, 192; advocates for new styles, 32; bebop (*see* bebop and bop); cool jazz, 12, 15, 31, 190–91, 207, 232; crossover jazz (*see* crossover jazz); Dixieland jazz, 4, 27–28, 29, 130; early jazz, 15, 18, 27–29, 179, 190; experimental/"outside" (*see* experimental/"outside" jazz); free jazz (*see* free jazz); jazz as still developing, 29; jazz fusion (*see* jazz fusion); Kansas City jazz, 28; Latin jazz, 15, 179, 199, 207–8, 209, 216; modern jazz, 23–24, 29, 54–55, 58–59 (*see also* bebop and bop; smooth/contemporary jazz); nearly jazz, 29; New Orleans jazz, 27–28, 54, 177, 189; opposition to new styles, 32; popular music vs., 30–31; progressive (*see* progressive/freeform jazz); ragtime, 27–28, 75; smooth jazz (*see* smooth/contemporary jazz); soul jazz (*see* soul jazz); "sweet" music vs. "hot" music and, 11, 26, 28, 30, 32, 50, 70, 261n68; swing (*see* swing); ubiquity of jazz elements in popular music, 28

jazz police, 21–22, 32, 118–19, 170–71, 173. *See also* gatekeepers

jazz programming services, 110, 136, 183–85, 201, 214, 230, 279n20

jazz radio, 108–34; broadcast paradigm and, 237–39, 246; commercial (*see* commercial radio); component parts of, 3; decline in radio as cultural force, 236–38; DJs (*see* DJs); in early days vs. the present, 246–47; golden age/peak of, 141–46, 154; iconic jazz figures and, 44, 47; ideology and, 9–18; jazz music in politics of, 15, 17, 21–22, 25; lack of scholarly research on, 16–18; late-night programming of jazz, 51, 70, 79, 86, 91–93, 101 7, 162, 190; modes in the U.S. 1950s and later, 4–5; moving beyond radio, 238–39, 244–49 (*see also* new media); musician visibility and, 6–7; noncommercial (*see* noncommercial radio); parties of radio-delivered music and, 13; pop radio vs., 85; power issues in, 2–9 (*see also* gatekeepers); programming (*see* programmers and programming; programming philosophies and theories); resistance to jazz across races, 67–70; station list circa 2020, 253–56; trends, 1957–1985, 91–94; types of jazz programs, 189–90

Jazz Times (magazine), 24
Jefferson, Al, 79–80
Jennings, Waylon, 127
Jim Crow: ASCAP and, 40; Black Codes and, 9; civil rights movement and, 80–81; "Crow Jim" debates, 12; Great Migration and, 9, 73–74, 121; Ku Klux Klan, 125
jive/hip street language, 25, 26, 40, 56–58, 65, 68–69, 70, 74, 77, 123
Johnny O, Sir, 91
Johnson, Aaron J.: black progressive radio at WAMU-FM (American University) and, 126; broadcast paradigm, 237–39, 246; live remote recording experience, 49; as performer in senior recital of Noble Jolley at Howard University, 214; as radio technician, 275n56; as trombonist at Yoshi's (Oakland, CA), 49; as tuba player at Town Hall concert (2009, New York), 49; as WRCT-FM DJ, 126, 143–44, 220
Johnson, Buddy (Woodrow Wilson), 63
Johnson, James P., 174
Johnson, Lyndon, 152
Johnson, Marcus, 191
Johnson, Plas, 4
Johnson, Stephanie Anne, 201
Johnson Publishing Company, 74, 105, 113
Jolley, Noble, 214
Jones, Jonah, 29, 47
Jones, Quincy, 4
Jordan, Louis, 8, 47
Joyner, Tom "Fly Jock," 73, 267n7
jukebox industry, 42–43, 263n35

Kallen, Kitty, 51
Kansas City jazz, 28
Kasem, Casey, 53
KATZ (St. Louis), 120–21
Katz, Jamie, 216
Katz, Mark, 18
KBCA-FM (Los Angeles), 100, 102, 108, 110, 111–12
KCEP-FM (Las Vegas), 190
KCRW-FM (Santa Monica College, CA), 111–12, 195, 201
KCSM (San Mateo, CA), 166
KDKA (Pittsburgh), 142
KDKO (Denver), 73
Keightley, Keir, 30, 96
Keith, Michael, 98
Keller, Marcello Sorce, 17–18
Kelley, Rubin D. G., 58

Kennard, William, 221, 224
Kennedy, Robert, 151
Kenny G, 31
Kent, Herb "The Cool Gent," 75
Kenton, Stan, 56, 65
Kentucky Club (New York), 47–48
Kerouac, Jack, 53
KFVD (Porterville, CA), 67
KFWB (Los Angeles), 39–40
KGIL (Los Angeles), 78
King, Martin Luther, Jr., 122, 126
Kinnison, William, 40
Kirk, Rahsaan Roland, 218
Kittross, John, 16
KJAZ-FM (San Francisco), 109, 114, 132
KJZZ (Bellevue, WA), 166
KKGO (Los Angeles), 112
KKJZ (Long Beach, CA), 112, 166
Klemmer, John, 31, 166
Klugh, Earl, 27, 129
KMPX (San Francisco), 99, 100
Knight, Gene, 190–91
KNKX (Seattle/Tacoma, WA), 200–201, 279n18
KNOB (Los Angeles), 108–11
Kouwenhoven, John A., 14
KOWL (Santa Monica, CA), 66
KPLU-FM (Pacific Lutheran University), 183–84, 191n, 196, 200–201, 213
KPRS (Kansas City), 71
KTSU-FM (Texas Southern University), 166, 219–20
KUHF-FM (University of Houston), 219
Ku Klux Klan, 125
KUOW-FM (Seattle), 200–201
KVTI-FM (Seattle/Tacoma, WA), 200
KXJZ (Sacramento, CA), 182, 184–85
KXLW (St. Louis), 120–21
KYW (Philadelphia), 28

Lacy, Frank, 174, 176
Ladd, Jim, 168
Lake, Oliver, 173, 200
The Landing (San Antonio), 190
LaPalm, Dick, 25, 86, 185, 186
Lasar, Matthew, 208
Last Poets, 77–78, 122, 126
Latin jazz, 15, 179, 199, 207–8, 209, 216
Latinx radio programming, 230–31
Lattisaw, Stacy, 86
La Vere's Chicago Loopers, 63
Layman, Will, 129
Lazarsfeld, Paul F., 211–12
Leadbelly, 125
Lee, Peggy, 29, 65
Lee, Valeria and Jim, 154

Levine, Saul, 108, 112
Levinson, Hy, 110
Levy, Morris, 65
Lewis, Ramsey, 11–12, 78, 90, 129, 130
Lewis, Yale, 157
libation, 178
Lincoln, Abbey, 125
Lincoln Center (New York), 49, 133, 173, 175, 189, 191, 199, 277n12
Lindsay, Drew, 158
Lion, Alfred, 53, 97
Lion, Lorraine, 58
Little Richard, 67
Live from Emmett's Place (streaming series), 7
live remotes, 36–39, 49–51, 54, 56, 64–65, 82–84, 111
Lloyd, Charles, 100
Lombardo, Guy, 8, 42
Lopes, Paul, 29–30
Lopez, Vincent, 42
Lott, Eric, 14–15
low-power FM (LPFM), 213, 220–31; Class D stations, 220, 221; establishment of, 197, 220–22; Jazz24 and, 201; list of jazz and smooth jazz stations, 222–24; number and growth of stations, 220, 222–24, 225; pirate radio vs., 221; religious and conservative interests and, 221–22; WETF-LP (South Bend, IN), 230–31; WOWD-LP (Takoma Park, MD), 225–28; WSFM-LP (Asheville, NC), 228–29
LPs, 5, 18–22, 53, 54, 86, 87, 90, 96, 100, 110, 111, 137–38, 167; limitations of 78 rpm records and, 20, 49, 137; origins of (1948), 137; single 45 rpm records vs., 137, 272–73n2. *See also* records and recordings
Lubinsky, Herman, 53
Lucas, Christopher, 221, 224

Mackey, Nathanial, 174–75
Mahavishnu Orchestra, 129
Mailer, Norman, 68
The Make-Believe Ballroom, 39–40, 65, 66, 262n14
Making Easy Listening (Anderson), 19
Malcolm X, 121, 122, 125
Mancini, Henry, 4, 110
Mangione, Chuck, 31, 187
Mankiewicz, Frank, 151–53
Mark, Sid, 113–14
Marsalis, Wynton, 173–74, 175
Martha Jean the Queen, 72
Martin, Michel, 210
Martin, Roberta, 12
Masekela, Hugh, 90
Massey, Malvin, 213

Index   303

mass media: commercial radio (*see* commercial radio); competition and, 45, 94; economies of scale and, 19–20, 45; motion pictures, 18, 28, 45, 66, 85, 236; musicology and, 17–18; noncommercial radio (*see* noncommercial radio); as public good, 45; records (*see* records and recordings); sonic culture combining records and high-fidelity audio equipment, 19; technological capabilities of, 18–22; television (*see* television)
Mathis, Johnny, 67
Mauldin, Manny, 40
May, Billy, 63, 85
Mayfield, Curtis, 122, 125
M-BASE, 176
McBride, Christian, 179, 189–90, 207, 241
McCann, Les, 100
McChesney, Robert Waterman, 202
McClendon, Gordon, 79
McCourt, Tom, 16
McCoy, Quincy, 129, 132–33
McCoy, Sid, 51, 75, 77, 78–79, 86
McDuff, "Brother" Jack, 90, 122
McGovern, George, 151
McPartland, Marian, 179
Merz, Charles, 18–19
Metronome (magazine), 57, 62
Miller, Glenn, 28–29
Miller, Marcus, 241
Millinder, Lucky, 8
Mingus, Charles, 10, 22, 100, 127
Mitchell, Charles, 127
Mitchell, Jack, 152
Mitchell, Jack W., 138
modernism/American modernism, 2, 10, 12, 29, 174
modern jazz, 23–24, 29, 54–55, 58–59. *See also* bebop and bop; smooth/contemporary jazz
Monk, Thelonius, 10, 47, 49, 58, 219
Monroe, Vaughn, 47
Monson, Ingrid, 10
Montgomery, Wes, 86, 90, 117
Moran, Jason, 200, 219
MOR (Middle of the Road) format, 8, 33, 47, 90, 93, 106, 107, 117–20, 145; as adult version of Top 40 format, 84, 86, 94, 99; DJ personality and, 52; rock and roll not allowed and, 67
Morgan, Lee, 4
Morgenstern, Dan, 54, 56, 57, 199–200
Morton, Jelly Roll, 171–72
motion pictures, 18, 28, 45, 66, 85, 236
Motown, 67, 100, 134
Mowod, Tony, 142
MTV, 67, 235
Muhammad, Idris, 100

Mulligan, Gerry, 68
Murray, Albert, 14, 173–74
Murray, Sunny, 195
Murray Street Productions, 191, 278n45
Muse Records, 129
musicians: DJs as professional, 51–52, 79, 112, 179; jazz radio in visibility of, 6–7; "long tail" economics and, 246, 248; new media and, 6–7, 245–46, 283n24. *See also* African American musicians
music industry (generally): jazz radio programming philosophy and, 9–10, 180, 185–86; tension between audience desires and, 180
MusicMaster, 184–85
musicology: jazz music and, 13, 17–18, 28, 32, 49; jazz radio programming philosophy and, 180–83; mass media and, 17–18; radio programming and, 166–67, 180–81, 182, 184, 186–87
Mutual Broadcasting System (MBS), 37
Myrick, Maxx, 188

narrowcasting, 107, 161–63, 188
National Association of Broadcasters, 221
National Association of Educational Broadcasters, 150
National Cable Satellite Corporation, 146
National Endowment for the Arts (NEA) Jazz Masters, 23, 54, 133, 191, 243–44
National Public Radio (NPR), 17, 129, 132–33, 242, 278n45; *All Things Considered*, 21, 155–56, 195, 197, 201, 214; financial crisis of 1983, 135, 151–54; founding (1970), 141–42, 147–48, 152, 153, 194; *Fresh Air*, 157–58, 189, 201; *Jazz Alive*, 49, 149, 154; low-power FM and, 221; *Morning Edition*, 144, 161, 195, 201, 210, 214; programming spending trends, 140–41; Sirius XM, 188, 237, 240, 241–42; *Toast of the Nation*, 49, 190
Navarro, Fats, 63
NBC: Blue Network, 37, 41, 95; corporate conflict determination (1934), 38; disk jockey vs. network model of programming, 42; Orange/Gold (West Coast) Network, 37; RCA as parent company of, 49; Red Network (former AT&T stations), 37, 51; transcription programs, 38, 39
NEA Jazz Masters, 23, 54, 133, 191, 243–44
Negro Appeal format. *See* Black Appeal/Negro Appeal format
Nesi, Tom, 216
Netflix, 236, 237
Newark Public Radio, 1, 195, 198–99. *See also* WBGO-FM
New England Public Radio, 230

Newman, David "Fathead," 76
new media: broadcast paradigm and, 246; democratizing influence of, 245; fee-based business model and, 240, 245–46; forms of, 237; internet music services, 184, 201, 207 (*see also* internet); lack of gatekeepers, 238, 245, 248; "long tail" economics and, 246, 248; media products as public goods, 245; musicians and, 6–7, 245–246, 283n24; music streaming, 7, 237, 239–40, 242–44; new radio/streaming services, 7, 191–92, 216–19, 236, 237, 239–40, 242–44, 283n21; peer-to-peer file sharing, 237; types of, 237, 239, 245–46; YouTube music, 7, 237, 240. *See also* internet
New Orleans jazz, 27–28, 54, 177, 189
New York Public Radio, 149, 165, 198
New York Times, 68, 165
Nichols, Red, 42
Nicholson, Stuart, 243
Nielsen data (now Arbitron), 240, 242
Niles, Chuck, 112
Nixon, Richard, 8, 99, 124
Nnamdi, Kojo, 124
noncommercial radio, 135–233; budget imperatives and, 142; classical and jazz music as staples of, 141–42; college radio (*see* college radio); commercial radio tactics used in, 161–62; community radio (*see* community radio); conservative vs. progressive programming and, 10, 15, 22, 171–78, 248; decline of commercial radio and, 5, 45, 235–36; as DIY radio in early years, 142; early subsidies by colleges and universities, 142; financial pressures on, 231–33; format (*see* radio formats); ideology in programming, 10; jazz and classical music excluded from programming, 168–69; jazz arrival in the 1970s, 5–6, 15, 16; jazz audience and, 139–41; jazz golden age/peak years on, 141–46; jazz move from commercial stations, 132–34; jazz movement from commercial radio, 91–96; jazz police and, 170–71, 173; jazz program types, 189–90; jazz station list (circa 2020), 253–56; local vs. network production and, 148–49; low-power radio (*see* low-power FM); mission of "serving the public interest," 138, 142, 154, 195; omnibus/variety programming, 139, 142–43, 148; origins of, 3–4; ownership/management models, 195; partnership with jazz music, 5–6; in Pittsburgh, 142–44; professionalization trend and, 2, 142, 150, 151, 154–67, 195, 212–13; programming influences, 170–71; public radio (*see* public radio); subscriber memberships, 147–48, 153–54, 188, 191, 232; in Washington, DC, 144–46. *See also* FM radio
Norman, Tony, 210
Norton, Jon, 182
Novick, Harry, 121–22
Novick, Morris, 121–22
NTI (news, talk, and information) programming, 140, 144–46, 148, 161, 165–66, 169, 200–201, 204, 232, 236, 242

O'Day, Anita, 68
O'Jays, 86
omnibus/variety programming, 4, 36–39, 41, 50–51, 69, 72, 85, 139, 142–43, 148
On the Road (Kerouac), 53
oppositional pairs programming philosophy, 180
Orange/Gold (West Coast) Network, 37
Orkin, 115
Ottenhoff, Bob, 1
"outside" jazz. *See* experimental/"outside" jazz
Owens, Jesse, 112

Pacifica Radio Network (PRN), 123, 126, 131–32, 160, 205, 208–12, 213; *Democracy Now!*, 196, 208, 211, 214, 228; financial instabilities of, 210; influence on community radio, 195, 196; licensing of stations, 195, 196; nature of, 196; Pacifica Foundation as owner of, 195, 208; programming and, 196, 208–9; stations within, 196, 203, 208; WPFW-FM (Washington, DC), 209–12
Pacific Public Media, 201
Pandora, 240
Panken, Ted, 219
Paradise, Sal, 53
Parker, Charlie, 47, 63, 65, 216, 217
Parker, William, 176
Parlocha, Bob, 179, 191–92, 278n47
Partridge, Marika, 225, 228
Paul, Billy, 86
payola, 21, 45, 55, 58, 69, 240, 272n69, 277n22
Pelleyá, Maggie, 207
Pepper, John, 72
Peterson, Oscar, 166–67
Pet Milk, 78
Pew Research, 221
Phillips, Esther, 104–5
Phillips, Michael, 228
Pickney, Warren R., 18
pirate radio stations, 221
Pleasure, King, 35
Plique, Eddie, 40
podcasts, 200, 236, 238, 241, 242, 282n8
Pop format, 63, 85, 90, 186

pop music/pop vocal style: decline of jazz on radio and, 47, 86; gap between jazz and, 62–63; jazz instrumentation and, 47, 117; record industry and, 19
Porcello, Thomas, 18
Porter, Gregory, 168
Porter, Tom, 203
post-bop jazz, 15, 28, 31, 171–73, 192, 195, 200, 207, 232, 247, 248
post-modernism, 10
Powell, Adam Clayton, Jr., 64
Powell, Bill, 142
Powell, Bud, 47
Preminger, Otto, 66
Price, Jonathan, 228
Price, Lloyd, 85
Prima, Louis, 29, 47
primitivism, 10, 12, 28, 29, 68, 96, 246–47
programmers and programming: conservative vs. progressive discourse, 10, 15, 22, 171–78, 248; DJ role in, 22–24, 45, 46, 52–59, 73–77, 79, 94–96, 97, 106–7, 117, 132; ethnic (*see* ethnic programming); free-form/underground/progressive radio, 4, 5; gatekeeper function, 20–21, 22–23; jazz programming on noncommercial radio, 141–46, 170–92; jazz programming services, 51, 110, 136, 183–85, 201, 214, 228, 230, 279n20; of listener digital libraries, 167; modal music research, 183–85; musicology and, 166–67, 180–81, 182, 184, 186–87; new radio/streaming services and, 7, 53, 191–92, 216–19, 236, 237, 239–40, 242–44, 283n21; omnibus/variety programming, 4, 36–39, 41, 50–51, 69, 72, 85, 139, 142–43, 148; philosophies and theories (*see* programming philosophies and theories); prestige and influence in field, 6; programmer, as term, 178; programming clocks and, 2; progressive (*see* progressive programming); volume of new releases and, 6, 46
programming philosophies and theories, 178–92; aesthetic philosophy, 10, 180–81, 187–88; audience philosophy, 180, 181–82; business-related aspects of, 9, 188–92; conflicts among philosophies, 180, 186–88; independence of programmers, 178; industry philosophy, 180, 185–86; management role and, 179; oppositional pairs in, 180; research philosophy, 180, 182–85; station format and, 178–79
program/music/jazz directors: audience research and, 160–61; control over playlists, 114, 117–19, 122–23; role of, 179; station library and format restrictions, 2, 6, 67,

179, 186, 188. *See also* programming philosophies and theories
progressive/free-form jazz, 99–101, 142; music styles in, 15; nature of, 15; programming controls and research tools for, 100–103, 107; progressive vs. conservative camps and, 22
progressive programming: conservative vs. progressive camps and, 10, 15, 22, 171–78, 248; in free-form/underground/progressive radio, 4, 5, 15, 143, 168, 208–9; nature of, 15, 171, 172; underground/progressive radio movement and, 99–101
Prohibition, 68
Pruter, Robert, 75–76
PRX (Public Radio Exchange), 17, 153, 190, 192, 197, 200–201, 210, 230
Public Broadcasting Act (1967), 135, 150, 220
Public Broadcasting System (PBS): *Jazz* (2001 documentary), 172, 173–74; *PBS NewsHour*, 157–59, 163
public radio, 197–201; American Public Media, 161, 197; American Public Radio, 153; audience growth, 168; changes in jazz and, 247–48; community radio vs., 154–56, 195, 204 (*see also* community radio); consensus around "melodic" jazz, 247; demographics of audience, 140, 148; diminished federal funding in the 1980s, 146–49; diversity problems, 165–66; FM broadcasting and growth of, 16, 19; jazz and classical music excluded from programming, 168–69; jazz music arrival in the 1970s, 15, 17; KNKX (Seattle/Tacoma, WA), 200–201; licensing of stations, 195–96; NTI (news, talk, and information) programming, 140, 144–46, 148, 161, 165–66, 169, 200–201, 204, 232, 236, 242; ownership/management models, 195–96; podcasts and web features, 184, 191, 200, 201, 236, 238, 241, 242, 282n8; professionalization of, 150, 151, 154–61, 200; PRX (Public Radio Exchange), 17, 153, 190, 192, 197, 200–201, 210, 230; Public Broadcasting Act (1967) and, 135, 150, 220; Public Radio International (PRI), 153, 190, 210, 230, 278n45; radio usage hours and, 139–40; rigidity in approach to music, 247; WBGO-FM (Newark), 197–200. *See also* Corporation for Public Broadcasting (CPB); National Public Radio (NPR)
Public Radio International (PRI), 153, 190, 210, 230, 278n45
PubMusic (streaming service), 192
Pullen, Don, 15
Purvis, Jack, 62
Purvis (Marks), Betty Lou (Bettelou), 56, 62–64

Quiet Storm formats, 126

Ra, Sun, 10
race: as barrier for African American experimentalists, 7; in commercial and noncommercial eras of radio, 7–8, 17; of jazz listeners, 165–66; jazz programming and, 171; music-industrial complex and, 7; resistance to jazz across races, 67–70. *See also* entries beginning with *"African American"*; ethnic programming
race music, 65, 264n47
Radio and the Struggle for Civil Rights in the South (Ward), 7
radio formats: AOR (album-oriented rock), 59, 97, 99, 100, 119, 120, 142, 207, 269n59; Black Appeal/Negro Appeal (*see* Black Appeal/Negro Appeal format); CHR (Contemporary Hits Radio), 167–68, 269n59; Country and Western/Country, 42, 52, 85, 93, 107, 112, 127, 128; Easy Listening (*see* Easy Listening/Good Music format); Gospel, 60, 85, 215, 223, 224; MOR (*see* MOR (Middle of the Road) format); NTI (*see* NTI (news, talk, and information) programming); Pop, 63, 85, 90, 186; R&B (Rhythm & Blues), 8, 67–68, 86, 87–90; Religious, 85; Soul, 93, 105, 107, 191; Top 40 (*see* Top 40 format); Triple A (Adult Album Alternative) format, 144, 148; Urban Adult Contemporary, 67–68, 268n35; Urban Contemporary, 67–68, 120n, 123, 126, 145–46, 161, 167–68, 215n, 268n35
Radio Free Dixie (Tyson), 125
radio.net, 242, 243
Radio Research Consortium, *Audience 2010* report, 166
radio station managers, 64, 82, 91, 95–96, 150, 181, 182, 205, 209, 235; payola and, 21, 45, 58, 69, 240, 272n69, 277n22; professionalization of operations and, 2, 67, 142, 150, 151, 154–61, 195, 212–13
ragtime, 27–28, 75
rap: appearance in the 1970s, 86; precursor of, 77–78; "rapping" DJs, 77–78; record industry and, 19; resistance to, 86; signifying and, 77–78
Rawls, Lou, 86
Razaf, Andy, 9
Razlogova, Elena, 76
R&B (Rhythm & Blues) format, 8, 67–68, 86, 87–90
RCA, 28–29, 36–38, 49, 131
RCA Victor Record Company, 38
Reagan, Ronald, 151–52
record promoters, 5, 7, 23–25, 45–46; payola and, 21, 45, 58, 69, 240, 272n69, 277n22

records and recordings: buying vs. renting music, 239–40; CDs, 6, 20, 167, 185, 187–88, 239–40, 243; checks on growth of, 41; commercial radio growth and, 18–20, 36–39; decline in the late 1990s, 19; development and spread of jazz music and, 18; distribution cost as barrier to entry, 20; hit records vs. hit songs, 42–45; jazz DJ impacts on sales, 25–26; limitations of 78 rpm records, 20, 49, 137; live performances replaced by, 35; live remotes vs., 36–39, 49–51, 54, 56, 64–65, 82–84, 111; LPs (*see* LPs); microgroove technology, 96, 272–73n2; partnership with radio, 45–47; private record collections and libraries, 19, 95, 179; radio in promoting, 19–20; sales (1945), 44, 47; stages of record industry, 19; transcription programs, 36, 38–39, 46, 49–50, 52, 58, 59; types of record charts, 45; types of recordings, 20
Red Network (former AT&T stations), 37, 51
Reinhardt, Django, 44–45
religious broadcasters, 138, 147, 221
Religious format, 85
research philosophy of programming, 100, 182–85
rhythm and blues (R&B): decline of jazz on radio and, 75, 85, 86, 87–89; as ethnic programming, 57–58; nature of, 50; performed by jazz musicians, 8; pioneering radio program and, 67; replacement of race music and, 264n47; resistance to, 69; smooth jazz as instrumental, 32; soul jazz and, 31. *See also* R&B (Rhythm & Blues) format
Rhythm Planet (Schnabel), 111–12
Rich, Jammin' Jay (Jai Rich), 112
Richardson, Jerome, 105
Rise of a Jazz Art World (Lopes), 30
Rivers, Sam, 130
Roach, Max, 125
Robbins, Fred (Fred Rubin), 57–59
Robinson, Jackie, 62
Robinson, Smokey, 126
rock and roll/rock music: AOR (album-oriented rock) format, 59, 97, 99, 100, 119, 120, 142, 207, 269n59; decline of jazz on radio and, 86; early years of, 45, 78; MOR format vs., 67; record industry and, 19; resistance to, 67, 69, 70
Rodriguez, Ramon, 230
Rollins, O. Wayne, 115
Rollins, Sonny, 86, 90, 177, 191
Rollins Broadcasting, 64, 115
Roosevelt, Eleanor, 64
Roosevelt, Franklin D., 35
Rothenbuhler, Eric W., 16, 139
Rounsaville, 115, 119

Index   307

Rourke, Constance, 14
Roussel, Jennifer Houlihan, 165
Rucker, Ursula, 178
Russell, Ross, 53
Russo, Alexander, 38

Sanctified Shells, 49
Sanders, Pharaoh, 49
Sapper, Neal, 181
satellite radio, 3, 110, 152, 179, 191, 196; C-SPAN, 146, 212; Sirius XM, 188, 237, 240, 241–42
Savage, Barbara, 7, 267n22
Savitt, Jan, 29
Savoy label, 53
Sayama, Kogyo, 112
Schaap, Phil, 23, 216, 218, 219, 278n42
Schaefer, John, 276n84
Schmitt, Al, 97
Schnabel, Tom, 111–12
Schneider, Maria, 243–44
Schwan, Dave, 191
Schwartz, Jonathan, 165
Scott, Raymond, 26
Scott, Tom, 100
Scott-Heron, Gil, 4, 49, 77–78, 126
Seaway Broadcasting, 113
Segal, David, 73
Sesac, 178
Shaw, Woody, 187
sheet music, 42–43, 263n35
Sherrell, Charles, 115–16
Shields, Del, 122
Shorter, Wayne, 78
Siemering, Bill, 147–48
signifying, 77–79
Silver, Horace, 11–12, 80
Silverstein, Joseph, 40
Simmering, Bill, 194
Simone, Nina, 27, 86, 90, 122, 125
Simpson, Kim, 100
Sinatra, Frank, 4, 29, 64, 85, 114, 241
Sinatra, Nancy, 21, 111
Singleton, Zutty, 20
Sinnett, Jae, 179
Sirius XM, 188, 237, 240, 241–42
Slaughter, Vernon, 129
Smalls (New York), 244
Smiley, Tavis, 210
Smith, Kate, 47, 51–52
Smith, Keely, 29
Smithsonian Jazz Masterworks Orchestra, 133
smooth/contemporary jazz, 15, 16, 126–28, 133, 167; black college radio and, 32; classification controversy and, 31–32; and conservative vs. progressive jazz, 173, 175, 177; decline of format in commercial radio, 32, 235, 261n80; as instrumental R&B, 32; nature of, 32, 177; origins of, 11; origins of term, 31–32; "real" jazz vs., 115–16. *See also* crossover jazz
social media, 6, 24, 78, 173; controversies concerning, 245–46; influencers in, 25, 239, 240, 260n59; YouTube, 7, 237, 240. *See also* internet
Sonderling Broadcasting, 115, 127, 131
song pluggers, 21, 44, 239
Soul format, 93, 105, 107, 191
soul jazz, 11–12, 15, 122, 133, 232; black church music/gospel and, 13, 31; blues and, 12, 31; elements of, 31; jazz industry revival of the 1960s and, 13; principles of, 90
soul music, 105, 113, 207–8; jazz instrumentation of, 85; origin of, 13, 31; record industry and, 19; white-owned "soul radio" stations, 86, 115, 121, 122, 127, 131
sound studies, 18
Spaulding, Norm, 76
Speidel Broadcasting, 115, 122
Sponsor (magazine), 52–53, 66
Spotify, 237, 239, 240
Spyro Gyra, 31, 129
Stallings, Carl, 85
Stanton, Frank, 211–12
Station Research Group, 138
Stein, Sleepy, 110
Sterling, Christopher, 16
Stern, Marc, 208
Sterne, Jonathan, 18
Sting, 168
Stolen Moments (Schnabel), 111–12
Storz, Todd, 79
streaming: algorithmic playlists, 53, 239, 240; *Live from Emmett's Place* (streaming series), 7; music streaming, 7, 237, 239–40, 242–44; Netflix and, 236, 237; new radio/streaming services, 7, 191–92, 216–19, 236, 237, 239–40, 242–44, 283n21; YouTube, 7, 237, 240
Strode, Tolley, 112
suburban growth, 2, 9, 94, 96, 140
Sutton, Percy, 121
"sweet" music styles, 28, 30, 32
swing music, 8, 15, 54; African American origins vs. white practitioners, 28–29; as "big business" in the record industry, 19; as brand name, 27; popular music vs., 29; small band vs. big band, 29
Szwed, John, 11

Tate, Grady, 104
Taylor, Billy, 56, 85, 122, 149, 179

Taylor, Cecil, 145, 173, 186
Taylor, Creed, 25–26, 31, 130
Taylor, Timothy Dean, 18
television: cable systems, 35, 214, 236–37; disruptions in network radio and, 19, 115, 236–37, 247; as dominant mass medium, 94; educational/public broadcasting, 135–36, 150, 152 (*see also* Public Broadcasting System); full evening schedules (1948) and, 3; gatekeeping function and, 20; jazz music on, 28, 85, 122; MTV, 67, 235; Netflix and on-demand-programming, 236, 237; new media and, 237; postwar development of, 15–16, 35–36, 45, 50–51, 150, 247; reruns, 38
Tesser, Neil, 191
Thielemans, Toots, 4
Thomas, Carla, 13
Thomas, Thomas J., 138, 163–66
Thompson, Charles, 58
Thompson, Lucky, 218
Tidal, 237, 239
Timmons, Bobby, 11–12
Top 40 format, 4, 8, 62, 67, 78, 93, 118, 120, 131; DJ personality and, 52, 107; MOR as adult version of, 84, 86, 94, 99, 119; as new business model, 50; origins of, 79; programming controls and research tools for, 100–101
Torin, "Symphony" Sid (Sidney Tarnopol), 23, 69, 77, 127, 180–81; as icon of bebop and beat cultures, 53–57, 181; WJZ (later WABC, New York) and, 56, 64–65; *Zippy the Pinhead* cartoon and, 53, 54
Torry, Frank, 219
Town Hall (New York), 49, 174
transcription programs, 36, 38–39, 46, 49–50, 52, 58, 59
transistor radios, 16, 94, 238
Triangle Music Publishers, 42, 43
Triple A (Adult Album Alternative) format, 144, 148
Turner, Douglas, 190
Turner, Ike, 67
Turner, Joe, 125
Turre, Steve, 49
Tynan, John, 12–13
Tyson, Timothy, 125

Union of Soviet Socialist Republics, 10–11
United Broadcasting, 79–80, 115
University of Pittsburgh student survey (2017), 237–38
university radio: college radio vs., 195, 212–13; HBCU radio stations, 176, 190, 206–7, 214–16, 219–20, 279n32; licensing of stations, 195–96; professionally staffed university-owned stations and, 195; university-owned stations, 136
Univision, 165
Urban Adult Contemporary format, 67–68, 268n35
Urban Contemporary format, 67–68, 120n, 123, 126, 145–46, 161, 167–68, 215n, 268n35
U.S. Department of Commerce, Federal Radio Commission (FRC), 37–38, 258n11, 262n7
U.S. Department of Justice, 45
U.S. Federal Communications Commission (FCC): AM/FM distribution of radio stations (1955), 71; Communications Act (1934) and, 8; community radio and, 105, 197; disclosure of "mechanical broadcasting" and, 37–38, 39; establishment of low-power FM stations (2000), 197, 220–22; first FM Class D licenses (1948), 220, 221; FM bands reserved for educational/noncommercial use (1945), 3, 5, 135, 136, 138, 149–50; FM broadcasting launch, 5, 35, 69, 96; legislation enabling public radio (1967), 135, 150, 220; nonduplication/simulcast rules, 93, 97, 122; post-war approval of new radio licenses, 71; repeal of net neutrality ruling (2017), 244; role in frequency assignment, 262n6

Vallee, Rudy, 42
Van Gelder, Rudy, 97
vaudeville, 10, 40
Vaughan, Sarah, 51, 62–65, 82, 83, 86–90, 177
Vee-Jay records, 74, 78
Vega, Ray, 179
Venezie, Andrew "Herschel," 142
venue bookers, 6–7, 185
Venuti, Joe, 63
Vermont Public Radio, 179
Viacom, 127
Village Gate (New York), 127–29
Villanueva, Eliud, 230
Vision Orchestra, 176
Voice of America shortwave broadcast, 41
Voice Over (Barlow), 7
Voting Rights Act (1965), 121

WAAF (Chicago), 40, 74, 86, 101–5, 112–13, 117–18, 119
WABC (formerly WJZ, New York), 41, 56, 64–65
WABE (Atlanta Board of Education), 196
WAIT (Chicago), 77, 112–13
Wald, Elijah, 20
Walker, Gary, 23, 179, 199

Index 309

Walker, Jesse, 151
Walker, T-Bone, 66
Waller, Fats, 9, 17, 36
WAMO (formerly WHOD, Pittsburgh), 60–62, 79, 110, 142
WAMU-FM (American University), 124, 126, 141, 144–45, 156–59, 164–65, 195–96
WANN (Annapolis, MD), 23, 64, 80–84
Ward, Brian, 7, 25, 204
Warner Brothers, 85
Warnock, Tom, 153
Washington, Dinah, 4, 47, 65, 82, 86–90
Washington, Grover, Jr., 31, 123, 133, 187
Washington, Harold, 21
Washington, Kenny, 179
Washington Educational Telecommunications Association, 145
Washington Post, 121, 124
Watanabe, Carl, 182
Waters, Ethel, 36
Watkins, Mel, 77
Watson, Phil, 123
Watters, Lu, 29
WAZZ-FM (Pittsburgh), 110, 119
WBAI (New York), 131–32, 196, 208
WBAP (Fort Worth), 69
WBBM (Chicago), 41
WBEE (Harvey, IL), 40, 74, 113, 114–17, 119
WBEZ-FM (Chicago), 113
WBFO (Buffalo, NY), 149
WBGO-FM (Newark Public Radio), 23, 49, 139, 156, 166, 179, 186, 189–90, 195, 217; management concerns, 1–3, 242; mission statement, 198–99; profile, 197–200; revenues and expenses, 198
WBJC-FM (Baltimore Community College), 100, 103, 195
WBLS-FM (New York), 23, 66, 121, 122–23, 127, 177–78
WBNX (Bronx), 54
WBUR-FM (Boston), 148, 161, 162
WCAP (Washington, DC), 39–40
WCAR (AM then FM, Detroit), 110
WCFL (Chicago), 78, 79, 86, 117
WCHB (Detroit), 71
WCLK-FM (Clark Atlanta University), 190, 191, 206–7
WCUY-FM (Cleveland), 119
WDCB (Chicago), 139, 166
WDCU-FM (University of the District of Columbia), 96, 144, 145–46, 212, 213, 280n54
WDES (New York), 70
WDIA (Memphis), 3, 7, 70, 72, 73
WDJY (Washington, DC), 145
WDNA-FM (Miami), 192, 196, 207–8

WDUQ-FM (Duquesne University), 143–44, 166, 184, 192, 204, 213, 280n54
Weather Report, 123
WEBB (Baltimore), 70
Webb, Chick, 67
Weheliye, Alexander G., 18
WERD (Atlanta), 71
WESA-FM (Pittsburgh, formerly WDUQ-FM), 143–44, 204
West, Cornell, 210
West, Hollie, 144–45
WETA-FM (Washington, DC), 144–45, 157–58, 164–65, 195
WETF-LP (South Bend, IN), 230–31
WEUP (Huntsville, AL), 71
WEVD (Fairfield, CT), 56
WFIU (Bloomington, IN), 230
WFMT (Chicago), 117, 191–92, 207, 214, 230
WGBH-FM (Boston), 148, 161, 163, 195, 274n25
WGEE (Indianapolis), 115
WGES (later WYNR, Chicago), 74, 75–76, 78, 79
WGLT-FM (Illinois State University), 182, 195
WGMS (Washington, DC), 145
WGN (Chicago), 77
WGRT (Chicago), 101–5, 113, 269nn61–63
WGTB-FM (Georgetown University), 144–45, 146, 213
WGTS-FM (Takoma Park, MD), 49
WHA (University of Wisconsin), 212
WHAM (Rochester, NY), 91, 106
WHAT-FM (Philadelphia), 60, 70, 108, 113–14, 119, 132
WHBI (New York), 57
Wheelin' on Beale (Cantor), 7
WHFC (Chicago), 40, 74
Whiteman, Paul, 15, 26, 42, 51–52
WHN (New York), 47–49, 54, 57
WHOD (later WAMO. Pittsburgh), 60–62, 79, 110, 142
WHOM (Elizabeth, NJ), 54
WHRV-FM (Norfolk, VA), 179
WHUR-FM (Howard University, formerly WTOP-FM, Washington, DC), 49, 121, 123–24, 126, 144, 145–46, 271n40
WHYY (Philadelphia), 195
Wilkerson, Ed, 21
Wilkinson, Christopher, 28
Williams, Cootie, 47
Williams, Gilbert, 78
Williams, Mary Lou, 174
Williams, Nat D., 72
Williams, Robert and Mabel, 125–26
Williams, Sonja, 79
Wilner, Spike, 244

Wilson, Gerald, 112
Wilson, Nancy, 4, 86–90
Winchester, Simon, 141
WINS (New York), 57
WINX (Washington, DC), 64
WITH (Baltimore), 70
WJAB-FM (Alabama A&M), 190–91
WJPC (Chicago), 105, 113
WJSU-FM (Jackson State University), 191
WJSV (now WTOP, Washington, DC), 41, 263n26
WJZ (later WABC, New York), 41, 56, 64–65
WJZZ-FM (Bridgeport, CT), 119
WKCR-FM (Columbia University), 23, 131–32, 186, 196, 216–19
WLIB AM/FM (New York), 63–64, 66, 68–69, 108, 119, 121–22, 126, 127
WLIN-FM (Detroit), 110
WLMD (Laurel, MD), 144
WLTT (Bethesda, MD), 145
WMAL-AM (Washington, DC), 24, 95–96, 144, 145–46
WMAQ (Chicago), 38, 51, 77, 78
WMBM (Miami), 119
WMCA (New York), 48–49, 54, 64–65
WMGM (New York), 54
WMPP (Chicago), 113
WNER (Denver), 78
WNEW (New York), 39–40, 48–49, 57, 122
WNJR (Newark), 64–65, 115
WNOP (Cincinnati), 108, 119
WNUS (Chicago), 79
WNYC-FM (New York), 49, 165–66, 198, 276n84
WNYR (formerly WGES, Chicago), 74, 75–76, 78, 79
WOBS (Jacksonville, FL), 79
Wolff, Francis, 130
"Wolfman" Jack (Robert Smith), 77
women DJs: Yvonne Daniels, 51, 77, 79, 86, 117; Mary Dee Dudley (Mary Elizabeth Goode), 59–62, 79, 265n74; Martha Jean the Queen, 72; Bettelou Purvis (Marks) as music director and, 56, 62–64; at WSDM-FM (Chicago), 117–19
Wonder, Stevie, 123
WOOK (Washington, DC), 64, 65, 79–80, 260n56, 268n28
WOR (New York), 48–49, 54
World Broadcasting System, 39
world jazz, 16
WOV (New Rochelle, NY), 57–58
WOWD-LP (Takoma Park, MD), 145, 178, 225–28
WPFW-FM (Washington, DC), 144–45, 166, 196, 203, 208, 209–12

WPGH-AM (Pittsburgh), 62–63
WQED-FM (Pittsburgh), 143–44, 274n25
WQXR (New York), 68, 165, 198, 276n83
WRAP (Norfolk, VA), 115
WRC (Washington, DC), 144
WRCT-FM (Carnegie Mellon University), 126, 143–44, 196, 220
WREK-FM (Georgia Tech), 213
WRFG-FM (Radio Free Georgia, Atlanta), 196, 204–7
WRGM (Richmond, VA), 119
WRVR-FM (New York), 3, 119, 126–32, 198
WSAI (Cincinnati), 41
WSBC (Chicago), 40, 74
WSBL-LP (South Bend, IN), 230
WSCI (Charleston, SC), 195
WSDM-FM (Chicago), 79, 117–19
WSFM-LP (Asheville, NC), 228–29
WSHA-FM (Shaw University), 213, 214
WSID (Baltimore), 64
WSOK (Augusta, GA), 122
WTOP (formerly WJSV, Washington, DC), 41, 263n26
WTOP-FM (later WHUR-FM, Washington, DC), 49, 121, 123–24, 126, 144, 145–46, 271n40
Wu, Tim, 236
WUMR-FM (University of Memphis), 213
WUOM (University of Michigan), 196
WUPY-FM (Boston), 119
WVAS-FM (Alabama State University), 190–91
WVOE (Chadbourn, NC), 71
WVON (Chicago), 78, 113, 116, 117
WVSP-FM (Warrenton, NC), 154–56
WWDB-FM (Philadelphia), 114, 119
WWDC (Washington, DC), 41, 95–96
WWIN (Baltimore), 70, 91
WWRC (Washington, DC), 145–46
WWRL (New York), 127
WYDD-FM (Pittsburgh), 142, 143
WYEP-FM (Pittsburgh), 143–44, 151, 192, 204, 213
WYNR (formerly WGES, Chicago), 74, 75–76, 78, 79
WZUM-FM (Pittsburgh), 139, 184, 192

XM 70, 188

Yates, Sterling, 142
Yoshi's (Oakland, CA), 49
Young, Lester, 35, 47, 68, 199–200
YouTube, 7, 237, 240

Zippy the Pinhead cartoon, 53, 54

AARON J. JOHNSON is an associate professor of music at the University of Pittsburgh.

The University of Illinois Press
is a founding member of the
Association of University Presses.

Composed in 11.5/13 Adobe Garamond Pro
with Avenir LT Std display
by Kirsten Dennison
at the University of Illinois Press
Manufactured by Versa Press, Inc.

University of Illinois Press
1325 South Oak Street
Champaign, IL 61820-6903
www.press.uillinois.edu